Presidential Campaigning and Social Media

An Analysis of the 2012 Campaign

Edited by

JOHN ALLEN HENDRICKS
Stephen F. Austin State University

and

DAN SCHILL
James Madison University

New York   Oxford
OXFORD UNIVERSITY PRESS

Oxford University Press is a department of the University of Oxford.
It furthers the University's objective of excellence in research,
scholarship, and education by publishing worldwide.

Oxford New York
Auckland Cape Town Dar es Salaam Hong Kong Karachi
Kuala Lumpur Madrid Melbourne Mexico City Nairobi
New Delhi Shanghai Taipei Toronto

With offices in
Argentina Austria Brazil Chile Czech Republic France Greece
Guatemala Hungary Italy Japan Poland Portugal Singapore
South Korea Switzerland Thailand Turkey Ukraine Vietnam

For titles covered by Section 112 of the US Higher Education
Opportunity Act, please visit www.oup.com/us/he for the
latest information about pricing and alternate formats.

Published in the United States of America by
Oxford University Press
198 Madison Avenue, New York, NY 10016
http://www.oup.com

Library of Congress Cataloging-in-Publication Data
Hendricks, John Allen.
  Presidential campaigning and social media : an analysis of the 2012
campaign / edited by John Allen Hendricks, Stephen F. Austin State University
and Dan Schill, James Madison University.
      pages cm.
  ISBN 978-0-19-935584-6
  1. Presidents--United States--Election--2012. 2. Presidential candidates--United States.
3. Communication in politics--Technological innovations--United States. 4. Social media--
Political aspects--United States. 5. Internet in political campaigns--United States. I. Title.
  JK5262012 .H46 2014
  324.973'0932--dc23
                                                                    2013037514

Printing number: 9 8 7 6 5 4 3 2 1

Printed in the United States of America
on acid-free paper

Dedication

This book is dedicated to the memory of Lynda Lee Kaid (1948–2011), who was a prolific political communication scholar, having authored/ edited over 30 books and nearly 200 peer-reviewed articles and book chapters. Dr. Kaid was also an admired teacher of thousands of students, an award-winning mentor who chaired 41 doctoral dissertations during her career, and the recipient of a University of Florida university-wide Outstanding Doctoral Mentoring and Advising award for 2010–2011. Appropriately so, Dr. Kaid was named by *Communication Quarterly* as one of the most prolific and productive scholars in the discipline. She was a most-valued friend to the majority of scholars who contributed studies to this book. Above all of her many accomplishments, she was simply our friend—she is greatly missed and will always remain in our thoughts.

BRIEF CONTENTS

CONTENTS

PART I   SOCIAL MEDIA AND POLITICAL
COMMUNICATION

Chapter 10   **YouTube/OurTube/TheirTube: Official and Unofficial Online Campaign Advertising, Negativity, and Popularity**   140

Jacob Groshek and Stephanie Brookes

PART IV   **SOCIAL MEDIA AND THE PRESIDENTIAL GENERAL ELECTION**

Chapter 11   **The Spirals of Newly Transcending Political Voices: Social Media Purify the Atmosphere of Political Dialogues in Cyberspace**   154

Hyun Jung Yun

PART V SOCIAL MEDIA AND VOTER/MEDIA ENGAGEMENT

LIST OF TABLES, FIGURES
AND CHAPTER APPENDICES

Tables

Figures

Chapter Appendices

FOREWORD

Social media are revolutionizing the American electoral process. Their integral role in facilitating campaign communication, networking, collaboration, and activation has evolved rapidly. A novelty in the 2008 presidential contest, social media gained traction in the 2010 midterm elections and became established as a standard element of candidate strategy, voter engagement, and media reporting in 2012. Social networking sites (SNSs); video sharing platforms; and full-service, multimedia Web sites have been institutionalized as campaign media requisites. New media are now ubiquitous in campaigns, and their effects are far-reaching.

The 2008 election was a defining moment for campaign media. Most notable was the extent to which voters spontaneously exploited the opportunities offered by social media for becoming involved in the presidential campaign outside the purview of campaign committees and political parties. Voters, especially young people, were excited by the possibility of using social media platforms, such as Facebook (and to a lesser extent the nascent Twitter), in groundbreaking ways, such as to share information, express opinions, and work for or against candidates. Citizen-created campaign clips, mashups, and ads were popular on video-sharing sites like YouTube. Voters established online organizations with people who shared their views or group identities; these organizations performed functions traditionally consigned to political parties, such as setting the issue agenda, facilitating voter registration, and organizing get-out-the-vote drives. Social media provided alternative mechanisms for accomplishing traditional campaign tasks, such as fundraising, volunteer recruitment, publicity, event organizing, and advertising. The appeal of social media was boosted by the fact that it offers options for engagement that often are more convenient and accessible to citizens than taking part in election activities offline.

The Obama campaign took advantage of voters' participation via social media in 2008 by encouraging citizens' efforts to organize volunteers and to create messages to distribute in their own networks. Obama's team incorporated citizen-initiated strategies into its game plan, a move that contributed to their candidate's electoral success. Social media's prominence and novelty prompted the traditional press to report heavily on digital communication as a category of election news. Journalists relied on social media as sources of campaign information and incorporated social media tools into their reporting repertoire. With fewer professional journalists "on the bus" with the candidates, citizens provided eyewitness accounts from the campaign trail.

The amount of social media activity and content in the 2012 election far exceeded 2008 levels. The potential audience for campaign social media was substantial. According to studies by Edison Research and the Pew Research Center, 56% of Americans had a profile on an SNS during the election, although a smaller percentage used these sites intentionally for campaign-related purposes. Both the Obama and Romney campaigns employed digital media specialists who were charged with devising strategies that effectively integrated technology into their campaign schemes. The Obama campaign made a substantial investment to implement an aggressive social media operation, nearly tripling the amount it spent on digital media in 2008. Romney's organization considered social media to be less of a priority than the Obama campaign and dedicated fewer resources to digital campaigning. According to the Project for Excellence in Journalism (PEJ), the Obama campaign tweeted an average of 29 times daily compared to a single daily tweet from the Romney campaign. In addition, Obama had twice as many Web site posts and YouTube videos than did Romney.

The dynamics underpinning the social media campaign in 2012 were decidedly different than in 2008. Top-down control by political and media organizations largely supplanted the populist imperative that characterized social media use in the previous presidential election. Voters were not as inspired by the candidates, and consequently were less inclined to innovate with social media on their behalf. Instead, supporters were encouraged to post material on the sites controlled by candidates and political parties. The campaign committees and the Democratic and Republican parties set as their social media priorities getting their message across, promoting their candidates' brand, fundraising, and attracting media attention. Their social media teams pushed out a tremendous amount of content to voters through a range of platforms, such as Pinterest, Reddit, Google+, Tumblr, and Foursquare, many of which did not exist four years earlier. While the campaigns were quick to hop on the latest social media bandwagon, they did little to explore innovative uses of these media that might have invested voters more solidly in the election or stimulated active engagement. Instead, social media functioned as campaign loudspeakers shouting messages to anyone who would listen.

The candidates' social media reflected their respective personal styles. Obama's digital communication tried to be hip and edgy, while Romney's was more restrained. Both Obama and Romney were perceived by voters as being distant, and they took to social media to change this image by sharing their favorite things—films, music, food, and more. Their campaigns also published snapshots depicting the candidates in intimate settings. An aide posted Twitter photos of Romney eating a peanut butter sandwich and playing with his grandchildren as the campaign came to a close. The Obama campaign circulated photos of the president sharing personal time with daughters, Sasha and Malia. To appeal to young voters who heavily populate social media, the campaigns kept digital scrapbooks on Tumblr and Pinterest. They tweeted references to popular culture icons, such as Kim Kardashian, and television programs, including *Modern Family* and *Friday Night Lights*. They launched remixed video clips with commentary and posted captioned memes on microblogging sites, such as Tumblr. The campaigns' social media managers posted real time reactions to key events, like the debates, which piqued the interest of younger voters, who posted hundreds of thousands of responses.

The news media stepped up its social media efforts markedly in 2012. The Web sites of mainstream media organizations incorporated multiple social media platforms with high tech features that allowed professional journalists, pundits, and citizens to post and disseminate information. Some journalists, such as CNN's Wolf Blitzer, became social media devotees who both contributed to and reported on digital media in the election. The press treated social media as a barometer for measuring shifts in campaign momentum despite concerns about the accuracy of this approach. The number of Facebook likes and Twitter followers became a metric for assessing the candidates' popularity—a contest that Obama won handily, with over 20 million more Facebook likes and 19 million more Twitter followers than Romney, according to the PEJ. The campaigns sought to control the communications agenda by posting social media content that would attract the attention of mainstream media outlets, hoping that they would propagate their messages; often, the campaigns were successful.

This brief overview does not do justice to the scope and complexity of social media in presidential elections. Social media platforms are multiplying, the applications are continually expanding, and the political functions are intensifying. The authors in this impressive volume move forward our understanding of social media in elections at both the state and national level in important ways and establish new baselines for research. This volume provides an historical context for considering social media's role in campaigns. It explores social media in primary campaigns, where much of the experimentation with political applications of digital platforms takes place, and it examines the dynamics of social media use during general elections. This text considers political learning, knowledge acquisition, and opinion formation through social media during the 2012 campaign, as well as voter and media engagement via social media. In so doing, this volume tackles prominent related issues, such as communication effects across different types of platforms and the significance of campaign social media for young people. This collection is a welcome contribution to new media scholarship.

Diana Owen
Washington, D.C.
Georgetown University

PREFACE

This book is an examination of how political communication has evolved in the 21st century and of the role of new media technologies in the American democratic process. Particularly, it provides a detailed examination of the role that social media and social networking sites (SNSs) such as Facebook, Twitter, You-Tube, Tumblr, Google Plus+, Instagram, Pinterest, and others played in the 2012 Republican presidential primaries and the general election campaign between former governor Mitt Romney, a Massachusetts Republican, and incumbent president Barack Obama, a former Democratic senator from Illinois. The book's chapters are divided into five areas of focus that include social media's role in: (1) the process of political communication, (2) political knowledge, (3) presidential primary elections, (4) the presidential general election, and (5) voter and media engagement throughout all stages of the 2012 campaign.

In 2008, then Senator Barack Obama became the first truly "21st-century communicator" and established a precedent for how future contenders for the White House and political offices below the Oval Office must communicate and interact with the electorate. In fact, Claire Cain Miller, a journalist for the *New York Times*, observed in November 2008 that: "One of the many ways that the election of Barack Obama as president has echoed that of John F. Kennedy is his use of a new medium that will forever change politics. For Mr. Kennedy, it was television. For Mr. Obama, it is the Internet." Politicians must now campaign with Facebook pages, YouTube channels, and Twitter accounts. In 2012, politicians utilized almost every type of new media technology that existed in order to reach voters of all ages, ethnicities, socio-economic backgrounds, sexual orientations, etc., to inspire and motivate Americans to participate in this country's democratic process of electing its leaders. Using both quantitative and qualitative methodological approaches, this book thoroughly examines the 2012 campaign's use of each form of social media technology and SNSs and considers which strategies proved effective in connecting with and motivating the electorate to vote.

As politics and new media technologies are becoming increasingly interdependent in modern elections, it is prudent to reflect on this symbiotic relationship. The 2012 campaign was characterized by a convergence of new technologies and new ways of communicating with and motivating the electorate. For example, during the 2008 presidential campaign, Twitter did not play a significant role; but, in contrast, Twitter was a primary means used by politicians to communicate with the electorate in 2012. Considering the convergence of these factors in the 2012 election, this book examines the ways in which new technologies were used by candidates, the media, and the voters. New media technologies have established themselves as influential and important communication tools in political campaigning, and this book strives to help better define the role of social media/new media not only in the 2012 presidential campaign, but also in future campaigns. This book will have wide appeal to students and scholars in political science, communication/media studies, and information technology studies. Because of the continued proliferation of new media technologies and the rapid adoption rates by consumers of these new technologies, this book should easily have a wide appeal for anyone seeking to better understand technology's role in 21st-century electioneering.

ACKNOWLEDGMENTS

The editors wish to express sincere appreciation to each contributor of this book for their wonderful work on each study and their eagerness and diligence to assist at all stages to ensure that this project was successfully completed. It is the collective interest and desire to better understand political communication among the contributors that made this book possible.

The editors wish to express appreciation to Jennifer Carpenter, executive editor of politics in the Higher Education Division at Oxford University Press in New York, who was very supportive of this project from its outset. Also, the editors wish to thank Maegan Sherlock, associate editor of politics in the Higher Education Division, whose guidance was valued throughout the process, especially because she fielded so many questions throughout the writing and editing stages. Everyone at Oxford University Press offered prompt and professional assistance at every juncture. Moreover, the editors want to thank the reviewers whose thoughtful and insightful comments and recommendations made this book much better and robust: Chris Burnett, California State University, Long Beach; Johanna Dunaway, Louisiana State University; Matthew Eshbaugh-Soha, University of North Texas; Michael Charles Grillo, University of Louisville; Lindsay Hoffman, University of Delaware; Rob Mellen Jr., Mississippi State University; Michael K. Romano, Western Michigan University; Carlos E. Diaz Rosillo, Harvard University; and John Barry Ryan, Florida State University.

John Allen Hendricks wishes to acknowledge the continued support of Stephen F. Austin State University (SFA) in Nacogdoches, Texas. SFA understands and values the need to balance scholarly pursuits with administrative and teaching responsibilities. Dan Schill would like to recognize his colleagues at James Madison University and to thank the innovators, investors, staffers, users, advocates, politicians, journalists, and programmers who developed and implemented the new communication technologies analyzed in this book.

Lastly, but perhaps most importantly, the editors wish to express gratefulness and love to their families for their continued support and understanding for the many hours that were spent at a computer focused on this book. John Allen Hendricks owes a debt of gratitude to his wife, Dr. Stacy Hendricks, and to his children, Abby and Haydyn. Dan Schill remains indebted to Jessica, Ellie, and Bennett.

John Allen Hendricks
Nacogdoches, Texas

Dan Schill
Harrisonburg, Virginia

ABOUT THE EDITORS

John Allen Hendricks (Ph.D., The University of Southern Mississippi) is chair of the Department of Mass Communication at Stephen F. Austin State University (SFA) in Nacogdoches, Texas, and he holds the rank of professor. The department includes the academic units of strategic communication (advertising/public relations), radio/television, and journalism/photojournalism/new media.

He is the former director of the Division of Communication & Contemporary Culture at SFA, which included the academic units of media studies, communication studies, philosophy, Greek, and Latin. Dr. Hendricks is the former chair of the Department of Communication and Theatre at Southeastern Oklahoma State University, which included the academic units of media studies, communication studies, and theatre, where he held the rank of professor. He has ten years of experience as an academic unit leader.

Dr. Hendricks has published six books on the topic of social media/new media technologies in politics and society, including: *Communicator-in-Chief: How Barack Obama Used New Media Technology to Win the White House* (with Robert E. Denton, Jr.), which was the recipient of the National Communication Association's Applied Research Division's 2011 Distinguished Scholarly Book Award; *Techno Politics in Presidential Campaigning: New Voices, New Technologies, and New Voters* (with Lynda Lee Kaid); *Social Media: Usage and Impact* (with Hana Noor Al-Deen); and *Social Media and Strategic Communications* (with Hana Noor Al-Deen).

Dr. Hendricks serves as a member of the 2013–2014 Broadcast Education Association's (BEA) Executive Committee after having served for four years as a member of the BEA Board of Directors representing Texas, Oklahoma, Kansas, Missouri, and Arkansas from 2009–2013. He is past president of the Oklahoma Broadcast Education Association (OBEA), as well as former chair of the Southern States Communication Association's (SSCA) Political Communication and Mass Communication Divisions.

Dan Schill (Ph.D., University of Kansas) is an associate professor in the School of Communication Studies at James Madison University. Dr. Schill currently teaches courses in advocacy, political communication, and media and politics. His research program investigates how political messages are created, shaped, and communicated by newsmakers, how those messages are covered and framed by the mass media, and how the messages are received and processed by audiences.

His book *Stagecraft and Statecraft: Advance and Media Events in Political Communication* was the first of its kind to comprehensively study the techniques, functions, and effects of media events in political affairs. Dr. Schill's work has appeared in *American Behavioral Scientist, Review of Communication, Rhetoric & Public Affairs, PS: Political Science & Politics,* and *Mass Communication and Society.* He has also received top paper awards from the Political Communication Divisions of the International Communication Association, National Communication Association, and the Central States Communication Association.

In addition to his academic research, Dr. Schill frequently conducts research for media outlets with Dr. Rita Kirk from Southern Methodist University. Since 2008, he and Dr. Kirk have organized and moderated on-air dial focus groups for CNN and provided real time analysis of debates, speeches, and ads. His research and analysis has also appeared in *The Wall Street Journal, Chicago Tribune, Chronicle of Higher Education,* and other national and regional media outlets. He spent the 2009–2010 academic year working on telecommunications and Internet policy issues for the United States Senate as an American Political Science Association Congressional Fellow.

ABOUT THE CONTRIBUTORS

Monica Ancu (Ph.D., University of Florida) is an assistant professor and under-graduate program coordinator in the Department of Journalism and Media Studies at the University of South Florida. She studies the role of online technologies, especially online social media, in political campaigns. Within this framework, she investigates how political candidates and voters use social network Web sites, blogs, podcasts, online advertising, etc., and how these online technologies affect political communication and political behavior. Her research has appeared in *Journalism Studies, American Behavioral Scientist, Journal of Broadcasting & Electronic Media,* as well as in several books.

Emily Kay Balanoff (Ph.D., University of Texas, Austin) is an assistant professor of Political Science at Texas State University. Balanoff's primary research interests are in organizational communication, civic engagement, and the nonprofit and voluntary sector. She has taught undergraduate courses in public personnel ad-ministration and graduate courses in nonprofit and voluntary sector theory and ethics. Her current work in public administration examines how nonprofits express and maintain public values. Dr. Balanoff has presented work at various regional and national conferences and is a board member of the Section for Women in Public Administration.

Jody C Baumgartner (Ph.D., Miami University) is an associate professor of politi-cal science at East Carolina University. His research focuses on the vice presidency, political humor, and various aspects of presidential campaigns.

Stephanie Brookes (Ph.D., University of Melbourne) is lecturer in media and communications at Monash University in Melbourne, Australia. Her research inter-ests are election campaign language; constructions of national identity in political discourse; and the intersection of local, national and global identity in news media. She has published peer-reviewed papers on Australian election campaign language, media coverage, and national identity, and she is the coauthor of the chapter on government advertising in *Government Communication in Australia*. She teaches Australian media and journalism studies, global media theory, and media policy.

Raluca Cozma (Ph.D., Louisiana State University) is an assistant professor at the Greenlee School of Journalism and Communication at Iowa State University. Cozma's research interests include political communication, foreign correspondence, and social media, and her work has been published in venues such as the *Journal of Broadcasting & Electronic Media, Newspaper Research Journal, Journalism Studies,* and The *Harvard International Journal of Press/Politics*.

Daniela V. Dimitrova (Ph.D., University of Florida) is an associate professor in the Greenlee School of Journalism and Communication at Iowa State University, where she teaches classes in international communication, political communication, multimedia production, and communication technology and social change. Her research interests focus on political communication, new media technologies, and the news framing of political events. Dimitrova's scholarly record includes more than 40 peer-reviewed publications in journals such as *Communication Research,* The *Harvard International Journal of Press/Politics, International Communication Gazette, Journalism & Mass Communication Quarterly, New Media & Society, Journal of Computer-Mediated Communication,* and *American Behavioral Scientist*. She is a member of the Association for Education in Journalism and Mass Communication, which is the largest U.S. organization for journalism educators, and she recently served as head of its Communication Technology Division.

David A. Dulio (Ph.D., American University) is professor and chair of Political Science at Oakland University in Rochester, Michigan. Dulio has published eight books, including *Cases in Congressional Campaigns: Riding the Wave* and *Vital Signs: Perspectives on the Health of American Campaigning*. He teaches courses on campaigns and elections, Congress, and political parties and interest groups.

Juliana Fernandes (Ph.D., University of Florida) is an assistant professor in the Department of Strategic Communication at the University of Miami. Her research interests include the affective impact of advertising, social media, and international political communication.

Jacob Groshek (Ph.D., Indiana University) is an assistant professor at Boston University. His research interests include the democratic utility of communication technologies and the ways in which the structure, content, and uses of online and mobile media may influence political change. Additional research pursuits include applied econometric analyses, data mining, public sentiment, and media ethics. He has over 20 peer-reviewed publications, and his work is featured in *Journal of Communication, New Media & Society, International Communication Gazette,* and *Journalism,* among others. Jacob also sits on the editorial board of *Communication*

Yearbook and has served as head of the Communication Technology Division of the Association for Education in Journalism and Mass Communication.

Gary Hanson (M.A., Kent State University) is a professor in the School of Journalism & Mass Communication at Kent State University. His research interests include the impact of new media on traditional media practices, new communication technologies, journalism ethics, and issues of journalistic accuracy.

Paul Haridakis (Ph.D., Kent State University) is a professor in the School of Communication Studies at Kent State University. His research interests include media use and effects; social media and other new communication technologies; media law, freedom of speech; mediated sports; and media history.

Joshua Hawthorne (B.A., University of Illinois) is a graduate student in communication at the University of Missouri working on his master's degree. His interests include political uses of social media and the influence of uncivil political messages on political violence.

Spiro Kiousis (Ph.D., University of Texas, Austin) is executive associate dean of the College of Journalism and Communications at the University of Florida and a professor in the Department of Public Relations. Kiousis was Research Foundation Professor from 2009–2011. His current research interests include political public relations, political communication, and new media.

Rita Kirk (Ph.D., University of Missouri) is the director of the Cary M. Maguire Center for Ethics & Public Responsibility and a professor in the Division of Communication Studies at Southern Methodist University. She is an Altshuler Distinguished Teaching Professor and a Meadows Distinguished Teaching Professor. As an academic, she is recognized for her analysis of political and persuasive campaigns. She is the author of three award-winning books and numerous articles, including *Political Empiricism: Communications Strategies in State and Regional Elections; Hate Speech* (with coeditor David Slayden), a book analyzing the implications of hate discourse in public communication; and *Solo Acts: The Death of Discourse in a Wired World.* Specializing in communication strategy, she has more than 25 years of experience as a strategist for city council, mayoral, state, U.S. Representative, and gubernatorial races. In addition to her political consulting, she serves as a communications consultant to several national and multinational corporations on public policy matters.

Neta Kligler-Vilenchik (M.A., University of Southern California) is a doctoral candidate at the University of Southern California Annenberg School for Communication and Journalism. Her work examines changing models of youth citizenship in contexts of new media and popular culture. Her recent research projects have examined the civic practices encouraged through participatory cultures and fan communities.

Mei-Chen Lin (Ph.D., University of Kansas) is an associate professor in the School of Communication Studies at Kent State University. Her research interests include intergroup communication and identity management, communication and aging, intergenerational communication, and new communication technologies.

Jessica Mahone (M.A., East Tennessee State University) is a doctoral candidate in political communication at the University of Florida. Mahone's research interests include media and social movements, credibility and non-institutional political groups, and political advertising.

Roxana Maiorescu (Ph.D., Purdue University) is an assistant professor in the Department of Marketing Communication at Emerson College. Her research interests include the strategic use of social media to enhance corporate identification, global crisis communication, corporate social responsibility, and ethical business practices. Roxana's work has been published by Sage and has appeared in peer-reviewed journals, including the *Business Research Yearbook* and the *International Journal of Interdisciplinary Research*. She has presented her work at national and international conferences such the National Communication Association Convention, the International Academy of Business Disciplines, the International Public Relations Research Conference, and the Association for Education in Journalism and Mass Communication.

Jennifer L. McCullough (Ph.D., The Ohio State University) is an assistant professor in the School of Communication Studies at Kent State University. Her research interests include media use and effects, media and children, parental mediation, consumer communication, and new communication technologies.

Sarah Turner McGowen (M.A., Northeastern State University) is a doctoral candidate in communication at the University of Missouri. Her research interests surround the intersection of gender, media, and politics.

David S. Morris (M.A., University of Virginia) is a doctoral candidate in the Department of Sociology at the University of Virginia. His research focuses on educational inequality and social stratification, with particular interests in student behavior, school discipline, family life, and political participation.

Jonathan S. Morris (Ph.D., Purdue University) is an associate professor of Political Science at East Carolina University. His research focuses on the media and politics, especially political humor and cable news. He is coeditor of *Laughing Matters: Humor and American Politics in the Media Age,* and he has published in several journals, including *Political Research Quarterly, Public Opinion Quarterly,* and *Political Behavior.* His teaching interests are in American government, political communication, and political analysis.

Eisa Al Nashmi (Ph.D., University of Florida) is an assistant professor in the Department of Mass Communication at Kuwait University. His research interests include online journalism, new media in the Middle East, and political communication.

Cynthia Opheim (Ph.D., University of Texas, Austin) is associate provost for Academic Affairs and a professor of Political Science at Texas State University. Her research focus is American politics with an emphasis on legislative process, political parties, comparative state politics, and the role of the Internet in politics. She has published articles in leading academic journals such as the *Legislative Studies Quarterly, Regional and Federal Studies,* and *Public Administration Review.* She has taught both graduate and undergraduate courses on the U.S. Congress as well as the senior capstone course on American politics. She has directed and is a regular participant in the Texas State in England Study Abroad program in which she teaches courses comparing the British parliamentary and American presidential systems. Dr. Opheim served as chair of the Political Science Department from 1996–2003 and interim chair of geography from 2004–2005. She has served as both vice president and president of the Southwestern Political Science Association.

Diana Owen (Ph.D., University of Wisconsin-Madison) is associate professor of political science and director of American studies at Georgetown University. She teaches in the Communication, Culture, and Technology graduate program of which she is a cofounder. She is the author of *Media Messages in American Presidential Elections, New Media and American Politics* (with Richard Davis), and *American Government and Politics in the Information Age* (with David Paletz and Timothy Cook). She is the coeditor of *The Internet and Politics: Citizens, Voters, and Activists* (with Sarah Oates and Rachel Gibson) and *Making a Difference: The Internet and Elections in Comparative Perspective* (with Richard Davis, Stephen Ward, and David Taras). She is the author of numerous journal articles and book chapters in the fields of media and politics, political socialization and civic education, elections and voting behavior, and political psychology/sociology. She is the research editor of *Electronic Media and Politics.*

David Lynn Painter (Ph.D., University of Florida) is a course director in the new media journalism and public relations Master of Arts programs at Full Sail University. His research interests include online political communication and political advertising.

LaChrystal D. Ricke (Ph.D., University of Kansas) is an assistant professor of mass communication at Sam Houston State University in Texas. Her primary area of research is the intersection of Web 2.0 technologies—specifically YouTube—and political communication and civic engagement. Her research has appeared in the *Journal of Information Technology and Politics,* the *Encyclopedia of Social Media and Politics,* and in the book *Politics and Popular Culture.* Her primary teaching interests are mass media theory and criticism.

Jesper Strömbäck (Ph.D., Stockholm University) is a Lubbe Nordström professor and chair of journalism as well as a professor of media and communications at Mid Sweden University. He has published more than 100 journal articles, book chapters, and books on political communication, political news journalism, and strategic political communication.

Emma Svensson (M.A., Lund University) is a doctoral candidate in political communication at Mid Sweden University. Her research interests concern strategic political communication in general and political public relations in particular.

Kjerstin Thorson (Ph.D., University of Wisconsin-Madison) is an assistant professor of journalism at the University of Southern California. Her research explores the effects of digital and social media on political engagement, activism and persuasion, especially among youth. Recent research projects have investigated uses of Facebook around the 2012 election, video activism in the Occupy Movement, and the contributions of media use in shifting conceptions of politics among young adults.

Terri L. Towner (Ph.D., Purdue University) is an assistant professor of political science at Oakland University in Rochester, Michigan. Towner's research focuses on the influence of new media on political attitudes, the role of race and ethnicity in politics, attitudes toward the Iraq War, and the pedagogical value of social networks. Her work has been published in journals such as The *Journal of Political Marketing, New Media & Society,* and The *Howard Journal of Communications.* She teaches courses on public opinion, political behavior, politics and the Internet, and quantitative methodology.

Emily K. Vraga (Ph.D., University of Wisconsin-Madison) is an assistant professor in the Department of Communication at George Mason University. Her research examines how individual predispositions such as partisan identity influence the processing of media content, particularly in the evolving digital environment. Recent projects have explored the use of social media in promoting political and social engagement, the role of dissonance in explaining response to incongruent information, and the impact of tone in judging content credibility.

Benjamin R. Warner (Ph.D., University of Kansas) is an assistant professor of communication at the University of Missouri. His research interests include political extremism, incivility, and political uses of digital media.

Andrew Paul Williams (Ph.D., University of Florida) is a writer, researcher, communication consultant, and social media strategist who approaches his work from international and interdisciplinary perspectives. He is president/founder of Williams Media Management, LLC. He researches the use of new media and evolving technologies—primarily in the context of political communication—and analyzes the ways in which mass media, organizations, and audiences frame issues, objects, and events. His work has been published in journals such as *Journal of Political Marketing, Journal of International Business Disciplines, American Behavioral Scientist, Harvard International Journal of Press/Politics, Journalism Studies,* and *Mass Communication and Society.* He is the coeditor of the book *The Internet Election: Perspectives of the Web in Campaign 2004.* Williams has presented many speeches and findings from his research at leading international communication and political science conferences. He has received top paper awards at the annual conferences of the Broadcast Education Association and the International Communication Association. He taught communications classes at Virginia Tech, University of Florida, and Flagler College. Williams has been recognized for his outstanding teaching by the International Communication Association. As a journalist, his work has also been published as feature articles in magazines and newspapers such as *Where, Jacksonville Magazine, Financial News & Daily Record,* and The *Clay County Leader.*

Hyun Jung Yun (Ph.D., University of Florida) is an associate professor of political science at Texas State University. Her research is dedicated to interdisciplinary approaches across political communication, public opinion, geopolitics, and applied methodology. Her research has been published in several leading journals, such as *American Behavioral Scientist* and *Journalism Studies.* Additionally, she has authored several book chapters that examined the media coverage of policy issues and political candidates across different political regions to observe the relationship between voters' embedded political characteristics and political information effects. She has served as the data analyst and research manager of several grant-supported and inter-university collaborated projects since 2004. She teaches senior and graduate level courses with her concentration focusing on political communication and applied quantitative methodology.

CHAPTER 1

The Presidential Campaign of 2012: New Media Technologies Used to Interact and Engage with the Electorate

John Allen Hendricks and Dan Schill

O n Election Day 2012, public opinion polls and commentators described the election as too close to call, and political watchers wondered if incumbent president Barack Obama would be reelected or whether former Massachusetts governor Mitt Romney would come out ahead. It was seen as neck and neck. For example, the Gallup (2012) poll's final pre-election survey estimated 49 percent of voters backing Romney and 48 percent backing Obama. Five days before the election, Steve Lombardo (2012, para. 1) predicted, "it is now pretty clear that—barring a destabilizing external event—Mitt Romney will likely win the national popular vote for president." Of course, Obama soundly defeated Romney in the electoral college and bested Romney by over 5 million votes in the popular vote count.

But leading up to the election, perhaps the most calm—or maybe relieved—group was Obama's number crunchers and forecasters sheltered in The Cave, a windowless room in the campaign's Chicago headquarters. The Obama campaign never really felt behind and did not think the race was close at the end because they spent more time, effort, and money on polling, modeling, and get-out-the-vote efforts than ever before. As part of its digital campaign, the Obama campaign recruited the best young minds in the booming fields of behavioral science, big data, and analytics and had them work 16 hours a day for 16 months in an effort to determine how every single wavering voter in the country would vote and how to persuade them to their side (Rutenberg, 2013). This group developed the most comprehensive and sophisticated voter model in the country, and the model turned out to be strikingly accurate. The Obama campaign's forecasting model—internally code-named the "Golden Report" for its summary report routinely sent to senior aides—successfully predicted Obama's vote share to within half a percentage point in 6 of the top-10 battleground states (Iowa, New Hampshire, Colorado, Florida, Nevada, and Wisconsin), within one percentage point in 3 swing states (Virginia,

North Carolina, and Pennsylvania), and within 2 points in Ohio (Green, 2013b). These models also proved to be more accurate than the traditional tracking polls conducted by the Obama campaign (Green, 2013a).

The foundation for Golden was "ID calls"— the 4,000 to 9,000 phone calls the campaign would place to voters in battleground states each day. These short four-question surveys, which totaled nearly one million by Election Day, allowed the campaign to update its model daily and to make more detailed predictive models than ever before. While campaigns have long used voter file databases, the Obama campaign innovated both in terms of integration and scale. The Cave's modeling gave every registered voter a "support score" from 0 to 100 (with 100 being a certain Obama supporter) in order to make voter contact and canvassing more efficient. In terms of integration, the campaign merged door-to-door voter contact information from the Democratic National Committee going back to 1992 with data from the 2008 Election Day voter-tracking system (called Houdini) and with demographic and attitudinal data from consumer preference databases. Most importantly, the master database was constantly updated with information from canvassing, online behavior tracking, and social networking sites (SNSs). By mining and modeling the data in this master database, the campaign tried to cal-culate the likelihood of whether each registered voter would support Obama (the previously mentioned support score), the odds that they might volunteer or donate, and the chances that each of the 180 million profiled individuals would vote early. The tech unit worked feverously to integrate all of this data into a simple set of services that acted as an interface to a unified data store that could be used for all of the campaign's applications and assist the field, political, and other units. This software project—named Narwhal, after the tusked whale—was constantly behind schedule and ultimately too complex to finish before Election Day, but bits and pieces of Narwhal were completed and used in other software, such as the canvassing application called Dashboard.

Using these methods, the Obama campaign identified roughly 15 million voters in swing states who were most persuadable, and Campaign Manager Jim Messina ordered the campaign to focus a majority of its efforts on winning over these voters, one by one if needed (Rutenberg, 2013). The campaign tried to link traditionally online communication tactics with offline engagement methods and used data to inform all campaign decisions. Messina said:

> There's always been two campaigns since the Internet was invented, the campaign online and the campaign on the doors. What I wanted was, I didn't care where you organized, what time you organized, how you organized, as long as I could track it, I can measure it, and I can encourage you to do more of it (cited in Balz, 2013, para. 13).

Traditional political communication channels such as television advertising and door-to-door canvassing would be very important (and the Obama campaign used data to optimize those efforts), but digital communications—namely social media like Facebook, Twitter, and YouTube—would be more important than ever. After the campaign, Teddy Goff, digital director for Obama 2012, described

Facebook as "the most significant new addition to the voter-contact arsenal that's come around in years, since the phone call" (cited in Madrigal, 2012).

To locate and persuade these targeted voters, the Obama team started with supporters who signed into the campaign Web site through Facebook. The campaign then asked for permission to scan their Facebook friends lists, photos, and news feeds. Once granted consent, the campaign could access millions of names and profiles that could be matched against the campaign's list of persuadable voters. After this, the campaign asked the self-identified supporters to reach out to their undecided friends and urge them to register, vote Democratic, volunteer, or donate. Individuals fitting persuadable voter profiles were likely to see targeted content spilling into their newsfeeds from the campaign and their friends' Facebook posts. The Obama digital unit had over 200 staff members who generated a constant stream of videos, e-mails, texts, tweets, Facebook posts, and other online content. In the end, the Obama campaign said one million people used its Facebook application by Election Day (Judd, 2012a), and this targeted, person-to-person contact on Facebook reached 5 million voters, most of whom were younger and more difficult to reach through traditional methods, such as telephone calls and door-knocking campaigns (Judd, 2012b). In total, one-fifth of the campaign's overall media budget—$109 million—was spent on digital advertising (Alter, 2013).

During and after the election, many claims were made about the importance of data, digital communications, and social media. Journalist Jonathan Alter (2013), for instance, wrote:

> The 2012 cycle will likely be seen as the first 'data campaign.' Just as Franklin Roosevelt and John F. Kennedy have been viewed by historians as the first presidents to master radio and television, respectively, Barack Obama will likely be seen as the president who pioneered the use of digital technology that, in various forms, will now be a permanent part of politics around the world. (p. iv)

The purpose of this book is to test these claims and to empirically examine, describe, and analyze the role of social media in the 2012 campaign. This chapter begins this examination by providing an overview of Internet and SNS usage in the 2012 presidential primaries and general campaign.

As the forthcoming chapters lay out, this book finds that social media played a central role in the 2012 Republican primary and the 2012 general election— social media influenced the race by educating voters, setting media agendas, and effecting participation, but SNSs themselves were not determinative in the election outcome. This is similar to what other researchers have observed when measuring different 2012 election effects. John Sides and Lynn Vavreck (2013), for example, found that advertising spending and field office activity was not determinative in 2012 because neither side had a large advantage in campaign resources, both sides ran reasonably effective campaigns, and because Obama benefitted as an incumbent running amidst modest economic growth. The same can be said about the candidates' social media use—both sides invested in digital communications and ran reasonably effective campaigns, and social media use was only one factor in the multifaceted election.

Importantly, this book doesn't take a side in the ongoing debate about whether social media, and online communication in general, is "good" or "bad" for our politics and public sphere. It is unquestionable that our politics and public dialogue are changing in many complicated and multidimensional ways, and a heated debate has emerged about these changes. On one side are optimist thinkers associated with technological utopianism and related philosophies (e.g., Johnson, 2012; Schmidt & Cohen, 2013) who affirm that technology will empower individuals and solve many of the world's problems. On the other side are digital pessimists who attack over-extended Internet-centrism (e.g., Morozov, 2013) and argue that technology inflicts unattended consequences on our privacy, civic engagement, and morality. Of course, there are also those who hold a middle position (e.g., Mele, 2013), describing the positive and negative outcomes of these changes. This book is not a polemic or think piece, as is common in books published on this topic. Instead, each chapter empirically studies social media use through quantitative, qualitative, or mixed methods. Indeed, commentators on all sides of this debate may find data points in any given chapter to support their arguments, which suggests that social media use is complex, dynamic, and has many outcomes that we do not yet understand.

THE 2012 REPUBLICAN PRIMARY AND SOCIAL MEDIA

From its early stages, the 2012 race was waged on social media outlets. Notably, candidates formally announced their intent to run for president using new media technologies (Mehta, 2011). "Politicians have long adapted to new platforms to press their agendas, from Franklin D. Roosevelt's embrace of fireside chats on the radio in the 1930s and 1940s to John F. Kennedy's use of television decades later. Adoption of online innovation has occurred much more rapidly," asserted Seema Mehta (2011, para. 9).

In 2012, the Democratic Party had an incumbent in the White House, former Illinois senator Barack Obama, who was seeking a second term after having had a first term wherein domestic policy was front and center due to a poor economy that demanded his primary and consistent attention. A number of current and former Republican governors, senators, and House members emerged to seek their party's nomination and serve as its nominee to run in the general election against President Obama. In the end, the Democrats nominated Barack Obama to serve as their nominee, while the Republicans nominated former Massachusetts governor Mitt Romney as their nominee.

Although the Republicans eventually supported Governor Romney, who was described as looking "like Hollywood's idea of a president" (Freedland, 2012, para. 5) and was one of the wealthiest individuals to ever run for the presidency, his path to the nomination was far from easy. Governor Romney faced a challenging and grueling 2012 Republican primary process that not only included 22 debates but also had a wide-ranging cast of individuals and rivals with varying backgrounds and qualifications who were also seeking the party's nomination. That cast of candidates included the following: 1) Minnesota congresswoman

Michele Bachmann; 2) former Godfather's Pizza CEO Herman Cain; 3) former U.S. Speaker of the House of Representatives Newt Gingrich; 4) Jon Huntsman, Jr., former Utah governor and former U.S. ambassador to China under President Obama; 5) Texas congressman Ron Paul; 6) Texas governor Rick Perry; 7) former Louisiana congressman and governor Buddy Roemer; and 8) Rick Santorum, former U.S. senator from Pennsylvania. While Romney was backed by many in the Republican establishment, he faced frequent challenges by colorful competitors endorsed by the Tea Party, religious groups, and libertarian-minded party members. At various points during the primary, five candidates (Romney, Perry, Cain, Gingrich, and Santorum) led in the polls (Real Clear Politics, 2012). Jonathan Freedland (2012) declared: "The field of [Republican] rivals included outlandish characters who seemed absurd to outsiders: pizza magnate Herman Cain, evolution-denying congresswoman Michele Bachmann, Texas governor Rick Perry, who could not remember which three government departments he planned to shut down" (para. 5).

As a result of Obama's success with new media technologies and social media in 2008 (Hendricks & Denton, 2010), the conservative candidates learned that they should use all available communication channels to engage and interact with the electorate and involve individuals in the political process. In fact, Sujan Patel (2012) stated: "It's clear that the 2012 Republican primary candidates took these lessons [of the 2008 campaign] to heart, as social media involvement has never been higher during an election cycle" (para. 2). Illustrating the ability of social media to reach and to engage with the electorate, the Obama campaign team reported that by the end of the 2008 presidential campaign there had been an astonishing 1 billion viewings on the campaign's YouTube channel (Pew Research Center, 2012), and Republicans hoped to replicate Obama's successes.

To leverage the power of social media to reach the electorate and engage with potential supporters, each of the Republican primary candidates utilized some form of social networking platform. However, simply having a static presence on social media did not suffice, as one must have an effective and continuous presence on SNSs and have a successful social media communication strategy. Newt Gingrich had 1.4 million Twitter followers, which gave the appearance that he had strong support among his party's base; however, it was learned that half of those followers were not Twitter accounts that even originated from the United States (Sifry, 2012). Observers noted that after Rick Santorum performed so well in the Iowa caucuses and interested individuals started visiting his Web site, the site actually crashed, and visitors were unable to access the page (Stirland & Judd, 2012).

Early in the Republican presidential primary, Pesante (2011) criticized the Republican candidates' use of social media technology and offered astute advice:

> I . . . have a problem with what I've seen from these potential GOP candidates and it is simple: too much reaction and not enough proactive social media strategy. Anyone can use their Twitter, YouTube or Facebook accounts to rant, blow off steam, voice their opinions and point fingers. It takes a measured, responsible candidate to mobilize people through social networking sites where they then translate into the foot soldiers necessary to win an election . . . I don't think any

Republican presidential hopefuls are harnessing the power of social media to their fullest ability. Stop reacting and attacking and start using your SNSs to discuss your platform and the issues. (paras. 7–8)

Brown (2012) similarly noted that social media "followers," "likes," and "views" did not always translate into actual votes. For example, leading up to the Iowa caucuses on January 3, 2012, Governor Romney had 1.2 million Facebook followers, Congressman Ron Paul had more than 600,000 followers, and Rick Santorum had just under 61,000 followers. Moreover, Texas governor Rick Perry released a YouTube advertisement that garnered more than 7.5 million views. But, when the state's caucuses were over, Santorum beat Romney by only 8 votes, Paul came in third place, and Perry decided to return to Texas to assess his bid for the presidency because he did so poorly. Leading up to the New Hampshire primary, *The Washington Post*'s "Mention Machine," which tracked what people were talking about on social media, indicated that Ron Paul was the most talked about of all the Republican candidates, yet he placed second in the New Hampshire primary, behind Romney. Accordingly, a mere presence on social media does not suffice for electoral success. A controversial video may generate page views, but dedicated supporters in primary states, a compelling message, and a competent candidate mattered more on caucus and primary nights. In other words, an effective and well-targeted social media strategy was more important.

SOCIAL MEDIA PLATFORMS

All of the presidential candidates, not only during the Republican primary but also during the general election campaign, used the three most popular SNSs: Facebook, YouTube, and Twitter. Of the top 500 Web sites visited by Americans, Facebook ranks second, only behind Google, with over 163 million American users (Alexa.com, 2012). Facebook is designed to connect friends and acquaintances with a constant newsfeed of status updates, photos, videos, links to webpages, and other items of interest that connect this vast network of individuals (Socialbakers.com, 2012).

YouTube, a SNS designed to upload, share, and comment on videos, ranks as the third most visited Web site by Americans and has more than 800 million unique visits to the site each month (YouTube, 2012; Alexa.com, 2012).

Twitter, with more than one billion users, is the tenth most visited Web site by Americans (Alexa.com, 2012). Like texting on a smartphone, Twitter has an online interface that allows users to post short comments (140 characters per entry), also known as "tweets," and to follow the comments of other users (Wasserman, 2012).

Social media use in the 2012 presidential campaign was not limited to these three sites. Popular sites used by Obama and Romney (and citizens) included: 1) Pinterest, the fourteenth most visited Web site by Americans, allows users to identify and "pin" their favorite things to share with friends; 2) Tumblr, the eighteenth most visited Web site by Americans, is a blog-hosting platform where users share photos and multimedia; and, 3) Instagram, the forty-eighth most visited site by Americans, allows users to upload and customize photos (Alexa.com, 2012).

Other sites were also significant, but less important in the overall landscape. For instance, Obama made headlines when he held a digital question-and-answer session with young tech-savvy voters of the Reddit Web community, and it was so successful that Obama made a return visit to ask for last-minute votes (Rodriguez, 2012). Showing its mobilization potential, 30,000 Redditors registered to vote after Obama inserted a link to the Obama voter registration page during his Q&A session (Madrigal, 2012).

E-mail also remained an important digital communications channel. Notably, as anyone who signed up to receive campaign e-mail messages experienced, the campaigns sent hundreds of millions of e-mail messages to raise money and mobilize supporters, and the majority of the $690 million that Obama raised online came via e-mail solicitation (Green, 2012). In total, nearly $7 billion was spent on the 2012 election (Schouten, 2013). Thomas (2011) asserted, "[E-mail] is still king when it comes to fundraising" (para. 21). In 2012, the campaigns turned e-mail solicitation into a science through A/B comparison testing. In late June of 2012, when the Obama campaign was running low on money, for example, the team tested 13 versions of an e-mail message from the president on a sample of their e-mail list. Several subject lines were tested, including "Would love to meet you," "Do this for Michelle," and "Some scary numbers," but the winner of the test was "I will be outspent." That message went on to raise $2.6 million in a single day when e-mailed to the entire list (Alter, 2013).

Enabling this growth in social media use was the rapid adoption of smartphones. In 2012, 45% of adults owned smartphones, 55% went online using their phones, and the average adult sent more than 41 text messages per day (Rainie, 2012). Facebook, Twitter, and other social networking services were integrated into popular smartphone operating systems, such as Apple's iOS and Google's Android. This allowed users to quickly and easily check their e-mail and SNS feeds. The campaigns also developed smartphone apps for reaching out to supporters and disseminating messages and media. One simple but important innovation from Obama's digital team was a quick donate mobile app that raised $75 million by allowing supporters to give with one click instead of filling out paperwork or online forms. According to the campaign, donors who used the frictionless, quick donate app gave 4 times as often and 3 times as much money as those who didn't (Alter, 2013).

In 2012, a majority of Americans used social media. Surveys have found that 69% of all adults online used SNSs, with 66% using Facebook (Brenner, 2012) and 13% using Twitter (Smith, 2012). Interestingly, 54% of online adults accessed Twitter via their smartphones. Regarding YouTube and other video sharing sites, 55% of registered voters watched a political video in 2012, 52% received a video recommendation via an SNS, and 19% made a video recommendation to a friend (Smith & Duggan, 2012). These percentages are significant, since it is estimated that Internet usage in the U.S. exceeds more than 245 million individuals (Internet Usage, 2012). Importantly, social media allowed the candidates to bypass the filtering and gate-keeping abilities of traditional media and reach the electorate directly (and for citizens to communicate with each other). The Pew Research

Center (2012) asserted: "In 2012, in short, voters are playing an increasingly large role in helping to communicate campaign messages, while the role of the traditional news media as an authority or validator has only lessened" (p. 4). Few would debate social media's prominent role in the 2012 campaign. Even former Democratic president Bill Clinton concluded, "The way the Obama campaign won Florida, won Ohio, won this election by more than projected was the combination of technology, social media and personal contact" (cited in Tau, 2013, para. 5).

GENERAL ELECTION

Although pollsters predicted the 2012 election would be very close, social media analytics indicated otherwise: "President Obama dominated the social media battle, and ended up winning the presidency" (Adams, 2012, para. 1). Adams declared that social media engagement is a proxy for voter engagement and that social media analytics have predictive abilities when determining who will win political elections: "candidates who win the social media volume battle will win the election, and the social media volume battle was overwhelmingly won by Obama" (para. 8). Obama and Romney used Facebook, Twitter, and YouTube, but also expanded their SNS footprint by engaging and interacting with the electorate via Tumblr, Pinterest, Google+ (launched in 2011 as an SNS similar to Facebook), and Spotify (a commercial music-streaming service that allowed both candidates to share with the electorate what their favorite music was via their Spotify accounts).

Although the Republican primary did not prove Adams' (2012) theory accurate, the results of the general election did provide some interesting data to consider and apply toward Adams' notion that social media analytics have some predictive abilities as to which candidate will win. As of November 1, 2012, Obama's YouTube channel exceeded 262 million video views and 254,807 subscribers, compared to Romney's 29.3 million video views and 27,633 subscribers—a difference of more than 227,000 subscribers. On Election Day, Obama had just over 33 million Facebook "likes" compared to Romney's 12 million "likes"—a difference of 21 million. And in the end, Obama had 20 million more Twitter followers than Romney (Kasperkevic, 2012). The Obama campaign team far outpaced the Romney campaign team when it came to social media staff; comparatively, the Obama campaign headquarters had 750 people dedicated to working on the social/digital media team while Romney's campaign headquarters only had a staff of 87 people (Rogers, 2012). Not only did Obama's team have a head start and more staff than Romney's digital team, but the Obama team had a more effective social media strategy of attracting and engaging supporters.

As described earlier in this chapter, the president was far ahead of his Republican challenger in digital and social media use. Mehta (2011) observed:

> Obama's emphasis on social media in his first campaign left him with a treasure trove of millions of cellphone numbers and email addresses. Those supporters were the first to be formally notified of his reelection bid and directed to a [Web site] listing local Obama events, volunteer opportunities and ways to donate money. (para. 25)

Building on their 2008 success, the Obama campaign had several innovations in the social media space in 2012. The main innovation was integrating the massive voter file with information from social media and mobile contacts with polling data, fundraising databases, field outreach files, and consumer databases so that the campaign could target and hyper-personalize the messages for each contact (Harris, 2012; Scherer, 2012). The campaign employed a large team of data scientists "better able to decide who could be most easily persuaded to vote for the first time, to donate money, to get active knocking on doors or perhaps even to switch sides" (Harris, 2012, para. 4) on a voter-by-voter basis. For the first time, Facebook was used on a mass scale to replicate the traditional door-knocking efforts of field organizers. As Scherer (2012) described:

> In the final weeks of the campaign, people who had downloaded an app were sent messages with pictures of their friends in swing states. They were told to click a button to automatically urge those targeted voters to take certain actions, such as registering to vote, voting early or getting to the polls. The campaign found that roughly 1 in 5 people contacted by a Facebook pal acted on the request, in large part because the message came from someone they knew. (para. 12)

And Obama's Facebook followers have tremendous reach. According to Teddy Goff, Obama's digital director, "the nearly 34 million Facebook users who 'like' Barack Obama on the social networking sites are friends with 98% of the U.S. Facebook population, making it an effective tool to reach out to younger voters" (cited in Miller, 2012, para. 10).

PRESIDENTIAL CAMPAIGNING AND SOCIAL MEDIA

The 2012 presidential campaign was considered by many observers to be the "social media" campaign. Friess (2012) declared: "This was the first presidential cycle in which the full complement of social media tools were mature enough to alter the canvas of American elections in ways that may not have seemed to matter at the time" (para. 2). The SNSs were abuzz throughout the 2012 presidential campaign with "political memes"—satirical, hyperbolic, and sometimes caustic images and quotations that caught attention from the campaign trail and spread through social media. Political memes are described by Fitzpatrick (2012) as "the democratization of political cartoons" (para. 3). One popular "Texts from Hillary" Tumblr meme showed a photo of Governor Romney sending a text message to Hillary Clinton asking: "Any advice?" with the juxtaposition of a photo of Clinton texting back to the governor on her smartphone: "Drink."

Social media memes often developed in real time and captured media and public attention. For instance, speaking immediately before Romney on the final night of the Republican national convention, actor and Republican Clint Eastwood used his time at the podium to talk to an empty chair that was supposed to be an imaginary Barack Obama. The incident included Eastwood rambling aimlessly, or "Eastwooding," as it came to be known, which confused not only the Republicans in the convention arena, but also those watching the performance on television.

An appearance by a popular and beloved conservative actor that was designed to be one of the highlights of the convention was ultimately deemed by observers and political analysts to be a huge negative for Romney as thousands mocked the speech on Facebook and Twitter (with the #Eastwooding tag). Kroll (2012) declared that Eastwood "delivered one of the most bizarre political convention speeches in American history" (para. 1). Fully embracing the power of social media, Eastwood's performance prompted the Obama campaign to create its own meme in response with a photo of President Obama sitting in a chair labeled "The President" in the White House Cabinet Room, with the text simply saying, "This seat's taken." Barbaro and Shear (2012) of the *New York Times* stated: "Mr. Eastwood's rambling and off-color appearance just moments before the biggest speech of Mr. Romney's life instantly became a Twitter and cable-news sensation, which drowned out much of the usual post-convention analysis that [Romney's] campaign had hoped to bask in" (para. 6).

One of the most damaging social media incidents for Governor Romney was the so-called "47%" video that was secretly recorded, posted anonymously on YouTube, and later promoted by *Mother Jones* magazine. The video went viral and showed Romney saying to a group of wealthy donors to his campaign that:

> There are 47 percent of the people who will vote for the president no matter what. All right—there are 47 percent who are with him, who are dependent on government, who believe that, that they are victims, who believe that government has the responsibility to care for them. Who believe that they are entitled to health care, to food, to housing. My job is not to worry about those people. I'll never convince them they should take personal responsibility and care for their lives.

Romney was forced to respond, as the video became the topic de rigueur and was prominently highlighted in Obama attack ads. The video aligned perfectly with the caricature of an out-of-touch plutocrat, which not only did the Obama camp attempt to label Romney, but so did Romney's challengers in the Republican primary. David Corn (2012), of *Mother Jones* magazine, who first wrote about the video, asserted: "That moment, when millions of Americans saw the candidate denigrating nearly half the electorate as 'victims' who do not take 'personal responsibility and care for their lives,' is widely seen as having upended the campaign" (para. 1). This pivotal moment—where a bartender surreptitiously recorded a video on his smartphone and an anonymous person posted it to YouTube—would not have happened without social media.

The Obama campaign was not free of mistakes and damaging political memes that circulated throughout social media. One of the most damaging memes for President Obama was the "You Didn't Build That" video clip. During a speech in Virginia in July 2012, Obama stated:

> Look, if you've been successful, you didn't get there on your own. You didn't get there on your own. I'm always struck by people who think, well, it must be because I was just so smart. There are a lot of smart people out there. It must be because I worked harder than everybody else. Let me tell you something—there are a whole bunch of hardworking people out there. If you were successful,

somebody along the line gave you some help. There was a great teacher somewhere in your life. Somebody helped to create this unbelievable American system that we have that allowed you to thrive. Somebody invested in roads and bridges. If you've got a business—you didn't build that. Somebody else made that happen. The Internet didn't get invented on its own. Government research created the Internet so that all the companies could make money off the Internet. (Remarks by President Obama, 2012, para. 79)

The Romney campaign and its supporters capitalized in ads, digital content, and fundraising e-mails using video that highlighted the president's words, "you didn't build that." Governor Romney's campaign even built a backdrop with large letters that read "WE DID BUILD THAT" to use during speeches, and "We Built It" was the theme of the first day of the Republican convention. Related to this incident, one meme had a photo of God creating Earth and the Biblical scripture of Genesis 1:1: "In the beginning, God created the heavens and the earth," with a photo of Obama saying to God, "You didn't build that. Somebody else made that happen."

SOCIAL MEDIA AND CHANGING AMERICAN DEMOGRAPHICS

Social media usage among racial and ethnic minorities in America is at an all-time high; and, importantly, the American minority population used certain social media technology, such as Twitter, more than white Americans during the 2012 presidential campaign (Smith, 2012). Indeed, adoption rates are growing at an un-precedented pace, all while minority and youth demographics are engaging social media in much higher numbers and concentrations than white and older Americans. For instance, Smith (2012) found that Hispanics and African Americans were more likely than Caucasians to use Twitter. Smith stated: "One in ten African-American internet users now visit Twitter on a typical day–that is double the rate for Latinos and nearly four times the rate for whites" (p. 3).

The demographic groups who used social media at the highest rates were also the groups most likely to vote for President Obama.

Although the demographic change was well underway during the 2008 election, that change was even more prominent in the 2012 presidential campaign. Hispanic Americans made up 17% of the U.S. population and consisted of 10% of the vote in the 2012 election. Hispanic Americans overwhelmingly voted for Obama with 71% of the vote, while Romney only received 27% of the Hispanic vote. Black Americans made up 12% of the U.S. population and consisted of 13% of the vote in the 2012 election. Black Americans overwhelmingly voted for Obama with 93% of the vote, while Romney only received 6% of the African American vote in the 2012 election. In comparison, White Americans made up 63% of the U.S. population and made up 72% of the 2012 vote and supported Romney with 59% of the vote, compared to Obama receiving 39% of the vote. Single women, who made up 23% of the 2012 vote, supported Obama 67% to Romney's 31%; compared to married women, who made up 31% of the vote and supported Romney 53% to Obama's 46%. Interestingly, 54% of single women identified themselves as Democrats, compared to 36% of married women who identified themselves as Democrats. Overall, however, American women were more likely to be Democrats than Republicans. In total, Obama won a whopping 80% of nonwhite voters in the 2012 presidential election (Cass & Benac, 2012).

Not only is the American population experiencing a change in ethnic diversity, but it is also experiencing the political emergence of a new generation—the Millennial Generation. This generation includes those born between the years of 1982 to 2003. The Millennials are the largest generation in American history, even larger than the Baby Boom generation. This is a generation that is politically active and will emerge as a voting bloc to be reckoned with in future elections, if not already. Winograd and Hais (2008) assert that the Millennial Generation will create a civic realignment in America that will drastically reshape the political landscape for decades. They note, however, that "the political party that will benefit from the coming realignment is not preordained" (p. 107). Interestingly, and perhaps foretelling for both the 2008 and 2012 presidential elections, the Democratic Party was solidly supported by this voting bloc. In 2012, the youth vote, or those under the age of 30, went overwhelmingly to Obama with 60% of the vote compared to Romney's 37% (CIRCLE, 2012).

Winograd and Hais (2008) state: "The campaigns, candidates, and events of the rest of this decade will determine which party gains the life-long allegiance of this new generation and, with it, a dominant advantage in the next civic era of American politics" (p. 108). Political parties and strategists not only need to be concerned with the youth vote, but also the previously mentioned shifts occurring among many other voting demographics. Prior to the 2012 election, The *Wall Street Journal*'s Gerald Seib (2011) observed:

> The core constituencies of the Democratic party—minorities, working women, educated voters in urban areas, younger voters—all are growing as a share of the electorate. Meanwhile, the white vote, where Republicans have done best, and where Mr. Obama's support has been sliding, continues to shrink as a share of the overall electorate. (para. 3)

Accordingly, Seib (2011) asserted: ". . . it ought to spell good times for Democrats for years to come" (para. 4). Nonetheless, as noted, the allegiance of future voters aligning themselves with the Democratic Party is not preordained. Importantly though, for political parties to keep the party faithfuls and simultaneously attract newcomers, such as the Millennial Generation and the growing minority population, politicians must create effective communication strategies to reach these voting blocs. And to reach these voting blocs with effective communication strategies, politicians must fully embrace digital communication and SNSs and be poised to change and adapt to new technological innovations and swiftly adopt new savvy social networking applications. This is especially true for Republicans, who have lagged significantly behind Democrats in digital advocacy adoption (Draper, 2013). The politicians and political parties who are "early adopters," or at least have assembled a digital media team of "early adopters," will most likely be the successful politicians in the next civic era of American politics.

OVERVIEW OF THE BOOK

The book is organized into five sections. The first section begins with this chapter and is an overview of the role, functions, and effects of social media in political communication generally and in the 2012 presidential election specifically. The section continues in Chapter 2, where based on a statewide survey of potential Iowa caucus goers, Daniela Dimitrova writes that social media was not associated with participation among the older Republican caucus goers in Iowa, although Web sites were a critically important information source.

In Chapter 3, Emma Svensson, Spiro Kiousis, and Jesper Strömbäck investigate the extent to which the Obama and the Romney campaigns used social media to cultivate relationships during the 2012 election campaign. Although social media allows two-way communication between voters and their representatives, the 2012 campaigns primarily used SNSs for one-way fundraising and get-out-the-vote and persuasion messages. After analyzing both the Romney and Obama social media usage strategies, the Pew Research Center (2012) came to a similar conclusion, observing: "In theory, digital technology allows leaders to engage in a new level of 'conversation' with voters, transforming campaigning into something more dynamic, more of a dialogue, than it was in the 20th century. For the most, however, the presidential candidates are using their direct messaging mainly as a way to push their messages out" (pp. 1–2). So, while social media channels do have unique properties and functions, in many political situations they are merely another channel to reach voters and now one part of a larger, integrated communications strategy.

The second section incorporates three chapters on political knowledge and usage and examines the impact of social media on young voters. For instance, in Chapter 4, Jody Baumgartner, David Morris, and Jonathan Morris show that some forms of young adults' SNS usage during the 2012 Republican primary, such as following a political figure or posting a political message, were associated with a higher level of political knowledge, but relying on SNSs as a primary information source was linked with less political knowledge. Testing similar questions during the general election, in Chapter 5, Terri Towner and David Dulio discuss how Facebook, Google+, and Twitter can have significant negative effects on political knowledge among young voters, and that SNSs are currently used more to mobilize supporters and fundraise than to convert and educate undecided voters. In Chapter 6, Kjerstin Thorson, Emily Vraga, and Neta Kligler-Vilenchik draw on in-depth interviews with young Facebook users in the run-up to the election to discover that Facebook political etiquette restrains partisan, opinionated content and encourages humor and information sharing.

Sections three and four comprise chapters exploring social media in the primary election and general election, respectively. In Chapter 7, Raluca Cozma surveys Twitter users in the 2012 Republican primary and proposes that the combination of both information seeking and social interaction is what makes Twitter a popular outlet for political communication. In Chapter 8, Paul Haridakis, Gary Hanson, Mei-Chen Lin, and Jennifer McCullough, having surveyed voters before the Ohio Republican primary, describe how social media are now accepted sources of political information, but most voters still rely more on television and the Internet.

In Chapter 9, Hyun Jung Yun, Cynthia Opheim, and Emily Kay Balanoff compare SNS use across "red," "blue," and "purple" states and learn that partisan, ideological, and geographic context play a significant role in the political usage of SNSs and the levels of trust, efficacy, and selectivity of the information. Specifically, they show that politically engaged individuals in swing states were more likely to post their opinions to social networks, were more interested in politics, and had a greater sense of political information efficacy and a heightened cynicism toward the political system than individuals in non-swing states.

YouTube was an important source of information in the Republican primaries. In Chapter 10, Jacob Groshek and Stephanie Brookes examine political advertising on YouTube during the primaries and describe how negative ads were viewed more frequently than positive ads and that negativity was related to increased audience engagement in the form of comments, "likes," and "favorites."

Turning to section four and the general election, in Chapter 11, Hyun Jung Yun explains how socio-economic and political minorities, such as ethnic minorities, young voters, and minority political party members are more likely to adopt social media as a venue of political expression and participation. Building on his previous work on campaign e-mails, in Chapter 12, Andrew Paul Williams and Roxana Maiorescu content analyze candidate e-mails and observe that e-mail was an important communication channel for outreach, fundraising, and getting voters to turn out to the polls in 2012.

Many questions remain about the influence of social media on the attitudes, knowledge levels, and behaviors of social media users. Several studies in this book address these questions. For instance, in an experiment presented in Chapter 13, David Lynn Painter, Juliana Fernandes, Jessica Mahone, and Eisa Al Nashmi reveal that expressing a political opinion on an SNS increases the election's salience and the feeling that one's knowledge is sufficient to engage in the politics.

Section five considers how social media were used as tools for voter and media engagement. In Chapter 14, for example, Dan Schill and Rita Kirk conclude that campaign and journalist Twitter use during presidential debates increased inter-media agenda setting and further blurred the distinction between old and new media. And looking at the connection between online social media engagement and offline political participation in Chapter 15, Monica Ancu finds that SNS users have higher campaign interest and higher campaign involvement; however, most of that involvement is online participation.

In Chapter 16, Benjamin Warner, Joshua Hawthorne, and Sarah Turner McGowen set out to uncover what characteristics make young people most likely to use social media as a form of political participation. They show that as long as young people believe they have something worth saying, they are willing to express themselves through social media, regardless of their partisanship or trust in the political system. The book concludes with Chapter 17, where LaChrystal Ricke reviews campaign YouTube use during the general election and determines that both the Obama and Romney campaigns were successful in leveraging YouTube to engage voters through information sharing and distributing campaign messages and advertisements with potential supporters and voters.

CHAPTER 2

The Evolution of Digital Media Use in Election Campaigns: New Functions and Cumulative Impact

Daniela V. Dimitrova

The use and importance of digital media in election campaigns has grown steadily over the past few election cycles. Back in the 1992 campaign, political candidates placed information online, although, at the time, the Internet was not yet widely adopted among the American public (Bimber & Davis, 2003). E-mail, political information Web sites, and blogs quickly became popular, and by the time of the 2000 presidential election, candidate sites were widely accepted as a common campaign tool, which led observers to declare 2000 as the first Internet election (Foot & Schneider, 2006). The medium continued to evolve and be used for political purposes in the 2004 campaign, with both candidates and political parties slowly realizing digital media's potential to reach and mobilize voters (Mossberger, Tolbert, & McNeal, 2008). In 2008, newer online tools, such as social networking and microblogging, gained popularity and were used successfully by the Obama campaign to mobilize and organize supporters (Hendricks & Denton, 2010; Hendricks & Kaid, 2011; Plouffe, 2009). While some saw 2008 as the "Facebook election," others noted that 2012 was the "Twitter election" (C-Span, 2012). Digital media continued to evolve and engage voters (Rainie & Smith, 2012).

This chapter focuses on the evolution of Internet tools and their use in political campaigns. It discusses the unique characteristics that distinguish digital media from traditional mass media and argues that various social media tools might have differential impacts on voters contingent upon the voters' characteristics. Finally, the chapter reports the results of a telephone survey conducted prior to the 2012 Iowa caucuses that examines the effects of digital media on Iowa voters.

SOCIAL MEDIA GROWTH, AGE, AND PARTISANSHIP

There is no doubt that both the number of those using digital media and the frequency with which they use it has steadily increased over time in the United States. A Pew report from April 2012 observed an overall increase in social networking site (SNS) usage in every age group for the period between 2005 and 2012

(Zickhur & Madden, 2012). Not surprisingly, American youth between the ages of 18 and 29 had the most SNS usage overall, but other age groups experienced increases, as shown in Figure 2.1 (Zickhur & Madden, 2012).

Despite the increasing popularity of social media and SNS, older Americans lagged behind younger age groups in their adoption of SNS technologies. According to the 2012 Pew data, half of adults ages 65 and older remain disconnected from the Internet. As of February 2012, about one-third of Internet users in the over-65 demographic reported using SNS, and only 18% of that cohort does so on a typical day (Zickhur & Madden, 2012). Among adults who are currently ages 76 and older, the statistics are even lower, as only 20% of the Internet users in that cohort use SNS and only 8% of them do so on a typical day.

The Internet usage statistics just covered demonstrate that SNSs and social media are currently used primarily by the younger generations, especially the 18- to 29-year-old age group, and SNS use seems to be negatively related to age. Still, the question remains: are social media being used by voters for political purposes? During the 2010 campaign, more than one-fifth of American adults used SNSs to get information about the campaign or the election; only 2% of the online users used Twitter for the same purposes (Smith, 2011). Data from the 2010 midterm elections also show that demographically those who use social media for political purposes tend to be younger and more educated than the rest of the online population. Specifically, 42% were under the age of 30 and 41% had a college degree,

Percent of American adults age 18+ who use the Internet

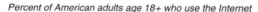

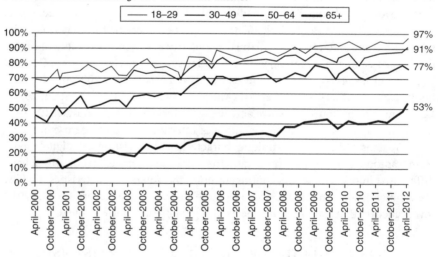

Figure 2.1 Internet Use by Age Group, 2000–2012

From "Older adults and Internet use" by K. Zickhur and M. Madden, June 6, 2012, Pew Internet & American Life Project, p. 4. Retrieved from http://pewinternet.org/~/media//Files/Reports/2012/PIP_Older_adults_ and_Internet_use.pdf. Reprinted with permission.

SOURCE: Pew Internet & American Life Project Surveys, April 2000–April 2012.

MORE: http://pewinternet.org/Trend-Data/Internet-Adoption.aspx

although they looked quite similar to the rest of the online population in terms of race, gender, and income (Smith, 2011).

In March 2012, similar patterns in the use of SNSs and political activities online were observed. Overall, the survey found that 80% of American adults used the Internet, and 66% of those online adults used SNSs such as Facebook, LinkedIn, or Google+. That amounts to more than half of the entire U.S. population who are SNS users. Interestingly, when it comes to SNS users, those who describe their political ideology as moderate or liberal are more likely than conservatives to use SNSs: 74% of Internet users who describe themselves as liberal use SNSs, and 70% of Internet users who describe themselves as moderate are SNS users—that compares with 60% of conservative SNS users, as shown in this chart (see Figure 2.2).

To summarize, frequency of use of social media remains much higher among younger Internet users. Furthermore, those with strong liberal tendencies are more likely than those with conservative tendencies to use SNSs for political purposes (Rainie & Smith, 2012). It is no surprise that the most engaged political participants on SNSs are those with strong political predispositions. They could be at opposite ends of the ideological spectrum, yet their experiences concerning political material on SNSs are quite similar (Rainie & Smith, 2012). At the same time, very liberal users seem more inclined to employ SNSs than their conservative counterparts. In general, Democrats, more than Republicans, also seem to think

Percent of SNS users in each party/group who say that SNS are "very important" or "somewhat important" for each activity

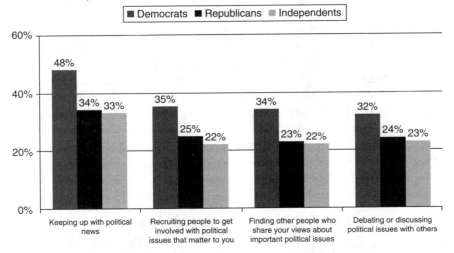

Figure 2.2 Social Networking Democrats Think the Sites are More Important for Political Activities

From "Politics on social networking sites," by L. Rainie and A. Smith, September 4, 2012, Pew Internet & American Life Project, p. 2. Retrieved from http://pewInternet.org/~/media//Files/Reports/2012/PIP_PoliticalLifeonSocialNetworkingSites.pdf. Reprinted with permission.

SOURCE: Pew Research Center's Internet & American Life Project January 20–February 19, 2012 tracking survey. N for social networking site users = 1,047. N for SNS-using Democrats = 523. N for SNS-using Republicans = 457. N for SNS-using independents = 547. Survey was conducted on landline and cell phones and in English and Spanish.

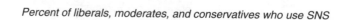

Percent of liberals, moderates, and conservatives who use SNS

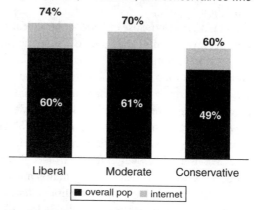

Figure 2.3 Who Uses Social Networking Sites
From "Politics on social networking sites," by L. Rainie and A. Smith, September 4, 2012, Pew Internet & American Life Project, p. 6. Retrieved from http://pewInternet.org/~/media//Files/Reports/2012/PIP_PoliticalLifeonSocialNetworkingSites.pdf. Reprinted with permission.
SOURCE: Pew Research Center's Internet & American Life Project January 20–February 19, 2012 tracking survey. N for overall survey = 2,253. N for internet users = 1,729. Survey was conducted on landline and cell phones and in English and Spanish.

that SNSs are more important for political activities, including recruiting people to get involved in political issues and for debating politics online (see Figure 2.3).

Certainly, the potential for mobilization on SNSs exists (Hirzalla, van Zoonen, & de Ridder, 2011). Aggressive comments or views that are in sharp contrast with what a user already believes, however, may have a negative effect on the receiver and diminish mobilization efforts. According to survey statistics leading up to the 2012 presidential election, 18% of SNS users have blocked, "unfriended," or hidden someone on the site because the person either posted too much about politics, disagreed with political posts, or bothered friends about politics (Rainie & Smith, 2012). Conversely, 16% of SNS users have friended someone whose political posts have appealed to them (Rainie & Smith, 2012). That suggests voters may be offended by too much political activity on SNSs—especially if it disagrees with their personal political views.

CHARACTERISTICS OF DIGITAL MEDIA

There are a number of unique characteristics that distinguish digital media from traditional mass media. Below, a brief summary is provided of how digital media might allow voters to become more engaged in the political process.

Multiple Opportunities for Political Engagement
There has been plenty of discussion about the fact the Internet and its technologies allow the average voter multiple and diverse opportunities for political engagement online (Bucy & Gregson, 2001; Kirk & Schill, 2011; Quintelier & Vissers, 2008).

Some of these opportunities involve participation in online polls, watching and commenting on online debates about politics, blogging or posting on someone else's blog, or engaging with political topics on SNSs. Individuals can engage in online political activities from the convenience of their own computers, which enhances their participation. The sheer number of people who use social media is astounding. According to Nielsen statistics, by the end of 2011, there were over 181 million blogs around the world, and three of the top ten social networks in the U.S. were blogs (Nielsen, 2012). The reach of social media is indeed global.

While there is some debate whether online political activities translate into meaningful political action in the "physical" world, there is an increasing body of research that confirms this is occurring (Bakker & de Vreese, 2011; Hirzalla et al., 2011; Mossberger et al., 2008; Vitak et al., 2011). A meta-analysis of previous studies on the effects of the Internet on political and civic engagement found that about half of the studies had reported statistically significant positive effects on different types of offline engagement (Boulianne, 2009). The studies reviewed also employed different determinants of Internet use/activities, different population groups, and different output variables. The meta-analysis concludes that the positive effects of Internet use on political engagement seem to be greater when online news is used as a measure and that these effects increase over time.

Research in the United States has shown that social media impacts engagement both online and offline (Bachmann, Kaufhold, Lewis, & Gil de Zúñiga, 2010; Kenski & Stroud, 2006; Mossberger et al., 2008; Vitak et al., 2011; Weber, Loumakis, & Bergman, 2003). International studies corroborate these findings: published research about digital media effects in Belgium, the Netherlands, and Sweden has demonstrated a statistically significant impact of one or more of these digital media tools on political participation (Bakker & de Vreese, 2011; Dimitrova, Shehata, Strömbäck, & Nord, 2014; Quintelier & Vissers, 2008).

The realization that digital media in general, and SNSs in particular, may have a tangible impact on voters is perhaps a reason why President Obama chose to appear in a first-of-a-kind Google Hangouts meeting as well as on Reddit/Ask Me Anything as he was competing for a second term in the 2012 election. Keenly aware of the power of social media, Obama also chose to announce his victory to a second term in the White House with a succinct Twitter message: "Four more years," accompanied by a picture of him and the First Lady hugging. The hug photo quickly became the most "retweeted" tweet in the world to date (Fitzgerald, 2012).

Lower Cost of Citizen Participation

Much has been written about the fact that the Internet lowers the cost of participation for citizens, both in terms of time and of effort (Bimber & Davis, 2003; Quintelier & Vissers, 2008; Mossberger et al., 2008). This is especially true now, in the age of the mobile citizen who can easily check his or her Twitter feed while waiting in line somewhere and get an updated tweet from their favorite candidate. These mobile citizens may be less likely to pick up a hard copy of the *New York Times,* but they do seem more inclined to look at the digital version of the paper, read the user comments online, and "like," "share," "post," or "retweet" an article that got their attention.

There is clearly an abundance of easily accessible information about politics and civic life in the digital era. Arguably, this unprecedented wealth of information may have the potential to contribute to a more informed electorate, a more engaged public, and a more transparent political process, as well as more accountable politicians (Bimber & Davis, 2003; Foot & Schneider, 2006; Prior, 2007).

While there is an abundance of choices in the current media environment, one should not conclude that this immediately translates into a more politically engaged citizenry. In fact, some scholars have shown that in this highly saturated information age, the public's political involvement has become more unequal with some using the new choices to increase political engagement and others turning away from political content (Prior, 2007). Compared with the pre-Internet era, it is easier now for voters who are not engaged in politics to further disengage by turning to entertainment media rather than news. Relatedly, there is also some evidence that the proliferation of media choices has contributed to higher political partisanship (Prior, 2007, 2013).

Interactivity

Perhaps the most unique feature of social media is the interactivity (Foot & Schneider, 2006). Unlike traditional media, which follows the one-to-many dissemination model, digital and social media allow—and often encourage—two-way communication between sender and receiver. Foot and Schneider's (2006) typology illustrates this well by distinguishing between the following digital media functions: (1) informing, (2) involving, (3) connecting, and (4) mobilizing. Any kind of digital media tool—a blog, an e-mail, or an SNS—allows the public to get involved and connect through direct (albeit mediated) contact with politicians and campaigns. This connection between politicians and voters may be highly empowering (Foot & Schneider, 2006). At the very least, such sites make the campaign and the political system as a whole appear more accessible to the average citizen, and that perception of accessibility can be legitimizing mechanism (Bucy & Gregson, 2001).

Data Tracking and Data Mining

The 2012 presidential election also pointed to the importance of data tracking and data mining in election campaigns. Regardless of whether one supports or opposes these trends, this is clearly something politicians will expand upon in the future. The goal of the Obama campaign in 2012 was to improve on the data mining methods developed in the 2008 Iowa caucuses, according to former Clinton advisor JoDee Winterhof, and allow campaign volunteers to efficiently connect with those who are truly Independents (cited in O'Brien, 2012). Data mining also allowed the Democratic Party to place an emphasis on identifying potential supporters who were less likely to vote and to make a concerted effort to get them to vote (Rutenberg & Zeleny, 2012). Another unprecedented case of data mining was the tracking of user activity immediately after or even during political events, such as the party nominating conventions during the 2012 presidential race. Undoubtedly, this "invisible" side of data tracking and data mining will continue to influence the outcomes of future elections.

Differential Impacts

Although scholars see the potential of social media as a whole to empower the average citizen and invigorate the political process, a clear distinction is rarely made between the different SNS tools. The question remains, do all of these digital media tools have the same impact or do they differ in their primary functions and audience effects? Using Foot and Schneider's (2006) online media functions, Dimitrova et al. (2011) proposed a digital media typology that distinguishes between (1) online news sites, (2) political candidate Web sites, and (3) social media sites, based on the primary functions performed by each. In the future, it may be helpful to further distinguish between the various digital media tools, including (1) email, (2) Web sites of political candidates/parties, (3) traditional blogs, (4) microblogs (such as Twitter), and (5) SNSs such as Facebook, Tumblr, and Pinterest. It would be worthwhile to connect such typologies with research on what motivates users to visit the different types of social media sites. Previous studies have demonstrated that the primary motivation in the case of SNSs is social interaction, although surveillance and information functions are cited as important gratifications, as well (Ancu & Cozma, 2009; Kaye & Johnson, 2002). Entertainment is another reason people use social media—especially younger users—and that particular motivation can be connected to visiting sites such as YouTube (Ancu & Cozma, 2009). Making the distinction between gratifications sought and gratifications obtained from digital media use would also allow scholars to better understand how specific motivations and gratifications influence political participation and civic engagement in the offline world.

METHOD

The Iowa caucuses represent an important national media event and an opportunity to "litmus test" candidate appeal among voters (Plouffe, 2009; Redlawsk, Tolbert, & Donovan, 2010). Since the 1970s, the Iowa caucuses have been established as the first step in the presidential nominating process in the United States and have become a "uniquely American Olympic contest" (Winebrenner & Goldford, 2010, p. 4). While their direct policy impact and effects on the final selection of candidates has been debated, it is widely accepted that the caucuses have helped shift the focus away from political parties to the candidates themselves and winnow down the potential party nominees (Adkins & Dowdle, 2001; Redlawsk et al., 2010; Winebrenner & Goldford, 2010). The Iowa caucuses can put presidential hopefuls in the national spotlight and give visibility to lesser-known candidates in particular, as was the case with Obama's 2008 race (Plouffe, 2009).

A study was conducted that focused on the 2012 Iowa presidential caucuses to determine whether digital media tools exert a significant effect on political participation. Data come from two telephone surveys conducted by Iowa State University's Center for Survey Statistics and Methodology before the 2012 Republican caucuses; the data collection period was November 1–13, 2011 (Wave 1), and December 8–18, 2011 (Wave 2). Since the Democratic nominee was already clear, the survey targeted Iowa adults who were registered as either Republicans or

Independents. The Iowa voter registry was obtained in August 2011 from the Iowa Secretary of State. To create the sample frame, voters who were inactive and who were registered as Democrats were removed. The resulting list contained 1,315,981 registered active Republicans (610,033) and Independents (705,948). The telephone numbers in the list were reported by voters at the time of their registration, and therefore included both landlines and cell phone numbers.

A stratified, systematic sampling design was used to select the initial sample to ensure spread across the range of variations in age, voter activity, geography, gender, and party affiliation. A variable was created to represent whether a voter was 35 years or younger and a second defined whether a voter had attended one or more of the last five primaries. The target sample size for Republicans and Independents was on a 2:1 ratio, and samples were drawn separately for each party. Within parties, sample size allocation incorporated an oversampling of primary attendees in order to maximize the chances of reaching likely Caucus attendees. The stratified design was implemented using a systematic probability proportional to size selection scheme.

A total of 1,256 respondents (979 registered Republicans and 277 registered Independents) completed the first wave of the survey and 940 respondents (740 registered Republicans and 200 registered Independents) completed the second wave of the survey. This translates into a response rate of 16% for the first survey and a cooperation rate of 75% for the second survey (American Association for Public Opinion Research [AAPOR], 2008). Only 787 of the second-wave respondents reported that they use the Internet for political information, so the following analysis focuses on those respondents only.

In order to test the impact on political participation, a series of multiple regression tests following a hierarchical regression model were employed. The variable used to gauge participation was voters' likelihood to attend the 2012 Iowa caucuses. This variable was measured by a five-point Likert-type scale ranging from the answer "definitely will attend the Caucus" to "definitely will not attend the Caucus" (with the midpoint being "unsure").

Three sets of predictors were entered in a hierarchical regression analysis in the following order: demographics and political predispositions (Block 1), frequency of use of traditional media (Block 2), and frequency of use of digital media (Block 3).

Of special interest to this study was the use of digital media. The variables used to measure digital media use were modeled after the work of Dimitrova et al. (2011) and were designed to include a range of different online activities measured by four-point scales. Respondents were asked how frequently ("always," "sometimes," "rarely," or "never") they engaged in the following: (1) reading online news sites such as the *New York Times*; (2) visiting political party/candidate Web sites; (3) reading political blogs; (4) commenting or posting on blogs about politics; (5) following a politician or political party on Twitter; (6) following a politician or political party on Facebook; and (7) following a politician or political party on YouTube.

Following the Drew and Weaver (2006) study, traditional media effects were gauged by asking how frequently respondents received political news from the following sources: (1) newspapers; (2) radio; (3) national television newscasts, such as ABC, CBS, or NBC; (4) cable television newscasts, such as MSNBC, CNN, or FOX News; (5) local television newscasts; (6) late night comedy shows; and (7) campaign advertising. Answers were recorded by choosing from the options "never," "hardly ever," "sometimes," and "regularly."

The demographic variables included age, gender, education, and income level, while political predispositions were measured by three indicators—ideological orientation (seven-point scale where 1 = "extremely conservative" and 7 = "extremely liberal"), interpersonal discussion about politics (four-point scale), and attention paid to the campaign (four-point scale).

RESULTS

Before addressing the results of the regression analysis, let's examine sample composition. Looking at the demographic characteristics of the respondents, it becomes clear that the sample of registered Republicans and Independents was relatively high in age ($M = 61.89$, $SD = 16.11$), ranging from 19 to 97 years old. There was roughly equal gender balance, with females making up 50.9% of the sample, and the sample respondents were relatively well educated ($M = 3.21$ on a five-point scale, $SD = 1.03$). Education categories included less than high school, high school graduate, some college or technical training, bachelor's degree, and post-graduate work or degree. Average income was between $50,000 and $75,000. To summarize, the survey respondents as a whole were relatively well educated, middle income, and older than the general population of Iowa. They also reported following the campaign fairly closely ($M = 3.19$, $SD = .76$).

The results of the multiple regression tests are reported in Table 2.1. Looking at the first model, it becomes clear that none of the demographic predictors (other than age) had a significant effect on caucus attendance. Perhaps not surprisingly, those who were older were significantly more likely ($\beta = -.01$, $SD = .00$, $p < .000$) to attend the Iowa caucuses (see Table 2.1, Model 1). The political predisposition variables, on the other hand, were all statistically significant. Those who paid more attention to the campaign ($\beta = .53$, $SD = .07$, $p < .000$) identified as more conservative ($\beta = -.21$, $SD = .04$, $p < .000$), more frequently engaged in interpersonal discussion about politics ($\beta = .18$, $SD = .05$, $p < .01$), and were more likely to participate in the caucus.

Model 2 reports the effects of traditional media use on caucus attendance. The only statistically significant coefficient was that for radio news ($\beta = .18$, $SD = .05$, $p < .000$), although the overall R-squared for the model increased from .15 to .17 when adding the traditional media variables, and that change was significant at the $p < .01$ level.

Turning to the effects of digital media, which was the primary area of interest, one will notice very few significant regression coefficients in the final model.

Table 2.1 Effects of Digital Media on Political Participation

	MODEL 1	MODEL 2	MODEL 3
Constant	1.40** (.42)	1.00* (.45)	.17 (.52)
Age	−.01** (.00)	−.01* (.00)	−.01 (.00)
Gender	−.00 (.11)	.03 (.11)	.07 (.11)
Education	.06 (.06)	.07 (.06)	.05 (.06)
Income	.06 (.04)	.04 (.04)	.06 (.04)
Ideological Orientation	−.21*** (.04)	−.16** (.05)	−.14** (.05)
Interpersonal Discussion	.18** (.05)	.14** (.05)	.12* (.05)
Attention to Campaign	.53*** (.07)	.43*** (.08)	.38*** (.08)
Network News		−.09 (.06)	−.09 (.06)
Cable News		.07 (.05)	.06 (.05)
Local News		−.01 (.06)	−.00 (.06)
Late-Night Comedy		−.07 (.07)	−.08 (.07)
Newspapers		−.01 (.05)	−.02 (.05)
Radio News		.18*** (.05)	.18*** (.05)
Campaign Advertising		.09 (.05)	.09 (.05)
Online News Sites			.04 (.07)
Party Web Sites			.16* (.08)
Reading Blogs			−.03 (.08)
Commenting on Blogs			.04 (.17)
Facebook			.07 (.13)
Twitter			.34 (.24)
YouTube			.03 (.14)
R^2	.15	.17	.19
R^2 Change		.02**	.02*

Table reports results from hierarchical OLS regression analysis. $N = 787$. Estimates are unstandardized regression coefficients with standard errors in parentheses. *$p < .05$. **$p < .01$. ***$p < .001$.

Source: Phone survey of registered Iowa Republicans and Independents, December 8–18, 2011; N = 940.

Seven digital media variables were included in the analysis, ranging from visiting online news sites to following political candidate/party on YouTube. The only variable that emerged as statistically significant was visiting political party Web sites (see Table 2.1). Visiting party Web sites had a positive beta coefficient ($\beta = .16$, $SD = .08$, $p < .05$), which indicates that higher frequency of use of political party Web sites is associated with higher likelihood of caucus attendance. None of the social media predictors were significant in any of the three models. These findings are consistent with previous studies of Iowa voters (e.g., Groshek & Dimitrova, 2011). Ideological orientation, interpersonal discussion, attention to the campaign, and listening to radio news remain significant in the final regression model.

It is important to note that the R-squared from Model 2 to Model 3 increased by two percent (see Table 2.1). This overall increase in the predictive power of the model was statistically significant at the $p < .05$ level, indicating that the digital media variables set as a whole made a meaningful contribution to the final regression model.

DISCUSSION

What is learned from the empirical results of the pre-caucus survey? When it comes to political participation in the Iowa caucuses, it appears that social media is yet to become the major determining factor for our respondents. The regression results reported in this study point to the fact that (1) the strength of people's ideological beliefs, (2) interpersonal discussion about politics, and (3) their engagement with the campaign remain the most important determinants. In other words, when controlling for demographic differences and media use, personal political predispositions emerge as the decisive influence on voter participation. This is consistent with the political communication literature that stresses the significance of factors such as party affiliation, ideological identification, political efficacy and interest in politics in determining voting decisions (Mossberger et al., 2008).

While this may suggest that digital media, despite their potential, play no role in people's political decision making, such a conclusion may be premature. Clearly, social networking services were not overwhelmingly important to the respondents' political activity—at least for the Iowa population examined in this study. None of the social media variables by themselves were significant predictors of participation in a statistical sense. However, the group of digital media variables as a whole significantly contributed to political participation in the first-in-the-nation Iowa caucuses. Therefore, the potential of social media to engage the public should not be underestimated, but the results found should be put in context: the data for our sample show an older group of respondents who are similar to the national statistics of older adults—in other words, they rely on social media much less frequently than the 18 to 29 year old age group (Zickhur & Madden, 2012). The older adults also reported being engaged in the campaign already and talking about politics with their family and friends on a regular basis. It is feasible that for this type of voter neither traditional nor digital media play a very significant role.

The one digital media variable that was statistically significant in this analysis was use of political party/candidate Web sites. Those Iowa voters who visited party/candidate Web sites with greater frequency were more inclined to attend the caucus, holding all other variables constant. In other words, the frequency of use of political party/candidate Web sites had a unique contribution to people's likelihood of caucus attendance. This finding is in line with the theoretical expectations that digital media may serve as a mobilization tool for the party base (Bimber & Davis, 2003; Hirzalla et al., 2011; Dimitrova et al., 2011). It also reinforces the importance of politicians' sites as vehicles not only to get information out to the public but to engage their supporters in a more meaningful way (Mossberger et al., 2008; Prior, 2007).

The key implication for political candidates and their campaigns is not to ignore digital media during the Iowa caucuses. In particular, future contenders should spend time on their Web sites during the primary season, making sure they create a consistent message and portray an appealing image to voters. This might be especially critical for lesser-known candidates who will need to establish an online presence and use their official Web sites as tools for voter mobilization.

Getting your supporters engaged in the first-in-the-nation caucuses may be the ticket to party nomination and future success in the national election. It seems that SNS efforts may be comparatively less important at these early stages of the campaign, but the candidates/parties still need to invest in developing and maintaining their sites to help them win in the primaries.

An anecdotal examination of the Web sites of the main political contenders in the 2012 election—Mitt Romney and Barack Obama—shows that their campaigns were well aware of the importance of these sites. Both candidates' Web sites were strikingly similar and tried to accomplish a number of different goals beyond simply providing information and policy stances to the electorate. Going back to the Foot and Schneider (2006) typology, a casual observer would have noticed quickly that both Obama and Romney's sites tried to involve, connect, and mobilize their supporters. They offered opportunities to (1) donate through the Web site, (2) hear the candidate speak, (3) see ads for the candidate or the opposing candidate, (4) sign up to be a volunteer, and (5) to buy candidate caps, buttons, and T-shirts; they also allowed visitors to share their personal stories, among many other options.

These examples show that, at least at the current stage of development (as of 2012), the boundaries between Web sites and SNSs become rather blurry. In other words, the candidate's own site may offer many features typical of Facebook or a political blog. That makes the distinction between traditional candidate Web sites and SNSs somewhat arbitrary. Future studies may want to develop more precise indicators of digital engagement not simply by asking what *types* of Web sites people visit, but what exact *activities* they do while online. Such distinctions may allow researchers to capture more accurately the effects of the broadly defined digital media on the American voter.

In conclusion, one thing that everyone agrees the Obama campaign did well in 2008—and did even better in 2012—was connect with potential supporters identified from multiple data sources. This, coupled with the immediate real-time responses to voters' reactions on Facebook and Twitter, helped enable the Democratic Party to get the vote out. The results of the 2012 election seem to suggest a possible return to the "retail politics" of the past, where politicians must engage one-on-one with voters in order to move ahead in the polls. Social media certainly facilitates such engagement.

As the popularity of social media grows over time and today's youth enter the next age cohort, we are likely to see the importance of digital and social media tools increase further. The young generation of 2012 is not only accustomed to—but is often addicted to—being connected to the Internet and to each other 24/7. There is no doubt that any candidate running for political office in the future will need to employ social media and other emerging digital platforms in order to reach these potential voters.

Future politicians will not only need to learn how to use social media, but they must also know how to use them effectively. They will need to understand the inherent differences between the various digital media tools, engage potential voters, and mobilize supporters by turning each of their followers into a political messenger on their behalf. As Facebook policy manager Adam Conner noted a few months before the 2012 election, candidates should recognize that in the new digital era the old motto *"all politics is local"* has been replaced by the slogan *"all politics is social"* (C-Span, 2012). If this is indeed the case, the new battleground of the future would undeniably be the virtual world of social media.

CHAPTER 3

Creating a Win–Win Situation? Relationship Cultivation and the Use of Social Media in the 2012 Campaign

Emma Svensson, Spiro Kiousis, and Jesper Strömbäck

Political parties and candidates have always been fast to adopt new communication technologies in election campaigning: newspapers in the mid-19th century, radio in the 1920s, television in the 1950s, and the Internet at the end of the 20th century. In the 2004 Democratic primary, Howard Dean took the use of Internet one step further when he successfully used the Internet for raising micro-donations and to organize supporters (Schneider & Foot, 2006). In the 2008 presidential election, the next step was taken when social media were innovatively used, mainly by the Obama campaign, to mobilize and organize volunteers and supporters (Hendricks & Denton, 2010). These developments have fueled a trend where digital media in general, and social media in particular, have become increasingly important in election campaigns across the world (Hendricks & Denton, 2010; Hendricks & Kaid, 2011; Sweetser, 2011).

The key question, then, is not if, or even how much, political parties and candidates use digital and social media when election campaigning. The key question is rather how, and based on what strategies, that they do this. This chapter will explore this question, with a particular focus on whether the Obama and Romney campaigns used social media strategically to build and maintain relationships with supporters and volunteers.

During the last couple of decades, relationship management and relationship marketing has become one of the key theoretical perspectives in both public relations and marketing (Egan, 2011; Gummesson, 2012; Heath, 2001; Ledingham, 2003). Even though there are similarities between relationship management and relationship marketing, these perspectives have seldom been combined, and there is even less research applying them in political contexts (but see Ledingham, 2011; Levenshus, 2010). At the same time, digital and social media offer campaigns unprecedented possibilities to interact and connect—to cultivate relationships—with key publics unfiltered by the mass media (Harfoush, 2009; Sweetser, 2011).

Against this background, the purpose of this chapter is to synthesize and operationalize the theories of relationship management and relationship marketing, and to investigate the extent to which the Obama and the Romney campaigns used social media to cultivate relationships during the 2012 election campaign.

THE PROMISE OF DIGITAL AND SOCIAL MEDIA

Since the mid-1990s, digital communication has become an increasingly integral part of presidential election campaigns (Dimitrova, Shehata, Strömbäck, & Nord, 2014). From the perspective of political campaigns, digital and social media offer at least four primary functions: (1) informing voters, (2) involving supporters, (3) connecting online users with political actors, and (4) mobilizing voters (Foot & Schneider, 2006). Digital and social media, therefore, also allow political campaigns unprecedented opportunities to build and maintain relationships with key publics, since they can connect directly with volunteers, supporters, and voters without having to go through the mass media (Aula, 2011; Bortree & Seltzer, 2009; Briones, Kuch, Fisher Liu, & Jin, 2011; Levenshus, 2010; Park & Reber, 2008; Sundar, 2007). The rise of digital and social media has thus made relationship management and relationship marketing both more relevant and potentially more efficient strategies than before.

Relationship marketing and relationship management can be conceived of as strategic approaches used by an organization to achieve its mission (Hallahan, Holtzhausen, van Ruler, Verčič, & Sriramesh, 2007; Strömbäck & Kiousis, 2011). Relationship marketing is concerned with creating and maintaining relationships with customers (and other publics) in order to determine the value proposition that a product or service should offer (Gummesson, 2012), while relationship managemet is concerned with building and maintaning relationships with key publics in order to keep them positive towards the organization and to create a favorable climate of opinion (Metzler, 2001). Digital and social media's potential for interactivity (Perlmutter, 2008) can facilitate a flow of input and output between parties in order to reach a mutually beneficial relationship (Yang & Lim, 2009) and can thus be a potentially effective tool when attempting to involve, connect, mobilize, and inform voters, a key public for electoral campaigns.

Different types of media carry different primary functions, and one way to distinguish between them is to classify them based on their level of interactivity (Trent, Friedenberg, & Denton, 2011). For instance, social media such as Facebook offer higher levels of interactivity (Marken, 2005; Perlmutter, 2008) than e-mail, while all digital media controlled by the campaigns offer more interactivity than mass media. On the other hand, mass media offer the campaigns the opportunity to reach out to larger groups of the electorate, as well as to shape the overall perception of the campaigns and the overall climate of opinion.

In this sense, the medium shapes and should shape the message. Different media have different logics and are conducive of different messages and different strategies; what works in one medium might not work in another medium. The same holds true with respect to different publics. Not all publics are alike, and the more messages that can be adapted to different publics, in form and content, the greater the prospects of involving, mobilizing, connecting with, and informing those publics.

One key quality distinguishing different publics from each other is based on their level of engagement with the campaign (Hutton, Goodman, Alexander, & Genest, 2001; Kiousis & Strömbäck, 2011). The more engaged different publics are, or could be expected to be, the more important it becomes to develop strategies as well as to use media and messages aimed at cultivating relationships with them. When publics are less engaged and more distant, it becomes more important to cultivate a favorable reputation. This suggests that digital media might be particularly important when reaching out to and mobilizing those close to the campaigns—supporters and volunteers—and it can be expected that both the Obama and the Romney campaign made use of relationship strategies during the 2012 presidential election.

In order to investigate the extent to which the Obama and Romney campaigns actually used social media to cultivate relationships, it is necessary to first probe deeper into the philosophy, input, outcomes, and maintenance of relationship cultivation. The rest of this section is, therefore, devoted to discussing their applicability in the context of election campaigns.

THE PHILOSOPHY—MUTUAL BENEFICIAL VALUE

Relationship cultivation is concerned with the management of relationships "between organizations and publics, organizations and organizations, and publics and other publics," through communication as well as behavior (Ledingham, 2011, p. 236; Ledingham & Bruning, 1998). Relationships are an ongoing exchange process (Buttle, 2001; Ledingham, 2011; Schurr & Ozanne, 1985) theoretically based on mutually beneficial exchanges and interdependency (Grönroos, 1999; Hung, 2005; Payne & Frow, 2005).

Exchange is a core dimension, but as Grönroos (1999) argues, an exclusive focus on exchange might be too narrow: "A relationship is also a *mindset*; hence, a relationship includes much more than exchange" (p. 238). In order to talk about actual relationships, they also have to be perceived as mutually beneficial, which can be defined as a win-win situation for all the parties involved (Grönroos, 1999; Payne & Frow, 2005). The win-win zone is, according to Hung (2005), composed of "exchange relationship," "covenantal relationship," and "mutual communal relationship." *Exchange theory* posits that favors must be returned to the same values or in equivalent goods (Clark & Mills, 1979; 1993), while *covenantal relationship* emphasizes the exchange of opinions between the parties, both being committed to a common good (Bennett, 2001). In a *mutual communal relationship*, both sides show concern for the other: "Mutual communal, covenantal, and exchange relationships can help an organization develop a win-win relationship with publics because, in these three types of relationships, both the organization and publics can benefit to the highest degree without being exploited" (Hung, 2005, p. 417).

"Mutual" does not, however, have to be symmetrical, as is often posed by scholars in public relations (Grunig, Grunig, & Dozier, 2002; Ledingham & Bruning, 2000). It can also be a state where those involved in the relationship experience satisfaction with the relationship. In this context, the concept of "expectations" highlights how a relationship can be mutually beneficial in different ways. When entering a relationship—and it may be with a newfound friend, a company, or when volunteering in a presidential campaign—publics have different expectations with respect to the relationship itself as well as with respect to the outcomes. When individuals actively choose to support or volunteer for a candidate, we can expect that they do it with the knowledge that it is the candidate's objectives that are going to be reached, with their help. In this context, the win-win zone can thus be understood as a situation where the candidate needs help to win the election and where volunteers help the candidate with whom they share values and beliefs to a position where the candidate can exercise power in order to pursue those policies. In such a situation, everyone can experience satisfaction with the relationship, even though it may not be symmetrical.

Input—The Willingness to Adopt

When an organization wants to develop and maintain relationships, it has to be willing, and open, to change, as well as adapt to its publics (Barnes, 1994; Holmlund, 2008; Payne & Frow, 2005). What the relationship requires is not only active participation from both sides, but also room and opportunity for co-creation, dialogue, and contact. This means that an organization has to engage with and seek to understand and gain knowledge about the other party in the relationship (Gummesson, 2012; Holmlund, 2008), for instance by understanding what makes the public want to have a relationship with the organization and what outcomes the public seeks. The organization has to determine what value it has to offer, what value the public wants (Christopher, Payne, & Ballantyne, 2008), and subsequently make a value proposal (Gummesson, 2012).

These demands on listening to those involved in the relationship and being willing to adopt the campaign and the policy platform to the views of key publics is possible to live up to, albeit mainly in earlier phases of an election cycle (Lees-Marshment, 2006). The closer to Election Day the campaign gets, the smaller the scope for the candidate to engage in dialogue with those groups that she or he represents. During the final election campaign, the candidate usually has a policy platform that she or he is committed to, and would risk major criticisms if changing the policies too much. It can therefore be argued that the policy platform as well as the candidate is the value proposition that the campaign offers. In addition, it is also possible to move the requirement of co-creation from the shaping of policies to the shaping of the campaign itself.

Outcomes—Long-term Commitment, Trust, and Loyalty

The outcomes of a relationship are probably the part of relationship cultivation that has received the most academic attention thus far, especially in the marketing literature where the measuring of the quality of relationships and their effect on profitability is common (Athanasopoulou, 2009; Rauyruen & Miller, 2007).

Trust and commitment are commonly mentioned outcomes of high quality relationships (Grunig et al., 2002; Grunig & Huang, 2000; Hon & Grunig, 1999;

Holmlund, 2008; Ledingham & Bruning, 1998). In a classic article, Morgan and Hunt (1994) identified commitment and trust as key mediating variables in quality relationship outcomes. Commitment, they argue, exists only when the relationship is considered important, while trust exists, "when one party has confidence in an exchange partner's reliability and integrity" (Morgan & Hunt, 1994, p. 23).

Trust is not just important for understanding high quality relationships, but also as a key concept both in political science and public relations. In the former, trust is seen as a crucial variable when choosing which candidate to support since it builds on the believed ability to handle problems (Petrocik, Benoit, & Hansen, 2003/04). In public relations, trust is foremost discussed in the context of crises. The notion of having trust capital is highlighted as critical for how well the organization can handle a crisis in the eyes of the publics (Coombs, 2010; Falkheimer & Heide, 2010). During an election campaign, candidates are not just exposed to internal crises but also, for instance, negative ads or media misrepresentation that can make supporters and volunteers question the candidate and lose trust.

Trust and commitment can also be seen as products of other relationship outcomes such as control mutuality (Grunig et al., 2002; Grunig & Huang, 2000; Hon & Grunig, 1999), shared value (Egan, 2011), and met expectations and satisfaction (Grunig et al., 2002; Grunig & Huang, 2000; Holmund, 2008; Hon & Grunig, 1999). Thus, in order for a public to gain trust in a political campaign, it must first feel that there is control mutuality, that it shares values with the candidate, and that its expectation of the relationship is met, which subsequently might lead to satisfaction (Egan, 2011; Gummesson, 2012). In an election campaign, volunteers function as speakers and constitute an important part of the face toward other publics. This implies that volunteers can be expected to be more engaged and active in promoting the candidates if they are satisfied with the relationship. At the same time, it should also be noted that political candidates are not per se dependent on long-term commitments, especially not when running for office for the last time.

Maintenance—Strategies for Sustaining and Strengthening the Relationship

One basic relationship strategy based on exchanges is collaboration or cooperation (Gummesson, 2012; Holmlund, 2008). That is, engaging in solving problems or helping each other (Grunig et al., 2002; Hon & Grunig, 1999). In election campaigns, presidential candidates are dependent on volunteers to carry out tasks such as voter registration, encouraging people to commit to vote, disseminating campaign messages, and so on. One step further is inviting the non-organizational party to engage in co-creation (Grönroos, 2000; Prahalad & Ramaswamy, 2004; Payne & Frow, 2005) of the campaign, a strategy that forces the organization to be open by letting volunteers be involved in creating messages.

Transparency and openness are general requirements for relationship cultivation (Egan, 2011; Grunig et al., 2002; Hon & Grunig, 1999; Ledingham & Bruning, 1998). In order to cultivate high-quality relationships with publics, political campaigns have to share at least some information with their publics (Barnes, 1994), as well as provide some access to the decision-making processes (Grunig et al., 2002). Like the covenantal relationship posits, parties engaged in a relationship have to be open to each other, share thoughts and concerns as well as satisfaction and dissatisfaction (Grunig et al., 2002). In order to get publics to actually be open, the political campaign can show assurances of legitimacy, which is a way to demonstrate to the other party that whatever possible concerns it may have are legitimate and that the campaign is committed to the relationship (Grunig et al., 2002; Hon & Grunig, 1999).

Parties in a relationship need access points where they can interact and communicate. The usage of different platforms such as Facebook, Twitter, and e-mail offers the possibility for easy contact and flexible response (Christopher et al., 2008). These access points also provide a channel for feedback (Egan, 2011; Morris, Brunyee, & Page, 1998) and at the same time a way for the campaign to gain knowledge about the publics in order to determine value and create a win-win situation.

Through networking (Gummesson, 2012; Grunig et al., 2002; Hon & Grunig, 1999), the organization has the opportunity to use other organizations, celebrities, or other politicians and officials to attract publics and show similarities in their beliefs and values. Finally, rewarding systems can be used to get people to stay in the relationship by offering them privileges (Nguyen & Mutum, 2012) that other publics do not have access to. All this can be perceived as important aspects of strategies aimed at building long-term commitment, trust and loyalty (i.e., maintain beneficial relationships with key publics).

As noted, while relationship management and relationship marketing have become increasingly prominent theoretical perspectives in public relations and marketing respectively, they have seldom been combined, and research applying them in political contexts is even more scarce. Hence, the purpose of this chapter is to synthesize theories of relationship management and relationship marketing and to investigate the extent to which the Obama and the Romney campaigns used social media to cultivate relationships during the 2012 election campaign. We have reviewed key aspects of the literature on relationship management and relationship marketing, as well as on the importance of digital and social media for building and maintaining relationships with key publics, such as volunteers and supporters. Based on this review, we hypothesize that both the Obama and the Romney campaigns (1) used relationship cultivation strategies in volunteer e-mails, Facebook updates, and tweets, (2) used more strategies based on exchange than on covenantal and mutual communal relationships, and (3) used different strategies in different channels.

METHOD

In order to investigate the extent to which the Obama and the Romney campaigns used social media to cultivate relationships during the 2012 election campaign, a quantitative content analysis was conducted. By the end of the Republican primaries, the researchers signed up to be volunteers in order to get those e-mails that both campaigns sent to their volunteers. The content data were thus collected from the Obama and Romney campaigns' volunteer e-mails, as well as official Facebook sites and Twitter accounts, where the unit of analysis was an e-mail, an update on Facebook, or a tweet. The time frame of the study was March 6, 2012, to November 6, 2012 (i.e., the time period from the end of Republican primaries to the national election). Twitter, which has large volumes of data, was systematically sampled (40% of tweets), while all e-mails and all Facebook updates during the time period were analyzed. The sample consists of a total of 2,039 e-mails, Facebook updates, and tweets. From the Obama campaign, a total of 975 messages were collected: 281 e-mails, 240 Facebook updates, and 454 tweets. From the Romney campaign, a total of 1,064 messages were collected: 364 e-mails, 368 Facebook updates, and 332 tweets.

Relationship Cultivation Strategy Measurements

The variables used to measure relationship cultivation strategies are based on the maintenance strategies discussed in the literature review. These are as follows: collaboration, co-creation, openness, assurances, feedback, common interest, networking, and rewarding systems. *Collaboration* was operationalized as the campaigns inviting supporters to share tasks and/or asking for help (Hon & Grunig, 1999; Gummesson, 2012; Holmlund, 2008). Specifically, seven subcategories of asking for help were developed based on a review of the campaigns' communications: donate, vote, volunteer, sign a petition, join a call, talk to friends/family, and share/retweet. *Co-creation* was operationalized as the campaign inviting supporters to shape the campaign and/or campaign messages (Grönroos, 2000; Prahalad & Ramaswamy, 2004; Payne & Frow, 2005). *Openness* was operationalized as the campaign displaying acts of self-disclosure and sharing thoughts and feelings, both positive and negative (Egan, 2011; Ledingham & Bruning, 1998; Grunig et al., 2002; Hon & Grunig, 1999). *Assurances* were operationalized as the campaigns showing concern about the other party, acknowledging its work, and expressing appreciation for the supporters' efforts (Grunig et al., 2002; Hon & Grunig, 1999). *Feedback* was operationalized as the campaigns showing openness for feedback, providing systems for feedback and/or asking for feedback (Egan, 2011; Morris et al., 1998). *Common interest* was operationalized as the campaigns stressing common interests with respect to issues, issue positions, ideology, and/or getting the candidate elected. *Networking* was operationalized as the campaigns building networks or coalitions with the same groups or opinion leaders as their supporters (Gummesson, 2012; Grunig et al., 2002; Hon & Grunig, 1999), for example, nongovernmental organizations (NGO), think tanks, and endorsements from celebrities and officials. *Rewarding systems* was operationalized as advantages or privileges offered only to supporters (Nguyen & Mutum, 2012). It was divided into "hard" privileges (free gifts or prizes, such as a campaign banners) and "soft" privileges (invites to special events or dinners with the candidate).

Each campaign message was coded using this relationship cultivation strategy framework. Each strategy was coded as either present or absent in every e-mail, Facebook update, or tweet. Pearson's chi-square was subsequently used to test the significance of differences between the campaigns and the channels.

To test for intercoder reliability, a reliability test was conducted by one of the authors and an independent coder, coding 10% of each source of the data. Holsti's score (Holsti, 1969) and Scott's Pi (Scott, 1955) were used to assess reliability. Holsti's score was .92, while Scott's Pi was .79.

RESULTS

To win a highly competitive election, political campaigns need to make the most efficient use of different campaign strategies and tactics, using scarce resources as effectively as possible. They also need to develop different strategies for different media and different publics, based on different media's inner logics and the public's levels of engagement (Harfoush, 2009; Levenshus, 2010; Strömbäck, Grandien, & Falasca, 2012; Sweetser, 2011). Thus, we expect both the Obama and the Romney campaign to have used different relationship cultivation strategies when campaigning through digital and social media.

The results show that both the Obama and the Romney campaign did use some relationship cultivation strategies (Table 3.1). The most commonly used strategy by both campaigns was, by far, *collaboration* (57.1% of Obama messages and 44.6% of Romney messages used collaboration). For the Obama campaign, the second most commonly used strategy was stressing *common interests*, whereas for Romney it was *rewarding systems*. The third most used by Obama was *rewarding systems*, and for Romney it was stressing *common interests*. These were, however, the only frequently used relationship cultivation strategies as all other strategies occurred in 6.2% or less of campaign messages. The chi-square comparison shows that there were some statistically significant differences between how the Obama and Romney campaign used cultivation strategies.

Table 3.1 Presence of Relationship Cultivation Strategies in E-mails, Facebook Updates, and Tweets by Campaign

STRATEGIES	OBAMA		ROMNEY	
	FREQUENCY	%	FREQUENCY	%
Collaboration*	556	57.1	475	44.6
Common interest	127	13	146	13.7
Assurances***	60	6.2	33	3.1
Openness***	50	5.1	22	2.1
Rewarding system***	76	7.8	173	16.3
Co-creation	8	0.8	8	0.8
Feedback	5	0.5	—	—
Networking	36	3.7	23	2.2
N	975		1064	

Note: $*p < .05$; $**p < .01$; $***p < .001$ indicate statistically significant differences between Obama's and Romney's strategies.
Source: Fall 2012 Presidential Election Content Analysis Conducted by Authors.

Collaboration (i.e., asking publics to share tasks and help the campaign) (Grunig et al., 2002; Gummesson, 2012; Hon & Grunig, 1999), can be perceived as the easiest step for a campaign to take when building a relationship. It can also be seen as a good example of an exchange relationship (Clark & Mills, 1979; 1993), where the mutual benefit would be that expectations from both parties are met. This is, however, a rather shallow understanding of relationships, and in order to talk about an actual relationship, it also has to include a mindset, an exchange of opinions, and both parties being committed to a common good (Bennett, 2001; Hung, 2005). Stressing common interests can be seen as an expression of an endeavor for a perceived common good. In the campaign context, stressing *common interest* equals the value proposition (i.e., a supporter is a supporter because she or he agrees with the candidate's ideology and/or policy positions and is willing to work in order to get the candidate elected). *Common interest* is a strategy that campaigns can use to underline the importance of the election, and it is a strategy that was used in those messages calling for *collaboration*: 33.3% for Obama and 25% for Romney (see Table 3.1).

Rewarding systems was the second most used strategy by the Romney campaign and the third most used by the Obama campaign. Dividing rewarding systems by "hard" and "soft" privileges, we find that soft privilege was used foremost in volunteer e-mails and that hard privilege was not used in any broader sense (see Tables 3.2 and 3.3).

When soft rewarding system was used, they were all used in combination with collaboration. That is, in order for supporters to have a chance to obtain an advantage or privilege (e.g., a dinner with the candidate, the vice presidential candidate, or the presidential candidate's wife, etc.), they had to invest something with the campaign, whether it be a donation or volunteering. This strategy can be viewed more as a maintenance strategy than relationship building, and it was often used as an incentive to get supporters to engage more in collaborative actions.

In order to reach the win-win situation, there also has to be a willingness to listen to the other party and show concern (Bennett, 2001; Hung, 2005). Since assurances is a way for the campaign to show supporters that possible concerns that they may have are legitimate and that the campaign is committed to the relationship,

Table 3.2 Rewarding System by Channel: Obama

SYSTEMS	EMAIL		FACEBOOK		TWITTER	
	FREQUENCY	%	FREQUENCY	%	FREQUENCY	%
Soft***	66	23.5	2	0.8	—	—
Hard**	3	1.1	1	0.4	1	0.2
N		281		240		454

Note: *$p < .05$; **$p < .01$; ***$p < .001$ indicate statistically significant differences between different channels. *N* indicates total number of emails, Facebook updates and tweets.

Source: Fall 2012 Presidential Election Content Analysis Conducted by Authors.

Table 3.3 Rewarding System by Channel: Romney

SYSTEMS	EMAIL		FACEBOOK		TWITTER	
	FREQUENCY	%	FREQUENCY	%	FREQUENCY	%
Soft***	118	32.4	13	3.5	8	2.4
Hard**	21	5.8	9	2.4	4	1.2
N		364		368		332

Note: *$p < .05$; **$p < .01$; ***$p < .001$ indicate statistically significant differences between different channels. N indicates total number of e-mails, Facebook updates, and tweets.
Source: Fall 2012 Presidential Election Content Analysis Conducted by Authors.

it is important for the quality of the relationship that *assurances* are expressed (Grunig et al., 2002; Hon & Grunig, 1999). However, the rather low frequency with which *assurances* were expressed (see Table 3.1) suggests that exchanges, rather than relationship quality, was at the core of the campaign strategies.

Another point that is noteworthy is that the Romney campaign never asked for *feedback*, whereas the Obama campaign did it five times. Keeping in mind the previous discussion on the campaigns' relationships with their publics, feedback from supporters did not solely have to be about policies and policy platforms; they could also be about the campaign as it was continuously creating and recreating itself through new ads, attacks, talking points, etc. Since the communication platforms included in this study all offer easy ways to interact, give flexible responses (Christopher et al., 2008; Egan, 2011; Morris et al., 1998; Trent et al., 2011), and gain knowledge about supporters and their opinions, it is notable that *feedback* was not used more. However, it is a strategy that demands more work by the campaigns, and the absence of requests for feedback could thus be a sign of the high pressure of presidential election campaigns and the persistent lack of time.

Different Strategies in Different Channels

Both marketing and public relations emphasize that different channels, as well as different communication strategies, should be used based on which publics an organization wants to communicate with (Hutton et al., 2001; Kiousis & Strömbäck, 2011). Still, while the campaigns used different relationship cultivation strategies in different channels, *collaboration* was the single most used strategy in all channels (see Tables 3.4 and 3.5). *Common interest* was the strategy that the Obama campaign used second most in both e-mails and Twitter, while it was third place among the strategies used on Facebook. For the Romney campaign, *common interest* was the third most used strategy in e-mails and Facebook and the fourth on Twitter. Chi-square comparison shows that there was a significant difference between how relationship cultivation strategies were used in the different channels, both by Obama and Romney.

Regarding the other strategies, there was no concordance either between which strategies were used by the same campaign in the different channels or

Table 3.4 Relationship Cultivation Strategies by Channel: Obama

STRATEGIES	EMAIL FREQUENCY	%	FACEBOOK FREQUENCY	%	TWITTER FREQUENCY	%
Collaboration***	269	95.7	124	51.7	67	1.8
Common Interest***	114	40.6	3	1.7	9	2
Assurances***	60	13.2	1	0.4	1	0.2
Openness***	32	11.4	10	4.2	8	1.8
Rewarding system***	72	25.6	3	1.3	1	0.2
Co-creation*	6	2.1	—	—	2	0.4
Feedback	3	1.1	2	0.8	—	—
Networking***	36	9.3	10	4.2	—	—
N	281		240		454	

Note: * $p < .05$; **$p < .01$; *** $p < .001$ indicate statistically significant differences between different channels. N indicates total number of emails, Facebook updates and tweets.
Source: Fall 2012 Presidential Election Content Analysis Conducted by Authors.

Table 3.5 Relationship Cultivation Strategies by Channel: Romney

STRATEGIES	E-MAIL FREQUENCY	%	FACEBOOK FREQUENCY	%	TWITTER FREQUENCY	%
Collaboration***	304	83.5	97	26.4	47	14.2
Common Interest***	123	33.8	15	4.1	8	2.4
Assurances***	26	7.1	3	0.8	3	0.9
Openness	3	0.8	10	2.7	9	2.7
Rewarding system***	139	38.2	22	6	12	3.6
Co-creation	2	0.5	2	0.5	4	1.2
Feedback	—	—	—	—	—	—
Networking***	3	0.8	—	—	16	4.8
N	364		368		332	

Note: * $p < .05$; **$p < .01$; *** $p < .001$ indicate statistically significant differences between different channels. N indicates total number of e-mails, Facebook updates and tweets.
Source: Fall 2012 Presidential Election Content Analysis Conducted by Authors.

between the campaigns. At the same time, the frequency with which other strategies were used was comparatively low. A strategy that does emerge prominently, however, is rewarding systems, as discussed above.

Even though the data does not tell us whom the publics in the different channels were nor whom the campaigns wanted to communicate with, the results show that both campaigns used different strategies in different channels. One way to explain this is to apply the relationship-reputation continuum discussed earlier. Relationship cultivation strategies offer tools to build and maintain relationships with key publics (Ledingham & Bruning, 1998) and one of the key publics for election campaigns are their volunteers. If the campaigns believe that different channels offer possibilities to communicate with different publics, not just key publics, there is no reason to use relationship cultivation strategies in all channels (Christopher et al., 2008; Hon & Grunig, 1999). Not only do different publics demand different strategies (Hutton et al., 2001; Kiousis & Strömbäck, 2011), but if the campaigns believe that they communicate with different publics in different channels, a different set of strategies can be—and were—used. Consequently, persons who sign up for volunteer e-mails can be expected to be among the most active and engaged in the campaign. Both Facebook and Twitter are open platforms and thus more suited for other types of communication than those aimed solely at key publics. On communication platforms that facilitate the dissemination of information and campaign frames, campaigns have the opportunity to communicate and connect with publics such as supporters, asking for types of collaboration that do not demand much activity from the supporter (like a donation or "share"), and also reach non-supporters such as voters who might be undecided, and "observers" such as the media.

Consequently, there might be a conflict between the notion that social media such as Facebook and Twitter offer higher levels of interactivity than e-mail and are more conducive for relationship cultivation (Trent et al., 2011), as suggested by the finding that relationship strategies were mostly used in e-mails. Although relationship cultivation strategies are tools for engaging in interaction with the publics, this strategy was used mostly in the communication channel that offers the least interactivity among those investigated here.

Helping the Candidate: Different Types of Collaboration

There are many ways in which supporters can share tasks with the campaign, and the collaboration strategy was divided into seven categories in order to more closely investigate what kind of collaboration the campaigns were seeking: *donation, volunteer, share/retweet, vote, talk to family/friends, sign a petition, or join a call.* The results are presented in Tables 3.6 and 3.7.

The most common type of collaboration was to ask supporters to *donate* to the campaign. Presidential campaigns are extremely expensive, and the candidates are dependent upon contributions in order to be able to run for the presidency, which therefore makes this type of collaboration essential. When looking at what other relationship cultivation strategies the campaigns used when asking for donations, the results show the following: the Obama campaign combined asking for donations with stressing *common interests* and offering *soft rewards* in 44.7% and 31% of the donate messages, respectively, while the Romney campaign did so in 44.5% and 40.2% of the donate messages, respectively.

For Obama, the second most requested help was to *share* (on Facebook) or retweet (on Twitter), a task that Romney also asked his supporters to do. Getting

Table 3.6 Different Types of Collaboration by Channel: Obama

TYPES OF COLLABORATION	E-MAIL		FACEBOOK		TWITTER	
	FREQUENCY	%	FREQUENCY	%	FREQUENCY	%
Donate***	205	73	12	5	3	0.7
Volunteer***	37	12.2	12	5	18	4
Share***	25	8.9	56	23.3	14	3.1
Vote	15	5.3	16	6.7	31	6.8
Talk to***	26	9.3	18	7.5	7	1.5
Sign Petition***	15	5.3	4	1.7	1	0.2
Join***	16	5.7	23	9.6	1	0.2
N	281		240		454	

Note: *$p < .05$; **$p < .01$; ***$p < .001$ indicate statistically significant differences between different channels. N indicates total number of e-mails, Facebook updates and tweets.

Source: Fall 2012 Presidential Election Content Analysis Conducted by Authors.

Table 3.7 Different Types of Collaboration by Channel: Romney

TYPES OF COLLABORATION	EMAIL		FACEBOOK		TWITTER	
	FREQUENCY	%	FREQUENCY	%	FREQUENCY	%
Donate***	254	69.8	21	5.7	10	3
Volunteer***	40	11	17	4.6	7	2.1
Share***	4	1.1	24	6.5	8	2.4
Vote	5	1.4	11	3	11	3.3
Talk to family	6	1.6	4	1.1	1	0.3
Sign Petition	1	0.3	7	1.9	5	1.5
Join	13	3.6	10	5.2	7	2.1
N	364		368		332	

Note: *$p < .05$; **$p < .01$; ***$p < .001$ indicate statistically significant differences between different channels. N indicates total number of emails, Facebook updates and tweets.

Source: Fall 2012 Presidential Election Content Analysis Conducted by Authors.

supporters to share campaign messages is a way for the campaign to reach more voters. It is also a way to build more confidence for the message—and subsequently for the candidate—when the message is delivered by someone known to the recipient (Hovland, Janis, & Kelley, 1953). The offline way to share is to *talk to family/friends*, a type of collaboration that Obama used in the *share* messages (72% in Facebook and in 73% in e-mails). Romney, on the other hand, used *talk to family/friends* in less than 1.6% of his campaign messages. This may suggest that

(1) the Romney campaign did not account for the fact that about 25% of the American population does not use the Internet and that among those who do use the Internet, only 52% use Facebook every day, and only 8% use Twitter every day (Pew Research Center, 2011); and/or (2) they realized that the threshold for sharing or retweeting may be much lower than engaging in actual face-to-face conversations. Both Obama and Romney used Twitter mostly to encourage people to *vote*. This was only done—of course—under the later phase of the election campaigns, which, again, suggests that Twitter was not used for relationship cultivation in any greater sense.

Lastly, presidential election campaigns also depend, to a great extent, on grassroots volunteering for canvassing, making phone calls, registering voters, etc. Asking supporters to *volunteer* was also the third most common type of task the Romney campaign used (2.1%), while it was second for the Obama campaign (4%). The Romney campaign used *hard rewards* as an incentive for getting supporters to sign up for volunteering in 25% of the campaign messages, while no such incentives were made by the Obama campaign.

DISCUSSION

During the last decades, relationship management and relationship marketing has become increasingly prominent within public relations and marketing, respectively, and with the rise of digital and social media, it has often been assumed that political campaigns use these media to cultivate relationships with key publics such as supporters and volunteers. In contrast, this study suggests that the use of social media by the Obama and the Romney campaigns was not primarily based on relationship cultivation strategies.

This is not to say that relationship cultivation was absent. Both the Obama campaign and the Romney campaign did use some relationship cultivation strategies in the 2012 election. Collaboration was, as expected, the most used strategy, whereas openness, feedback, and co-creation were not used in any broader sense. What this suggests is rather that the kind of relationship the campaigns attempted to cultivate was almost exclusively focused on exchanges. The candidates' got help with fund-raising, disseminating information, and canvassing, whereas supporters and volunteers got to work for a person with whom they shared beliefs and wanted to see elected (i.e., they had a mutual common interest and depended on each other for reaching that interest). However, this also suggests that the campaigns lacked the mindset (Grönroos, 1996) for having an actual relationship with their supporters and volunteers. Interestingly, the results also suggest that while the campaigns did use different strategies in different channels, they used relationship cultivation strategies mostly in the channel that offered the least interactivity among those investigated (i.e., e-mails).

What these results suggest is that it is questionable whether it is valid to describe how the campaigns use digital and social media as part of relationship cultivation strategies. It can also be questioned whether the communication carried out in these channels is that much different from the communication performed in other channels or through other activities, as Metzger and Maruggi (2009) suggest: "Have a message. Know where to find the target audience. Connect with that audience, offering a mutually beneficial two-way relationship. Nurture that relationship. Then ask for the vote. This is not new. It is just old-fashioned campaigning" (p. 154).

In the end, digital and social media might largely constitute another set of channels and platforms for communication rather than a revolution in terms of overall campaign strategies. As suggested by Metzger & Maruggi (2009) after the 2008 presidential campaign: "there is little evidence that any of these social media venues actually drove discussion, participation, or outcomes. The bottom line is that social media tools are only tools" (p. 141). While these platforms do offer opportunities for higher interactivity with a lower threshold than other media, the opportunities are more often perceived than realized. The opportunity to interact and engage in actual relationships is, as suggested by our results, often not taken (Dimitrova et al., 2014; Kent, 2008; Rybalko & Seltzer, 2010).

At the same time, it might also be questioned how great the need is for candidates in a presidential election campaign to really engage in long-term relationships with supporters and volunteers. When the campaigns are in full swing, the scope for different publics involved in a relationship to influence the campaigns is by necessity limited. The key point here is also that it perhaps is more realistic for political candidates to engage in relationships with key publics (and thus for scholars to study them) earlier in the campaign cycle (i.e., in a context which offers greater opportunities to open up for feedback, for co-creation of the policy platform, for the political actor to fulfill their role as a representative for the citizens, and to listen to the publics and their opinions). Along the same line, what the candidate needs in an election campaign is not primarily long lasting loyalty but donations, help to disseminate information, help with canvassing and mobilization, etc. From that perspective, what the Obama and Romney campaigns did through e-mail, Twitter, and Facebook during the 2012 election might be rational, although it focused more on one-way communication and letting supporters and volunteers work on the candidates' reputations rather than relationship cultivation.

What this might suggest is that scholars as well as practitioners might tend to use the concept of "relationships" far too broadly, including theories, strategies, and practices that do not constitute a relationship in a proper sense. As this study shows, relationship cultivation strategies were primarily used in volunteer e-mails (i.e., in a channel where the campaigns could communicate directly with their volunteers). However, not even in this channel is it possible to talk about a win-win situation, and even less so on Facebook and Twitter. When using the concept relationship as a description, including publics that are actually not that close to the organization, it risks being stretched too far. If we are to use concepts such as relationships with actual meaning, then they should be reserved for situations where campaigns or organizations have a relationship with a key public, a relationship that is built on a mutually beneficial interdependency, which is also covenantal and mutually communal. In other cases, reputation cultivation might be a more valid description than relationship cultivation (Hutton et al., 2001; Kiousis & Strömbäck, 2011).

Having said this, it might very well be the case that the Obama and Romney campaigns did make a greater use of relationship cultivation strategies in their communication with other publics than those reached through ordinary volunteer e-mails, Facebook, or Twitter, such as larger donors, representatives of key interest groups, and coalition members, or those who had shown greater commitment by repeatedly giving campaign contributions or participating in different campaign activities. If so, what these results suggest is not that the campaign strategy that guided the Obama and the Romney campaign overall should be described as reputation cultivation rather than relationship cultivation, but rather that campaign communication through Facebook, Twitter, and e-mails to those who mainly signed up for messages was less about relationship and more about reputation cultivation and mobilizing people to become more involved. For those who decided to become more involved, both campaigns might have used social media to engage further in relationship cultivation than this study suggests.

CHAPTER 4

Of Networks and Knowledge: Young Adults and the Early 2012 Republican Presidential Primaries and Caucuses

Jody C Baumgartner, David S. Morris,
and Jonathan S. Morris

In 2008, Barack Obama proved extraordinarily adept in his use of social networking Web sites in order to connect with supporters, especially younger supporters, throughout the campaign (Baumgartner & Morris, 2010). By 2012, a majority of Americans under the age of 65—of all demographic groupings—were connected via one or more of the various social networks (Brenner, 2012). This fact suggests that social networking sites (SNS) represent even more of an opportunity for candidates and parties to stay connected with supporters and reach out to potential new supporters. It also suggests that there may be some benefits for citizens in terms of staying connected and becoming more engaged with political campaigns.

To assess if this is the case, this study compares knowledge of the field of candidates in the early Republican presidential nomination season by users and nonusers of social media using survey data collected in January of 2012. The particular focus is on young people and the different ways they use SNSs for political purposes and how this may relate to their political knowledge. How much do young people use social media for information about public affairs, relative to other information sources? In what other ways do young people use these sites? Importantly, how does that affect their overall knowledge of the candidates and their campaigns?

The relationship between SNS use and political knowledge is an especially important question in the context of a presidential nomination season when no incumbent is running. Political knowledge is particularly important in the primary process because nominations are intraparty affairs, thus citizens cannot rely on party labels as information shortcuts. Therefore, the question of whether citizens can and do learn about the numerous candidates via SNSs is important from a democratic perspective. The focus on young people provides a critical test case for the democratic potential of social media because younger adults use social media with greater frequency than their older counterparts. If a relationship exists between political knowledge and social media, it may likely exist among this age cohort, especially considering the growing centrality of potential young voters and SNS use at the grassroots level of recent presidential campaigns. Do young people use this medium for news about politics during the nomination season? If they do, how? And how helpful—if at all—are SNSs in informing their voting choices?

In the next section, the literature review examines the relationship between SNS use and political engagement, with an emphasis on the political knowledge of users. Specifically, the study focuses on the fact that much of the existing scholarship does not adequately account for the fact that social media use is multifaceted. Following this, the data collection method is outlined. Finally, analysis of the findings is presented. It shows that some forms of young adults' SNS usage is associated with a higher level of political knowledge. However, this is not the case with all forms of social media use. In the end, we conclude that, like traditional social networks, the intensity of SNS engagement largely determines the political consequences.

SOCIAL NETWORKS AND KNOWLEDGE

Political Internet use has been widely examined for well over a decade (Bimber, 1998; Johnson & Kaye, 2003; Krueger, 2002; Quintelier & Vissers, 2008; Tolbert & McNeal, 2003). But, as the Internet has evolved and the tools and platforms available to users have expanded, research has begun to recognize that the medium is multifaceted, offering a variety of ways to consume information as well as to engage with other users. In response, researchers have begun to focus on specific aspects of Internet usage and how it relates to political engagement.

One such aspect, the use of SNSs such as Facebook and Twitter, has attracted a good deal of attention from social scientists of late. SNSs allow users to gather, share, create, and instantly disseminate information, rather than passively consume prepackaged information online. Use of these sites has seen explosive growth. According to data presented by Brenner (2012), the percentage of Internet users using SNS increased from eight to 65% between 2005 and 2011, and daily usage increased from two to 43%. For young adults, the numbers are even more staggering: the percentage of 18- to 29-year-olds using SNS increased from 9% to 83% between 2005 and 2011 (Brenner, 2012). Twitter, newer to the social media scene than Facebook and many other SNS, has seen everyday usage quadruple from two to eight percent for online adults between the end of 2010 and beginning of 2012 (Brenner, 2012).

The interactivity and expanding reach of SNS provides obvious potential benefits for candidates, parties, and the electorate, triggering scholarly examinations of the relationship between SNS usage and various forms of political engagement. Of the 40% of Americans who used the Internet to get news about the 2008 presidential election, 10% used SNSs in some political fashion. During the 2010 congressional elections, 21% used SNSs to engage politically. For young adults this was even more evident, with 42% of 18- to 29-year olds using SNSs for political purposes.

Some research suggests that the use of SNSs is positively associated with democratic norms in the form of decreased political cynicism and greater confidence in one's political knowledge and ability to participate (Hanson, Haridakis, Cunningham, Sharma, & Ponder, 2010; Sweetser & Kaid, 2008). Some research focusing on frequency of use suggests further potential democratic benefits, indicating that active social media users are likely to gather information about political candidates (Utz, 2009). However, other research suggests that the gathering and sharing of information about politics on SNSs may not be associated with greater levels of political knowledge. For example, in one study, social media users appeared no more likely than non-users to know which party is more conservative, which party holds the majority in Congress, and the name of the Chief Justice of the Supreme Court (Baumgartner & Morris, 2010; see also Kushin & Yamamoto, 2010).

Recent research on the uses and effects of SNSs on political participation and knowledge paint a picture of an online platform that provides individuals an opportunity to engage in the political system online and offline (Bode, 2012; Ellison, Steinfield, & Lampe, 2007; Valenquela, Park, & Kee, 2009). But existing research, mainly by virtue of the rapidly changing nature of the medium and adoption and usage patterns by individuals, has some shortcomings.

One such shortcoming is that most of the research is based on activity that took place during the 2008 presidential campaign, when the use of SNSs—by citizens and politicians (Smith, 2011)—was less developed and widespread than it was in 2012. Bode (2012), for example, examined Facebook usage in the 2008 presidential nomination season, when only 32% of Internet users reported having a profile on any SNS (Pew Research Center, 2008). By the 2012 primary season, this number had increased to 58% (Pew Research Center, 2012b). Another is that much of the research does not adequately account for variations in patterns of social media use. Checking a Facebook page once a week is quite different than posting to Facebook and/or Twitter several times a day or "following" or "liking" a politician or celebrity. These different forms of social media activity should be specified when including SNS use either as a dependent or independent variable.

Another development not fully accounted for in the literature is the effect of using SNSs as a primary source of news and information. According to Brenner (2012), the percentage of online adults who had ever used SNSs was 29%, while the percentage who had used them the previous day was just 13% (in 2008). By 2011, online adults who used SNSs was up to 65%, and the percentage of those who had used them the previous day had more than tripled to 43%. Increased use of social media by individuals can open up the possibility that some are being exposed to new information from an ever-broadening social network (Pasek, More, & Romer, 2009). Although individuals tend to gravitate toward online information outlets that concur with already held political leanings (Lawrence, Sides, & Farrell, 2010), SNSs have the unique capacity for joining disparate social networks (often referred to as weak social ties or "bridging" social capital) for the sharing of political ideas and information (Ellison et al., 2007; Granovetter, 1983; Putnam, 2000; Steinfeld et al., 2009). It is possible that more diverse social networks brought about by increased use of SNSs could lead to increased exposure to new, useful, and interesting political information. This, in turn, could contribute to higher levels of political knowledge.

However, this may not necessarily be the case. For example, it is possible that few really consider SNSs as a primary source of news and information. The point is that there is a great deal of variation in how often individuals use social media, and differing levels of usage provide differing opportunities for political engagement and learning. This, too, is an important factor to consider when examining SNS usage and political knowledge acquisition.

Finally, research on SNS use does not fully capture the fact that the partisan gap in SNS usage has narrowed considerably over the past few years. Initially, SNS were embraced by Democratic campaigns and voters more than by Republicans, as evidenced by the Obama campaign's successful use of social media to reach and galvanize supporters in 2008 (Fernandes et al., 2010; Woolley, Limperos, & Oliver, 2010). Indeed, in 2008, 36% of online Democrats used SNSs, compared to 21% of Republicans (Smith & Rainie, 2008). But by 2010, Republicans had caught up with Democratic SNS usage, with GOP supporters just as likely as supporters of the Democratic Party to use SNSs.

AGE AND SOCIAL NETWORK USAGE PATTERNS

While SNS use has become a significant part of the lives of many Americans across all segments of the population, this study's interest is in patterns of use among young adults. This particular age demographic is of interest for a few reasons. First, it is clear that online SNS use has infiltrated everyday life among young adults more than any other age group. Table 4.1 uses data from the Pew Research Center (2012a) and shows usage of Facebook and Twitter among 18- to 24-year-olds compared to the rest of the population. As can be seen, 93% of adults under the age of 25 use Facebook, almost double the percentage of adults over the age of 24 (50%). Twitter usage is less frequent but still much more prevalent among young adults (26%) than those 25 and older (8%).

Table 4.1 Social Networking Site Usage by Age

PERCENTAGE WHO:	AGE: 18–24	AGE: 25 AND OLDER
Use Facebook	93%	50%
Use Twitter	26	8
Say they learn about the election from Facebook at least sometime	44	15
Say they learn about the election from Twitter at least sometime	11	3
Follow candidate updates on Twitter or Facebook	20	4

Data from Pew Research Center. 2012b. Early January Communication Study, Jan 4–8, 2012.

Source: Pew Research Center Early January Communication Study, Jan 4–8, 2012b.

It is also clear that young adults are more likely than their older counterparts to use SNSs to acquire political information. Table 4.1 shows that young adults are approximately three times more likely than older adults to report having learned about the race for the 2012 Republican presidential nomination from Facebook and Twitter. Of those between the ages of 18 and 24, 44% said that they learned about the nomination campaign from Facebook at least sometimes, while 11% claim to have learned something from Twitter. Older adults, however, reported learning from these sites at much lower rates, with 15% saying that they learned about the nomination campaign from Facebook at least sometimes and only 3% reporting learning from Twitter. In addition, five times as many young adults reported following political candidates on Facebook and Twitter than did older adults (20% as opposed to 4%).

These data offer a good starting point for understanding SNS usage in context of an early presidential primary season. It is clear that a significant number of young adults use SNSs to follow political candidates and campaigns. Importantly, close to half of these young adults claim to have learned something about the campaign from these sites. What remains to be seen is what they actually did learn and what types of information they retain. The next section outlines the expectations in this regard.

SOCIAL MEDIA USE AND CAMPAIGN KNOWLEDGE: EXPECTATIONS

SNSs have been a welcome and dynamic component of the Internet when it comes to organizing and galvanizing a base for political and social movements. In 2011, civil resistance efforts in Tunisia, Egypt, and Iran relied on social media to share information, organize political activity, and get their messages out to the international community (Stepanova, 2011). The use of SNSs to aid political and social movements is not isolated to the Arab Spring of 2011, as evidenced by student demonstrations against governmental cuts to higher education in the United Kingdom (Theocharis, 2011). While social media and SNSs are not necessary components of social movements, their potential to facilitate political activity has been established.

The use of SNSs for political purposes on behalf of parties and the electorate was relatively new during the 2008 and 2010 election campaigns. It is possible that social media implementation strategies by campaigns and political groups, as well as the expectations and capabilities for political participation for individuals, have changed over the past few years. In this respect, SNS users during previous election cycles were pioneers in the use of these sites as a political tool. It is therefore conceivable that users in 2012 were better equipped with a sense of what these sites offered and what they were capable of politically. This is true with respect to all age groups, including young people—both Republican and Democrat. Early primary voters tend to be more knowledgeable about the candidates compared to the rest of the public during the onset of the campaign season, but this stage is still important in introducing the field to all potential voters (Pfau, Diedrich, Larson, & Van Winkle, 1993), and the electronic media plays a significant role in this process (Farnsworth & Lichter, 2011). The early adoption of SNSs may be expected to contribute to greater retention of political information, even if the SNS use may not be used expressly with the goal of obtaining news about political candidates (Baum, 2003; Popkin, 1991). This study, therefore, expected to find that in the context of the 2012 Republican primary, social media use would be associated with greater knowledge of the candidates and the campaign.

The next section discusses the manner in which data were collected to test the expectations regarding how political knowledge related to various types of SNS usage during the 2012 Republican nomination season. This is followed by an analysis and a discussion of the results.

METHOD

Data for this analysis were collected by way of an online Web survey. The survey began on January 4, 2012, the day after the Republican Iowa caucuses, and ended on January 20, 2012, the day before the South Carolina Republican primary. The New Hampshire Republican primary was held on January 10, 2012. Relatively few Americans closely follow news about the presidential campaign prior to the election year itself, but more are doing so by the time the first few caucuses and primaries of the campaign season (e.g., Iowa and New Hampshire) occur (Baumgartner & Morris, 2007). Therefore, the timing of the survey allowed for a good test of how well knowledge of the campaign and candidates associate with SNS use.

This study was a collaborative effort on the part of political scientists and communication scholars from seven major public universities. Each member of the research team contributed the e-mail addresses of all undergraduate students at their respective institution, creating a pool of over 120,000 potential respondents. E-mails were then sent to each student, inviting them to participate in the "2012 American Values Survey." The survey was described as "a research project that looks at what young adults think about various political issues," and the data was to be used to "help . . . better understand what people your age think about politics." The e-mail explained that participation was completely voluntary and included standard assurances about confidentiality of individual responses. No monetary or other incentive (e.g., course credit) was offered to potential respondents, but an additional appeal was made that focused on the idea that many "people in the media . . . think they know what you think and care about. We want to find out from you—the source . . . this is your chance to speak out about what's important to YOU." In addition to the first e-mail, two shorter e-mails were subsequently sent, reminding students of the project and again asking for their help.

In all, 3,450 completed surveys were returned. Because the focus of this research was on 18 to 24 year olds, respondents over the age of 24 were dropped from the final data set. This yielded a total of 2,166 participants. While the response rate was relatively low, this is not particularly unusual for Internet surveys among college students, who are being asked with increasing frequency to complete surveys. Research suggests that this is resulting in a certain amount of survey fatigue among students (Porter & Whitcomb, 2003; Porter, Whitcomb, & Weitzer, 2004). While respondents were self-selected, the sample has the advantage of having been drawn from multiple public universities across the country, making it more representative.

ANALYSIS: POLITICAL USE OF SOCIAL NETWORKING SITES AND POLITICAL KNOWLEDGE

How do young adults use SNSs to follow and engage in politics during a primary season? While SNS usage among those in the United States under the age of 25 is almost ubiquitous, the manner in which these Web sites are used and the degree to which they are used varies considerably compared with other sources of news and information sites. Table 4.2 demonstrates how the frequency of SNS use for the acquisition of news and information compares with that of more conventional news sites. In this regard, SNSs compare quite favorably with other sources of news. On average, respondents got news from SNSs more than three times per week, more than from television, radio, and print media. According to our data, only Web sites are used more frequently than SNSs for gathering news, suggesting that SNSs are not simply recreational tools but that they may be a significant source of news and information for young adults.

However, as suggested earlier, SNSs do not serve only as sources of news and information. A significant number of young adults use SNSs for other politically oriented activities. Table 4.3 shows the frequency of three SNS activities that go beyond simply using Facebook and/or Twitter as one of many sources of news or

Table 4.2 News Habits in a Typical Week

DURING A TYPICAL WEEK, CAN YOU TELL US ABOUT HOW MANY DAYS YOU . . .	AVG. DAYS PER WEEK
Watch the evening television news on ABC, CBS, or NBC?	1.1
Watch local television news?	1.3
Watch news on CNN?	.90
Watch news on the Fox News Channel?	.8
Watch news on MSNBC?	.7
Listen to news on the radio?	1.6
Watch/read news on a news organization's (e.g., CNN, NY Times) Web site?	3.7
Watch/read news on the Internet on some other type of Web site?	3.8
Read a printed newspaper?	1.6
Get news from a social networking Web sites such as Facebook?	3.1

Source: 2012 American Values Study (January 4–20, 2012).

information. The first is the tendency to use Facebook or Twitter as a primary news source. This was determined by asking subjects, "How have you been getting most of your news about the current campaign for president of the United States—from television, newspapers, radio, or the Internet?" Those who listed the Internet were asked, "In the previous question, were you referring to an Internet site that is a news site from a newspaper or television station? Or is it a blog, an SNS such as Facebook.com, or something else?" Twitter and Facebook were both unique response options, in addition to newspaper sites, television station sites, blogs, or "other."

As Table 4.3 shows, 10% of all the respondents reported using either Facebook (9%) or Twitter (1%) as their primary news source, indicating that one-in-ten young people relied on these sites for most of their news about the campaign. This percentage compares favorably to newspaper sites (23%), television station sites (8%), blogs (3%), and other sites, which would include portals such as Google, Yahoo, MSN, or blogs (18%). It also compares favorably to the rest of the sample, who reported primarily relying on non-Internet sources such as television (21%), print newspapers (5%), and radio (6%).

Table 4.3 also shows the percentage of respondents who use SNSs to follow politicians. "Following" a political figure on Twitter or "liking" that person on Facebook enables an SNS user to receive updates, information, and perspectives directly from that individual. In this manner, SNS followers receive what is akin to a steady stream of mini-press releases from politicians of their choice, which is a process of information gathering that goes well beyond being consumers of news in general. While only 6% of the sample reported following a political figure on Twitter, 19% had "liked" at least one politician on Facebook. In total, 23% of the respondents used at least one of the two methods to follow political figures, totaling almost a quarter of the sample.

The final aspect of SNS usage summarized in Table 4.3 is the practice of posting political messages. Of respondents, 11% had posted political messages on

Table 4.3 Social Networking Site Usage in the 2012 Primary Campaign

PERCENTAGE OF RESPONDENTS WHO REPORT HAVING:	PERCENTAGE
Primary News Source	
• Used Twitter as their primary news source	1%
• Used Facebook as their primary news source	9%
Following and Liking	
• Followed a political figure on Twitter	6%
• Liked a political figure on Facebook	19%
Posting	
• Recently posted a political message on Twitter	11%
• Recently posted a political message on Facebook	43%

Source: 2012 American Values Study (January 4–20, 2012).

Twitter, and 43% reported posting similar messages on Facebook. In all, 45% of the sample reported posting political messages on either Twitter or on Facebook, indicating that this was a fairly common practice among the sample of young adults.

Overall, the findings from Tables 4.2 and 4.3 demonstrate that Facebook and Twitter—particularly Facebook—are somewhat common tools young adults use for acquiring and disseminating news and information about politics, following the posts of political figures, and posting political comments online during presidential primaries. In fact, these practices seem as common as most other forms of news-gathering, although still falling below newspaper and television Web sites and cable and network television. But, does the tendency to use SNSs in some form or another associate with higher levels of political knowledge?

In order to examine the relationship between SNS usage and political knowledge, the familiarity with Republican candidates for president during the early nomination season was examined. Specifically, two aspects of candidate knowledge were investigated: candidate attributes and name recall. In order to measure knowledge of candidate attributes, a series of multiple choice questions were asked in which respondents were questioned to correctly identify the candidate that fit a particular profile. This approach yields a measure of candidate "familiarity" (Bartels, 1988). Table 4.4 summarizes these questions along with the percentage of respondents who answered each question correctly. To create a composite measure of candidate attribute knowledge, an additive index of the number of questions correctly answered (a scale of zero to five) was created. Higher values represent higher levels of candidate attribute knowledge.

Candidate name recall, on the other hand, was measured in an open-ended fashion. Respondents were asked, "Several candidates are seeking the REPUBLICAN PARTY'S nomination for president in 2012. For various reasons not all citizens know who is running. In the boxes below, please list as many of the candidate LAST names that you can remember. If you are not sure of the correct spelling,

Table 4.4 Candidate Attribute Knowledge

QUESTION: "OF THE SEVERAL CANDIDATES SEEKING THE REPUBLICAN NOMINATION FOR PRESIDENT IN 2012, DO YOU HAPPEN TO KNOW WHICH OF THE CANDIDATES . . ."	PERCENT CORRECT
Is a member of the U.S. House of Representatives from Minnesota? (Michelle Bachman)	52.3%
Is the current governor of Texas? (Rick Perry)	67.7%
Was formerly a Speaker of the House of Representatives? (Newt Gingrich)	60.4%
Was formerly a member of the Senate from Pennsylvania? (Rick Santorum)	31.5%
Was formerly the governor of Massachusetts? (Mitt Romney)	60.5%
Average number of correct answers	*2.7*

Source: 2012 American Values Study (January 4–20, 2012).

don't worry—just do your best." Each response was coded and recorded as correct or incorrect. Misspelled names were counted provided they could be reasonably attributed to a candidate. The variable derived from this measure is a count of the number of candidate names accurately recalled by the respondents. Higher values represent higher levels of knowledge of the field of candidates. This gives a dimension of candidate knowledge that is associated with name recall rather than name identification, which typically is measured by asking respondents to identify candidate names on a list. Asking respondents to list names in an unstructured format is a more accurate measure of candidate salience and also minimizes the tendency of respondents to falsely claim that they recognize a name that they actually do not (Lenart, 1997). The average number of candidate names correctly identified by the sample was 4.6. Figure 4.1 summarizes the distribution of the number of correct responses by respondents.

Using the variable summarized in Table 4.4 (candidate attribute knowledge) and Figure 4.1 (candidate name recall) as dependent variables, an explanatory model of political knowledge was constructed. As both dependent variables are the number of correct answers provided or recalled, the proper model fit is a maximum likelihood event count model, specifically, a Poisson regression analysis (Long, 1997). Our predictors of interest are the measures of SNS usage discussed in the previous section. These measures include the typical number of days per week an individual gets news from SNSs such as Facebook. These were measured separately on a scale of 0 to 7 (number of days in a typical week). In addition, three dummy variables (1 = yes; 0 = no) were included: (1) whether or not an individual used Facebook or Twitter as their primary source of news; (2) whether or not an individual had "friended" or "followed" a political figure on

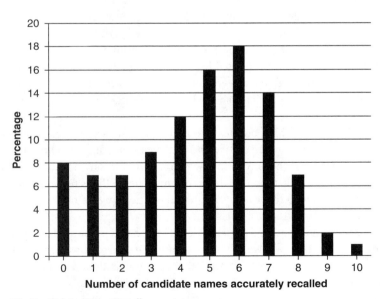

Figure 4.1 Candidate Name Recall
SOURCE: 2012 American Values Study (January 4–20, 2012).

Facebook or Twitter; and (3) whether an individual had posted a political message on Facebook or Twitter.

The models controlled for other variables as well, including party identification (1 = strong Democrat; 4 = Independent/don't know; 7 = strong Republican), political ideology (1 = very liberal; 2 = liberal; 3 = moderate/don't know; 4 = conservative; 5 = very conservative), gender (1 = male; 0 = female), race (1 = white; 0 = other), and annual family income (0 = $0–$25,000; 1 = $25,001–$35,000; . . . 4 = $75,001–$100,000; . . . 7 = over $200,000). Additionally, because other political activity may overlap with electronic political participation on SNSs, a variable for traditional political participation was included. This variable was constructed by asking respondents whether or not they had participated in various political activities in the past year (e.g., writing a politician, attending political rallies or public meetings, signing petitions, working for parties or interest groups, etc.). This index ranged from 0 (lowest level of engagement) to 10 (highest level of engagement).

The findings from the Poisson regression models are listed in Table 4.5. The first sets of estimates are for candidate attribute knowledge and the second are for name recall. It is clear that the models do not differ significantly, thus indicating the strong likelihood that both dependent variables are measuring very similar concepts (campaign knowledge), which is not surprising. However, when it comes to the effect of the different measures of SNS usage on the dependent variables, considerable variation exists.

When the media exposure variables are examined, the number of days an individual gets news from SNSs is unrelated to their level of political knowledge. This is also the case for network and local television news exposure and print newspaper usage. Cable news and Internet news exposure, on the other hand, are both positively associated with candidate knowledge and name recall.

The next form of SNS usage listed in Table 4.5 tells a different story. As already mentioned, the measures of media reliance are dummy variables constructed to reflect whether or not an individual listed a given media outlet as their primary source of news (the reference category in the model is reliance on television as a primary source). The coefficients show that reliance on SNSs negatively associates with political knowledge.

Both of the active SNS political engagement variables in Table 4.5 (posting and friending/following) are positive and statistically significant. Those who post political messages and those who follow political figures on Facebook or Twitter are more knowledgeable than those who do not. These effects remain statistically significant even though the level of traditional political engagement has been controlled, which is also positive and significant.

It also warrants mention that party identification and political ideology did not significantly impact knowledge of the candidates. Of course, those who participate in primaries and caucuses are likely to be more partisan and more politically knowledgeable than nonparticipants (Norrander, 1986). Also, partisan and ideological individuals should be more knowledgeable of their own field of candidates than candidates from the other party (Norrander, 1996). However, this particular study

Table 4.5 Campaign Knowledge by Media Exposure

VARIABLE	CANDIDATE ATTRIBUTE KNOWLEDGE INDEX	CANDIDATE NAME RECALL
Media Exposure Variables		
• Social Networking Sites	−.00 (.01)	.00 (.00)
• Cable TV News	.02 (.00)**	.01 (.00)**
• Network TV News	−.01 (.01)	−.00 (.01)
• Local TV News	−.01 (.01)	−.01 (.01)
• Internet News	.07 (.01)**	.05 (.00)**
• Print Newspaper	.01 (.01)	.00 (.01)
Primary Source of News & Information		
• Social Networking Sites	−.13 (.06)*	−.15 (.04)**
• Other Internet News	.03 (.03)	.00 (.03)
• Newspaper	.01 (.07)	.01 (.05)
• Radio News	.15 (.06)**	.05 (.05)
Political Engagement Variables		
• SN: Post Political Messages	.07 (.03)*	.08 (.02)**
• SN: Friend/Follow Politicians	.14 (.03)**	.09 (.02)**
• Traditional Engagement	.03 (.01)**	.02 (.01)**
Control Variables		
• Party Identification	−.00 (.01)	−.00 (.01)
• Political Ideology	.02 (.02)	−.00 (.01)
• Race	.09 (.03)**	.03 (.02)
• Gender	.25 (.03)**	.17 (.02)**
• Family Income	.02 (.01)**	.02 (.01)**
Constant	.22 (.06)**	1.05 (.05)**
Chi Squared	691.66**	574.89**
Log Likelihood	−4088.68	−4749.20
N	2166	2166

Note: Cell entries are Poisson regression coefficients with standard errors in parentheses. **$p \leq .01$, *$p \leq .05$ (two-tailed test)

Source: 2012 American Values Study (January 4–20, 2012).

examines a sample of the general population early in the nomination process. In this early stage, the mass public learns a significant amount about the candidates as information quickly surges in the media, thus lessening the impact of party identification and ideology (Keeter & Zukin, 1983).

Overall, the findings in Table 4.5 show that those who use SNSs for news are no more knowledgeable about politics than anyone else. Those who use these sites as a primary source of news are, it appears, less knowledgeable. But individuals who use SNSs to engage in politics beyond simple news-gathering are indeed more knowledgeable, even when other variables are statistically controlled.

DISCUSSION

It is clear that SNSs provide presidential candidates and parties with more opportunities to personally reach out to and connect with citizens than might otherwise be possible, at least in the context of a national presidential campaign. The use of these sites for political purposes was in its infancy in previous elections, but since the 2012 presidential election, such use has evolved into a more developed, widely used, and institutionalized form of political information gathering and dissemination. Both of these interrelated developments suggest greater opportunities for citizens to learn about political candidates, issues, and campaigns. And while this study did not test citizens' learning, it did seek to determine whether, in context to the 2012 Republican presidential nomination campaign, social media use would be linked to greater political knowledge. Was this the case? The evidence is mixed.

This study focused on the political uses of social media for young adults. First, it was demonstrated that 18- to 24-year-olds regularly use SNSs for news-gathering. The use of these sites is second only to nonsocial Internet sources, such as news Web sites. In fact, the study found that 10% of the sample used social media as its primary news source regarding the presidential elections in early 2012. Specifically, 23% of our sample followed or received updates directly from a political figure on an SNS, which is a more active use than merely getting news. Furthermore, 45% had recently posted a political message about the 2012 Republican presidential nomination campaign on Facebook or Twitter, which could be argued to be an even more active use than getting frequent updates via SNSs.

The study then turned to whether political uses of social media were related to levels of political knowledge during the 2012 Republican presidential nomination process. Here, it was found that those who use SNSs for news were no more knowledgeable about politics than anyone else, and those who use these sites as a primary source of news are less knowledgeable than those who use other media as a primary source. This latter point is hardly surprising. Individuals who claim Facebook or Twitter were their primary sources of news likely follow very little news. On the other hand, individuals who use SNSs in a more actively political fashion, like following a political figure or posting a political message, were more politically knowledgeable. This, too, makes some sense. More politically engaged and knowledgeable individuals are more likely to engage in political activity. This fits with Markus Prior's (2007) argument that a fragmented media environment that offers greater choice increases the divide between knowledgeable and less knowledgeable citizens, as informed citizens have greater access to political news, and the uninformed can easily avoid it. In the broadcast media world of the pre-1990s, the lack of media choice created the opportunity for disinterested and disengaged citizens to passively obtain some political information as an incidental byproduct of simply turning on the television or the radio. In the current fragmented media environment, however, it is easier to shut out the world of public affairs all together if so desired.

These findings make clear that use of social media in politics is more developed and has become a widely used and institutionalized political tool for campaigns and the electorate, and this is true for supporters of both parties. More young people are using social media to gather and share political information and in some cases use it as a primary news source. As discussed in the outset of this study, SNS usage has increased dramatically in a relatively short period of time. The majority of adult Internet users engage in some sort of SNS, and SNS usage is reaching full penetration among those under the age of 30 (Pew Research Center, 2012a). This means that any positive or negative effects of using SNSs for political purposes will likely become more widespread in the near future. Furthermore, the study's data were collected during a presidential nomination season when citizens were less engaged in the campaign. Because of this, the relationship between social media use and political knowledge may be underestimated. Of course, it is also possible that this is not the case, considering that the general public is less knowledgeable about the candidates for president during the primary season compared to the general election campaign. It would be worthwhile for future studies to consider differentiations between how the relationship between SNS usage and various forms of political knowledge vary across stages of the presidential election campaign.

In the end, however, this study leaves several questions unanswered. For example, it cannot demonstrate that the use or non-use of social media caused a change (positive or negative) in levels of political knowledge. For this, knowledge would need to be measured at two points in time. Moreover, there are limitations to the convenience sample of college students, as well as the how the survey was administered. Because the study solicited participation online and only from college undergraduates, it is certainly the case that the sample is likely to be more engaged and knowledgeable than young adults who may not have an e-mail address nor complete online surveys. Of course, this problem is common in social science research (Peterson, 2001), but future studies examining online activity should work to widen the sample pool. Also, as noted, the results paint a somewhat contradictory picture. Can social media improve citizens' understanding and awareness of politics, or is it a hindrance? In the end, this might be the wrong question. Other technological innovations have previously been hailed as a panacea for political engagement and have subsequently failed to live up to expectations. Whether an individual derives some democratic benefit from social media—at least for young adults in a nominating election—seems to depend in large part on how it is used.

CHAPTER 5

Technology Takeover? Campaign Learning during the 2012 Presidential Election

Terri L. Towner and David A. Dulio

As technology relates to political campaigns, the more things change, the more they seem to stay the same. For the last several election cycles, the use of technology has been growing by leaps and bounds. In the mid-1990s, campaigns used the Web basically as digital yard signs (Casey, 1996). In the late 1990s and early 2000s, candidates such as John McCain and Howard Dean discovered the fundraising power of the online world. More recently, candidates, led by Barack Obama in 2008, have begun to employ different social media applications; Obama even launched his own social networking site (SNS) in 2008, called MyBarackObama.com, or MyBO, which was modeled after Facebook. The pace with which technology is employed in political campaigns can be seen in the fact that at the time Barack Obama announced his candidacy for president, the first iPhone had yet to be released. In addition, as is typical with any change in campaign technology, use typically begins with presidential campaigns and trickles down to campaigns down the ballot.

The 2012 campaign was no different in this respect. More candidates began to employ some of the newest technology and tools, including looking beyond Facebook and YouTube to Reddit, Google+, Tumblr, and others. No other campaign saw as much discussion of technology as did the presidential race, and once again the Obama campaign led the way with its innovation. (We should note that the Romney campaign was also heavily invested in online activities, but the campaign will be remembered more for its mistakes in this area—including launching an app that misspelled America and a disappointing voter-turnout effort on Election Day—than for its innovation.) The Obama team devoted unprecedented resources to the collection of data through the use of social media. In fact, the digital division in the Obama campaign was their largest department; it hired several "nonpolitical tech innovators" and even invested in a full-time digital director in nearly all of the battleground states (Romano, 2012, para. 25). A key to this effort was "a more complex symbiosis between the campaign and Facebook" (Romano, 2012, para. 27) compared to 2008, which allowed the campaign to leverage the increased amount of personal data collected by Facebook.

Another dynamic that does not seem to change each election cycle is the prediction that the Web will change the way campaigns are waged. At the center of the Obama campaign's efforts was campaign manager Jim Messina who drew on relationships with tech-savvy experts to craft the Obama plan. One important contact for Messina was Google's executive chairman, Eric Schmidt, who commented during the campaign:

> In 2008, most people didn't operate on [Facebook and Twitter]. The difference now is, first and foremost, the growth of Facebook, which is much, much more deeply penetrated into things. The other obvious ones are the growth of YouTube and Twitter. The smart people were using them in 2008; now everyone's using them. You can imagine the implications of that. You can run political campaigns on the sum of those tools (as cited in Green, 2012, para. 18).

The Obama campaign claims it had access to roughly 20% of the total number of votes they needed to win the 2008 campaign simply through their list of 13 million e-mail addresses of supporters. Some estimated that they might reach 50% or 70% of the votes needed to win in 2012 with their enhanced digital effort (Green, 2012). During the campaign, Harvard professor Nicco Mele offered the following: "If the Obama campaign can combine its data efforts with the way people now live their lives online, a new kind of political engagement—and political persuasion—is possible" (quoted in Romano, 2012, para. 20).

In this chapter, we begin to investigate these types of claims of redefined campaigning. Are Web and social media tools changing political engagement and persuasion? We focus on what the public garners in terms of information during the campaign. Specifically, we focus on some of the most information-starved individuals—young Americans. In particular, we are interested in whether or not the use of specific types of Internet-information sources influence young Americans' knowledge of candidates. To do so, we revisit some of the questions we initially asked after the 2008 campaign (Towner & Dulio, 2011).

Given the varying features and designs of online newspapers, television network Web sites, presidential candidate Web sites, Facebook, Google+, YouTube, Twitter, Tumblr, and political blogs, we argue that each online source contributes differently to various knowledge structures. Indeed, "Facebooking" is qualitatively different from watching a political video on YouTube. Each of these online sources has different features, functions, and purposes, but their comparative effects are rarely examined. Much of the previous literature is rather limited, as it examines the effects of one online source or lumps many online sources together into one latent variable. We examine what effects paying attention to several specific forms of online media have on political knowledge. Next, we outline a series of research questions and hypotheses based on prior research.

POLITICAL KNOWLEDGE

If there is one thing political scientists can agree on, it is that much of the public is woefully uninformed about politics. Results pointing to this conclusion have been consistent in empirical research dating back to the earliest studies on the topic in the

1940s (Delli Carpini & Keeter, 1996). Some studies have gone well beyond the simple question of what facts an individual can recall (Graber, 1996; Neuman, Just, & Crigler, 1992) and moved into what individuals possess in terms of personal knowledge about candidates (Chaffee, Zhao, & Leshner, 1994), knowledge of current events (Price & Zaller, 1993), and issue knowledge about candidates (Patterson, 1980).

Not all information is considered the same, however. Political knowledge is comprised of two categories, differentiated and integrated: differentiated knowledge is linked to the factual recall of names, issues, and events; integrated knowledge is an individual's ability to link the differentiated items together (Neuman, 1981). While a lack of sophisticated knowledge among the American public persists even in the face of more and more information sources, certain segments of the population are more informed than others. Those with more wealth (Tichenor, Donahue, & Olien, 1970) and those who are more educated (Delli Carpini & Keeter, 1996) are more likely to be informed than other groups of Americans.

TYPE OF INFORMATION SOURCE

As noted, over the course of the last several election cycles, the Web has been ballyhooed as a boon for increasing political knowledge. As such, scholars have begun to investigate these claims and hypotheses. The results of these studies are mixed. Some studies have found that the Web is an important information source and use is positively related to political knowledge (Drew & Weaver, 2006; Kenski & Stroud, 2006; Norris, 2000; Shah, McLeod, & Yoon, 2001; Sotirovic & McLoed, 2004; Xenos & Moy, 2007). Other studies indicate that Web usage does not contribute to political knowledge (DiMaggio, Hargittai, Neuman, & Robinson, 2001; Jennings & Zeitner, 2003; Johnson, Briama, & Sothirajah, 1999; Wei & Ven-hwei, 2008). Interestingly, one study found that searching the Internet for entertainment purposes significantly *lowers* knowledge levels (Scheufele & Nisbet, 2002).

Findings related to knowledge from offline media sources are also mixed. Some studies have found that factual knowledge (Becker & Dunwoody, 1982; Dalrymple & Scheufele, 2007; Pettey, 1988) and party issue knowledge (Chaffee, Zhao, & Leshner, 1994; Eveland & Scheufele, 2000; Patterson & McClure, 1976; Weaver & Drew, 1993) are linked with reading hard-copy newspapers. No link, however, has been identified between newspaper usage and candidate likes and dislikes and ideological knowledge. (Dalrymple & Scheufele, 2007; Eveland & Scheufele, 2000). But television viewing often does boost an individual's knowledge of candidates and issues (Becker & Dunwoody, 1982; Chaffee et al., 1994; Lowden, Anderson, Dozier, & Lauzen, 1994; Weaver & Drew, 1993; Zaoh & Chaffee, 1995).

As argued earlier (Towner & Dulio, 2011), the Web offers a number of different types of information sources and tools to campaigns. Investigating use of the Internet in total is not a useful way of examining online effects. Rather, each kind of information source—presidential candidate Web sites, video-sharing Web sites, and online social networks, for example—may have its own impact on the public. With this in mind, we offer a series of research questions and hypotheses that examine potential effects of different information sources, both online and offline, and within those categories.

RESEARCH QUESTIONS AND HYPOTHESES

Online newspapers have become a major source of political information relating to candidates, issues, and parties. Both national newspapers, such as *NYTimes.com* and *Washingtonpost.com*, and local newspapers devoted sections of their sites exclusively to the 2012 election. These special sections included the latest public opinion polls, exit polls, videos, staff-generated interviews with candidates, candidate profiles, in-depth information on candidate issues, campaign-specific blogs, and information on voter registration and polling locations. Much of this material offered hyperlinks to online archives, past and recent stories, related articles and videos, and readers' forums, blogs, and commentary. This nonlinear format gives online readers more choice and control regarding how they receive the news and what information they read (see Eveland, Marton, & Seo, 2004; Tewksbury & Althaus, 2000). Linear and nonlinear newspaper formats have different implications for audience recall and learning (Eveland et al., 2004; Eveland, Seo, & Marton, 2002). One study (Tewksbury & Althaus, 2000) observed that hard-copy rather than online newspaper usage was associated with higher levels of factual knowledge. Dalrymple and Scheufele (2007) found that both hard-copy and online newspapers significantly increased factual political knowledge, whereas only online newspaper usage increased candidate issue stance knowledge and candidate likes and dislikes. During the 2008 presidential campaign, Towner and Dulio (2011), however, found that no relationship between attention to campaign information in hard-copy and online newspapers and factual and issue stance knowledge. In general, the effects of online newspapers regarding political knowledge are fairly mixed. Hence, we investigate the following research question:

> RQ1: Does attention to online newspapers increase levels of political factual recall knowledge, candidate issue stance knowledge, and candidate likes among young adults?

Similar to online newspapers, television network Web sites, such as CBS, CNN, and ABC, offer mainstream news that is often reported on their affiliated television channels. These sites include numerous articles, video clips, photographs, blogs, advertisements, and links to other Web pages, archives, and related content. Many television sites also had special sections dedicated to comprehensive 2012 election coverage. These sections featured interactive electoral maps, live streaming video of candidate debates and speeches, public opinion polls, candidate profiles, in-depth analysis of candidates and political issues, and online chats with guest commentators and readers. Despite the frequent use of television network sites during recent elections (see Owen, 2010; Schonfeld, 2008), the influence of these sources on political attitudes and behaviors has been unexamined by scholars. Thus, we investigate the following research question:

> RQ2: Does attention to television network Web sites increase levels of political factual recall knowledge, candidate issue stance knowledge, and candidate likes among young adults?

In 2012, both presidential candidates had regularly updated Web sites (Rosenstiel & Mitchell, 2012a). Web sites may be important source of information for voters, particularly for young adults (Carlin, 2008). Web site content includes biographical sketches, contact information, family photos, links to speeches, issue and policy positions, complementary news stories, and opportunities to donate money, volunteer, plan events, and register to vote (Bimber & Davis, 2003; Davis, 1999, 2005; Selnow, 1998; Tedesco, Miller, & Spiker, 1999). Despite these features, some scholars suggest that candidate Web sites simply mirror traditional campaign tactics used offline (Bimber & Davis, 2003; Margolis & Resnick, 2000), whereas others argue that these Web sites offer distinctive features not found offline (Foot & Schneider, 2002; Hughes & Hill, 1998; Norris, 2001). For example, the presentation of issue positions is the most unique part of candidate Web sites; but many online strategies are similar to offline campaigning (Xenos & Foot, 2005). In the 2012 campaigns, candidates' Web sites were the central hub of digital messaging, as many citizens used the Web sites to donate money, join a community, volunteer, and read articles. In fact, a majority of the candidates' digital posts on other social networking and video-sharing sites linked users to their, the candidates', Web sites (Rosenstiel & Mitchell, 2012a).

Information obtained from candidate Web sites can influence voters. Hansen and Benoit (2005), for instance, found that viewing presidential candidate Web sites in the 2000 general election altered perceptions of a candidate's character, policy positions, leadership, and global feelings. In an experimental study of presidential candidate Web sites in 2000, Bimber and Davis (2003) reported that subjects learned something new about the presidential candidate's issue positions and about the candidate as a person. Yet subjects viewing these sites were more likely to learn about issue positions than about the candidate as a person. Bimber and Davis also found that exposure to candidate Web sites did not influence how much the subject liked or disliked the candidate. Other experimental research, however, observed that interactivity with candidate Web sites during the 2000 presidential primary increased candidate likeability and knowledge of the candidates (Ahem, Stomer-Galley, & Neuman, 2000). More recently, Towner and Dulio (2011) found that more attention to candidate Web sites resulted in higher candidate issue stance knowledge, but candidate Web sites had no influence on factual knowledge or how much the respondent liked or disliked the candidate. Therefore, we expect that:

> H1: Attention to presidential candidate Web sites will have no influence on factual knowledge (H1a). Attention to candidate Web sites will positively influence candidate issue stance knowledge (H1b). Attention to candidate Web sites will not influence candidate likes (H1c).

Since the 2006 midterm elections, SNSs, particularly Facebook, have emerged as a vital campaign tool. Facebook enables candidates and supporters to post campaign events, comments, announcements, links, notes, videos, photos, and infographics (information graphics). Candidates use social networks to mobilize voters, promote voter registration, recruit campaign volunteers, and receive exposure (Gueorguieva, 2008; Williams & Gulati, 2008). Presidential candidates' Facebook fan pages included biographical and contact information, candidate interests, family photos, photos from the campaign trail, videos of stump speeches and rallies, event listings, notes from the candidate and campaign staff, information on voter registration and polling locations, and opportunities to donate money and volunteer. In 2012, Facebook was commonly used to get-out-the-vote, but rarely used for direct candidate–voter interaction. Candidates continue to use a top-down or one-way approach to campaigning on Facebook rather than two-way campaigning (Rosenstiel & Mitchell, 2012a). During the 2012 campaign, the incumbent president (Obama) had far more Facebook fans than Romney. The Obama and Romney campaigns, however, were relatively close in terms of the level of activity on Facebook, averaging about two posts per day. The Romney campaign was often more active on Facebook than the Obama campaign, particularly when it came to posting content, as well as liking, sharing, and commenting on content (Rosenstiel & Mitchell, 2012a; SocialBakers.com, 2012).

Despite the increasing use of social networking in campaigning, research is skeptical about its effects on users' political knowledge. Many users employ their sites for sharing and communication rather than news or information gathering, as many of the sites' political activities are "social" or a blend of communication and entertainment known as "communitainment" (see Cornfield, 2010; Rainie, Smith, Scholzman, Brady, & Verba, 2012; Rosenstiel & Mitchell, 2012a). Studies reveal that younger Americans who obtain news and information from social networks learn very little information about politics and candidates (Baumgartner & Morris, 2010; Groshek & Dimitrova, 2011; Pasek, More, & Romer, 2009; Towner & Dulio, 2011). In fact, Towner and Dulio (2011) showed that citizens who pay more attention to social networks during the campaign period have less factual and issue stance knowledge. Based on the latter research, we anticipate that:

H2: Attention to Facebook will decrease factual (H2a) and issue-stance knowledge (H2b). Attention to Facebook will not influence candidate likes (H2c).

One of the newest social networks used by both candidates in the 2012 presidential campaign was Google+. Google+ is similar to Facebook, as it allows users to send messages to friends, share links and pictures, and chat. Obama and Romney posted content in their "stream" about voter mobilization, campaign donations, early voting, videos of supporters and stump speeches, and general announcements. Unlike Facebook, Google+ allows users to create "circles" to segment their audience and share content with specific people. In addition, Google+ can facilitate a group video chat, dubbed as a "Google Hangout." Obama and Romney both held several Google Hangouts, usually with hand-picked participants and a moderator. By November 2012, Obama had twice as many followers on Google+ than Romney (CircleCount.com, 2012). In general, Obama and Romney used Google+ and Facebook in similar ways and for similar means. Thus, we anticipate that:

H3: Attention to Google+ will decrease factual (H3a) and issue-stance knowledge (H3b). Attention to Google+ will not influence candidate likes (H3c).

During the 2012 presidential election, YouTube was the most popular video-sharing Web site (Rosenstiel & Mitchell, 2012a, 2012b; Smith & Duggan, 2012). Both candidates used YouTube, but the Obama campaign posted slightly more videos and had more video viewers and channel subscribers than the Romney campaign. Yet, Romney's video posts often generated more commentary (Rosenstiel & Mitchell, 2012a). Candidate channels included biographical information, updates from campaign staff, "insider" information, candidate endorsements, and other material. Much of the content on candidates' YouTube channels, such as stump speeches, rallies, interviews, and television commercials, was posted by the presidential campaigns. Moreover, citizens could post text or video responses to clips posted by the campaigns, creating a video Web log (or "vblog"). YouTube also featured videos about the presidential race created by the general public, which included issue-related commentaries, videos from the campaign trail, attacks on the opponent, satirical or humorous sketches, and other information not written or created by trained journalists. Therefore, all types of political information could be accessed on YouTube—from a campaign's latest television ad to satire. That is, online videos did not always contain substantive political information. Indeed, some of the most-watched political videos are humorous or parody videos dealing with political issues (Smith & Duggan, 2012). Madden (2007) reported that young adults are more likely to watch comedy and humorous online videos than news videos. Young adults also consume more music, animation or cartoons, movies or television shows, and sports videos than older adults. Thus, individuals may view YouTube videos for mainly entertainment purposes (see Haridakis & Hanson, 2009). Studies conducted during the 2008 presidential campaign season found that respondents who got news and information from video-sharing Web sites learned very little information about politics and the candidates (Baumgartner & Morris, 2010; Groshek & Dimitrova, 2011; Towner & Dulio, 2011). In addition, Towner and Dulio (2011) showed that attention to video-sharing sites during the 2008 campaign increased attitudes toward Obama, but not McCain. We expect that:

> H4: Attention to YouTube will have no influence on factual (H4a) and issue-stance knowledge (H4b). Attention to video-sharing sites will not influence candidate likes (H4c).

While a relatively new tool in the 2008 presidential election, Twitter was one of the most widely used microblogging tools in the 2012 campaign (Rainie et al., 2012; Rosenstiel & Mitchell, 2012b). Twitter has a ticker-like screen, allowing users to post comments, or "tweets," in 140 characters or less. Obama's and Romney's tweets focused on influencing vote choice, campaign involvement, and getting out the vote. Due to the 140-character limit, candidates had little space to post detailed, substantive content on Twitter. Policy issues were rarely mentioned (see Ancu, 2011). According to several sources (Rosenstiel & Mitchell, 2012a; SocialBakers.com, 2012), Obama continued to outpace his Republican challenger in raw number of tweets (and number of followers). Yet, Romney's tweets were slightly more likely to be shared and retweeted by users (SocialBakers.com, 2012). Again, the candidates rarely replied to, commented on, or retweeted content from citizens, limiting themselves to one-way communication on Twitter (Rosenstiel & Mitchell, 2012a). Few studies examine how Twitter content influences political knowledge; thus, we investigate the following research question:

RQ3: Does attention to Twitter increase levels of political factual recall knowledge, candidate issue stance knowledge, and candidate likes among young adults?

Tumblr was also a newcomer in the 2012 presidential elections. A year before Election Day, Obama opened a Tumblr account. Romney followed in May 2012. Tumblr is similar to Twitter in that it is a blogging platform. Yet, Tumblr allows users to post media, such as audio, photos, and video, directly into their blog or "Tumblelog." In addition, users' blog posts are viewed in one large stream rather than one, isolated post. Obama and Romney's Tumblelogs consisted of short quotes, reblogs, letters from supporters, photos from the campaign, infographics, videos of speeches, and GIFs. The Obama campaign mastered animated GIFs, posting hundreds during the campaign period. Romney focused less on video and photos and used more text on Tumblr. Both campaigns relied on infographics to visually display policy issues, largely comparing the candidates on a particular issue. Overall, Obama posted much more content on Tumblr than Romney (Alfonso, 2012). The Obama team was also more likely to interact with Tumblr users by taking submissions and reblogging others whereas Romney's campaign simply blogged content. To date, no studies examine how Tumblr content influences political knowledge; thus, we investigate the following research question:

RQ4: Does attention to Tumblr increase levels of political factual recall knowledge, candidate issue stance knowledge, and candidate likes among young adults?

Blogs are not new to the political scene. Well-known bloggers, such as Markos Moulitsas of *Daily Kos* and Ed Morrissey of *Captain's Corner*, have been blogging about political topics for a decade or so. Since then, other influential blogs have developed, particularly *The Huffington Post, Little Green Footballs*, and many more. Blogs can be described as a Web page with a series of posts from bloggers and users, appearing in reverse-chronological order. During recent political campaigns, blogs have consisted of ideological commentary, partisan debates, scrutiny of the electoral process, and negative commentary and attacks on political candidates. Thus, blogs are often home to intense "negative" campaigning (Fung, Vraga, & Thorson, 2010). Unlike mainstream media, blogs do not strive for professionally objective and balanced news coverage. Instead, blogs usually have a political slant or bias. As a result, they are often attacked for not publishing accurate, high-quality information. Despite this, many citizens consider blogs as independent from corporate-controlled media (Andrews, 2003; Regan, 2003; Singer, 2006) and a solution to media bias, providing news and perspectives unavailable or ignored by traditional outlets (Johnson & Kaye, 2004; Rogers, 2005; Wall, 2006). In fact, blog users consider blogs as a more credible news source than any other medium (Johnson & Kaye, 2004). In 2012, 33% of Americans regularly or sometimes read political blogs (Kohut, Doherty, Dimock, & Keeter, 2012). The influence of blogs on political attitudes is rarely examined. Some research finds that blog readers are more likely to participate politically (Lawrence, Sides, & Farrell, 2010); yet, there is no research on blog attention and knowledge. We examine the following research question:

> RQ5: Does attention to political blogs increase levels of political factual recall knowledge, candidate issue stance knowledge, and candidate likes among young adults?

Last, we do not propose formal research questions or hypotheses regarding the effects of attention to television, hard-copy newspapers, and radio, as previous research shows that these offline sources have little or no relationship with political knowledge.

METHOD

Data for this study were collected in the fall of 2012 (September 25, 2012 to October 7, 2012) from undergraduate students at a medium-sized public university in the Midwest. The online survey was conducted during the height of the 2012 campaign. Thus, we believe our survey is a good test of attention to online information sources and political knowledge among young people, as political interest and use of online information sources are likely higher during this period than during the primaries or nonelection periods. The study and online survey were advertised via e-mail to over 1,000 students enrolled in introductory-level political science, sociology, and psychology courses. This recruitment method elicited 595 responses, a response rate of 52%. (Six hundred and eighty-two respondents clicked on the survey link. We removed 70 respondents for non-completion. We also removed 16 respondents who were not U.S. citizens and 1 respondent who was under 18 years old.) The respondents were relatively representative of the typical young, college student. The average age of respondents was 20.92 years ($SD = 5.00$). Of these, 37% were first-year college students, 70% were women, and 78% identified themselves as Caucasian. The sample's disciplinary background represents a broad range of majors from the liberal arts and sciences: biology (5%), political science (7%), social work (8%), psychology (12%), health sciences (12%), nursing (14%), and various other fields. As far as party affiliation, 35% identified themselves as either a strong Democrat or a Democrat, and 26% self-identified as either a strong Republican or a Republican.

Dependent Variables

We examined three measures of knowledge, representing both differentiated and integrated knowledge. Our first dependent variable was political factual recall knowledge (differentiated). The items measuring factual knowledge included a battery of six true/false statements. These asked respondents (1) if Joe Biden was the current Vice President, (2) if it was Congress' responsibility to determine a law constitutional, (3) if a two-thirds vote is required in the U.S. Senate and House to override a presidential veto, (4) if the Democratic Party had the most members in the House of Representatives in Washington last month, (5) if the Republican Party was more conservative than the Democratic Party at the national level, and (6) if John Roberts is Chief Justice of the U.S. Supreme Court. These were subsequently recoded into an additive factual knowledge scale ($\alpha = .58$) ranging from zero (all incorrect answers) to 6 (all correct answers).

Our second dependent variable was candidate issue stance knowledge (integrated). Six items were selected to measure candidate issue stance knowledge, including (1) raising taxes on the highest income Americans, (2) repealing the Affordable Care Act or healthcare reform, (3) allowing illegal immigrants who were brought to the U.S. as children to remain in the country, (4) creating a program that provides future retirees with a fixed payment for purchasing private coverage or traditional Medicare, (5) withdrawing troops from Afghanistan by 2014, and (6) raising the retirement age and creating a personal retirement investment account for younger workers. Respondents were asked to identify which of the two presidential candidates promised each of these proposals. The latter issues were selected because they were central to the campaign, as shown by media coverage. These items were recoded into an additive candidate issue stance knowledge scale ($\alpha = .74$) ranging from 0 (all incorrect answers) to 6 (all correct answers).

The third dependent variable was candidate likes (integrated). This variable taps how much the respondent liked and disliked the candidate. To measure the latter, respondents were asked to indicate how much they liked or disliked each presidential candidate on a scale ranging from 0 (strongly dislike) to 10 (strongly like). An overall measure of candidate likes and dislikes was also created by averaging both Romney and Obama likes/dislikes together.

Control Variables

Based on previous research (Delli Carpini & Keeter, 1996; McLeod, Scheufele, & Moy, 1999; Verba, Schlozman, & Brady, 1995), we included two categories of control measures. Key demographic variables, such as gender (1 = *male*, 0 = *female*), year in school (1 = *freshmen*, 2 = *sophomore*, 3 = *junior*, 4 = *senior*), and race (1 = *White*, 0 = *non-White*) were introduced into the analysis. Also, two predispositions, political interest and party identification, were included. For political interest, we asked, "Some people don't pay much attention to political campaigns. How about you? Would you say that you have been very much interested, somewhat interested or not much interested in the political campaigns so far this year?" (1 = *not interested at all*, 3 = *moderately interested*, 5 = *extremely interested*). To measure partisan attachment, we used two questions: (1) "Generally speaking, do you usually think of yourself as a Republican, a Democrat, an Independent, or something else?" and (2) "Would you call yourself a strong Democrat/Republican or a not-very-strong Democrat/Republican?" Answers to both questions were combined into a five-point scale (1 = *strong Democrat*, 2 = *Democrat*, 3 = *Independent, Don't know, No preference*, 4 = *Republican*, 5 = *strong Republican*).

Media Use Variables

Our independent variables were attention to campaign information in offline and online media. For offline media, we assessed attention to television, hard-copy newspapers, and radio. Regarding online media, we evaluated attention to nine sources on the Internet. We asked respondents the following question: "How much attention did you pay to information on 'television' about the campaign for President?" (1 = *none*, 2 = *very little*, 3 = *some*, 4 = *quite a bit*, 5 = *a great deal*). In subsequent questions, the word "television" was replaced with the words "hard-copy newspapers," "radio," "online newspapers," "Facebook," "Google+," "Twitter," "Tumblr," "YouTube," "political blog," "television network Web sites," and "presidential candidate Web sites." Descriptive statistics for all variables are noted in Table 5.1.

Testing Procedures

We tested our hypotheses using hierarchical ordinary least squares (OLS) regressions with political factual recall knowledge, candidate issue stance knowledge, and candidate likes as the dependent variables. We entered four blocks of predictors, beginning with demographic variables, predispositions, attention to offline media, and attention to online media variables. This method allowed us to examine how much each block contributed to explaining the variance, while controlling for each previously entered set of variables. Given the nature of the dependent variables in Table 5.2, ordered probit would also be an adequate method of estimation besides OLS regression. Thus, we estimated these models using both techniques and did not find significant differences. For ease of interpretation, we present the results of the OLS regressions.

Table 5.1 Descriptive Statistics

MEASURE	MEAN	STANDARD DEVIATION	CRONBACH'S ALPHA
Political Factual Recall Knowledge	3.77	1.46	.58
Candidate Issue Stance Knowledge	3.39	1.89	.74
Obama Likes	5.70	3.06	
Romney Likes	4.42	2.89	
Overall Candidate Likes and Dislikes	4.59	1.49	
Television	3.31	1.18	
Hard-copy Newspaper	2.17	1.17	
Radio	2.58	1.20	
Online Newspaper	2.28	1.25	
Television Network Web sites	2.21	1.26	
Presidential Candidate Web sites	1.81	1.13	
Facebook	2.37	1.24	
Google+	1.75	1.14	
YouTube	2.04	1.19	
Twitter	1.89	1.25	
Tumblr	1.43	.953	
Political Blogs	1.69	1.05	
Party Identification	2.89	1.23	
Political Interest	2.67	1.15	
Year in School	2.14	1.07	

Source: "All Politics is Socially Networked," N = 595 respondents, +/− 2.9% margin of error, September 25–October 7, 2012. Survey data collected by the authors.

Table 5.2 Predictors of Factual Political Knowledge and Candidate Issue Stance Knowledge

	FACTUAL POLITICAL KNOWLEDGE	ISSUE STANCE KNOWLEDGE
Demographics		
Male	.650** (.141)	.479*** (.186)
Race	−.124 (.166)	.185 (.217)
Year in School	.120** (.059)	.218*** (.077)
Incremental R² %	8.00***	5.10***
Predispositions		
Republican	.078 (.053)	.028 (.069)
Interest	.305*** (.063)	.423*** (.083)
Incremental R² %	9.80***	12.0***
Offline Media		
Television	.018 (.067)	.001 (.090)
Hard-copy newspaper	.078 (.064)	.055 (.085)
Radio	.010 (.062)	−.010 (.083)
Incremental R² %	1.00	1.10
Online Media		
Online newspaper	.266*** (.064)	.255*** (.085)
TV network Web sites	−.028 (.065)	.155* (.086)
Presidential candidate Web sites	−.122* (.074)	−.109 (.098)
Facebook	−.110* (.063)	−.117* (.083)
Google+	−.126** (.064)	−.082 (.085)
YouTube	.043 (.068)	.043 (.089)
Twitter	.057 (.059)	.022 (.079)
Tumblr	.045 (.072)	−.120* (.094)
Blogs	.018 (.078)	.069 (.102)
Incremental R² %	5.40***	3.80**
Final R² %	24.2	22.8
N	530	533

Note: All estimates are unstandardized ordinary least squares coefficients, with standard errors in parentheses. *$p < .10$. **$p < .05$. ***$p < .01$ (two-tailed).

Source: "All Politics is Socially Networked," N = 595 respondents, +/− 2.9% margin of error, September 25–October 7, 2012. Survey data collected by the authors.

RESULTS

Before addressing our hypotheses, we examined how often our respondents paid attention to different forms of offline and online media for information about the presidential campaign. Table 5.1 shows that young adults paid the most attention to traditional sources, particularly television, followed by radio rather than online outlets. Facebook and online newspapers were the top online sources for campaign information. Newer online sources, such as Google+ and Tumblr, received the least attention from respondents.

Table 5.2 presents the results of the regression models predicting political factual recall knowledge and candidate issue stance knowledge. The results show that demographics accounted for a large percent of the incremental variance for both factual (R^2 change = 8.0, $p < .000$) and issue stance knowledge (R^2 change = 5.1, $p < .000$). Examining the variables in the demographic block, we found that gender and year in school were significantly linked to both knowledge types. This suggests that respondents who were males and upperclassmen were more likely to have higher factual and issue stance knowledge. Race, however, was not associated with either factual or candidate issue stance knowledge. Predispositions demonstrated the strongest relationship with knowledge, adding an incremental 9.8% ($p < .000$) and 12.0% ($p < .000$) of the variance for factual and issue stance knowledge, respectively. In the predispositions block, more interested young adults were more likely to correctly answer factual and candidate issue stance questions. Respondent party identification was not associated with the two types of knowledge.

In the offline media block, we found that the traditional media variables did not influence factual and issue stance knowledge, as the R^2 change as well as the predictors were not statistically significant. Specifically, respondents who reported more attention to campaign information on television, hard-copy newspapers, and radio did not demonstrate higher levels of factual or candidate issue stance knowledge. In the online media block, there was a statistically significant effect for factual (R^2 change = 5.4, $p < .000$) and issue stance knowledge (R^2 change = 3.8, $p < .05$). We found that attention to online newspapers was strongly related to factual and issue stance knowledge (RQ1). That is, respondents who paid more attention to information about the presidential campaign in online newspapers were significantly more knowledgeable about political facts ($\beta = .266$, $p < .01$) and candidate issues ($\beta = .255$, $p < .01$). In addition to online newspapers, this analysis showed that only one other online media source increased political knowledge. Specifically, attention to television network Web sites boosted candidate issue stance knowledge among young people ($\beta = .155$, $p < .10$). Attention to television network Web sites did not have a significant impact on factual knowledge, however (RQ2). Unexpectedly (H1a), we found that attention to campaign information on presidential candidate Web sites was associated with significant decreases in factual knowledge ($\beta = -.122$, $p < .10$). In contrast with prior research (Bimber & Davis, 2003; Towner & Dulio, 2011), however, attention to candidate Web sites had no influence on candidate issue stance knowledge (H1b). As expected (H2a and H2b), respondents who paid more attention to Facebook were significantly less informed about factual information ($\beta = -.110$, $p < .10$) and issue knowledge ($\beta = -.117$, $p < .10$). Similar to Facebook, those who paid more attention to Google+ for campaign information were also less knowledgeable about political facts ($\beta = -.126$, $p < .05$) (H3a). Attention to Google+, however, was unrelated to candidate issue stance knowledge (although the coefficient was also negative) (H3b). The latter results are consistent with studies suggesting that online social networks, such as Facebook and Google+, are more for socializing and communicating rather than learning about political information (Baumgartner & Morris, 2010; Cornfield, 2010; Towner & Dulio, 2011). Table 5.2 also shows that attention to Twitter (RQ3), and Tumblr (RQ4) were not associated with factual knowledge, but those young people who paid attention to Tumblr were significantly less informed about candidate issue stances ($\beta = -.120, p < .10$). As we anticipated, YouTube (H4a and H4b) and political-blog attention (H5a and H5b) were unrelated to factual and issue stance knowledge among young people.

Table 5.3 displays OLS results when candidate likes were regressed against the same predictors used in Table 5.2. Predispositional variables accounted for almost half of the variance in Obama (R^2 change $= 37.9, p < .000$) and Romney (R^2 change $= 45.7, p < .000$) likes. As shown in columns 1 and 2, party identification was clearly the strongest predictor of candidate likes, with Democrats liking Obama more and Republicans favoring Romney. In the demographic block, race was also a strong predictor of

Table 5.3 Predictors of Candidate Likes

	OBAMA LIKES	ROMNEY LIKES	OVERALL LIKES
Demographics			
Male	−.077 (.270)	−.446* (.260)	−.376** (.175)
Race	−1.27*** (.305)	.280 (.325)	−.420** (.212)
Year in School	−.098 (.110)	.091 (.106)	.024 (.070)
Incremental R^2 %	9.50***	3.30***	3.60***
Predispositions			
Republican	−1.67*** (.105)	1.64*** (.099)	−.044 (.070)
Interest	−.006 (.122)	.085 (.113)	−.065 (.077)
Incremental R^2 %	37.9***	45.7***	0.10
Offline Media			
Television	.015 (.130)	.181 (.124)	.128 (.085)
Hard-copy newspaper	.175 (.122)	−.207* (.117)	.053 (.079)
Radio	.014 (.124)	−.065 (.117)	−.069 (.082)
Incremental R^2 %	0.20	0.70	2.20*
Online Media			
Online newspaper	−.204* (.122)	−.004 (.118)	−.072 (.080)
TV network Web sites	.154 (.123)	.120 (.124)	.100 (.082)
Presidential candidate Web sites	.093 (.140)	.223* (.145)	.132 (.099)
Facebook	.061 (.118)	.024 (.118)	.117 (.079)
Google+	−.278** (.121)	−.038 (.120)	−.198*** (.080)
YouTube	.062 (.126)	−.080 (.128)	.066 (.086)
Twitter	.104 (.110)	.067 (.114)	.082 (.075)
Tumblr	.061 (.129)	−.073 (.140)	−.080 (.089)
Blogs	−.200* (.147)	−.044 (.140)	−.154 (.102)
Incremental R^2 %	1.60	0.80	4.60*
Final R^2 %	49.2	50.5	10.5
N	486	454	408

Note: All estimates are unstandardized ordinary least squares coefficients, with standard errors in parentheses. *$p < .10$. **$p < .05$. ***$p < .01$ (two-tailed).

Source: "All Politics is Socially Networked," N = 595 respondents, +/− 2.9% margin of error, September 25–October 7, 2012. Survey data collected by the authors.

Obama likes, with non-whites liking Obama more. Race did not influence Romney likes, but gender was significantly related to attitudes toward Romney. That is, women were less likely to like Romney. Year in school and campaign interest were not related to attitudes toward Obama and Romney. The third and fourth blocks bring in offline and online media variables, with no significant R^2 change for Obama and Romney likes. In general, more attention to traditional media did not influence candidate attitudes for either Obama or Romney, which is entirely consistent with past research (Dalrymple & Scheufele, 2007; Eveland & Scheufele, 2000). In column 2, however, we found that more attention to hard-copy newspapers decreased attitudes toward Romney ($\beta = -.207, p < .10$). While attention to hard-copy newspapers did not influence Obama likes, we found that respondents paying attention to online newspapers had significantly lower attitudes toward Obama ($\beta = -.204, p < .10$). In contrast to our expectations (H3c), we found that attention to Google+ ($\beta = -.278, p < .05$) significantly lowered feelings about Obama. Similarly, political blogs ($\beta = -.200, p < .10$) also had a significant, negative influence on attitudes toward Obama (RQ5). Column 2 shows that the latter media sources had no influence on Romney likes. In fact, many of the remaining online sources, such as Facebook, Twitter, Tumblr, YouTube, and television network Web sites, had no impact on attitudes toward Obama and Romney. Noticeably few media sources had a positive influence on candidate likes. One exception was attention to presidential candidate Web sites, which had a positive influence on attitudes toward Romney ($\beta = .223, p < .10$). When the two indices were combined to create a comprehensive measure of candidate likes (column 3), we found that only attention to presidential campaign information on Google+ had a significant, negative effect ($\beta = -.187, p < .01$). Based on these findings, we can conclude that attention to campaign information on both online and offline media sources largely decreased attitudes toward candidates. The one exception was presidential candidate Web sites in Romney's case (see column 2).

DISCUSSION

In short, our findings are mixed about the influence of different media sources on young Americans' information levels. This is not supportive evidence for those who believe that the Web and social media tools are improving the way voters receive and gather information during a campaign. This is not to say, however, that the Web and social media tools are not influencing campaigning. Indeed, Web-based tools have a significant impact on some areas of campaigning; we have simply not come to the point of campaigning where young voters are seeing many informational benefits from the Web.

One of the most interesting aspects of our results is the opposite influence of hard-copy newspapers and online newspapers, with the former having no impact on knowledge but the latter showing an important impact. For the segment of the population we studied, we are likely seeing a shift in the way information is collected for at least two reasons. First, younger Americans are more likely to use online sources of information. The degree to which college students employ smart phones, tablets, and laptops certainly influences the way in which they collect information. Second, traditional hard-copy newspapers are simply disappearing on two fronts. First, the circulation of traditional newspapers has been decreasing for years, and some have stopped printing daily copies. For example, a Pew study reported that newspapers have been experiencing a decline in circulation for 17 consecutive six-month periods (Edmonds, Guskin, Rosenstiel, & Mitchell, 2012). In addition, the number of young Americans who read newspapers has been declining since the late 1990s and remains the age group least likely to read a daily paper. This effect may be transferable to the general population as well since each age group shows similar declines over the same period. Second, some newspapers have gone to online only or a hybrid model where hard-copy editions are only printed certain weekdays. This effect is likely more important for the individuals in our study given that three such papers in the general geographic area of where the study was done have moved in this direction. The effect we see in our results may be driven by young Americans' reliance on new tools like smart phones and tablets, but it also may be out of necessity—online newspapers are sometimes the only game in town.

We also must revisit the clear lack of positive effects that social media tools, particularly Facebook, Google+, and Twitter have on both knowledge (factual and candidate issue positions) and attitudes toward the candidates. Not only does using these tools not lead to increased knowledge about the candidates, politics in general, or candidate liking, some have a significant negative impact. (One exception is that the use of presidential candidate Web sites had a significant positive effect on attitudes toward Romney.) The predictions that these tools can be used to persuade voters to vote for a particular candidate are not supported by these findings.

Maybe we should not be surprised by these findings. When one thinks about who uses these tools and what they are used for—persuasion of voters is not likely. Take Facebook, for example. Who is most likely to visit the Facebook page of a candidate? Is it an undecided voter who labels themselves an Independent, or a committed supporter who wants to learn how to get involved in the campaign? Arguably, it is the latter, and they are already going to vote for that candidate in all likelihood.

This gets to the principal importance of Web and social media tools in campaigns today. Rather than information sources that can persuade uncommitted voters, these tools are most effective as extensions of traditional campaign activities like fundraising, organizing volunteers, and identifying and turning out voters. Indeed, the Obama campaign's "Dashboard" has been described as "a sophisticated and highly interactive platform that gives *supporters* a blue print for organizing, and communicating with each other and the campaign" (Romano, 2012; our emphasis, para. 7). Moreover, a post-election report noted the importance of these tools to the Obama campaign. A large part of the data collected via Facebook was put to use trying to replicate what field organizers have done for years by going door-to-door (Scherer, 2012). One Obama campaign official remarked about their use of Reddit: "Why did we put Barack Obama on Reddit? Because a whole bunch of our turnout targets were on Reddit" (Scherer, 2012, para. 16).

In short, American campaigns are not yet at the point where they have been taken over by social media tools for the purposes of persuading uncommitted voters by providing factual information. The importance of the Web in organizing campaigns, however, is undeniable. Here, we are at a point where campaigning can be taken over by technology.

CHAPTER 6

Don't Push Your Opinions on Me: Young Citizens and Political Etiquette on Facebook

Kjerstin Thorson, Emily K. Vraga, and Neta Kligler-Vilenchik

The past two decades of political communication research have been marked by renewed attention to the intertwined nature of interpersonal and mass mediated forms of communication. The characteristics of social media in particular defy scholarly temptation to divide media production from consumption or to attempt to study the effects of exposure to mass media content without attending to the interpersonal contexts within which such content is delivered. Facebook— or at least the Facebook that existed during election 2012, with its particular and impermanent cluster of affordances—simultaneously enables personal expression in a broadcast mode, relatively intimate interaction with friends, and exposure to professionally produced content from campaigns, brands, and news organizations (and that content itself might come directly from the source or arrive via the sharing choices of a friend). In late October 2012, a Facebook news feed might contain a post from the Romney campaign next to a video story from CNN, which could be next to pictures of a friend's trip to Maui or a baby's first haircut or a high school friend's angry exposition on President Obama's healthcare plan. Each piece of that content can, in turn, be read or ignored, "liked," commented on, or recirculated, a choice that is made not only based on what one thinks about the post itself but also on one's relationship to the source (e.g., best friend, grandfather, coworker).

Despite the current fascination with Facebook and other social media as spaces for the circulation of political information, the sociability of politics is nothing new. As Huckfeldt and Sprague (1987) noted in their study of offline political talk, "politics is a social activity imbedded within structured patterns of social interaction" (p. 1197). So what is new about Facebook as a context for campaign politics? We believe that too little work has been done to answer that question. Although there is widespread interest in Facebook as a potential site for political learning and engagement, and we are beginning to know a great deal from survey data about the extent to which individuals report seeing news on the site (e.g., Baumgartner & Morris, 2010), we as yet know little about the everyday political experiences of young citizens on Facebook. We are curious about how youth manage the incursion of politics into a space that, for most users, is known more as a home for every day social life than as either a news source or political soapbox.

In this chapter, the 2012 election is used as a context within which to explore the social life of political content on Facebook. We draw on twenty in-depth interviews with young adults, ages 18 to 29, conducted in the run-up to the election. In the interviews, respondents took us on a tour of their Facebook profile, answering questions about their lives, their political socialization experiences, their friends, and the kinds of content they value and share or dismiss and ignore. Our analyses of these data emphasize, first, the social pressures surrounding political discussion and content circulation within a space where multiple groups of "friends" from all areas of life are mixed together into one imagined audience. We observe the complex perceptions of political etiquette (Eliasoph, 1998) under conditions of social context collapse (Marwick & boyd, 2011). What we find is not only the presence of political content on Facebook—it is there, although it is not present on the pages of everyone we spoke to—and that the amount of such content varies across individuals (it does, and drastically), but that young adults have many remarkably consistent concerns about Facebook as a medium for political discussion. These beliefs can lead to the "evaporation" of certain kinds of partisan, opinionated political content from the site, even during a time when the media environment as a whole is consumed with politics (Eliasoph, 1998).

Second, we unpack the quite complex judgments of political content genres that stem from these notions of Facebook political etiquette. Our respondents distinguish not simply between opinionated and fact-based posts about politics but between "pushy" versus value-neutral content—and these judgments are lumped together across the kinds of sources that media scholars would normally differentiate, such as campaign content, news content, and postings by peers.

FACEBOOK AS A CONTEXT FOR DOING POLITICS

On November 6, 2012, more than 100 million Americans went to the polls to cast their ballot. More than nine million Facebook users shared this act with friends and family by clicking an "I voted" button on the site (Bakshy, 2012). An earlier experiment suggested that this message—showing people how many of their Facebook friends voted—increased the probability of a person turning out to vote (Bond et al., 2012), leading one of the authors to claim of the 2012 election: "it is absolutely plausible that Facebook drove a lot of the increase in young voter participation" (as cited in Rosen, 2012, para. 1). In fact, youth turnout (ages 18–29) was roughly the same in 2012 as it was in 2008 (about 50%), and, as overall voter turnout decreased, the youth vote comprised a greater share of the electorate in 2012 as compared to 2008 (CIRCLE, 2012).

This is not the first indication that social networking sites (SNS) like Facebook might contribute to political participation, particularly among youth.

Studies have proposed that social media hold potential for (a) political learning, primarily through incidental exposure to news content shared by friends or family (Baum, 2006; Baumgartner & Morris, 2010; Bode, 2010; Tewksbury, Weaver, & Maddex, 2001; Stelter, 2008), (b) political mobilization, hypothesized to occur through processes of normative contagion and expressive practice (Bond et al., 2012; Bode, Vraga, Borah, & Shah, 2013; Gil de Zuniga, Jung, & Valenzuela, 2012), and (c) as a space for political conversation both informal and deliberative in nature (Fernandes, Giurcanu, Bowers, & Neely, 2010; Shah et al., 2007).

Findings from these studies are mixed. Survey-based research suggests that posting news on Facebook is a relatively common activity, especially posting links to general interest news stories (Baresch, Knight, Harp, & Yaschur, 2011; Glynn, Huge, & Hoffman, 2012). Research also finds, however, that it is people who already engage in talk or action about politics and civic life who are more likely to make use of Facebook for such purposes (Park, Kee, & Valenzeula, 2009; Rainie, Smith, Schlozman, Brady, & Verba, 2012), reinforcing earlier concerns that expanding media choices might benefit the already engaged while providing the less interested with additional opportunities to opt out of public affairs information (Prior, 2005).

However, it is unclear if Facebook use fits this mold. Facebook news feeds vary in the amount of political content they contain, dependent as they are on both the practices of the Facebook user (e.g., choosing whether to view posts from the Obama campaign or the *New York Times*) and the content posting and circulation practices of one's friends, whose interests and preferences may be different than those of the user. The potential for exposure to political content on Facebook also varies over time as the affordances and usage practices of Facebook change (e.g., shifts in privacy settings, alterations to the algorithm that determines whose or how much content appears in the news feed). Thus, even as we set out to study how young adults engage with political content on Facebook, we are reminded that this experience is unique to each individual, embedded within their own personalized bubble (Pariser, 2011).

The literature, however, has paid scant attention to the social context within which incidental exposure occurs, and our current understanding as to *what kind* of political content spreads through Facebook is limited, as well. There is reason to believe that these two factors are intertwined. We know from decades of research on political talk that the social context within which politics is discussed has a shaping effect on the kind of conversations that occur (Eliasoph, 1998; Walsh, 2004; Knoke, 1990). In fact, the impossibility of fully understanding individual political behavior and responses to mass media content without considering networks of interpersonal relationships is a state of affairs that researchers in political science and communication have acknowledged, off and on and to varying degrees, since the early Columbia voting studies initially proposed a two-step flow theory of communication (Lazarsfeld, Berelson, & Gaudet, 1948).

But what kind of social context is Facebook, either for talking about politics or sharing political news? Facebook is a site based on technologies that collapse and combine friend networks and within which your own imagined audience only imperfectly overlaps with the audience of any other of your friends. Can we even think about shared norms of political expression under such a circumstance? The 2012 election serves as an ideal case through which to begin to explore such questions.

THE RESEARCH CONTEXT

In the 2012 election, social media were central not only for the dissemination of campaign-related materials—a photo of Barack and Michele Obama hugging, sent as the election results came in, was the most liked and shared social media post in history (Harding, 2012)—but also for user generated content, with political memes occupying the spotlight. Political content circulated on Facebook; indeed, Pew survey data tells us that for 36% of SNS users, these sites were important for informing citizens—although the same survey also finds that the vast majority of SNS users (84%) posted little or nothing about politics, with 59% saying that their friends post little to nothing, as well (Pew, 2012).

Facebook in the 2012 election was, thus, to echo Schramm, Lyle, and Parker's (1961) famous quote, a context in which some political content was likely for some young people some of the time, with little understood effects. Methodologically, it is hard to know not only how much politics different young people saw—this would depend on the makeup and characteristics of their respective network—but also how young people engage and interact with the content that was present during the election. This content and these practices are furthermore made largely inaccessible to researchers, due to the opaque practices of commercial companies like Facebook.

To address these questions, a Facebook-aided interview methodology was developed, and in-depth interviews with 20 people ages 18–29 were conducted (11 females, 9 males; mean age 22). We used purposive sampling in two locations on the East and West coasts, targeting participants who were college students or recent graduates and also Facebook users. Our goal for this study was to provide insight into exposure and reception of political content, therefore our respondents were chosen for that potential rather than for representativeness of the entire age cohort. The sample included a mix of more and less politically interested participants. After asking them about their life history and their socialization experiences around politics, we focused on their practices of Facebook use. As part of this section, we viewed together and talked through several days' worth of content on each participant's Facebook profile. We also conducted a mapping exercise in which participants were asked to think of the different types of content that appear on their Facebook newsfeeds, categorize these into different clusters, and map them on a continuum from "content I like least" to "content I like most." The interviews were conducted between September and November 2012, covering the period of the three presidential debates, the vice-presidential debate, and the election itself (two interviews occurred post-election). We predicted this would be a time when political content would be relatively salient on participants' Facebook news feeds. While this was true, for the majority of participants (80%), there was no news or politically related content in the last ten posts of their news feed.

Participants, who received twenty dollars for their participation, were informed ahead of time that the interview would be about their use of Facebook and that they would be viewing their Facebook profile together with the researcher. The semi-structured interview protocol, including the Facebook-assisted portion, was approved by the Institutional Review Board (IRB) at both university locations where the study was based. The interviews lasted approximately 60 to 90 minutes, and were audio recorded (with participants' permission) and later transcribed (for additional methodological details and the full questionnaire, see Appendix 6.1).

In analyzing the interview data, we sought recurring patterns in terms of how interviewees related to political content on Facebook, as well as their wider perceptions of Facebook as a social context. Eliasoph and Lichterman (2003) discuss the concept of "group style" in their analyses of offline social interactions within civic associations, defining these styles as "recurrent patterns of interactions that arise from a group's shared assumptions about what constitutes good or adequate participation in the group setting" (p. 737). We asked: Is there a "group style" that describes how young citizens relate to politics on Facebook? We draw both from the interview data as well as from the mapping exercise conducted by participants to answer this question. The remainder of the article is organized by the emergent themes, with respondents identified by pseudonym, age, and the date of the interview.

CONTEXT COLLAPSE AND THE NETWORKED AUDIENCE

Political content on Facebook can be viewed through a number of different lenses. Those studying incidental exposure focus on the way news content is shared. Scholars of deliberation might choose to analyze interactive exchanges, for example, in the comments underneath a post. Our starting point is an interest in the social life of political content on SNSs, so we begin with perceptions of Facebook as a site for political interaction.

Ethnographic studies of political talk find that the eruption of political discussion in everyday social settings is rare at best and vastly more likely to occur in certain social contexts rather than others (Eliasoph, 1998; Walsh, 2004). For most Americans, and in most social situations, political talk is risky and uncomfortable. Looking across a range of groups (activists, volunteers, and country-western dancers), Eliasoph (1998) observed that groups have an elaborate "political etiquette," a process of creating a context in which political conversation is deemed either valuable or undesirable. She argues: "people implicitly know that some face-to-face contexts invite public-spirited debate and conversation, and others do not; in contemporary U.S. society, most do not" (p. 6).

Heterogeneous social situations provide a particular challenge for political talk (Mutz, 2006). Lacking the speech norms that may emerge in established groups, people experience "social groundlessness" (Warren, 1996), an absence of known rules and standards with attendant discomfort. In offline settings as well as in interest-driven communities online, people tend to experience a limited amount of heterogeneity (of various sorts: partisanship, race and ethnicity, class) in their political discussion networks (McPherson, Smith-Lovin, & Cook, 2001). However, Facebook networks are often more heterogeneous than most offline social settings (Pew, 2012). Although Facebook networks are known to map to offline social networks (Hogan & Quan-Haase, 2010), Facebook "friends" include acquaintances from multiple, crisscrossed social networks developed over a life span—college friends, work friends, family, acquaintances of acquaintances—brought together as an entity only through their collective relationship to you. Wojcieszak and Rojas (2011) have described this phenomenon as creating an "egocentric public," bigger than a small group setting and defined simply through each member's relationship with a single person. Facebook and other social media flatten these multiple identities and groups into a single audience, producing "context collapse" by mixing together multiple audiences who in offline interactions might be quite distinct (Marwick & boyd, 2011). In their study of Twitter users, Marwick and boyd found that posting to a context collapsed audience is fraught with impression management issues that are distinct from those found in many face-to-face settings.

This study set out to examine how young adults perceive and construct the norms that guide political conversation on Facebook. In what follows, we present three key themes emergent from the interview data that, taken together, suggest that despite the differences that make each Facebook feed unique, many young adults hold a similar set of standards for appropriateness of political talk. According to these standards, political talk should be either avoided, or be kept tolerant to others' views, up to the point of neutrality. These norms lead to (1) self-censorship of potentially controversial or sensitive topics, (2) a preference for political content that is funny or satirical, and (3) the reinforcement of civic ideals of information awareness but a rejection of opinionated rants.

One Golden Rule

Our interview data reveal that respondents perceive context collapse quite readily when they are confronted with decisions to post or recirculate content that might offend, annoy, bore, or otherwise bother some among their Facebook network. The topic of politics, in particular, triggers active concerns over self-presentation across nearly all our respondents. These concerns are linked to the looming dangers of social context: the risk of offending others, of getting caught up in controversy or debate, or of your friends seeing you in an unflattering light. In their Twitter study, Marwick and boyd (2011) found that people engaged in acts of self-censorship and careful content balancing to preserve, on the one hand, a sense of authenticity and, on the other, to avoid offending a sliver of the mixed audience. We see similar strategies at work around politics on Facebook. Specifically, a majority of our respondents reported (1) engaging in self-censorship—that is, avoiding posts about politics altogether—and (2) adopting a blanket policy of valuing neutrality over opinion expression for all political content on Facebook.

In the first case, we find the old adage of no religion or politics at the dinner table, a conflict-avoidant attitude socialized offline, is alive and well for young adults using Facebook. One reason for this is to avoid risking an inflammatory response or inadvertently causing a controversy that might reflect badly on oneself. Elisa (21, Oct. 17) tells us: "There was one golden rule that I followed in high school and it was don't talk about politics and don't talk about religion with people unless you want to get into a huge debate." Bay, a twenty-two year old woman (Oct. 10), explains that on Facebook:

> I kind of try to stay away from that [partisan politics] because I don't want anyone to get like, not offended, but I don't want them to have to . . . I have like a lot of friends who vary in their political views. You can tell by their statuses and everything. I don't want to have to have certain friends look at me in a different way because I like some . . . I mean, politics can play a huge role in how, I mean, friends, I guess see you. They want their views to also match up with yours. I kind of stay away from that. It's kind of my personal opinion.

However, Carrie (22, Oct. 12) points out that for her, these subjects are not taboo altogether, but that such controversial issues should be tackled offline rather than discussed in the more public arena that Facebook represents,

> INTERVIEWER: You don't post news stories yourself, either?
> CARRIE: No. Nothing too controversial. I will gladly talk about it with friends. I will gladly tell you my opinion in any other way. I just don't like it where everyone can see it.

Here, Carrie is distinguishing her offline social interactions with friends as something of a backstage performance, in contrast to the "front stage" of Facebook (Goffman, 1959). We see this repeatedly in the interviews: For politics in particular, the imagined Facebook audience must be carefully navigated and dealt with delicately. Notably, this is not always true on Facebook. For many everyday posts, our respondents see Facebook as a much smaller world than the numbers of their Facebook friends (764 on average for our participants) would suggest, offering them the freedom to interact in a more relaxed manner. For example, Aideen (20, Sept. 15) describes posting an inside joke meant for only her close friends:

> I'll see stuff that someone posted to another friend's wall. I'm like, "Oh my god, yes." I'll like that and maybe comment on it. But if other people want to like and comment, then that's cool. It's only if they get the inside jokes. Some people just comment, and they're like, "What are you talking about?" I have no need to include them in the conversation. I just don't respond.

Aideen does not feel the need to censor her private joke, even though it, too, like a political statement, might only be appropriate for a limited subset of her friends. This suggests that perceptions of the imagined audience on Facebook are fluid, and that practices for addressing that audience shift by topic.

In addition to self-censorship, a second related strategy to avoid social discomfort around politics on Facebook is to adopt a policy of public neutrality. As Ashok (26, Oct. 16) puts it: "I think the reason why I'm more neutral is just because when you pick a side, you alienate the other group of people." These feelings, which are widespread among our respondents, have the broader result that many think that polite political neutrality is the *only* correct orientation on Facebook.

Respondents are unwilling to post content that might make them look "one-sided" (Katie, 22, Oct. 11), and are offended by those who do. For example, Bay (22, Oct. 10) explains her disinclination to post any political content herself in this way: "I think in terms of politics, because now [in the run-up to the election] everyone is really getting into it, I want to stay away from . . . I don't want to push my opinion on other people. That's all I'm trying to say. I don't like it when other people try to do that, so I don't want to do that to other people."

Our respondents—nearly every one—scrupulously adhered to norms of tolerance for competing views, norms that are widespread among this generation (Pew, 2010). Part of this tolerance manifested in a heated dislike for attempts to persuade or to be pushy about one's political opinions. Bringing the discussion back to religion and politics, two long-standing sensitive topics within American political culture, Erin (21, Oct. 15) says:

> I really, really, really don't like when people push things on other people, which is why I take a step back from that if I can. If somebody asks me about something I'm more than happy to talk about it in detail but I just don't like to shove anything on anyone else. I guess part of that goes to Facebook because that's such a public thing and everybody sees that. I don't want that to be the only little blurb because my political views and my religious views are a lot more than that little blurb.

Thus, part of tolerance and respect for others' opinions often meant people circled back to the strategy of self-censorship, maintaining a polite silence, even on topics that they feel deeply about. As Erin further explains, "I don't talk about too much of politics because I have friends on both sides of the spectrum. And I respect my friends for that." Ultimately, the choice to not engage on the topic of politics to avoid seeming one-sided and offending people comes back to an unwillingness to judge or be judged for political attitudes: "I think also that, you know, people feel the way they feel and have a right to feel the way they feel" (Elisa, 21, Oct. 17).

These perceptions about the etiquette of sharing political content on Facebook have consequences for what our respondents "see" on Facebook. Almost all reported that few among their friends post about their political opinions. However, even once content makes it to Facebook, users have a lot of options in deciding whether—and how—to interact with content. In the next section, we explore how respondents perceive, group, and react to different types of content that may appear on their news feed throughout the course of the election period.

Keep Your Opinions to Yourself (Unless They're Funny)

In addition to the collapse of multiple group contexts, a second key feature of Facebook as a context for the exchange of political content is the flattening of multiple media genres. The Facebook owner has little control over the types of content she sees in her news feed, outside the choices she makes to keep or remove friends or to interact or refuse to interact with a particular individual. One friend may post only updates about his daily life. Another may actively share mobilization requests from a candidate or a non-profit organization. Yet another may share only jokes, or frequently post angry diatribes. If an individual "likes" an organization or a candidate's Facebook page, this content will also appear in the news feed alongside content posted by friends. Previous research suggests that such mixing of content is not without consequences. For example, credibility evaluations of news content are affected when balanced news appears next to opinionated commentary (Thorson, Vraga, & Ekdale, 2010).

We began exploring the idea of young people's classifications of political content through the mapping exercise conducted as part of the interview protocol. This was a pen-and-pencil exercise in which we asked participants to think of the different kinds of content they may see on their news feeds. Participants were asked to classify this content into "clusters" and map those on a continuum from the content they like most to that they like least. We expected to find content-based categories, similar to those used in a content analysis, such as "pictures of family and friends," "links to news items," or "status updates." Instead, we found that respondents clustered content by its tone or style. Under content young people enjoy, we saw clusters like "funny statuses," "funny banners," "memes," "humor," as well as pictures of family and friends. Under content people do not like, we saw clusters such as "political rants," "political rants/judge-y posts," and "status updates about politics." Yet politics-related content could also find itself in the liked content areas, when it is considered "worthwhile politics" or, alternatively, when it is in the form of links to news articles. And while respondents each had their own characterization of "worthwhile politics," Harry (19, Oct. 16) clarified that for him it meant "if somebody posts something worthwhile in terms of politics, like not necessarily their opinion but just kind of like 'I found this' or something like that . . . if they have something interesting, something that's not really commonly seen, stuff like that, I'll look at it." Content could also find itself in the liked category when it is delivered in humorous form: for instance, a funny *political* meme may be considered simply a funny meme and thus something liked, rather than a political "rant" that is disliked. Thus, our respondents did not think of "political content on Facebook" as belonging to one category, but rather made sub-divisions by tone.

Further, these content judgments are deeply entwined with the above-described beliefs about political etiquette. When it comes to politics on Facebook, it seems, it is not what you say, but how you say it. As Lisa (24, Oct. 17) puts it: "I like reading political posts that are funny and that are rhetorical and ironic like that. I don't like rants and raves. I don't like paragraphs that are telling people how they should vote. I get it, and I think, you know, dissemination of information is important. But I don't like it in that form."

These nuanced divisions of types of content meant most of our respondents rarely disparaged or avoided entire topics as appropriate or inappropriate for Facebook. Rather, we witnessed their skill at identifying different tones or stances of political content. They are likewise skilled in deciding how to use (or avoid) those in their own interactions. Across the respondents, we heard discussions of three main types of tones used with political content on Facebook. These categories structure the remainder of this section:

1. Opinionated content/rants—these are instances in which people state their own opinion on Facebook, often in a heated way. Such "rants" are disliked by the majority of our participants.

2. Neutral/informative—these are instances in which information is conveyed in a "neutral" manner, for example through links to news items or facts. These are generally seen by participants as positive, although they are not always read.

3. Funny content—when politics is presented in a humorous and creative way on Facebook, it is appreciated—and this is true both for political content and for other content.

Type 1: It Bothers Me When People Push It on Others

Scholars have long been concerned about the potential for negativity, aggression, and incivility to arise in political discussions, and the movement of political communication online has sharpened these worries (Ansolabehere & Iyengar, 1995; Mutz & Reeves, 2005; Ng & Detenber, 2005; Papacharissi, 2004), especially as incivility tends to breed more incivility (Andersson & Pearson, 1999; Edgerly, Vraga, Fung, Dalrymple, & Macafee, 2013). While incivility depends on context, it generally includes derogation of opponents, name-calling, and a lack of respect for others' positions and ideas (Brooks & Geer, 2007; Mutz & Reeves, 2005; Thorson et al., 2010). Incivility's effects are not uniformly negative. It can be entertaining (Mutz & Reeves, 2005), but it also encourages negative perceptions of online discussants and decreases the legitimacy of disagreement (Mutz, 2007; Ng & Detenber, 2005).

Interview respondents are also very concerned about incivility, although primarily as an instance of violating political etiquette on Facebook. The most common identification of a type of political expression was the "rant," which young people in our sample were overwhelmingly opposed to. As Laura (24, Oct. 12) said: "it just bothers me when people push it on others. Like, you are all dumb if you don't agree with this. That's an offensive post and that bugs me, because that's just people that need somewhere to put their rage and they put it on Facebook, that's all they're doing," a concern echoed by many of the other participants.

One way in which participants judged the tone depended on their assessments of the *intentions* of the person posting the message. We heard critiques of content designed to "rile" or "stir" people up, or that represented indiscriminate expressions of personal rage. Notably, such practices appeared to violate the etiquette of maintaining neutrality that most participants endorsed and were instead seen as a form of incivility: "On the Internet, everyone can become the bully" (Tom, 21, Sept. 28).

To further heighten this concern was the perception that many of these posts (or comments on the posts of others) might not indicate the poster's true opinions, but instead were an effort "just to sound educated or get a rise out of people without really caring or knowing why they're so into it" (Laura, 24, Oct. 12). Strong endorsement of (partisan) political opinions is seen as bomb throwing, rather than as a legitimate attempt at persuasion. Posters of political content are under suspicion as being insufficiently qualified to hold their opinions or to advocate them to others.

Type 2: Learning about Politics "Is Super Easy Now"

Despite the skepticism toward opinionated posting, many respondents claimed to value a different type of political content on Facebook—"neutral," informative content. In fact, in line with past findings (Baresch et al., 2011; Glynn et al., 2012; Pew, 2012), several respondents noted that Facebook was an important source of news during the campaign season. As Bay (22, Oct. 10) puts it: "I think [learning about politics] is super easy now. All I need to do is like with Facebook, all I need to do is check my news feed and if there's something really important, ten people have already talked about it in their status."

Several respondents reported that Facebook can serve as a gateway to encourage or remind people to look up news information in other contexts. In fact, this search for outside information can serve as a response to what is widely seen as the impossibility of trusting information provided on Facebook (due to concerns that even neutral-seeming content is often posted to advance a particular viewpoint). Thus, a Facebook news feed has at least the potential to notify users to major news trends or political issues, inciting people to gather more information from sources they trust:

> Sometimes on Facebook it prompts me to look up a specific news story if I see a lot of people are posting about something. When gas prices rose this week I went to go get gas and I was just so surprised at how expensive they were. [. . .] Then people started to say, why are gas prices so high? I was like, I need to look this up. There must be something. There wasn't any news article, but because people were posting it reminded me I need to go onto my news and see why this is happening (Carrie, 22, Oct. 12).

That said, most respondents reported regularly ignoring news content posted on their Facebook page. As we looked together with participants at their news feeds and asked what they would and would not click on, a recurring response we received was that people just scroll past news content:

> I do like seeing articles and I don't mind it because I can just choose to scroll down. I don't have to click on it, I don't have to read it, and I do like to see what people post because if I didn't have that I wouldn't see all the things that I do see and I do click on (Carrie, 22, Oct. 12).

While many respondents pointed to Facebook as a source of information and news, at the same time they also admit to being only minimally engaged with the information personally. They do not hesitate to skip over any information they are uninterested in. That said, for those youth who do have news content in their Facebook page (and not all did), mere exposure to headlines seems to create what Hermida (2010) has called "ambient awareness" of the news. For politics, this awareness, like the postings that help to create it, is often event-driven—consequent from a rush of posts during and after each debate, for example. For some, this awareness spurs more investigation of the topic, both via Facebook and through other sources, like Carrie's example with the gas prices mentioned before or, for example, Harry's assertion (19, Oct. 16): "If someone posts something about [the news] I kind of just Google it on my own or look it up . . . I don't go searching for news on Facebook." The extent to which Facebook postings spur additional information seeking cannot be settled by the qualitative data we present here. In their survey of 18–24 year olds around the 2008 election, Baumgartner and Morris (2010) found that although many reported using social network sites as a source for news, there was little evidence that such use was related to political knowledge. In our interviews, many respondents seemed satisfied to be made aware of current events and displayed little intention to learn more about many of the issues or stories that pop up on their feed. This may reflect a normative shift among this cohort toward what Schudson (1998) calls monitorial citizenship—a watchful, aware citizen ready to act when necessary rather than one who is routinely informed on the facts of the day. In the end, while being aware of politics and current events through social media may be perceived as "easy," for many, awareness is the highest bar achieved (Conroy, Feezell, & Guerrero, 2012).

Type 3: Anything That Makes Me Laugh

There is an important exception to the general rule of suspicion and dislike for opinionated content. That exception is reserved for humorous content. The love of funny content on Facebook was mentioned in nearly every interview, with respondents reporting enjoying "anything that makes me laugh" (Erin, 21, Oct. 15) and claiming they reserve their "likes" and comments for witty content and jokes among their friends. "It has to be fun otherwise it's not really worth sharing," said Ashok (26, Oct. 6). One respondent differentiated between political content that is "negative, braggy, preachy, self-centered versus funny, heart-warming, nice . . . I can listen to the news if I want to hear the preaching or the bragging" (Lisa, 24, Oct. 17). Our respondents also enjoyed funny memes, including those about politics: "Memes, exactly. I think they're fun. . . . Totally. I like all kinds. Political, current events, almost anything that will make me laugh I like. Yeah, I don't really mind them at all. I like them all" (Lisa, 24, Oct. 17).

This appreciation for funny content goes hand in hand with previous research, suggesting that humor has the potential to limit the negative effects of incivility and aggression within political contexts (Baron & Ball, 1974; Miron, Brummett, Ruggles, & Brehm, 2008; Vraga et al., 2012; Vraga et al., 2010). Further, humor can inspire people to pay more attention to dull messages (Kuiper, McKenzie, & Belanger, 1995), suggesting it might be a useful way to get people involved in political content (Baym, 2010). Humor might not only cut through the incivility and aggression often associated with political debate, but may itself provide a gateway to young people to learn about political events (Baym, 2005; Feldman & Young, 2008; Young & Tisinger, 2006).

In our interview data we identified several examples where respondents mentioned paying attention to political content primarily because they found it funny. The interview with Sandi (24) took place on October 3, 2012, the day of the first presidential debate. One of her friends shared a post from Barack Obama's Tumblr, using a reference to the pop culture movie *Mean Girls* in which the lead female character is asked by the guy she has a crush on for the date, and is told "it's October 3rd." As Sandi explained, the friend who posted this does not usually share political content: "she probably posted it more because it was a *Mean Girls* reference than because it was a political one."

Posting or sharing humorous content is thus viewed as something of a third path for many young people we talked to. Those who worry about offending their friends or appearing too partisan or opinionated will be political if they can do so in a funny manner. Katie (22, Oct. 11) prides herself on being politically neutral, although she identifies as a conservative. Despite this allegiance, she says of Romney, "I thought he won the debate, objectively, but I thought the funniest thing was the Big Bird comment. I posted about that. I think both sides would just think that that was randomly funny, not making fun of Mitt Romney, not saying Obama won, but something in the middle and funny about it." In general, she describes her political content as "either neutral, funny, or sarcastic on both sides. I very rarely, I don't think I've ever posted something that could be completely one-sided politically."

Like political neutrality, the strategy of humorous posting is therefore another approach to managing the networked audience. Humor seems to make political opinions more palatable, more acceptable in the Facebook context. This is true both for those who post such content in an effort to participate in election-related Facebook conversations, but also for those who are observing their friends' political posting. One respondent summed up his position by reminding us that, despite our scholarly interest in politics on Facebook, it is not perceived as a "political medium," at least for the general population of his Facebook friends.

> I just don't use Facebook as a political medium. If I do post anything that's kind of news-ish, I'll just post it to someone I think is interested and then the people that are also interested, that's fine. Generally, if I post stuff on Facebook, it's mostly funny stuff (James, 21, Oct. 15).

DISCUSSION

Throughout this chapter, we have drawn on several lines of inquiry in political communication and social interaction to better understand and contextualize our findings on young citizens' engagement with political content on Facebook. We end with an examination of what our findings suggest for these different areas, as well as ways in which our results point to areas ripe for further examination using representative data, testing the generalizability of the themes uncovered here.

This is not the first time emerging technology has forced scholars to reflect on what political interaction looks like in new media spaces, or consider the implications for our conceptualization of political life (see, for example, Bode,

Edgerly, Vraga, Sayre, & Shah, 2013). Questions about emerging media forms, their affordances, and their consequences for discussion and politics come up with every new technology and its own set of practices. Yet political communication scholarship may benefit from preserving previous insights, while carefully examining their application to new contexts, and make adjustments to theory where needed.

Most importantly, we argue that Facebook, like other SNSs, requires political communication researchers to rethink boundaries between exposure to content (such as reading the news) and interaction and engagement with politics, such as in the context of informal political talk. Most previous literature on engagement with politics on Facebook has depicted it mostly as a site where people may be *exposed* to political content. Our research suggests that this can be the case: Facebook indeed serves as a source of news for some young adults. However, our expectations about the value of incidental exposure must be tempered by a growing understanding of the complex environment within which such information is shared, producing a set of contextual variables that may well shape the reception of political content viewed on Facebook. Facebook is a social context, not a news aggregation site, and decisions to engage with content may depend as much on the social relations within (and outside of) Facebook as on the content itself.

In many ways, our findings reflect those of ethnographers examining informal political talk in offline social contexts (Eliasoph, 1998; Walsh, 2004; Gamson, 1992). Political conversation, including casual political talk, has been shown to matter for a range of democratic outcomes (Kim & Kim, 2008; Wyatt, Kim, & Katz, 2000). Such linkages have spurred scholars on a hunt for political talk: How much do Americans talk about politics? What kinds of contexts make it more likely that political talk will occur? And what are the potential implications of this kind of talk for valued outcomes like political knowledge and engagement?

These are some of the characteristics of what Eliasoph and Lichterman (2003) call "group style". Group style cues participants to what is and is not appropriate in the group context—should we talk about politics or not? Can we express our opinions? Attempt to mobilize or persuade? These messages are conveyed, enforced and reinforced through behavior, talk or laughter, as well as through resounding silence. Eliasoph (1998) finds moreover that sometimes politics may be relegated to the back stage of social situations, whispered behind the scenes rather than expressed out loud.

Our findings suggest that, at least among the young citizens we interviewed, willingness to talk about politics on Facebook is shaped by two factors: how appropriate they think it is to talk about politics in general, and their perception of Facebook as a social context. Consistent with previous research, we find some variability in people's general willingness to talk about politics, influenced by factors such as having discussed politics with their own parents around the dinner table or having a peer group in high school that cared passionately about social issues. On the other hand, despite the uniqueness of an individual Facebook network, comprised as it is of one's own particular slice of the world, there does seem to be a widely shared (and fairly limited) understanding of political etiquette on

Facebook—a form of group style. Yet it is a group style in which the group itself is an unknown, an imagined audience the perceptions of which shift depending on the topic you discuss. Politics, or at least electoral politics, lives in the realm of sensitive topics with the possibility of offending, and silence or neutrality are seen as the safest possible actions.

The majority of respondents identified Facebook as a social and entertainment space—and not one in which frequent political posts are appropriate. Over and over again in the interviews participants told us of their unwillingness to appear partisan or one-sided—and their dismay at their friends who breached this norm of neutrality. Respondents questioned the validity and objectivity of their friends' opinions, assuming that few among their acquaintances were sufficiently expert or neutral to make their posts worthy of trust. The posting of news content is similarly fraught. Many respondents said they appreciated seeing "neutral" informational content on Facebook and that it raised their awareness of what was happening in the election. That said, we find little evidence that these young citizens were learning about political events in any detail. News content is easily ignored. However, in at least a few instances respondents reported actually clicking on a news post to read the full story, or went to other sources to supplement their knowledge.

At the same time, politics on Facebook is not all front stage (where politics is taboo) or back stage (where it may be whispered). Instead, some forms of political content—particularly humor or neutral informative content—are acceptable, and some, like rants, are not. The widespread use of the vote sharing button on Facebook reminds us that reporting the act of voting is considered neutral as well (Bakshy, 2012). It is only attempts to push your vote choice on others that would violate political etiquette. It is also worth noting that in our interviews respondents used the term "politics" to refer quite narrowly to electoral or campaign politics—in no case did discussions of political content on Facebook lead to talk about broader notions of what might be political, such as posts from activist organizations or even non-profits. This is likely in part because of the timing of the interviews, during campaign season, but also because many youth—particularly the politically disengaged—are in general poorly resourced for imagining broader boundaries of the political (Thorson, 2012). It remains an open question as to whether modes of political etiquette on Facebook for campaign politics will hold for content such as the KONY 2012 video released by Invisible Children—to date, the "most viral video in history" (Wasserman, 2012, para. 1)—or other types of social change advocacy outside the bounds of national electoral politics.

We found that people do not generally unfriend others for political reasons, but they have another powerful act at their disposal: ignoring. In the Facebook context, where young people are engaging in complex impression management activities and are very conscious of friends' reactions to content, if a posting does not get reactions, many are unlikely to post again. Coupled with the Facebook algorithm, which adapts itself to the users' behavior and supplies more of the content users interact with, we may be seeing a cycle of passive selective exposure. As young people ignore political content, they may also see less of it in the future.

In our interviews, looking together with respondents at their Facebook news feeds, we indeed found political content. However, in every case, that content came from a specific few individuals in the Facebook network who engage in posting about politics. Most respondents were easily able to identify at least one friend or family member who, in their eyes, disregard the norms of the political etiquette and share political content on Facebook. Perhaps due to this disregard for social norms, these select few are not perceived as knights on white horses, bringing political information and thoughtful opinion to the needy. Rather they are perceived as loud, almost obnoxious—particularly when their posts move away from personal expression to "push" opinions on others and thus fly in the face of deeply entrenched norms of tolerance and respect. What are the consequences of seeing the political opinions only of a small number of loud voices? Rather than creating positive political outcomes, we fear this state of affairs may actually create a backlash and more evaporation of opinionated content.

In this context, humor offers an alternative route to political neutrality—a way to get people to swallow the "bitter pill" of politics. Our respondents enjoy humorous content and like it on their Facebook pages. The question remains: do they learn from it? Are they mobilized by it? Or does it make engagement with politics even harder? Some literature (Kim & Vishak, 2008; Young & Tisinger, 2006) shows that humorous news content appeals to those already knowledgeable, but can hinder learning. Others point to the positive effects of learning through humor, especially for the usually uninterested (Xenos & Becker, 2009). But over time, seeing politics only in humorous forms—enforced not only by user-driven content but even by campaigns' adoption of this practice, circulating memes and *Mean Girls* mash-ups as at least the Obama campaign did in 2012—may be shaping young people's expectations of political content into a "spiral of humor," such that political communication in other forms is increasingly not tolerated.

At the same time, our findings also point to some more optimistic directions. Within the broadcast era, the dominant model of citizenship was that of the dutiful citizen, who followed news and political content out of a sense of duty, as was expected of a good citizen (Schudson, 1998). With the fragmentation of the media environment and increasing media choice, this expectation has increasingly faded (Bennett, 1998), and citizens are attending to media content they enjoy most or are most interested in (Prior, 2005). Our study, drawing on interview data with a small sample of youth, provides some suggestion that on Facebook, at least within the highly politicized context of the 2012 elections, young people may again be socializing their peers into something like a dutiful citizen model, where being at least minimally informed about politics is almost a threshold to participate in the SNS equivalent of "watercooler conversations." These and other implications of this study are ripe for testing more broadly among a representative sample of youth.

Consider the case of 24 year old Laura (Oct. 12). She tells us:

> I never remember talking about politics at the table. I think the way I found the information was mostly through my friends. Like once it became something to talk about, even now, the only reason I really follow the election is because my

friends are talking to me about it. Not to sound like I don't care, but I definitely care more because other people want to talk about it. . . . I think it [Facebook] pressures people to care about politics, like me. More people post about Romney, and you're like, OK, what's this guy about? You're going to read his platform.

Yet Laura also senses the two-sidedness of the potential for political content on Facebook, tempering her optimistic perceptions with a critique of posts and posters she has observed. She continues,

> On the one side, I guess it's good because it encourages people to care a little more, but on the other side, people don't know what the hell they're talking about. They're just talking [about something they don't know about] and they just want somebody to validate them.
>
> INTERVIEWER: And which side do you think you fall on?
>
> LAURA: Both, because I think it is talking [without knowing anything], but at the same time, it inspires me to want to have an opinion of my own, so then I'll go read a source. It's probably a good thing.

These uncertainties about the role of Facebook in youth political engagement are reflected in our broader findings. Our interviews with young citizens show that doing politics on Facebook is particularly fraught because Facebook is primarily considered a social venue—and one in which context collapse makes navigation of social relationships sometimes difficult indeed. We expect future research to confirm that these social variables—worries about offending, a belief that politics doesn't belong at the dinner table—are key contingencies in the broader impact of social networking services, affecting the tone and amount of political discourse among this cohort.

APPENDIX 6.1: INTERVIEW GUIDE

Intro: Thank you very much for your participation in this research study. This study is interested in how young people use media, and particularly Facebook. We're interested in how people interact with Facebook, what kind of things they post, what they think about what others posted. We are really interested in your perspective so there are no right or wrong answers. This is a voluntary, informational interview. Please feel free to skip any questions that do not apply or you wish to skip, and please expand on areas that you think would help us get a better understanding of your experience. Also, I want to remind you that all your answers will not be associated with your name or you in any way, and that we will not record any identifying information about other people on your Facebook.

Please take a few minutes to look over this consent form.

Do you agree to having your interview audio recorded?

Life History (10–15 mins. Make sure to get Political Socialization, Political/ Volunteer Behavior Growing up)

[check for: age, occupation/major, education background, parents' occupations]

Tell me about yourself. How would you describe yourself? Where did you grow up? How long have you been here? What are you doing now?

What was your family like? Siblings? What did/do you parents do?

How about the kind of media you used when you were younger. As you were growing up, what did you watch, read, do on TV or the Internet or whatever? Has that changed as you grew up. How about now?

I'm particularly interested in how you perceived your parents as engaged or not in the world. Would you call them political? Did you/do you know if they supported certain candidates or parties? What ideas did you have about politics when you were a kid? Did you talk about politics? Were they "joiners?"

How about now, what does "being political" mean to you? Is that something that has ever been important to you? How would you describe your political views?

How do you feel about your ability to find out what's going on in the world? Is there any issue you think you know a lot about? How do you go about finding out about current events?

What do you think about people who get involved in causes? Do you have any friends like that?

Facebook-Aided Section
Tell me a little bit about you on FB.

- How long have you been on Facebook? Why did you join?
- How often do you go on Facebook?
- What do you mostly use it for?

As we open your Facebook account, I'd like to begin with a little exercise. Think about the different kinds of content that shows up on your Facebook news-feed, which other people or groups post. How would you categorize these contents into different "clusters"? (e.g. updates, funny pictures, links to news stories) Who tends to post what?

While you're doing that, I'll just jot down some information from your profile. [Jot down # of friends, # of photos, # of likes] Then transition to ask about map.

While discussing FB, make sure to cover:

- How do you decide who you want to be friends with?
- How do your organize your friends? Do you separate them into groups?
- Security settings on Facebook [distinguishing people who tightly control their Facebooks or don't]
- Are you a fan of any organizations, brands, etc.? Politicians? Issues?
- When you go on Facebook, where do you usually start/what do you do first?

- [Entry point to start talking about the news feed, e.g.:] Let's look at these first few posts. Can you tell me about who posted them, what they're about?
- What kind of news most interests you on your news feed? What do you pay most attention to? Are there things others alert your attention to?

[Stop for specific piece of content—preferably explicitly political]

- This looks like a news story. Who posted? Did you read? Do you ever read them? Which ones do you think you read? Why?
- Who is this person/org—post this kind of stuff a lot? Do you like it? Ever make you mad? Is this something you would share?
- What kind of things do you not like when people post?
- Is there a lot of news in your FB? How about politics?
  - Now that it's election season, do you see more of that kind of content?
  - Is that something you enjoy seeing?
  - Do you think other people enjoy that kind of content? Why/why not?

Walk me through the process of finding and deciding what to post.

- Have you ever looked for content specifically to post it? Can you think of a specific example?
- Do you ever share other people's content?
- How about when you post, what do you think about? How do you decide "this is worth sharing?" Adding your own comment? y/n
- What do you think about when adding your own comment?
- Do you have a particular audience in mind? Who do you think is reading what you post? Do you think about how people will respond?
- Do you pay attention to whether people comment on what you post, like it or retweet it?
- Have you ever not posted something you thought interesting because you were afraid of how someone might respond? How do you deal with people who can get angry or annoyed with your posts? Have you ever defriended someone because of what they post?
- What different kinds of things do you post?

Why do you think you post news stories/politics? Do a lot of people post that kind of content in your FB?

Do you use any social network sites besides FB? [Twitter?] [Pinterest?] How would you compare what you do there to what you do on FB?

Can we take a look at your 'likes' page? What kind of things do you like? Why? Do you 'like' any politicians?

What do you think of politicians who are using social media? Do you tend to friend/follow/become a fan of these politicians? What would make you more likely to engage with a politician on a social media networks?

What do you think politicians' goals are who use social media? Do you think
they are trying to engage with people in new ways or are they repeating the
same messages as they do in other contexts?

Did you ever deactivate your profile? Why? What did you miss most?

APPENDIX 6.2: FACEBOOK INTERVIEWS: INTERVIEW AID

Name of interviewer: Date:

Pseudonym of interviewee: Age:

From profile page:

# of friends:

# of photos:

# of likes:

Rough number of posts they posted in the last week:

Out of the 10 last posts, any about hard news?   Yes / No

If yes, how many?

If no, how far back is the first one?

CHAPTER 7

Uses and Gratifications of Following Candidates' Twitter Campaign during the 2012 U.S. Primaries

Raluca Cozma

Following a trend started in the 2008 election, all candidates vying for the Republican Party's presidential nomination were present on Twitter during the 2012 primaries. The growing popularity of the social networking site (SNS), which reached more than 500 million users in the summer of 2012, is no doubt one of the reasons politicians jumped on the social media bandwagon. In fact, some of the candidates maintained two accounts on Twitter: one created especially for the campaign and another for updating constituents on their existing office responsibilities. For instance, Texas governor Rick Perry tweeted from his existing @governorperry as well as his newer @teamperry account. Likewise, Jon Huntsman was active on both his traditional @jonhuntsman account and his campaign @jon2012hq profile.

With research increasingly indicating that political candidates' effective use of social media can translate into electoral success (Tumasjan, Sprenger, Sandner, & Welpe, 2010; Vergeer, Hermans, & Sams, 2011), this chapter examines the motivations and effects of following candidates' campaign activity on Twitter in the 2012 U.S. primaries. Understanding how social media cater to political uses and gratifications can inform future mobilization efforts and suggest better ways to engage the electorate, especially young voters, who are a sizeable demographic on Twitter: The most represented age cohort is the 18–to–29-year-old age group, followed by the 30–to–49-year-old age group (Smith & Brenner, 2012). An online survey of visitors to the profiles of the Republican candidates for nomination was conducted in the weeks leading up to and immediately following the Iowa caucuses (which took place January 3, 2012). The survey sought to uncover what attracted voters to candidates' Twitter accounts during the campaign, what social and political variables predicted users' various needs, and what effects these uses and gratifications had on related political engagement and attitudes. As more and more Americans gravitate toward the Web to consume political information, Twitter could be an efficient tool for them to learn about politicians' stands on issues and to get in touch with like-minded citizens. According to an October 2012 Pew study on social media and political engagement (Rainie et al., 2012), 60% of American adults use Facebook or Twitter, and 20% of those who use social media used the tools to follow elected officials and candidates for office. Social media use is even higher among adults under 30. No less than 92% of people in this age bracket use SNSs, a significant increase from the midterm election in 2010, when 73% of young adults logged into sites like Facebook or Twitter (Lenhart, Purcell, Smith, & Zickuhr, 2010). Why do citizens follow political candidates' micro-blogs and what do they get out of them? This is the central question of this chapter, informed by the uses and gratifications theory.

POLITICAL USES AND GRATIFICATIONS OF SOCIAL MEDIA

The uses and gratifications theoretical framework is ideal for studying motivations behind adoption and use of online technologies (Papacharissi & Rubin, 2000; Ruggiero, 2000). The theory has been revived lately to examine motives and communication behaviors of Internet users in general and of voters and political actors in particular. The theory assumes people are active users of media and that their media use is goal-oriented. For instance, when candidates first created campaign Web sites, they primarily attracted supporters and undecided voters seeking to satisfy their information needs (Bimber & Davis, 2003). Later, political blogs and more interactive online platforms appealed to voters with high political efficacy who needed to check the accuracy of traditional media reports (Kenski & Stroud, 2006), who needed a platform for self-expression (Kaye, 2005), or who wanted to interact with like-minded individuals (Kaye & Johnson, 2006). The premise of the uses and gratifications theory is not only that each medium serves different goals, which can vary from fantasy–escape to education–surveillance, but also that these goals, as well as social and demographic factors, can affect media consumption patterns and effects. For instance, in the 2008 election, younger people followed primary candidates' MySpace profiles for information and guidance more so than their older counterparts. In contrast, older voters befriended candidates on the SNS for entertainment motives (Ancu & Cozma, 2009). Regardless of demographics, MySpace candidate profiles gratified visitors' need for social interaction the most.

Unlike the use of campaign blogs in previous elections (Kaye & Johnson, 2002; 2006), which was driven primarily by cognitive needs, the main incentive for citizens to use SNSs for political purposes in more recent years seems to be the opportunity to network and meet like-minded peers. In more recent research, Parmelee and Bichard (2011) provided further empirical support for this hypothesis. According to their results, social interaction is the main reason people followed political leaders on Twitter during the 2010 election. Granted, in their national survey, the researchers used a very generous definition for political leaders, which included elected officials and candidates for public office, but also bloggers, columnists, pollsters, academics, and cable news and radio talk show hosts.

Given that earlier research (Postelnicu & Cozma, 2007; Sweetser & Weaver-Lariscy, 2007) on MySpace and Facebook comments left by voters on the social media profiles of the 2006 congressional candidates found that visitors to such profiles were motivated more by camaraderie and connection motives than by information-seeking needs, the first hypothesis of this chapter is formulated:

H1: Social interaction was the main gratification of following candidates' Twitter accounts during the 2012 primaries.

THE RELATIONSHIP BETWEEN POLITICAL ATTITUDES AND USES OF SOCIAL MEDIA

Previous research shows correlations between certain political attitudes and people's various uses of online political media. For instance, Kaye and Johnson (2002) found that online media consumers are more likely to have higher political efficacy than average voters, as the Internet allows them to voice opinions and concerns to elected officials and their peers. Political efficacy, which captures people's belief in their competence to understand political issues and affect the political process, has been found to predict use of online political media for information-seeking and guidance motivations (Kaye & Johnson, 2002; Kaye, 2005). Parmelee and Bichard (2011), however, found no correlation between efficacy and information needs; rather, they found that self-expression and social-interaction needs were higher for Twitter users with high efficacy.

Political communication scholarship is equally mixed when exploring the connections between people's affinity for politics and their motives for accessing online political content. Kaye and Johnson (2004) observed that political interest correlates with using political blogs to satisfy information-seeking needs. In the 2006 midterm elections, voters' interest in politics was significantly linked to the entertainment gratification of befriending candidates on MySpace (Ancu & Cozma, 2009). Parmelee and Bichard's Twitter study (2011), on the other hand, found that political interest is more likely to predict following political leaders' accounts to satisfy social interaction needs.

Other studies have found positive associations between informational uses of SNS and political engagement (Conroy, Feezell, & Guerrero, 2012; Gil de Zúñiga, Jung, & Valenzuela, 2012; Park, Kee, & Valenzuela, 2009; Valenzuela, Park, & Key, 2009). These positive correlations between informational uses of social media and political participation are, in part, explained by the easy access afforded by sites like Twitter to diverse and substantive content that could prompt reflection about political matters (Shah, Cho, Eveland, & Kwak, 2005; Shah et al., 2007) and by the creation of bridging networks that facilitate information flow across separate groups throughout a community (Kavanaugh, Reese, Carroll, & Rosson, 2005). Likewise, related uses and gratifications studies found that using new technologies for social interaction can serve as a potential mobilizer. Kwak, Shah, and Holbert (2004) found a positive correlation between engagement in public life and the use of media for networking and keeping in touch with friends and family. Social-utility use may therefore contribute to participatory democracy as much as using the same media for news and public affairs.

In light of these inconsistent findings regarding the effects of political attitudes on uses and gratifications of social media, the present study aims to answer the following research question:

RQ1: To what extent do uses and gratifications of following political candidates on Twitter correlate with certain demographics and political attitudes?

THE EFFECTS OF USES AND GRATIFICATIONS

While it is important to investigate upstream of media use to understand what factors may influence the gratifications people glean from online political content, it is equally enlightening to ask the "So what?" question and explore downstream of media use. Do people's various motivations behind following candidates on Twitter result in significant affective, cognitive, and behavioral effects? Several uses and gratifications researchers have explored the relationship among motives and many different kinds of effects, including "knowledge, dependency, attitudes, perceptions of social reality, agenda setting, discussion, and various political effects variables" (Palmgreen, 1984, p. 29). More recently, Sundar's (2004) uses and gratifications research indicates that interactive media are bound to enhance users' involvement with Web-based information because, by definition, interaction fosters engagement with content. For instance, Kaye and Johnson (2006) found that using online chat services makes people feel politically involved. Likewise, Shah et al. (2007) contend that online communication with political leaders and like-minded people empowers people and leads to increased political participation. As such, this study sets out to solve another piece of the social media puzzle by exploring whether certain motives for following political candidates on Twitter result in positive attitudes toward the candidates as well as increased online political participation:

RQ2: What is the relationship between various motives and the effects of following political candidates on Twitter in the 2012 primaries?

METHOD

An online survey was conducted among Twitter users during the 2012 primaries. The survey was active for a month, starting a week prior to the Iowa caucuses. Participants (political affiliation was not a factor in participation) were recruited using direct solicitation on Twitter and a snowball technique (where existing subjects recruit future subjects from their social network), resulting in 191 answers. Twitter settings no longer allow direct messaging to users who are not on one's follower list. The link to the survey was hence disseminated on the author's feed and directly messaged to several accounts on the author's follower list, which had more than 2,500 followers. The message included a request to retweet the link to the survey. Several popular accounts belonging to news or research organizations

(The *Des Moines Register*, several Iowan TV stations, Harvard's *Journalist's Resource, Survey Monkey, The National Communication Association, The International Studies Association*, etc.) as well as other users with fewer followers retweeted the invitation, which specifically indicated that the survey was aimed at Twitter users who followed presidential candidates on the SNSs. After filtering out noncitizens and incomplete questionnaires, the final sample size dropped to 153. Due to the diverse recruiting methods, the completion rate could not be estimated.

Measures

The motives for following political candidates on Twitter during the 2012 election were examined using an 8-item index derived from previous research about the Internet as a source of political information (Kaye & Johnson, 2002, 2006; Ancu & Cozma, 2009). The *uses and gratifications index* measured the reasons for participants' use of Twitter, using the eight following reasons: information seeking; engaging in discussions with candidates; finding out what other people have to say to candidates; meeting other candidate supporters; making up their minds about which candidate to support; passing time; feeling that Twitter is better than other sources of information; and because it is entertaining. Responses were measured on a 5-point scale from 1 (strongly disagree) to 5 (strongly agree). The eight items measuring this variable were factored by principal components analysis with Varimax rotation, and items were assigned to a particular factor if the primary loadings were greater than .60 (Stevens, 1986). Six of the eight items loaded into two factors, showing that the primary uses and gratifications of candidate profiles were *information seeking and interaction* and *entertainment*. Cumulatively, these two factors explain 62.72% of the variance in the motives for following political candidates on Twitter, with information seeking and social utility being the strongest factor (see Table 7.1). The other two items, one that measured *convenience* (using Twitter, because information is easy to obtain) and another that measured *guidance* (wanting to see what other people have to say about the candidate) did not cluster with any of the other motivations and were analyzed separately.

Political efficacy was measured with a four-item index (with a Cronbach's alpha of .92) adapted from Ancu and Cozma (2009). The statements gauged respondents' self-perceptions of how qualified they were to participate in politics, of how informed they were about politics compared to other people, of how able they were to understand the important political issues facing the country, and of how capable they were to talk with their friends about the presidential candidates. On the 5-point scale, where 5 (strongly agree) indicated high political efficacy and 1 (strongly disagree) low efficacy, the respondents' average score was 3.9 (SD = 1.02), indicating a relatively high level of self-confidence in their competence to understand politics.

Political engagement was measured using a summative score of nine items (Ancu & Cozma, 2009; ANES, 2004) that asked about Twitter users' visits to candidates' Web sites, their engagement in online political discussions, subscriptions to candidate communication, comments made on political blogs, election discussions with friends, donations and volunteering for campaigns, participation in

Table 7.1 Factor Analysis: Motivations for Visiting Profiles of Political Candidates on Twitter

	FACTOR 1	FACTOR 2
1. INFORMATION and SOCIAL NEEDS		
To find out more info about candidate	.790	.124
To decide which candidate to support	.730	.186
To engage in discussion with the candidate	.764	.063
To meet other supporters	.674	.173
2. ENTERTAINMENT NEEDS		
To pass time	.010	.926
For fun	.238	.852
3. GUIDANCE NEEDS		
To find out what other people have to say about the candidate.	.530	.595
4. CONVENIENCE NEEDS		
Because information is easy to obtain.	.591	.447
Eigenvalue	3.78	1.31
Variance explained	46.3%	16.4%

N=153

Source: Online Survey of Twitter Users during the 2012 Primaries, December 2011–January 2012.

political rallies and other campaign events, as well as watching of televised debates between the candidates. The additive score (on a 9-point scale) was rather low at 2.9 (Cronbach's alpha $= .84$, $SD = 2.5$).

Finally, *affinity for politics* was measured by asking respondents how interested they were in the primaries, using a 5-point scale from 1 (not at all) to 5 (very interested). The respondents showed high interest in the election, with an average score of 4.17 ($SD = 1.1$).

Among the independent variables, standard demographic questions included age, gender, education level, ethnicity, media use, and political affiliation. A quarter of the respondents were in the 20–25-year-old age group and 40% were in the 26–40-year-old age group, with the average age being 30 years old. This demographic breakdown is representative of the overall Twitter population (Smith & Brenner, 2012), as is the gender breakdown: 53% of respondents were women. In terms of ethnicity, however, the sample is less representative, with 86% being white, 3% black, 4% Hispanic, and 3% Asian. Findings on education levels were representative for the general Twitter population, with 42% having a post-graduate degree and 36% having a college degree. Pew data (Smith & Brenner, 2012) indicate that people who have more than a college degree tend to be heavy users of Twitter. In terms of political affiliation, 42% of respondents identified themselves as Democrat, 29% as Republican, and 21% as Independent.

For media use variables, respondents were separately asked, using a 5-point scale, how often in the past month they used daily newspapers ($M = 3.31, SD = 1.47$), television ($M = 3.81, SD = 1.24$), radio ($M = 3.05, SD = 1.46$), online news sites ($M = 4.36, SD = 1.08$), and Twitter ($M = 3.96, SD = 1.38$) for news. This group of respondents consists of heavy users of Twitter (77% said they log into their accounts several times a day), which explains why, among their *daily* sources of news, online news sites ranked first (64%), followed by Twitter (55%), and then television (33%).

In order to measure effects of following candidates on Twitter for various uses and gratifications, seven items measured *positive attitudes* (Cronbach's alpha = .89, $SD = .8$). After visiting a candidate's Twitter account, respondents were asked about their agreement with the following statements: whether they liked the candidate better, knew him better, wanted to learn more about him, how likely they were to volunteer for the candidate's campaign, attend a campaign event for the candidate or talk to a friend about the candidate, and how likely they were to vote for the candidate. On the 5-point scale from 1 (strongly disagree) to 5 (strongly agree), the respondents indicated moderate positive effects, with an average of 2.7.

Twitter political participation was measured as a summative score of 5 items that gauged whether respondents who followed candidates' accounts engaged in any of the following activities in the previous month: read friends' tweets about the primaries, retweeted a candidate's message, retweeted or replied to friends' messages about the primaries, posted original tweets about the election, and linked to campaign news in their tweets. The average score was 2.7 (Cronbach's alpha = .77, $SD = 1.7$), indicating that, on average, Twitter users engaged in about three of the five activities related to the campaign listed above.

RESULTS

The results of the factor analysis in Table 7.1 both lend credence to and reject hypothesis 1, which predicted social interaction would be the main gratification of following candidates' Twitter accounts. It turns out that respondents in this survey could not differentiate between their informational and social uses of Twitter. The two uses and gratifications are so strongly correlated that they clustered into a single factor. While the social interaction factor was indeed the strongest, it was also more complex than anticipated as it included the information-seeking dimension, which is usually measured as a separate variable.

To answer the second research question, the first column in Table 7.2 reports the results from an OLS regression analysis predicting informational and relational uses of Twitter from political efficacy, engagement, and interest while accounting for a host of control variables. It shows that political efficacy actually has a significant negative effect on informational and relational use of candidates' Twitter accounts ($\beta = -.244, p < .05$), whereas political engagement ($\beta = .159, p < .001$) and political interest ($\beta = .207, p < .001$) are positive predictors of informational and interaction uses. Being a woman was also positively associated with increased use of Twitter for information and social utility.

Table 7.2 OLS Predicting Uses and Gratifications of Following Candidate Twitter Accounts from Political Attitudes

	INFORMATION AND SOCIAL UTILITY	ENTERTAINMENT	CONVENIENCE	GUIDANCE
Political Attitudes				
Efficacy	−.244*	.201	−.216	.057
Engagement	.159**	.079	.086	.150*
Interest	.207**	.107	.166	.142
Control Variables				
Gender	.377*	.046	−.231	.341
Age	.031	−.169**	−.055	−.007
Education	.029	.181	.251	.064
Ethnicity	−.154	−.568	−.313	−.743*
Affiliation	−.113	.191	.030	.151
	$F = 4.673**$	$F = 2.072*$	$F = .87$	$F = 2.517$
	$R^2 = .26$	$R^2 = .14$	$R^2 = .06$	$R^2 = .16$

Note: Entries are standardized final regression coefficients. Female, Caucasian, and Republican are coded higher. *$p < .05$; **$p < .001$.

Source: Online Survey of Twitter Users during the 2012 Primaries, December 2011–January 2012.

Meanwhile, the second column in Table 7.2 reports the effects of the same variables on entertainment uses of Twitter, and only age made a significant difference. Younger respondents are more likely to visit candidates' Twitter account for entertainment purposes ($\beta = -.169, p < .001$). None of the independent variables are significantly associated with the use of Twitter for convenience motives (column 3, Table 7.2). Guidance uses (column 4, Table 7.2) are significantly predicted by political engagement ($\beta = .178, p <. 05$). Ethnicity is negatively correlated with guidance uses ($\beta = -.922, p <. 05$), which means that whites are less likely to follow candidates on Twitter in order to find out what other people have to say about the primaries and the politicians in the race.

To answer the second research question, another set of linear regressions (Table 7.3) was run in order to gauge the effects of each use and gratification of following Twitter candidate profiles. The coefficients in column 1 indicate that respondents who followed candidates for informational and social motives were more likely to engage in sharing political content on the SNS, such as retweeting candidates' and friends' messages about the primaries, crafting original tweets about the campaign, or linking to relevant election news in their tweets ($\beta = .620, p < .001$). In contrast, convenience uses of Twitter had a significant negative effect on political participation on the micro-blog ($\beta = -.352, p < .05$). People who only follow candidates because it is easy and convenient are less likely to engage in any related behaviors, such as sharing election-related content on Twitter.

Table 7.3 OLS Predicting Twitter Political Participation and Attitudes toward Candidates from Various Uses and Gratifications of Following Candidate Twitter Accounts

	TWITTER POLITICAL PARTICIPATION	POSITIVE ATTITUDES TOWARD CANDIDATES
Uses and Gratifications		
Information and Social Utility	.620**	.628**
Entertainment	.237	.098
Convenience	−.352*	−.017
Guidance	.243	−.026
	$F = 8.054$**	$F = 28.253$**
	$R^2 = .22$	$R^2 = .51$

Note: Entries are standardized final regression coefficients.

*$p < .05$; **$p < .001$.

Source: Online Survey of Twitter Users during the 2012 Primaries, December 2011–January 2012.

Informational and social uses of Twitter also predicted significant positive effects in terms of attitudes toward the candidates ($\beta = .628$, $p < .001$). People who followed candidates' accounts to seek information and build relationships were more likely to report knowing more about the candidates, wanting to know more about them, liking them better and even expressing intention to vote for these candidates. None of the other uses and gratifications reached statistical significance.

DISCUSSION

This study investigated what uses and gratifications drove people to the Twitter accounts of the Republican candidates in the 2012 primaries, what demographics and pre-existing political attitudes might explain those motivations, and what effects various uses of social media had on potential voters. The data analysis revealed that while social interaction remains the main appeal of political content on social media, this purpose can no longer be analyzed separately from the informational use of the same medium. In the 2012 primaries, people's information-seeking goals became intermingled with social interaction motives on Twitter. The factor analysis indicated that the main demand satisfied by Twitter is a complex one, encompassing both information and interaction needs. This finding brings some vindication to Twitter CEO Dick Costolo, who in various instances has tried to explain that the service his team created in 2006 is not just another SNS (New Rising Media, 2012) but an alternative news source, a complementary second screen for existing media as well as a new form of town square (Ingram, 2012). Costolo defended his statements by arguing that 40% of active Twitter users never tweet. They opt instead to use it as a source of information (New Rising Media, 2012). In this study, the users under examination both tweet and follow political candidates on the micro-blog. As such, they are not one-way receivers of information. Hearing from candidates and other people they follow is equally important as engaging with them. In fact, 40% of respondents said they retweeted or replied to candidate messages. The findings of this survey suggest that Twitter can be an effective campaign tool if it gratifies both cognitive and social needs. This motivation is especially high for those who are politically interested and engaged (not an apathetic crowd) and in turn translates into positive attitudes toward the candidate and essentially in free advertising (retweets and links to campaign news). Entertainment continues to be a motive for consuming online political content, especially for the younger users, who are accustomed to getting soft news from infotainment and late-night political talk shows (Holbert et al., 2007), but this goal is secondary to the informational and social use.

These main uses and gratifications identified in the analysis are somewhat in line with related studies of online political consumption, but some differences stand out. First of all, the fact that Twitter users do not distinguish between informational and social utility uses is a finding unique to this study, which might set Twitter apart from other SNSs before it. Research on MySpace in the previous election (Ancu & Cozma, 2009), for instance, found that voters did not necessarily visit candidates' profiles to learn about their stance on issues, but rather to find like-minded people and engage in conversation with them. Similarly, Baumgartner and Morris (2010) found that users of SNSs in the 2008 election tended to seek out views that corresponded with their own. Therefore, the followers of presidential candidates might have added the politicians to their Twitter lists as a means to express their political identity rather than to learn more about the candidate or in order to make a decision for ballot-casting day. That is not the case in the present study, where the sample captured more Democrats than Republicans following Republican candidates on Twitter, and the analysis revealed no differences in uses and gratifications by party affiliation. In Twitter research conducted during the 2010 midterm contests, Parmelee and Bichard (2011) found that social utility was the primary impetus for following political leaders (broadly defined) on Twitter, followed by entertainment and self-expression. Information-seeking needs only came in fourth. In contrast, informational uses emerged as the top motivation in the present study, suggesting that information seeking becomes a stronger appeal when the stakes are higher: in this case, deciding candidates for the highest office.

These findings on the uses and needs gratified by candidates' Twitter accounts may help explain Barack Obama's electoral success in 2008. Obama's team strategically used Twitter to connect with voters at an individual level (Hendricks & Denton, 2010). In contrast, candidate Hillary Clinton used Twitter as just another broadcasting medium and did not follow people back, thwarting Twitter users' need for interaction.

All of the political attitudes measured—political efficacy, political engagement, and political interest—had a sizeable effect on the main motivation of following candidates' accounts on Twitter, but not in the same direction. While political engagement and political interest predicted an increased likelihood of using Twitter for informational and social uses, which aligns with previous research discussed above, political efficacy had a negative effect. People who felt confident in their competence to understand politics were less likely to turn to Twitter for information and interaction with like-minded people. Separate t-tests ($F = 8.292, p < .001$) found that women scored significantly lower ($M = 3.9$ on a 5-point scale) in political efficacy compared to their male counterparts ($M = 4.3$), which is in line with existing scholarship (Kenski & Stroud, 2006; Tedesco, 2011). If we consider that regression analysis also found that women are more likely to turn to candidates' Twitter profiles to satisfy informational and social needs, we start to understand why low efficacy correlates with increased use of Twitter for information seeking and social interaction. Gender accounted for the strongest effect on that first factor, indicating a continued gender gap.

Although entertainment remains a strong appeal of social media, regression analysis found that it is mainly the younger cohorts that access candidates' Twitter profiles for entertainment. This finding contradicts similar research conducted on MySpace in the previous election cycle (Ancu & Cozma, 2009), when it was the older people who gravitated to that social medium simply because it was fun. With its stripped-down interface, Twitter lends itself better to updates from the campaign trail and to linking to campaign news. Consequently, its content was less "soft" than it tended to be on MySpace, where candidates were more likely to share personal information about their hobbies, favorite music, and books.

Not surprisingly, people who reported higher levels of political engagement were more likely to follow candidates on Twitter for guidance. Seeing what other people have to say about the candidates and the election can instruct their political activities, both online or offline. The only demographic that made a difference on guidance needs was ethnicity. Non-whites were significantly more likely to follow candidates on Twitter in order to gauge other people's opinions about the campaign. Given the increase in the Hispanic vote in the 2012 election and the fact that Hispanics are the most represented racial minority in the sample, the findings might be an indication that Twitter can serve as a welcoming sphere for demographic groups that historically relied less on traditional media. Indeed, a recent Pew study (Rainie et al., 2012) found that a higher proportion (within each racial group) of African Americans (22%) and Hispanics (17%) are present on Twitter, compared to white Americans (14%).

In the third part focusing on effects, this study reaffirms the importance of paying attention to people's uses and gratifications on various platforms. The respondents animated by informational and social-interaction motivations reported significant and sizable effects in positive attitudes toward the candidates they followed and in related behaviors (Twitter political participation). Using Twitter for informational and social needs resulted in an increased likelihood of liking the candidates better and even wanting to vote for them. Further supporting the finding that Twitter users are no longer content with one-way interactions, the people who followed the campaigns for information and interaction were also more likely to retweet candidates' messages, to tweet about and link to campaign news, thus creating an echo chamber for the politicians' information and ideas, and in fact providing free political advertising. To be successful, future Twitter campaigns should provide a mix of useful information and means of interacting with the candidates. Politicians who aim to increase their two-way communication with supporters on Twitter have a variety of tools at their disposal. They could follow people back to acknowledge their interest and sentiments, reply to followers' messages, mention followers in their tweets, issue calls for action and feedback, and contribute to trending topics of interest to their supporters by using hashtags.

Entertainment and guidance uses did not predict any considerable positive effects in attitudes or behaviors. People who followed candidates on Twitter simply because it is convenient reported a decreased likelihood in further engaging in election-related activities on Twitter. That makes sense. Convenience is the opposite of effort, and crafting tweets about the election, seeking relevant tweets to retweet to one's followers, and searching useful news stories to disseminate on one's Twitter account takes a certain expenditure of time and research.

All in all, the unique contribution of this study is the discovery that in high-stake political events like presidential primaries, Twitter appeals to people who are equally motivated by information and social interaction needs. This may be an indication that social media are maturing and becoming serious players in the media landscape. It also lends credence to a central tenet of the uses and gratifications theory that posits that prolonged experience with a medium results in more uses of that medium over time. While social interaction remains a strong pull (Ancu & Cozma, 2009; Parmelee & Bichard, 2011), SNSs seem to be growing into legitimate sources of information. This study puts both "social" and "media" back in "social media" but, due to its exploratory nature and the limitations of its sample, it invites further exploration of the motivations behind reading political content on sites like Twitter. As the medium matures and users become savvier, the motivations and patterns of its use are bound to diversify.

The study also contributes to the literature on the political consequences of Twitter contact between voters and candidates. The findings show that Twitter can influence the political process. The top motive for following candidates' tweets (information and social interaction) was correlated with strong affective and behavioral changes, and future studies could look into how exactly the candidates in the 2012 primaries performed on their Twitter profiles. Combined with the actual results of the election and the effects uncovered in this study, such content analysis could provide cues for strategic use of the platform in future campaigns.

CHAPTER 8

Fitting Social Media into the Media Landscape during a 2012 Republican Primary

Paul Haridakis, Gary Hanson, Mei-Chen Lin,
and Jennifer McCullough

Midway through the third presidential debate between Barack Obama and Mitt Romney, conservative pundit and author Ann Coulter tweeted the following message: "I approve of Romney's decision to be kind and gentle to the retard" (Coulter, 2012). Her message resonated with her followers, was derided by her critics, and the story became a central narrative in the traditional news media's coverage of the campaign (Grinberg, 2012). Her comment and the reaction to it illustrates the three roles that Twitter had come to occupy in the 2012 presidential election: (1) the ability to reach a network of personal followers, (2) the opportunity for campaigns and their surrogates to communicate with their core constituencies, and (3) the ability for comments that originate in the social media sphere to drive the agenda of the traditional news media. The Coulter tweet accomplished all three.

Social media have played a role in American politics for several presidential election cycles. One of the first notable examples was the use of YouTube by Democrat Howard Dean in 2004. In 2008, the Obama campaign made significant use of social media using a two-pronged approach: to educate the public and to mobilize its voters on Election Day (Cogburn & Espinoza-Vasquez, 2011). By 2012, the number of social media users had grown tenfold, and services such as Twitter emerged as a critical tool in political campaigns (Parker, 2012). Social media tools are seen as a way to generate cheap, easy publicity for campaigns (O'Brien, 2011) and to provide a sense of direct conversation with the candidates (Lee & Shin, 2012). One strain that runs through much of the research is that social media are tools of choice among younger voters (Rainie, Smith, Lehman-Schlozman, Brady, & Verba, 2012; Wortham, 2012).

The ability to communicate with like-minded individuals in the political sphere online is not a new phenomenon. Emerging in the late 1990s, Web logs (or blogs) have been an important form of Internet communication, facilitated by popular, open-source publishing tools such as Blogger and WordPress. Blogs made it possible for non-media affiliated groups and individuals to post information online. By 2004, blogs had become an important component of political communication. By the 2008 campaign, blogs were identified by researchers as useful sources of political information (Haridakis & Hanson, 2011). Microblogs are a miniature variant of blogs that have been described as having the flexibility of e-mail, the ubiquity of text messaging, and the immediacy of instant messaging (Ifukor, 2010).

Two stark differences make social media, such as microblogs or Facebook, unique in comparison to previous mass media used for political information. First, although they are channels of mass communication (like TV, newspapers, and radio), unlike these older mass media, they are designed for interpersonal communication within interest groups, as well. Social connection has long been a part of political media, however, the blending of mass and interpersonal connection in SNS may have extraordinary outcomes on political engagement. Second, social media can be used to communicate directly with media elites. Although people have long written letters to the editors of newspapers, called into talk radio shows, and written to broadcast stations, each of these media served as gatekeepers controlling whether the voice of the public was disseminated. Social media can eliminate that gatekeeper. In fact, social media users have become important sources of information for the media themselves, and the traditional media listen.

Johnson (2009) describes Twitter as a combination of three elements: social networks, live searching, and link-sharing. Twitter invites people to tweet the answer to the question "What are you doing?" or write about "what's happening?," which is the current invitation language that users see when they compose a new tweet. Java, Song, Finin, and Tseng (2007) conducted early research on Twitter. They described four main uses of the service: daily chatter, conversations, sharing information, and reporting news. Similar results were found in Zhao and Rosson's (2009) study. The length limit placed on Twitter messages (140 characters) may be its strongest attribute, as it discourages tangential comments and encourages posters to "speak their piece" quickly and efficiently, and users are able to extend their messages by link-sharing (Morris, 2009). The ability to connect users and followers in "near-real time" discussions has significant implications for political communication. It is no surprise, then, that November 6, 2012, Election Day, was the most tweeted event in U.S. political history, with more than 20 million tweets (Timpane, 2012).

While social media platforms share many characteristics, researchers are beginning to study the differences between Twitter and Facebook, the other major social network. Facebook is seen as a tool for organizing groups of people (Ladhani, 2011). Social media services such as Facebook are *friend dependent*, which suggests that people who interconnect with each other know each other or at least have a passing acquaintance. Twitter is more *follower dependent*. An influential microblogger can have millions of followers and not necessarily know any of them. This asymmetrical relationship between poster and follower and the potential ability of tweets to go "viral" makes Twitter more like a traditional one-to-many mass medium. In short, while there are differences among social media, a major similarity is that the simplicity of social media has lowered the barriers for participation (Java et al., 2007). Of course, not every citizen of voting age has a Twitter or Facebook account. But the number of users is growing—quadrupling since late 2010 (Smith & Brenner, 2012). The mainstream media cannot afford to ignore the content and impact of social media. The obvious conclusion is that a person no longer needs to be online with Twitter or Facebook to be touched by their power and reach.

But researchers are also sounding notes of caution. The impact of social media can be exaggerated or not representative of the entire voting public. Gayo-Avello (2011) raised an interesting point—that researchers and the public need to be careful not to turn social media into another *Literary Digest* poll, making a reference to a famous magazine poll in the 1930s that incorrectly predicted the outcome of a presidential contest because the sample of readers did not reflect the voting population as a whole.

Therefore, it is important to place the use of social media within the context of other media use. Facebook and Twitter are on the rise, but they have hardly supplanted television, radio, and newspapers as sources of political information. The ascendency of social media, however, does raise several important questions: How important are social media vis-à-vis other media? How do they complement other media as sources of political information? How do they satisfy voters' needs for information, and are those needs unique or similar to those satisfied by other media? Do different age groups choose their media sources differently? Are the worlds of Facebook and Twitter (and other online media) really the purview of the young? This chapter explores these questions.

Our analysis focuses on voters' media selection for political information, the motives for using media for political information, and the perceptions of media coverage of their preferred political party. Most importantly, we consider where social media fit in the new media environment as sources of political information when compared to other media sources that pre-date them. We chose to collect data immediately before the 2012 presidential primary election in Ohio. The Republican presidential field had effectively narrowed to two candidates—Mitt Romney and Rick Santorum. Santorum invested heavily in the state, but Romney prevailed by less than a percentage point. Both campaigns spent a significant amount of money on television advertising prior to the vote. The GOP primary played out against several factors in Ohio that made the election interesting to watch. The Republican Party took control of both houses of the state legislature in 2010 and elected a popular Republican governor. The state was the site of a major political battle over the rights of public employee unions. A Republican-led effort to curb union rights was ultimately overturned in a special election. Ohio was one of the states to mount a legal challenge against the Affordable Care Act, otherwise known as Obamacare. In addition, the national media were touting the fact that Ohio was going to prove to be a key swing state in the general election that would follow. It was against this background that voters headed to the polls in March 2012 as the GOP candidates battled for the state's 66 convention delegates.

MEDIA CHOICE

Modern presidential campaigns would not be possible without the mass media. Most voters rarely see their candidates for president in person. The information and opinions that they receive are most often filtered through one or more of the media included in this study. Scholars have long understood that interpersonal connection with other citizens, along with mass media, influence public opinion (Lippmann, 1922), mobilization, and how people make up their minds about which presidential candidate for whom to vote (Lazarsfeld, Berelson, & Gaudet, 1944). When people acquire political information from the media, they tend to share it interpersonally (Campus, Pasquino, & Vaccari, 2008; Yang & Stone, 2003), and that interpersonal communication is more influential in attitude change than are the media alone (Klapper, 1960; Lazarsfeld et al., 1944). But never before have there been the plethora of mediated social network channels that social media provide to connect voters.

The social media phenomenon is growing. In the months leading up to the 2012 presidential election, social media and/or microblogging sites were used by nearly 60% of American adults. More than two-thirds of those individuals were using those sites for some form of civic or political activity (Rainie et al., 2012).

But what do we know about how important these media are, exactly, and for whom? Demographically, we do know that age is an important factor influencing the choice of media for political fare and engagement. Research during presidential elections over the last decade has suggested that those over the age of 29 tended to turn to newspapers and TV more than did younger voters (Kaid, McKinney, & Tedesco, 2007), whereas younger voters were more likely to turn to the Internet for political fare than were their older counterparts (Sweetser & Kaid, 2008). As Internet blogs emerged as a new source of political fare, research suggested that bloggers tended to be under the age of 30 (Pew Internet and American Life Project, cited in Sweetser & Kaid, 2008). During the 2008 presidential campaign, it also was apparent that there were age differences in the use of social media as sources of political information. Specifically, Haridakis and Hanson (2011) found that first-time eligible voters (those 18–21 years old) used social media sites significantly more often than did their older counterparts. In fact, during the 2008 campaign season, Haridakis and Hanson found that of nine different media sources for political information (general Internet, TV, radio, newspapers, magazines, books, blogs, YouTube, and Social Network sites), social networking sites (SNS) were the least used for political information among those over the age of 35. While SNSs were used more by those under the age of 35, general Internet Web sites, TV, and newspapers were used more often even by these younger potential voters than was YouTube. Among those between the ages of 18 and 21, SNSs were the fifth most used source for political information, and among 22 to 35 year olds, SNSs were the seventh most used source. In light of such findings pertaining to age differences in media selection, in the current study, we were primarily interested in seeing if this media-selection pattern had changed between the 2008 election and the 2012 election season as these new media channels have matured.

MOTIVES FOR USING MEDIA
FOR POLITICAL INFORMATION

Prior research suggests that media use and effects are not merely the result of media exposure. Gleaning a better understanding of the media choices people make requires consideration of factors that influence that choice. One of these fundamental factors is audience motivation—that is, the motives (or reasons) driving media users' media selections. In an early précis, Lasswell (1948) suggested people use media for three overarching functions: surveillance, cultural transmission, and to help them make sense of their environment. Since then, researchers have identified numerous more specific motives people have for using media. For example, people use media generally for entertainment, information seeking, relaxation, passing the time, escape, mobilizing, and a host of other rather universal reasons, regardless of the medium selected.

Prior research also has identified certain motives that people have for selecting media to seek political information, specifically. Some of these include evaluation of candidates and their stance on issues, guidance in reaching a voting decision, information seeking, surveillance, entertainment, social utility, excitement, and reinforcement (Garramone, Harris, & Pizante, 1986; Haridakis & Hanson, 2011; Kaye & Johnson, 2002, 2004; McLeod & Becker, 1974).

In newer media environments that provide opportunities for interpersonal and group connection, there may be additional motives that pertain more to how people use media to communicate with others. Haridakis and Hanson (2011) found, for example, that people used media during a presidential campaign for purposes of self-expression. Outside of a political context, Hanson and Haridakis (2008) found people used YouTube, in part, for interpersonal interaction, social interaction, and for co-viewing with others.

PERCEPTIONS OF MEDIA BIAS

Although the choices of media for political information and the motives driving that selection are important, clearly people's perceptions of the media fare they consume also are likely to influence their political attitudes and participation. In the U.S., Americans expect the media to serve a fundamental role as the watchdogs of government—as a fourth estate, serving an important role in our system of checks and balances. But, as with public perceptions of the public servants who occupy the country's other three estates (the executive, judicial, and legislative branches of government), the public does not always have a positive view of the press. For example, a recent survey conducted by the Pew Research Center (2012a) indicated that the believability rating of every major news organization continues to decline. What is more, Republicans perceived the news, with the exception of Fox News, to be less credible than did Democrats. In fact, some research suggests that there is a rather general propensity among the public to view media coverage as biased against their ideological or other points of view (see Hwang, Pan, & Sun, 2008, for a review of some studies). This phenomenon sometimes has been referred to as hostile media perception or bias.

In this study, we wanted to assess the relationship between media selection patterns of members of different political parties and their perceptions of media bias toward their party and its candidates. For example, conservatives, in particular, seem to criticize mainstream media as promulgating a liberal bias. There has been much discussion about the "liberal media" in recent years. Although some research has suggested, in fact, that the media do convey partisan biases, other research has suggested that such claims are overstated and that the mainstream media are not rife with partisan biases (e.g., Ho et al., 2011). The question of whether the media do or do not promulgate partisan bias, while important, may be less important than the *perceptions* of bias among media users. Whether such perceptions are accurate or not, some have claimed that one's social (in the case of this study, political) identity can lead one to presume the media are hostile toward one's group (Coe et al., 2008; Oh, Park, & Wanta, 2011). Accordingly, we wanted to account for such perceptions in this study.

METHOD

Sample

Participants in the study included college students at an Ohio university who were enrolled in a large communication course that satisfied part of the university's liberal-education requirements and a quota sample of adults to which students in the course disseminated questionnaires after training by the researchers. Data were collected the week preceding the Ohio Republican primary. In all, the sample included 380 participants. In terms of age, 199 were 18–21, 37 were 22–35, 85 were 36–55, and 59 were 56 or older. There were 116 Republicans, 156 Democrats, and 89 Independents. Those who identified themselves as Republicans were older (39.71) on average than Democrats (32.37). Those who identified themselves as Independents were younger on average (29.01) than those who identified themselves as either Republican or Democrat.

Measures

Respondents were asked to report how often they used each of several media (1 = never; 5 = very often) to receive information about the political campaign. The media choices were TV, radio, newspapers, magazines, books, Internet (excluding social media), SNSs (e.g., Facebook), video sharing sites (e.g., YouTube), micro-blogs (e.g., Twitter), and online political blogs.

Motives for using media for information about the campaign were measured with a 72-item 5-point Likert scale comprised of media-use motive items derived from previous studies of politics (Haridakis & Hanson, 2011; Johnson & Kaye, 2003), social identity (Harwood, 1999), and the Internet (Papacharissi & Rubin, 2000). The participants were asked to indicate how much each of these items was like their own reasons for using the media for information about the political campaign. We subjected the motive items to principal components factor analysis with varimax rotation and identified five motive factors that accounted for 65.88% of the total variance. Motive 1, *passive entertainment* ($M = 2.11$, $SD = 0.84$, $\alpha = .96$)

explained 22.74% of the variance. It consisted of 18 items. These items reflected using political media fare to relax, escape, pass the time, and unwind; for companionship; out of habit; but also because it is thrilling, entertaining, exciting, "peps me up," and to get others to do something. Motive 2, *political identity* ($M = 2.34$, $SD = 0.92$, $\alpha = .94$) explained 17.42% of the variance and consisted of 12 items. These items reflected using media because of feelings of pride in one's party when the party does well; feelings of increased confidence, achievement, and self-esteem when one's party does well; and to belong to a group with similar others. Motive 3, *convenient information seeking* ($M = 3.13$, $SD = 0.93$, $\alpha = .87$) explained 8.93% of the variance. It consisted of 6 items that reflected using media as a convenient and easy way to search for information and to see what is out there. Motive 4, *issue and candidate evaluation* ($M = 3.40$, $SD = 0.76$, $\alpha = .87$) explained 8.93% of the variance. It consisted of 7 items reflecting using media to see what a candidate would do if elected, to help decide how to vote, to see what political leaders are like, to help decide important issues, to see where candidates stand, to find out how issues affect people like me, and to judge who is likely to win. Motive 5, *opinion leadership* ($M = 2.47$, $SD = 1.02$, $\alpha = .83$) explained 5.08% of the variance. It consisted of 3 items that reflected using media to participate in discussions, give input, and answer other people's questions.

We measured hostile media bias with an index we adapted from prior research (e.g., Hwang et al., 2008). Respondents rated their agreement with the six items ($1 =$ *strongly disagree*, $5 =$ *strongly agree*) that tapped their perceptions of the extent to which they perceived the national media as hostile toward their party (e.g., "The national media coverage is filled with partisan rhetoric hostile to my preferred party") and/or biased toward the opposing party (e.g., "The national media are biased toward the opposing party's candidates"). Responses to the six items were summed and averaged to create an index of hostile media bias perceptions ($M = 3.16$, $SD = 0.66$, $\alpha = .86$).

Statistical Analysis

We used one-way analysis of variance (ANOVA) to assess and compare differences among potential voters in four age groups—18–21, 22–35, 36–55, 56 and over—on all variables. We also used one-way ANOVA to compare differences among voters who identified themselves as either Republicans, Democrats, or Independents on all variables. In addition, we also examined frequencies of media use and correlations between selected media and perceptions of media bias.

RESULTS

Amount of Media Use

The majority of participants in our study appeared to be spending their time in front of screens. Our results show that citizens received their information about the Ohio Republican primary election primarily from TV (e.g., news programs and commercials) and the Internet (e.g., news and commentary sites, candidate and political Web sites). In the context of this study, it should be noted that social media (social networking $M = 2.42$, $SD = 1.41$; video sharing $M = 2.45$, $SD = 1.37$) and microblogging ($M = 1.82$, $SD = 1.22$) were not used widely as sources of political information, at least in relation to the other media studied. The relationship with other media is an important one in our view. Media users have a finite amount of time to spend with information media. How they spend that time on a particular media type in relation to the other media types is significant.

One can understand the changes in media habits by looking at the trend lines that emerged from our study (See Table 8.1). Consider the changes in six media types—three older, traditional media (newspapers, television, and radio) and three newer, more interactive media (Internet, social networks, and microblogging). Television continues to hold onto its position as a dominant source of political information. Television remains the major portal for key events and activities that surround a campaign: debates are televised to a wide national audience and hundreds of millions of dollars are used to purchase TV advertising ("Mad Money," 2012). But television use rises in terms of its relative position with other media as the population grows older. Younger media consumers' favorite appears to be the Internet.

The differences in media choice among age groups are even starker when looking at newspapers and radio, with each of these media occupying a stronger relative position for each successive age group.

The trend lines for newer media are a mirror image of their older counterparts (See Table 8.2). Internet use in general and online SNSs and microblogs occupy a stronger relative position with younger voters. However, across all age groups, the Internet (e.g., general news and commentary sites; political Web sites)

Table 8.1 Rank Order of Media Use for Political Information by Age Groups

18–21	22–35	36–55	56+
1. Internet	1. Internet	1. TV	1. TV
2. TV	2. TV	2. Internet	2. Newspapers
3. Social Networks	3. Newspapers	3. Newspapers	3. Radio
4. Video Sharing	4. Video Sharing	4. Radio	4. Internet
5. Newspapers	5. Social Networks	5. Video Sharing	5. Magazines
6. Microblogs	6. Radio	6. Magazines	6. Books
7. Radio	7. Magazines	7. Books	7. Video Sharing
8. Magazines	8. Microblogs	8. Social Networks	8. Social Networks
9. Books	9. Books	9. Political blogs	9. Political Blogs
10. Political blogs	10. Political blogs	10. Microblogs	10. Microblogs

Note: Each column reflects the rank order of each medium used (from the most often to the least often).

Source: This Figure was Created from Original Survey Data Collected by the Researchers During the 2012 Republican Primary Race in Ohio.

Table 8.2 Univariate Analysis of Variance of the Four Age Groups on Media Exposure

MEDIA SELECTION	F(df)	p	AGE GROUP 18–21	22–35	36–55	56+
TV	(3, 376) = 7.64	.000	3.14 (1.24)[b]	3.17 (1.20)[b]	3.42 (1.22)[b]	3.94 (1.05)[a]
Radio	(3, 376) = 13.98	.000	2.09 (1.01)[b]	2.58 (1.35)[b]	2.57 (1.11)[a]	3.05 (1.31)[a]
Newspapers	(3, 376) = 15.45	.000	2.62 (1.06)[c]	2.92 (1.06)[bc]	3.08 (1.25)[b]	3.67 (1.15)[a]
Magazines	(3, 376) = 2.07	.104	2.06 (1.05)[a]	2.33 (1.01)[a]	2.15 (1.03)[a]	2.41 (1.10)[a]
Books	(3, 375) = 6.13	.000	1.64 (.07)[b]	1.75 (.09)[b]	1.80 (1.00)[b]	2.22 (1.12)[a]
Internet	(3, 376) = 10.16	.000	3.65 (1.26)[a]	3.88 (1.08)[ab]	3.16 (1.27)[bc]	2.77 (1.37)[c]
Video Sharing	(3, 376) = 1.05	.37	1.79 (1.14)[a]	1.92 (1.14)[a]	1.65 (1.17)[a]	1.56 (1.01)[a]
Social Networking	(3, 376) = 9.51	.000	2.35 (1.38)[a]	2.29 (1.23)[ab]	1.75 (1.24)[b]	1.50 (1.04)[b]
Microblogging	(3, 376) = 9.54	.000	1.87 (1.19)[a]	1.71 (1.08)[ab]	1.35 (.91)[b]	1.18 (.58)[b]
Political Blogging	(3, 376) = .07	.98	1.35 (.80)[a]	1.33 (.70)[a]	1.35 (.82)[a]	1.39 (.84)[a]

Note: Standard deviation for each mean is included in the parentheses. Pairwise comparison results are indicated with superscripts.
Source: This Figure was Created from Original Survey Data Collected by the Researchers During the 2012 Republican Primary Race in Ohio.

is used more frequently for political purposes than those social media functions that are specifically designed for social interaction.

Another way to examine media use is to look at the percent of the various age cohorts who said they used a particular medium either "very often" or "often" for political purposes. Social network use ranged from 32% for the youngest participants to just 9% for the oldest. The use of microblogging sites showed a similar trend (19% for the youngest; 6% for the oldest). Not surprisingly, age can predict the popularity of more traditional media. Using a similar scale, 59% of the older participants favored newspapers compared to 20% of the youngest participants. Figure 8.1 illustrates media use across all age groups.

Although social media sites were not predominant sources of political information among participants in our sample, among those 18–21, social media had made the most inroads since the 2008 presidential campaign. Social networking and video sharing sites were the third and fourth most used media reported among members of this age group.

Age Differences and Similarities in Motives for Using Media for Political Information

Not surprisingly, *issue and candidate evaluation* and *information seeking* were the two most salient motives for using media for political information across the board (See Table 8.3). The means for these motives for the entire sample were both above the midpoint (3.0) of a five-point scale.

As was the case with media selection, we found age differences in the motives people in different age groups had for seeking political information from the

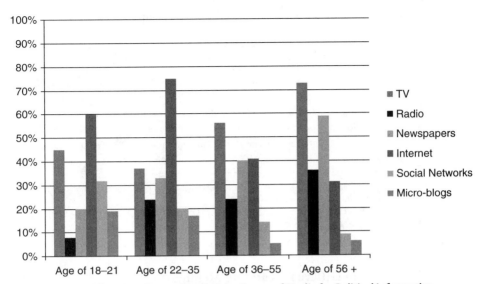

Figure 8.1 How Often Age Groups Use Various Forms of Media for Political Information
SOURCE: This figure was created from original survey data collected by the researchers during the 2012 Republican primary race in Ohio.

media (See Table 8.4). However, we found more similarities than differences. For those in the 18–21 and the 22–35-year-old age groups, opinion leadership was the third strongest motive for seeking political information from the media. For those in the 36–55 and 56 and older age groups, political identity was the third strongest motive, followed by opinion leadership.

Table 8.3 Univariate Analysis of Variance of the Four Age Groups on Motives to Use Media for Political Information

| MEDIA MOTIVES | F(df) | p | AGE GROUP | | | |
			18–21	22–35	36–55	56+
Passive entertainment	(3, 374) = 4.94	.002	2.13 (.84)[a]	2.39 (.76)[a]	1.80 (.71)[b]	2.22 (.91)[a]
Political identity	(3, 374) = 5.19	.002	2.23 (.91)[b]	2.13 (.97)[b]	2.30 (.86)[b]	2.71 (.84)[a]
Convenient information seeking	(3, 374) = 2.86	.037	3.01 (.96)[a]	3.43 (.72)[a]	3.13 (.90)[a]	3.31 (.85)[a]
Issue and candidate evaluation	(3, 375) = 5.32	.001	3.28 (.79)[b]	3.47 (.60)[ab]	3.39 (.73)[ab]	3.70 (.65)[a]
Opinion leadership	(3, 374) = 2.62	.051	2.44 (1.02)[a]	2.75 (.93)[a]	2.21 (1.01)[a]	2.60 (1.01)[a]

Note: Standard deviation for each mean is included in the parentheses. Pairwise comparison results are indicated with superscripts.
Source: This Figure was Created from Original Survey Data Collected by the Researchers During the 2012 Republican Primary Race in Ohio.

Table 8.4 Rank Order of Motives for Selecting Media for Political Information by Age Groups

18–21	22–35	36–55	56+
1. Issue/candidate evaluation	1. Issue/candidate evaluation	1. Issue/candidate evaluation	1. Issue/candidate evaluation
2. Information seeking	2. Information seeking	2. Information seeking	2. Information seeking
3. Opinion leadership	3. Opinion leadership	3. Political identity	3. Political identity
4. Political identity	4. Entertainment	4. Opinion leadership	4. Opinion leadership
5. Entertainment	5. Political identity	5. Entertainment	5. Entertainment

Note: Each column reflects the rank order of each motive indicated by participants in that age group (from "the exactly like me" to "not at all like me.").

Source: This Figure was Created from Original Survey Data Collected by the Researchers During the 2012 Republican Primary Race in Ohio.

Media-Selection Differences among Members of the Major Political Parties

We also examined some differences in media-use patterns among Democrats, Republicans, and Independents. The ranking of the top media choices was slightly different between Republicans and Democrats (although not statistically significant). The Internet was the top political media choice of Democrats and Independents. Television was the top choice for Republicans. We did find one significant difference of interest. Republican voters turned to radio as a source for political information more often than did their Democrat or Independent counterparts. The rank order for media use is highlighted in Table 8.5. ANOVA results are highlighted in Table 8.6.

Table 8.5 Rank Ordered Media Use by Political Party

DEMOCRAT	REPUBLICAN	INDEPENDENT
Internet	TV	Internet
TV	Internet	TV
Newspapers	Newspapers	Newspapers
Social Networking	Radio	Video Sharing
Video Sharing	Video Sharing	Social Networking
Radio	Social Networking	Radio
Magazines	Magazines	Magazines
Micro-blogging	Books	Micro-blogging
Books	Micro-blogging	Books
Blogs	Blogs	Blogs

Note: Each column reflects the rank order of each medium used (from the most often to the least often used).

Source: This Figure was Created from Original Survey Data Collected by the Researchers During the 2012 Republican Primary Race in Ohio.

Table 8.6 Univariate Analysis of Variance of the Three Political Parties on Media Exposure

MEDIA SELECTION	F(df)	p	DEMOCRATIC PARTY	REPUBLICAN PARTY	INDEPENDENT
			POLITICAL PARTY		
TV	(2, 348) = 6.33	.002	3.48 (1.12)[a]	3.61 (1.22)[a]	3.02 (1.29)[b]
Radio	(2, 348) = 4.55	.01	2.33 (1.11)[b]	2.68 (1.20)[a]	2.22 (1.20)[b]
Newspapers	(2, 348) = 2.72	.07	3.02 (1.09)[a]	3.08 (1.21)[a]	2.71 (1.26)[a]
Magazines	(2, 348) = 2.60	.08	2.28 (1.11)[a]	2.21 (1.02)[a]	1.97 (.98)[a]
Books	(2, 347) = 1.50	.23	1.83 (1.03)[a]	1.85 (1.02)[a]	1.63 (.79)[a]
Internet	(2, 348) = .22	.81	3.48 (1.27)[a]	3.38 (1.34)[a]	3.41 (1.34)[a]
Video Sharing	(2, 348) = .50	.61	2.51 (1.33)[a]	2.53 (1.43)[a]	2.34 (1.42)[a]
Social Networking	(2, 348) = 2.10	.12	2.59 (1.40)[a]	2.27 (1.43)[a]	2.31 (1.42)[a]
Micro-blogging	(2, 348) = .52	.60	1.90 (1.21)[a]	1.76 (1.19)[a]	1.78 (1.29)[a]
Political Blogging	(2, 348) = 1.91	.15	1.56 (.99)[a]	1.46 (.92)[a]	1.32 (.72)[a]

Note: Standard deviation for each mean is included in the parenthesis. Pairwise comparison results are indicated with superscripts.
Source: This Figure was Created from Original Survey Data Collected by the Researchers During the 2012 Republican Primary Race in Ohio.

Regardless of their preferred party affiliation, participants were not significantly different with respect to the motives they had for seeking political information except for the motive of political identity (See Table 8.7). Though Republicans were not significantly different than Democrats in seeking political information for purposes of political identity, members of both parties sought information for that reason significantly more often than did Independents.

Table 8.7 Univariate Analysis of Variance on Motives of Using Media by Political Party

MOTIVES	F(df)	p	DEMOCRATIC PARTY	REPUBLICAN PARTY	INDEPENDENT
			POLITICAL PARTY		
Passive Entertainment	(2, 346) = 1.54	.22	2.12 (.82)[a]	2.21 (.89)[a]	1.99 (.82)[a]
Political Identity	(2, 346) = 9.78	.000	2.44 (.92)[a]	2.51 (.83)[a]	1.99 (.85)[b]
Convenient Information Seeking	(2, 346) = 1.22	.30	3.13 (.95)[a]	3.21 (.85)[a]	3.00 (.94)[a]
Issue and Candidate Evaluation	(2, 347) = .34	.71	3.41 (.76)[a]	3.46 (.76)[a]	3.37 (.72)[a]
Opinion Leadership	(2, 346) = 1.14	.32	2.44 (.99)[a]	2.56 (.99)[a]	2.35 (.99)[a]

Note: Standard deviation for each mean is included in the parenthesis. Pairwise comparison results are indicated with superscripts.
Source: This Figure was Created from Original Survey Data Collected by the Researchers During the 2012 Republican Primary Race in Ohio.

In addition to looking at motives for turning to political media, we examined one background characteristic of voters related to how political partisans choose and evaluate media: Do party supporters perceive the media to be hostile toward their particular candidate/party? We found that Republicans were significantly more likely than Democrats or Independents to sense the presence of hostile media bias, $F(2, 348) = 7.98, p < .001$. Using a 5-point scale (5 = Strongly Agree; 1 = Strongly Disagree), the mean response for Republicans was 3.33 ($SD = .73$). The means for Democrats and Independents were 3.03 ($SD = .54$) and 3.07 ($SD = .61$) respectively.

DISCUSSION

The news media have been an important conduit for political information and dialog since the founding of the U.S.—newspapers since the 1700s, magazines since the 1800s, radio since the 1920s, TV since the 1950s, and the Internet since the 1990s (Benjamin, 1987; Kaid, 2002; Wells, 2008). The media landscape has changed in the 21st Century with the emergence and use of social media. This does not mean that social media are displacing or proving to be more important than older media. But, they are part of the media landscape and have emerged as sources of political communication in their own right. Social media are making significant strides, particularly among younger audiences.

As a result, television's long-held position as the major source of political information is facing some strong competition. The most popular choice for political information among our survey participants is a near dead heat between the Internet and television. Slightly more than half (52%) of all the respondents in the survey said they turned to the Web for political information either "very often" or "often"; 51% of all respondents said they turned to TV at the same levels (Newspapers ranked third overall, but its relative usage compared to the Internet and television dropped to 33% among the heaviest users).

In 2012 we found that social media had established themselves as acceptable sources of political information but most people still reported to be using TV and the Internet more often. Newspapers were relevant sources of political information among those in the 22–35 and 36–55 age groups, and for those 56 and older, radio was a predominant source of information. Perhaps the most glaring change was that social media (video sharing sites and SNSs) had overtaken other media (with the exception of TV and the Internet) as primary sources reported by those in the 18–21 year-old age group. One out of three potential younger voters said they turned to social media either "very often" or "often" for political information. Similarly, one in five estimated they used microblogging at the same rate. It is fair to speculate that this trend will continue.

Our results tend to support prior research. For example, Van Rees and Van Eijck (2003) found that participants over the age of 55 were more likely to use local television and newspapers as well as public television than their younger counterparts. Similarly, Taneja, Webster, Malthouse, and Ksiazek (2012) found older adults were more likely to use television than younger adults, but less likely to use the computer for work. The Pew Research Center (2012b) examined the use of traditional and digital news among different age groups and found that use of television and print newspaper use increased with age, while Twitter and social networking decreased with age. Our results were consistent with and tend to corroborate these findings.

The fact that social media were not the top choices for political information does not mean they were not without influence. First, it has been widely reported that mainstream media often turn to social media for newsworthy information. For example, Hodge (2010) detailed 10 big stories that were reported first by Twitter (e.g., the 2009 US Airways plane crash on the Hudson River and the violence at the 2009 G20 summit in London). Second, campaigns are bypassing mainstream media and using social media to communicate with the public directly. The result is that journalists often spend more time trolling social media than getting to know the candidates and their campaign staffs (for a discussion, see Enda, 2011). Accordingly, social media may have a strong indirect influence by affecting the political content of the mainstream media.

Another reason to be cautious about concluding that social media were not influential sources of political information is because they foster social connection among users. Decades of communication research (e.g., Hwang, 2012; Lazarsfeld et al., 1944; Rogers, 2003) has suggested that interpersonal and group communication among those in our social circles (i.e., networks) who we trust is likely to have an impact on our attitudes and behaviors (including political ones) than are the mainstream media. In fact, this is a central premise of perspectives such as the two-step flow of communication.

As in the case with media selection, one of the more significant findings regarding motives for using media for political information in the lead up to the Republican primary were the similarities across age groups. The primary reasons for using the media for political fare were *issue and candidate evaluation*, and *information seeking*. These results suggest that participants, regardless of age, were using media instrumentally to be informed and cognizant about the issues and candidates. It is interesting to note that while some observers have commented that politics is presented like a horse race (e.g., Sweetser & Kaid, 2008), which suggests that the entertainment value of the race is important, participants in this study did not for the most part report seeking political fare from the media for reasons of entertainment. The more salient reasons they had for turning to the media for politics—candidate and issue evaluation and information seeking—is a type of use that is much more in the spirit of Lasswell's (1948) surveillance and correlation functions the media serve for people.

Although *opinion leadership* was a bit stronger political media-use motive for those in the 18–21 age group and *political identity* was more salient for those 56 or older, these two motives were not predominant reasons for turning to the media for politics. Nonetheless, it is interesting that those over the age of 56 were significantly more likely to use media for political identity reasons than were those in the three younger age groups. It could be that the older an individual gets, the more one's political media use is shaped by one's political identity, which may have crystallized over the years.

It also is interesting to note that members of the different political parties did not differ significantly in their reasons for using media for political information. The only exception was that Independents reported that they were less likely to use media for purposes of political identity than were Republicans and Democrats. Of course, this is expected as those who are independent may lean toward a certain party, but by definition, have not committed to one.

We also found that Republicans were more likely than Democrats and Independents to feel the media were hostile toward their political party. While it is difficult to attribute this to the media, it is interesting to note that the only medium Republicans relied on significantly more than did Independents and Democrats was radio. This is an important factor to consider in future research, because it has been suggested that talk radio is dominated by conservative voices, such as Rush Limbaugh (Jones, 2004). Specifically, Jones (2004) found that among Republicans who listened to political talk radio, trust in the media was relatively low. While we did not focus on particular channels within media sources measured in this study, that should be a focus in future research. It could be that conservative Republicans turn to such conservative programs as an alternative to what they perceive as a liberal media bias in other media venues. Or, alternatively, that selection may result in perceptions of a mainstream media liberal bias. Or both could be true—Americans hostile to the media may tune into talk radio and talk radio may confirm and reinforce those attitudes.

Regardless of the direction of the relationship, the changing patterns of media used most often for politics could have other repercussions, as well. For example, the one perception of media users we measured here—the perception of whether the national media were hostile to one's party was related to selection of media chosen for political fare. Amount of Internet use, the source selected most often by those under the age of 56, correlated with hostile media bias perceptions ($r = .12$, $p < .05$). Newspaper use and radio use (media which were used more often by those over the age of 56) linked with hostile media bias perceptions ($r = .13$, $p > .05$ and $r = .19$, $p < .01$, respectively). Only one social media source, use of video sharing sites (e.g., YouTube), linked with hostile media bias perceptions ($r = .11$, $p < .05$). There was no relationship between hostile media bias and selection of SNSs, microblogs, or political blogs. Perhaps most importantly, TV use (the first or second ranked medium used across age groups) did not link with hostile media bias perceptions.

Some scholars have argued that newer media give people more opportunities to select media fare that reinforces their attitudes and predispositions. It could be that those who feel that the mainstream media are biased against their party turn to newer media that provide them with more options to engage in selective exposure to views that support their predispositions. It also is possible, however, that the newer channels they select influence such perceptions. As referenced above, future research should explore the direction of the relationship with respect to media choice to flesh that picture out more fully.

If such a perception affects or is affected by media selection, other perceptions and individual differences that have been found to be important to political communication and/or political participation (e.g., trust in government, political cynicism, political discussion) also may be differentially related to media selection for politics.

In conclusion, the power of the use of social and mobile media to mobilize became glaringly obvious on a world stage as the role the use of social and mobile media played in the Arab Spring uprisings that began in 2010 and other political mobilization around the world. The actual use of these media in the last half decade has demonstrated the profound effect of these interactive media on political advocacy, mobilization, change, or simply to give those who are socially and politically motivated an interactive channel to connect with like-minded others. No longer, as historically has been the case, are the media controlled by just a few with the licenses to control media access to media to just a few elites, candidates and political operatives. These new channels that provide socially and politically active people with a common interest with important tools with which to communicate with each other, has changed the media distribution process. In doing so, they provide important new forums for new voices in the political process (Hendricks & Kaid, 2011).

CHAPTER 9

Whose States Are Winning? The Adoption and Consequences of Social Media in Political Communication in the American States

Hyun Jung Yun, Cynthia Opheim, and Emily Kay Balanoff

The presidential election of 2008 saw a sharp rise in the use of social networking services (SNSs) to gather information about the candidates and in the number of opportunities for citizens to express their opinions and to participate in a wide variety of political activities. Nearly three-quarters of Internet users went online during the 2008 election to get news or discuss the candidates and issues (Smith, 2009). This constituted almost 55% of the adult population. Approximately one in ten Americans "friended" the presidential candidates on SNSs in 2008 (Smith, 2009). The popularity of such sites showed no signs of waning in 2012. During the presidential election, about 75% of American SNS users reported finding political content posted to their friends' sites (Rainie & Smith, 2012). Both presidential candidates posted to Facebook and other social media sites and "tweeted" with supporters as a part of their political campaign (Yaverbaum, 2012).

Although many factors may predict the patterns of SNSs' political adoption and utilization, it is likely that these patterns vary across different geographic, partisan, and ideological contexts. That patterns of use for traditional forms of political communication and the political consequences vary across geopolitical contexts in American politics is well established. Prior scholarship demonstrates that political culture and ideology are embedded within geographical regions and that political predisposition influences the way politicians and the electorate communicate; it also influences the ways in which people in the region utilize communication channels to learn, understand, and use political information (Benoit, McKinney, & Holbert, 2001; Yun, Jasperson, & Kaid, 2010). In spite of the technological advances represented by social media, the influence of the surrounding political climate on an individual's political communication is likely to persist. Therefore, these theories can and should be applied to online political communication.

In order to understand how this new form of digital political communication works across different political regions and ideological contexts, this study examined levels in the adoption of social media among blue, purple, and red states— that is, liberal, swing, and conservative states, respectively. It analyzed politically active social media users' political perceptions, political identities, and their attitudes towards cynicism, political efficacy, and political participation. It also examined the question of whether engaging in SNSs increases or reduces exposure to crosscutting views. The findings revealed that partisan, ideological, and geographic context play a significant role in the political usage of SNSs and the levels of trust, efficacy, and selectivity of political information. The increasing use of social networks in cyberspace to communicate political voices in "real time," combined with preexisting geopolitical attitudes, had great potential to enhance or change political outcomes of the 2012 presidential campaign and election.

THEORETICAL UNDERPINNINGS

The Growth of Social Media in Political Campaigns

The use of social media sites such as YouTube, Facebook, and MySpace, as well as of political blogs, has grown exponentially since the 2008 presidential campaign. Over 80% of American adults use the Internet, and 60% of those online participate in SNSs. Many of these SNSs are relatively new: MySpace went online in 2003 and Facebook in 2004 (Hanson, Haridakis, Cunningham, Sharma, & Ponder, 2010). These sites, and others like them, have become popular places for citizens to gather information, engage in political conversation, and engage in debate regarding the candidates and the issues.

While television remains the most important source for most Americans, there has been a gradual shift away from traditional media sources, such as newspapers and television, as individuals turn from the one-way broadcast of political information to the more interactive, conversational capabilities of the Internet. In 1996, only 3% of Americans listed the Internet as their primary source for political information; in 2008, this figure was 40% (Pew Research Center, 1996, 2008). Although a significant portion of this activity occurred on traditional news sites such as CNN.com or MSNBC.com (Milbery & Anderson, 2009), the use of non-legacy media sites sharply increased during the 2008 campaign (Parmelee, Davies, & McMahan, 2011).

Although social media come in a variety of formats, "the defining attribute of each is the fact that they are more user centered than traditional media counterparts" (Hanson et al., 2010, p. 585). Online SNSs allow voters to obtain information from one another, form like-minded groups that advocate particular candidates or issues, engage in online discussion or messaging, post videos, and blog about causes or issues (boyd, 2008; Price, Nir, & Cappella, 2006).

Candidates are also embracing social media as a campaign tool. The precedent-setting use of SNSs by the Obama campaign in 2008, no doubt, contributed to this trend. The Obama campaign drew from the resources of a database of almost 13 million e-mail addresses, a community blog, and a digital network of volunteers to raise money and build a grassroots organization. Both the Obama and McCain campaigns relied on digital networks for "get-out-the-vote drives." A "bottom-up" approach characterized these efforts as well; volunteers uploaded address books and sent targeted messages to friends and family in support of their candidate (Clark, 2010).

Given these developments, there would seem to be little doubt that access to SNSs can influence the political attitudes and behavior of citizens. But an important question persists: How much of this impact is filtered through a geopolitical context? In other words, are citizens remaking the political world online, or are they recreating existing patterns? Before addressing this question, it is important to discuss existing research examining the impact of the Internet on the public's trust, interest and efficacy, and participation.

SOCIAL MEDIA'S EFFECT ON POLITICAL ATTITUDES AND BEHAVIOR

Political Cynicism

Traditional media's role in effecting the level of cynicism in American institutions has been documented for nearly half a century. Much of this research argues that the media contributes to cynicism or distrust in the political system and, thus, discourages political participation. Higher levels of disengagement have been linked to both television viewing in general (Putnam, 1995) and campaign coverage, in particular (Hart, 1998; Hibbing & Theiss-Moore, 1995; Patterson, 1994, 2003; Sabato, 1993). Prominent studies of the latter attribute increased public cynicism from negative campaign ads (Kaid & Boydston, 1987), the media's reliance on a "horse race" frame in political coverage (Cappella & Jamieson, 1997), and the amount of political information exposure (Hill & McKee, 2005; Semetko, 2004).

While the positive relationship between television and cynicism appears robust, this relationship does not hold true under all conditions or for all types of media (Austin & Pinkleton, 1999; Lee, 2005; de Vreese, 2005). The relationship between news media exposure and cynicism may be contingent on the medium in question (Lee, 2005). All media are not created equally in this regard. A recent series of studies focusing on the interactive capabilities of the Internet (and social media, in particular) have shown that these new communication channels can reduce political cynicism (Kaid, McKinney, & Tedesco, 2000; Hanson et al., 2010) and contribute to increased levels of trust among users (Himelboim, Lariscy, Tinkham, & Sweetser, 2012; Zhang, Johnson, Seltzer, & Bichard, 2010). Additional studies, however, failed to demonstrate such connections (Kaid, 2002). And yet others show that the Internet's effect is mixed; it is positively associated with both political trust and cynicism (Lee, 2005; Postelnicu & Cozma, 2008). Individual political factors in the audience are suspected of exerting an influence on political attitudes and social media use. Weaver, Tinkham, and Sweetser (2011), for instance, link higher levels of political cynicism to political sophistication. And, while social media campaigns have been shown to attract the politically sophisticated (Himelboim et al., 2012), individuals engaged on SNSs are less likely to distrust political leaders (Hanson et al., 2010). Clark (2010) argued that social media may bolster one's faith in institutions and public figures because SNS users interact with political leaders and with one another.

Political Information Efficacy

Another important and established construct in political communication is political efficacy, particularly political information efficacy. Tedesco (2011) defines political information efficacy as confidence about one's own competence to understand, and to participate effectively, in politics. Alterations in the type of political information to which an individual is exposed lead to differences in the type of information processing. According to this theory, the source and medium of information play a key role in determining one's level of political efficacy (Kaid, McKinney, & Tedesco, 2007). Tedesco (2011) found that Internet messaging raised the level of political efficacy among younger social media users, particularly young men. This contradicts the findings of earlier studies, which held that low levels of political efficacy led to reduced levels of voting among young people (Kaid et al., 2007). Thus, it may be inferred that the use of the Internet and social media as a platform for news, information, and discussion was a factor in the change.

The link between political knowledge and information and electoral participation is a strong one. Kaid, McKinney, and Tedesco (2007) demonstrated that young voters exposed to political information on the Internet were more likely to seek out additional information sources and to indicate a greater likelihood of voting. Drawing on media system dependency theory, Tolbert and McNeal (2003) concluded that the variety of information sources on the Internet, combined with the speed and flexibility of obtaining information online, stimulates higher voter turnout. The implication is that the presence and availability of Internet resources encourages users to participate in offline as well as online political activities. However, Prior (2005) added an alternative perspective that stated that the positive relationship between Internet use and political knowledge and turnout depends on individuals' political interests. Internet users who are interested in politics are more likely to learn from the abundant political information on the Internet and participate in politics, while people who are politically uninterested can easily avoid political content on the Internet and seek their preferred non-political online information. Thus, the greater variety of information on the Internet could influence voter turnout and possibly increase the political knowledge gap among Internet users.

Taken together, the evidence indicates that citizen involvement with the Internet and with social media sites as sources of information and as an outlet for sharing opinions may be altering how media influence political attitudes and behavior. As the study of the effects of social media use matures, however, it is important to examine whether or not the findings discussed above are consistent across geographical and political contexts. Next, we investigate the literature in this regard.

Social Media, Geography, and Political Ideology

Whether or not the Internet and social media will reconfigure democratic politics or merely recreate preexisting patterns has given rise to speculation among academics and popular commentators (Dahlberg, 2007). At the heart of this discussion is the extent to which geography, partisanship, and political ideology or, in other words, the drivers of traditional politics will hold sway in this new media environment. Cyberspace advocates argue that the Internet's successes in democratizing politics are substantial. Hindman (2008), for instance, stated that cyber advocates believe that the Internet is "redistributing political influence . . . and involving citizens in political activities that were previously closed to them" (p. 6). Digital utopians envision social media platforms displacing rational and restrictive models of the public sphere and creating in their place a self-authorizing network of citizens who are no longer content to be mere passive consumers of political party spin or mass media news (Bennett, 2003; Dahlgren, 2009; Loader & Mercea, 2011; Papacharissi, 2010).

One reason that the Internet has generated such enthusiasm in this regard is the promise of social media to further enhance the quality of democratic deliberation by transcending the bounds of geography and physical space to connect people from different backgrounds and thus expose its users to crosscutting views (Brundidge, 2010; Kim, 2011). Papacharissi (2002) stated that "Utopian perspectives on the Internet speculate that computer-mediated political communication will facilitate grassroots democracy and bring people all across the world closer together. Geographic boundaries can be overcome and 'diasporic utopias' can flourish" (p. 16). Such communication diminishes not only the importance of geographic boundaries, but it also has the potential to destabilize the discursive boundaries that maintain dominant, hegemonic interests (Dahlberg, 2007).

Indeed, research supporting these theoretical contentions exists. Brundidge (2010), for example, claimed that the Internet weakens social barriers and promotes the "non-avoidance of encounters with political difference" (p. 972). Similarly, Kim (2011) indicated that exposure to political difference was not affected by demographic difference and that partisanship did not significantly influence the exposure to crosscutting viewpoints. Interestingly, Wojcieszak and Mutz (2009) found that crosscutting political discussion was more likely to occur in apolitical spaces than in political chat rooms or on political message boards.

Not everyone is quite as sanguine about the prospects of social media to reshape democratic politics. There is much to suggest that online forms of civic participation are and will continue to be shaped by the same deeply entrenched social and economic interests that drive traditional politics (Hill & Hughes, 1998; Sunstein, 2007). In other words, the differing political attitudes and behaviors of social media users reviewed in the preceding section may be attributed to the interaction between the prevailing partisan and ideological culture and exposure to political information as determined by an individual's geographic location.

Bishop (2008) found the influence of geographic location on political behavior to be rising, not waning. His argument, however, is nuanced. Place is an increasingly powerful predictor of political attitudes and voting behavior because contemporary Americans have sorted themselves into remarkably homogenous communities. Such "communities of interest" are different from traditional neighborhoods; today's like-minded enclaves reflect similar beliefs or ways of life rather than similarities in age, employment, or income (Bishop, 2008). Geography is more than mere location when considered in conjunction with social location (Gelman, 2008). Place, then, exerts power by increasing exposure to locally dominate views, reducing exposure to diverse viewpoints, and rewarding more extreme versions of group ideology.

Precedent for predicting the importance of geopolitical culture and partisanship can also be found in the work of prominent American politics scholars like Larry Bartels (2002) and political communication scholars Yun and her colleagues (2010) and William Benoit and his colleagues (2001). The combined insight of these researchers posits that the primary influence on political communication is an interaction between political information exposure and political predisposition (e.g., partisanship). Subsequent studies that built upon this claim showed that distribution of political information by the media and politicians is not consistent across states. Thus, people who are exposed to more political information in battleground states tend to be politically more knowledgeable and more analytical (Benoit et al., 2001; Druckman, 2004; Semetko, 2004; Wolak, 2006; Wright, 1998) and are more likely to change their views in light of new political information than are people with limited and selective media exposure in non-battleground states (Yun et al., 2010).

A similar claim can be made regarding the adoption of social media and the distribution of political information on the Internet. Geographic location can alter an individual's exposure to online political information. According to a digital report issued by the DCI Group (2011), there are variations in the levels of adoption of social media among the general public and politicians across the United States. For instance, Washington State ranked first and New Mexico ranked last in the number of Facebook users as a proportion of state population. The same DCI report found that 46 states have legislators using Twitter, 48 governors have a personalized Twitter presence, and more than one-third of state legislators have a Facebook profile. Herrnson, Stokes-Brown, and Hindman (2007) asserted that the strategic and structural circumstances of the race have a major impact on candidates' Internet use. They observed that presidential and congressional candidates were more likely than candidates for lower-level office to use the Internet, as were candidates who had younger and better-educated constituents. Partisan differences played a role in candidates' adoption of Facebook, according to Williams and Gulati (2012). Democratic Party candidates more rapidly adopted and actively used Facebook than Republicans. While a majority of both major party candidates maintained a Facebook presence, Democrats were, for instance, more likely to update their Facebook pages. Other drivers of adoption and implementation included competition, money, and the level of education in the district. Williams and Gulati (2012) summarized their findings thusly:

> Challengers and candidates for open seats were more likely to be early adopters, but incumbents used Facebook more extensively. Both higher adoption rates by

peers or competitors in the candidate's own state and a propensity to adopt earlier campaign technologies are strong positive motivators for early adoption, but irrelevant to usage (p. 1).

Research on online media consumption habits also suggests that the relationship between information exposure and political predisposition holds true in a digital environment. As the number of sources of political information increase, studies indicate that partisanship and political ideology determine media selection and consumers choose outlets that reflect and confirm their own political views (Lee, 2005). The pattern of selective exposure based on partisan affinity is even more pronounced among the more politically engaged (Iyengar & Han, 2009). The "networked individualism" heralded by Internet optimists becomes a sign of the social fragmentation that threatens to erode collective action and social responsibility (Loader & Mercea, 2011). Put differently, individuals expose themselves to like-minded perspectives that exacerbate fragmentation and polarization of attitudes (Sunstein, 2007; Stroud, 2010). Sunstein (2007) labeled this pattern of selectivity "enclave communication." Iyengar and Hahn (2009), for instance, uncovered strong ideological patterns in the selectivity of communication with news sources: Democrats and Republicans read and watched news on their preferred venues and avoided those with which they had no partisan affinity. From this perspective, the Internet offers citizens opportunities to filter what they read and hear and allows them to bypass contrasting viewpoints.

Political ideology and partisanship also influenced the attitudes and behavior of those engaged in political activity on social media, according to Rainie and Smith (2012). In the study, liberals were a bit more likely to use SNSs for political purposes, and they were inclined to block, "unfriend," or hide someone whose views were different than their own. Liberals were also more likely to have friends who regularly discuss politics on SNSs. Both liberals and conservatives were more likely than moderates to "self-censor" their comments, that is, avoid making political comments that might offend others. There was little difference in the percentage of liberals and conservatives who reported that they "never disagree" with their friends' political contributions and little difference between these two ideological groups in their responses to challenges to their views. Most stated that they ignored such challenges.

The literature reviewed demonstrates that differing political attitudes and behaviors of social media users may very well be attributed to the interaction between the prevailing partisan and ideological culture and exposure to political information as determined by an individual's geographic location. Our investigation now turns specifically to the examination of the political activity of social media users in a partisan context. The study documents the uses of social media in traditionally Republican, Democratic, and battleground states. It investigates the purposes and level of political utilizations of SNSs across these political climates and provides evidence for theoretical speculation on the effects of this usage on political attitudes, such as cynicism and political efficacy, as well as the effects on perceptions towards and exposure to different political viewpoints.

METHOD

Sample

From October of 2011 to April of 2012, 35 undergraduate students were provided information about important issues and current agendas in political communication and trained to conduct web-based surveys. The students were then divided into 7 different groups. Each group worked together to explore political content on personal SNSs, group SNSs, organizational SNSs, professionally affiliated SNSs, or via their personal SNSs, by joining groups or communities and by being friends or/and followers at SNSs. Each group randomly selected about 50 politically engaged individuals in social media, who actively participated in political discussions and forums about the current campaign or policy issues, posted political pictures or videos, initiated political activities, and/or led political groups via SNSs, and invited those politically active social media users to participate in the survey. Based on convenience for the respondent, the survey was administered either (1) via SNSs in real time, with the trained surveyor asking respondents each question; (2) as an e-mail attachment that respondents completed and then returned via their personal e-mail; or (3) in person by a trained surveyor at an official, off-line political meeting. The survey was in the field for 6 months and closed in April, which marked the end of the peak campaign season for the 2012 presidential primaries. Not surprisingly, surveyors experienced some difficulty (e.g., security restrictions, reaching the target samples of politically active individuals in social media), and, as a result, had a relatively low response rate and a high incompletion rate compared to other survey methods. This was likely due to the technological limitations and restrictions of web-based surveys compared to other survey techniques such as telephone, mail, or personal interviews (Wimmer & Dominick, 2011). The total number of respondents who completed the survey was 138.

To examine patterns in the political usage of SNSs across geopolitical regions, survey respondents were placed into one of three different categories: politically active SNS users living in either a red, purple, or blue state. There are multiple ways to determine the partisan nature of states. This study used the results of the last four presidential elections to classify the geographical division: If a state consistently voted for the Republican Party candidate in the last four presidential elections, the state was labeled as a red state; if a state consistently voted for the Democratic Party candidate in the last four presidential elections, the state was labeled as a blue state; and if a state voted at least once for a different party candidate in the last four presidential elections, the state was labeled as a purple state.

Using the classification method above, the sample contained unequal numbers of individuals across red ($n = 76$), purple ($n = 13$), and blue ($n = 49$) states. In addition, the random selection of individuals who were politically active on SNSs reflects the visibility of salient issues and the level of political opinions and activities of individuals or groups. Moreover, the levels and patterns of political opinions and activities of individuals might determine their willingness to participate in the survey and, thus, even more significantly magnify the difference in sample size across red, purple and blue states. To address these practical issues and in order to overcome the difference in the sample sizes among red, purple, and blue states for more reliable comparisons, the study weighted sample cases of the color of states assigning weighting factors of 5.846 and 1.551 to the cases of purple and blue states, respectively.

Variables and Measures

Respondents were asked to provide their geographical location (state) along with other demographic factors, such as political party affiliation, gender, race, age, and level of education. This information was used to control for these factors in the relationship between geopolitical circumstance and the political usage of SNSs. In addition, respondents were queried about their levels of general media usage, SNS usage, and the ways in which they utilized SNSs for political purposes.

The survey also measured the respondent's level of trust toward political information and friends on SNSs when exchanging political views, as well as their level of trust in SNSs compared to the mainstream media. To capture politically engaged SNS users' political opinions, attitudes, and behaviors, respondents were asked: to rate the status of their perceived personal political opinions versus the general American public and mainstream media; their level of political expression in both supportive and hostile contexts; the possibility of change to their political views and behaviors as a result of political discussions and activities on SNSs; and their level of political interest, information efficacy, and cynicism. Each component of the study was asked as a separate question or single item and measured in a Likert scale of 1-lowest values to 5-highest values, except the political information efficacy and cynicism scales.

The index of political information efficacy was created by merging 4 separate items and achieved a reliable Cronbach's Alpha value of .82. The statement items were: I consider myself well qualified to participate in politics; I think I am better informed about government and politics than most people; I feel that I have a pretty good understanding of the important political issues facing our country; and, if a friend asked me about the presidential election, I feel I would have enough information to help my friend figure out who to vote for. The index of political cynicism was created by merging 8 separate items and achieved a high Cronbach's Alpha reliability of .73. The 8 items were: vote has no influence on what politicians do; one never knows what politicians really think; people like me don't have any say about what government does; politicians and government seem complicated for a person like me; one can be confident politicians will always do the right thing; politicians often forget election promises after the campaign; politicians are more interested in power than what people think; and one cannot always trust what politicians say. These questions were measured on a Likert scale of 1-lowest values to 5-highest values, and new indexes were rescaled on the same 1-lowest to 5-highest scale.

Lastly, the survey inquired about the foremost uses and gratifications of political activities on SNSs. The answer option categories were: to seek political information; to have political networks; to have social networks; to share my political views with people who have similar views; to educate and enlighten people; to improve the current political situation; to change current public policies; and other. Then, respondents were asked an open-ended question about the potential and actual achievements of the expression of respondents' political views shared and distributed via SNSs. The answers were then summarized and categorized into 5 different parameters: change government and policy; distribute my voice, share opinion and educate others; educate myself; gain my personal interests; and no achievement. This study compared politically active social media users' political attitudes, identities and perceptions, uses and gratifications, and perceived achievements of their online political communication across red, purple, and blue states in order to understand different levels of the political adoption and application of social media by different geopolitical cultures.

RESULTS

Political Utilization and Legitimacy of SNSs

According to ANOVA (analysis of variance) and Bonferroni post-hoc tests, after controlling for other demographic factors, politically active SNS users in red ($M = 15.22, SD = 16.55$ per week) and blue ($M = 14.76, SD = 23.14$ per week) states were more likely to spend their time on any type of media than were politically active SNS users in purple states ($M = 7.73, SD = 13.49$ per week), $F(2, 213) = 3.53, p \leq .03$. In other words, political SNS users in non-battleground states are more likely to use media on a daily basis than political SNS users in battleground states (see Table 9.1).

Although there was no statistical difference in the amount of social media usage among individuals who are politically active on SNSs across individual

Table 9.1 Media Consumption Pattern

	OVERALL MEDIA USE		SNS USE		POLITICAL POSTS TO SNSs	
	F	P	F	P	F	P
Intercept	8.349	0.004	1.817	0.179	1.759	0.188
State Color	3.533	0.031	0.574	0.564	5.533	0.005
Political Party Affiliation	4.889	0.003	5.866	0.001	9.234	0.000
Gender	6.499	0.012	1.984	0.161	0.335	0.564
Race	1.398	0.236	0.573	0.683	6.035	0.000
Age	6.983	0.009	0.282	0.596	0.242	0.624
Education	16.227	0.000	15.181	0.000	10.396	0.002
	$R^2 = .212$		$R^2 = .157$		$R^2 = .441$	

Source: The Authors' Original Data on a Cross-sectional SNS Study Collected Between October 2011 and April 2012 (n = 138).

different states, respondents in purple states ($M = 19.34$, $SD = 15.33$ per week) were more likely to post their political opinions to SNSs than individuals in blue states ($M = 10.67$, $SD = 14.87$ per week) and red states ($M = 8.05$, $SD = 8.53$ per week), $F(2, 103) = 5.53$, $p \leq .01$. This suggests that politically active SNS users in battleground states tend to more actively distribute and share their political views via SNSs than politically active SNS users in non-battleground states (see Table 9.1).

In addition, individuals in purple states ($M = 3.35$, $SD = 1.00$) who were politically active on SNSs were more likely to believe that political discussions found on SNSs would change their political views compared to politically active SNS users in blue states ($M = 2.93$, $SD = .98$), $F(2, 248) = 4.699$, $p \leq .01$). Political SNS users in purple states ($M = 3.49$, $SD = 1.04$) more strongly believed that political discussions on SNS could also change their political behaviors than political SNS users in red ($M = 3.02$, $SD = 1.18$) and blue ($M = 2.68$, $SD = .98$) states, $F(2, 242) = 12.38$, $p \leq .01$ (see Table 9.2). Politically active SNS users in battleground states seem to perceive more power and legitimacy in SNSs' political influence on their political opinions and behaviors and are more likely to believe that they would be swayed by political discussions via SNSs than political SNS users in non-battleground states.

However, political SNS users who live in politically more liberal states were more likely to trust information, friends, and members of SNSs than political SNS users who live in politically moderate and conservative states. According to ANOVA and Bonferroni post-hoc tests, politically active individuals on SNSs in blue ($M = 3.18$, $SD = 1.09$) states tended to trust political information shared and distributed via SNSs more than politically active people on SNSs in red states ($M = 2.79$, $SD = 1.22$), $F(2, 248) = 3.24$, $p \leq .05$. Additionally, political SNS users in blue states ($M = 3.86$, $SD = 1.00$) were more likely to trust friends and

Table 9.2 Effects of SNS Political Discussion on Changes of Political Opinion and Behavior

	CHANGES IN POLITICAL VIEW		CHANGES IN POLITICAL BEHAVIOR	
	F	*P*	*F*	*P*
Intercept	91.751	0.000	64.763	0.000
State Color	4.699	0.010	12.376	0.000
Political Party Affiliation	3.904	0.010	5.964	0.001
Gender	0.016	0.899	0.121	0.728
Race	3.550	0.004	1.793	0.115
Age	0.094	0.759	2.075	0.151
Education	8.871	0.003	5.974	0.015
	$R^2 = .186$		$R^2 = .216$	

Source: The Authors' Original Data on a Cross-sectional SNS Study Collected Between October 2011 and April 2012 (n = 138).

members of SNSs when they exchange their political views than political SNS users in purple states ($M = 3.51$, $SD = 1.09$), this approached, but was not significant at the .05 alpha level, $F(2, 248) = 2.72$, $p \leq .07$. This tendency was consistent when the level of trust toward SNSs was compared to the level of trust toward the mainstream news. Politically active SNS users in blue states ($M = 3.47$, $SD = 1.00$) trusted political information provided by, and the opinions of, friends and members of their social networks more strongly than mainstream news coverage, compared to political SNS users in red states ($M = 2.97$, $SD = 1.16$), $F(2, 248) = 4.99$, $p \leq .01$ (see Table 9.3).

Political Interests, Information Efficacy, and Cynicism of Political SNS Users

Among individuals who were politically active on SNSs, people from purple states ($M = 5.89$, $SD = 4.81$) were more likely to express that they were interested in politics than people from blue ($M = 4.91$, $SD = .92$) and red states ($M = 4.21$, $SD = 1.10$), $F(2, 249) = 8.05$, $p \leq .01$. Although the statistical significance was somewhat weak, people from purple states ($M = 4.02$, $SD = .64$) had higher political efficacy and, thus, were more confident in their political participation than people in blue states ($M = 3.81$, $SD = .61$), $F(2, 249) = 2.36$, $p = .097$. However, people in purple states ($M = 3.53$, $SD = .61$) also expressed higher political cynicism than people in blue states ($M = 3.21$, $SD = .58$), $F(2, 240) = 7.04$, $p \leq .01$. The ANOVA and Bonferroni post-hoc tests results indicated that politically active SNS users in battleground states have higher degrees of political interest, efficacy, and cynicism than political SNS users in non-battleground states (see Table 9.4).

Table 9.3 Legitimacy of SNSs

	TRUST SNSs INFO		TRUST SNSs FRIENDS/MEMBERS		TRUST SNSs OVER MAINSTREAM MEDIA	
	F	P	F	P	F	P
Intercept	45.529	0.000	87.053	0.000	69.278	0.000
State Color	3.235	0.041	2.718	0.068	4.985	0.008
Political Party Affiliation	5.776	0.001	5.141	0.002	6.903	0.000
Gender	2.261	0.134	0.640	0.425	0.000	0.996
Race	1.870	0.100	1.611	0.158	0.430	0.827
Age	25.058	0.000	11.936	0.001	16.905	0.000
Education	10.282	0.002	8.035	0.005	13.631	0.000
	$R^2 = .225$		$R^2 = .177$		$R^2 = .192$	

Source: The Authors' Original Data on a Cross-sectional SNS Study Collected Between October 2011 and April 2012 (n = 138).

Table 9.4 Political Interest, Information Efficacy, and Cynicism of Political SNS Users

	POLITICAL INTEREST		POLITICAL EFFICACY		POLITICAL CYNICISM	
	F	P	F	P	F	P
Intercept	17.491	0.000	162.593	0.000	282.480	0.000
State Color	8.053	0.000	2.355	0.097	7.035	0.001
Political Party Affiliation	16.796	0.000	2.824	0.039	8.207	0.000
Gender	5.399	0.021	1.354	0.246	0.274	0.601
Race	3.620	0.004	6.713	0.000	4.207	0.001
Age	2.743	0.099	2.228	0.137	6.028	0.015
Education	0.131	0.718	4.505	0.035	24.262	0.000
	$R^2 = .300$		$R^2 = .227$		$R^2 = .307$	

Source: The Authors' Original Data on a Cross-sectional SNS Study Collected Between October 2011 and April 2012 (n = 138).

Perception and Expression of Political Opinions via SNSs

ANOVA and Bonferroni post-hoc tests also revealed that politically active SNS users in red states ($M = 2.99$, $SD = .99$) were more likely to believe that their political opinions were shared with the majority of the American public than politically active SNS users in blue states ($M = 2.54$, $SD = .87$), $F(2, 248) = 4.05$, $p \leq .02$. However, politically active SNS users in blue states ($M = 2.92$, $SD = .98$) were more likely to believe that the mainstream media was supportive of their political opinions and activities than political SNS users in purple states ($M = 2.44$, $SD = 1.08$), $F(2, 248) = 5.45$, $p \leq .01$. In contrast, politically active SNS users in purple states ($M = 3.31$, $SD = 1.09$) believed more strongly that the mainstream media were hostile to their political opinions and activities than politically active SNS users in blue states ($M = 2.93$, $SD = 1.07$), $F(2, 248) = 3.10$, $p = .047$. Moreover, people in purple states ($M = 3.96$, $SD = .67$) more strongly believe that the mainstream media coverage could give misinformation to the American public than people in blue states ($M = 3.55$, $SD = .99$), $F(2, 248) = 4.49$, $p \leq .01$ (see Table 9.5).

However, political SNS users who lived in Democrat-leaning states seem to be more sensitive to others' political views and less likely to express their political views when facing disagreement. According to ANOVA and Bonferroni post-hoc tests, controlling for other demographic factors, politically active SNS users in blue states ($M = 2.44$, $SD = 1.25$) were more reluctant to express their political views via SNSs when friends and members of SNSs had different views from their own than political SNS users in purple states ($M = 1.98$, $SD = .92$) when faced with the same situation, $F(2, 242) = 3.692$, $p \leq .03$. Moreover, the SNS users in blue states ($M = 2.19$, $SD = 1.29$) were even more reluctant to voice their political views in face-to-face meetings with friends and members of SNSs that disagreed with their views than politically active SNS users in the same face-to-face hostile circumstances in red ($M = 1.76$, $SD = .99$) and purple ($M = 1.71$, $SD = 1.00$) states, $F(2, 248) = 5.15$, $p \leq .01$ (see Table 9.6).

Table 9.5 Perception of Political Opinions via SNSs

	CONGRUENCE WITH AMERICAN PUBLIC		CONGRUENCE WITH MAINSTREAM MEDIA		INCONGRUENCE WITH MAINSTREAM MEDIA		MISINFORMATION BY MAINSTREAM MEDIA	
	F	P	F	P	F	P	F	P
Intercept	23.780	0.000	22.711	0.000	91.598	0.000	64.986	0.000
State Color	4.046	0.019	5.446	0.005	3.100	0.047	4.486	0.012
Political Party Affiliation	2.797	0.041	7.491	0.000	7.226	0.000	1.849	0.139
Gender	0.422	0.516	1.531	0.217	0.700	0.403	0.027	0.869
Race	3.654	0.003	0.201	0.962	1.726	0.129	1.142	0.339
Age	0.039	0.844	11.056	0.001	9.591	0.002	8.730	0.003
Education	4.104	0.044	24.280	0.000	25.479	0.000	0.398	0.529
	$R^2 = .142$		$R^2 = .229$		$R^2 = .236$		$R^2 = .131$	

Source: The Authors' Original Data on a Cross-sectional SNS Study Collected Between October 2011 and April 2012 (n = 138).

Table 9.6 Expression of Political Opinions via SNSs

	VOICE IN ONLINE		VOICE IN OFFLINE	
	F	P	F	P
Intercept	7.746	0.006	3.202	0.075
State Color	3.692	0.026	5.146	0.007
Political Party Affiliation	0.815	0.487	1.900	0.130
Gender	0.055	0.815	0.813	0.368
Race	2.541	0.029	5.803	0.000
Age	0.725	0.395	0.264	0.608
Education	11.390	0.001	9.052	0.003
	$R^2 = .137$		$R^2 = .177$	

Source: The Authors' Original data on a Cross-sectional SNS Study Collected Between October 2011 and April 2012 (n = 138).

Purpose and Gratification of Political SNS Users

The dominant reason that individuals were politically active via SNSs in blue states was to share their political views with like-mined people (29.3%). The most prevalent purpose of politically active SNS users in purple states was to share their political views with like-minded people (37.7%) and to change current public policies (23.4%). However, for SNS users in red states, no dominate rationale emerged, $\chi^2 = 58.33$, $p = .001$ (see Table 9.7).

When survey respondents were asked to describe the potential and actual achievements of their political activities on SNSs, individuals in all states pointed to changes in current government and policies, as well as sharing and distributing their opinions. However, individuals in red states (35.15%) were more likely to say

Table 9.7 Purposes of Social Media Use

	STATE COLOR		
PURPOSE	RED	PURPLE	BLUE
To seek political information	10.53% (n = 8)	7.79% (n = 6)	18.67% (n = 14)
To have political networks	5.26% (n = 4)	0.00% (n = 0)	4.00% (n = 3)
To have social networks	14.47% (n = 11)	7.79% (n = 6)	6.67% (n = 5)
To share my political views with people who have similar views	7.90% (n = 6)	37.66% (n = 29)	29.33% (n = 22)
To educate and enlighten people	15.79% (n = 12)	7.79% (n = 6)	12.00% (n = 9)
To improve the current political situation	18.42% (n = 14)	15.58% (n = 12)	18.67% (n = 14)
To change current public policies	7.90% (n = 6)	23.38% (n = 18)	4.00% (n = 3)
Other	19.74% (n = 15)	0.00% (n = 0)	6.67% (n = 5)

Source: The Authors' Original data on a Cross-sectional SNS Study Collected Between October 2011 and April 2012 (n = 138).

Table 9.8 Social Media Gratifications of Political SNS Users

	STATE COLOR		
ACHIEVEMENTS	RED	PURPLE	BLUE
Change government and policies	35.09% (n = 20)	30.26% (n = 23)	23.53% (n = 12)
Distribute my voice and share opinion & educate others	35.09% (n = 20)	53.95% (n = 41)	43.14% (n = 22)
Learn political information and educate myself	3.51% (n = 2)	0.00% (n = 0)	5.88% (n = 3)
Gain my personal interests	0.00% (n = 0)	7.90% (n = 6)	0.00% (n = 0)
None/No achievement	26.32% (n = 15)	7.90% (n = 6)	27.45% (n = 14)

Source: The Authors' Original Data on a Cross-sectional SNS Study Collected Between October 2011 and April 2012 (n = 138).

to change current government and policies, and individuals in purple states were more likely to say they shared their opinion and educated others (53.9%). Interestingly, more than a quarter of the politically active SNS users in blue (27.5%) and red (26.3%) states said they had nothing to achieve, implying a heightened level of disappointment regarding the outcomes of sharing their political opinions and activities on SNSs, $\chi^2 = 24.89, p = .002$ (see Table 9.8).

DISCUSSION

This study offers insight into the political utilization of social media and its consequences on the political perceptions, attitudes, and behaviors of politically engaged social media users. The results were filtered through the lens of ideology, and, not surprisingly, cultural and partisan factors helped to predict certain patterns. Politically engaged individuals in swing (purple) states were more likely to post their opinions to SNSs and more likely to feel that they can be influenced and influence others by this activity. Political SNS users in battleground states tended to be more interested in politics, have a greater sense of political information efficacy, a heightened cynicism toward the political system and its leaders, and perceive higher mainstream media bias against their political views than political SNS users in non-battleground states. These findings are reinforced by the fact that the politically active SNS users in battleground states believed that they achieved their primary goals of distributing their political opinion and educating others. In contrast, over a quarter of politically active SNS users in non-battleground states were disappointed by the prospects of their activities on SNSs; saying that nothing was or would be achieved by the use of social media.

The results provided here extend the findings of previous studies demonstrating that people in battleground states who are surrounded by mixed partisan climates and exposed to larger amounts of strategic campaign messages (e.g., negative advertising, campaign events) were more politically active, analytical and critical, attentive to new political information, and open and positive to political changes than people in partisan, non-battleground states with limited and selective political exposure (Benoit et al., 2001; Druckman, 2004; Semetko, 2004; Wolak, 2006; Wright, 1998; Yun et al., 2010). The implication is clear: political usage of SNSs in campaigns and elections is more effective and influential in battleground states than non-battleground states.

As in earlier surveys, there was evidence that politically engaged SNS users tended toward a more selective exposure to information. This was especially true for politically moderate and liberal individuals. Liberals, in particular, indicated a preference to retreat into "enclaves of communication." When asked "What is the main reason you are politically active via social networking sites?" the number one reason liberals offered was "to share my political views with people who have similar views." Politically engaged SNS users in liberal circumstances were more trusting of information and people on SNSs than their counterparts in politically neutral or conservative climates. However, when political SNS users in blue states disagreed with friends or other SNS members they were more reluctant than individuals in red or purple states to express their political views in both online and in-person discussions.

In-group identity theory, the theory of the spiral of silence and the related concept of thin social skins may help to explain such reticence (Eagly & Chaiken, 1993; Noelle-Neumann, 1993; Prislin & Wood, 2005). Broadly stated, these theories hold that people who believe that they share a strong political in-group identity with like-minded individuals become attached to their in-group (Turner, 1991) and, as a result, are reluctant to disagree with other members (Noelle-Neumann, 1993; Oshagan, 1996). While this tendency may enhance the homogenous voice among people who share in the group's identity (Turner, 1991), it can alienate and frustrate individuals with opposing views (Eagly & Chaiken, 1993). It is possible that this pattern of behavior first observed in face-to-face groups is now being replicated online; politically active liberals who use SNSs feel highly connected to their like-minded friends, and this sentiment allows them to trust information and people within their circles and makes them more sensitive to other voices within the group.

SNS users in blue states also tended to believe that the mainstream media was supportive of their political views, while people who were politically active on SNSs in conservative states felt that the American public supported their political views. This is yet another instance where a well-known pattern in legacy media is being replicated online. The hostile media phenomenon holds that individuals attending to mainstream media reports focus on the negative coverage of their political views as opposed to the positive coverage. This tendency foments the perception of media bias and, in the U.S., supports the familiar lament among political conservatives that the American mass media is liberal (Dalton, Beck, & Huckfeldt, 1998; Eveland & Shah, 2003). Moreover, political discussion tends to be more cynical rather than supportive and political leaders are always the target of political humor and criticism (Paletz, 2001). The incumbent Democratic president may have created the circumstances for a more negative political discussion targeting the current administration and Democrats, and thus the public perceived the inverse political mood that sounds more supportive of the opposition party. These perceptions can be more prevalent among people who interact with like-minded people within a social and political unity and group (Turner, 1991), just like politically active SNS users who exchange their political views with other friends and members of their SNSs.

While the SNS users in liberal or moderate political environments tended to participate in political discussions and activities on SNSs primarily to distribute and share their political views, and the SNS users in battleground states expressed a strong desire to "change current public policy," there was no dominant political purpose of SNS users in politically conservative climates. The political conservatives and liberals in non-battleground states tended to be more pessimistic about the effects of their online participation. This pattern suggests that the political usage of SNSs is more purposive in purple states than red and blue states (Moy, Pfau, & Kahlor, 1999).

Although the potential economic, social, and political impacts of SNSs are unlimited, the practical and theoretical outcomes and results are, as of yet, not well established. Therefore, it is too soon to generalize about the political role and function of SNSs. This study, however, makes a modest contribution to the construction of theoretical approaches and frameworks in SNSs' political utilizations upon which future studies may build.

CHAPTER 10

YouTube/OurTube/TheirTube: Official and Unofficial Online Campaign Advertising, Negativity, and Popularity

Jacob Groshek and Stephanie Brookes

YouTube is one of the most-used Web siteWeb sites in the world—in 2012, it ranked only behind Google and Facebook—and is the leading video-sharing Web site (Fitzgerald, 2012). With the slogan *Broadcast Yourself*, YouTube's 2005 launch promised users who registered the ability to create and share their own videos, and to comment on and share videos uploaded by others. Initially seen as primarily a source of entertainment, a space to watch music videos or movie clips and to share personal video blogs (vlogs) or mash-ups, YouTube has increasingly become populated with news and political videos that can prove influential in elections.

In the 2006 mid-term election cycle, for example, the "viral" spread of Virginian Senator George Allen's now-infamous "macaca moment" footage was seen as signaling the YouTube's potential capacity to shape campaign agendas and sway voters. This understanding seemed to be cemented in 2008, when YouTube's *YouChoose'08* was launched as central hub for political and election-related videos. The Obama campaign, alone, posted more than 1,900 ads to YouTube during 2008 (according to Ridout & colleagues' (2010) categorization); this output was augmented by enormously popular third-party videos, such as the celebrity-infused, will.i.am "Yes We Can" music video.

In the 2012 presidential election, the YouTube *Election Hub* (launched in August 2012) again provided a central place for users to find political news and other election videos, and also allowed citizens to browse or search for campaign and candidate-sponsored videos. However, the launch of *Election Hub* came after more than a year after the Republican primaries had begun. While YouTube hosted political debate and discussion during the general election, it also enabled the Republican primary candidates to share and upload political advertisements, speeches and other videos, and offered President Barack Obama, who was running uncontested in the Democratic primaries, a platform through which to communicate his re-election message with voters.

This chapter thus examines political advertising on YouTube during the 2012 primaries, undertaking an analysis of key features such as negativity, popularity, and content producers.

SOCIAL MEDIA, ELECTION CAMPAIGNS, AND POLITICAL ADVERTISING

The relationship between media coverage, technology, and election campaigns has been a source of interest for researchers across numerous disciplines, ranging from political science, media and communications, and history to linguistics and behavioral studies. The emergence of a "new" technology or innovation often sparks a wave of research that reconsiders both the form and content of political communication on the new medium and its potential effects on electoral outcomes, voter mobilization and efficacy, and the democratic system. The introduction of television, for example, prompted many studies, across disciplines, that assessed the impact of this new format on politics and campaigns.

As social and digital media technologies became increasingly ubiquitous in the first decade of the 21st century, academic and journalistic attention turned to examining whether these new communication channels might contribute to a recasting of the relationship between government, political parties and candidates, the media and citizens (e.g., Meyer, 2012; Parker, 2012). Participatory or "Web 2.0" technologies seemed to promise new kinds of political messages and interactions. Here (argued the cyber-optimists), increasingly inexpensive and easy-to-use technologies would unsettle monopolies over content production and distribution, blurring the lines between "producer" and "consumer" and making a new participatory media politics possible.

In this context, scholarly considerations of "online" political communication have explored the ability of citizens to connect and interact through social and other digital media (Papacharissi, 2009, 2010); while election-specific research increasingly considers the role and impact of these new media technologies (Williams & Tedesco, 2006). The most recent research shifts from an interest in campaign and candidate Web sites (Xenos & Bennett, 2007; Foot & Schneider, 2008; Schneider & Foot, 2006) to examine the ways that widespread social media might impact on campaign agendas, voter engagement and efficacy, and election outcomes (e.g., Shah et al., 2007). In an early study of YouTube and MySpace in the 2006 elections, Gueorguieva (2008) noted that "no research has been conducted on the use and impact of online social networks on election campaigns," due to the rapid and recent rise of these networks (p. 298).

The years since have seen a dramatic increase in attention to these technologies, especially in light of their prominence in the 2008 and 2010 election cycles (Lilleker & Jackson, 2011). This finding is evident in the recent publication of collections on "new media" in campaigns, and in the inclusion of studies of social and participatory media in edited works assessing campaigns more broadly (Hendricks & Kaid, 2011; Hendricks & Denton, 2010; Sabato, 2010; Panagopolous, 2009).

In this emerging field, attention has been paid to social networking sites (SNSs) such as Facebook and MySpace (Bode, 2012; Woolley et al., 2010; Baumgartner & Morris, 2010b), weblogs ('blogs') (Fung, Vraga, & Thorson, 2011; Snow, 2010), microblogs such as Twitter (Ancu, 2011; Solop, 2010), and video-sharing Web sites such as YouTube (Hanson, Haridakis, Cunningham, Sharma, & Parma, 2010; Powell, 2010).

YOUTUBE AND THE ONLINE CAMPAIGN

Within these studies of social and participatory media, a strand of research focuses specifically on video-sharing Web site YouTube, which has established itself as a significant player in the broader mediated campaign landscape. Researchers have pointed to its popularity as the most-used video-sharing Web site in the world, and the emerging political and journalistic consensus about the potential of online videos to influence politics and campaigns (Basulto, 2012; Wilson, 2012) as compelling more systematic scholarly attention. In particular, YouTube's emphasis on user-generated content has been a focus of early examinations of the rising popularity and influence of this open communication space (van Dijck, 2009; Burgess & Green, 2009), while attention has also been paid to its increasing embrace by political and corporate interests (May, 2010).

A wave of scholarly interest has accompanied YouTube's rising political prominence following the 2006 election cycle (the first after YouTube's 2005 launch), both internationally (Chen & Walsh, 2010; Carlson & Strandberg, 2008; Kalnes, 2009; Lev-On, 2012; Salmond, 2008) and in the United States. In 2010, a "YouTube and the 2008 Election Cycle" edition of the *Journal of Information Technology and Politics* confirmed that studies of YouTube had become a vital component of campaign research, alone and as part of broader considerations of the mediatized campaign environment. The concerns of the papers collected in that volume—how candidates use YouTube; the effects of YouTube on campaign outcomes and on democratic engagement and participation; the interactive trajectories of YouTube videos; and questions of methodology and approach to studying YouTube—provide a useful indicator of the emerging concerns of work in this field more broadly.

Research into the voices engaging in YouTube politics has identified that the video-sharing channel is being used extensively by "official" and institutional political actors, such as campaigns and candidates (Gulati & Williams, 2009; Davisson, 2009; Gueorguieva, 2008), to communicate with voters, fundraise, and mobilize supporters. This is supported by Dylko and colleagues (2011) who found, in a content analysis of political news content on YouTube, that the most popular videos tend to be created by or feature "elites," or consist of traditional news content. However, other studies have highlighted that influential content often comes from beyond political parties and candidates, and have explored genres such as political documentaries (Musser, 2009) and online spoofs and parodies (Tyron, 2008) created by "unofficial" users.

Emerging understandings of who is using YouTube to create, view or comment on videos, are further deepened by research into how and why it is used: for entertainment, for getting information about politics (Smith & Duggan, 2012), and as a "time-shifting" device for traditional media content (Hanson et al., 2010).

Political videos on YouTube have been analyzed with particular interest in YouTube's potential effect on campaigns (Karpf, 2010) and voters (Bal, Campbell, Payne, & Pitt, 2010; Davisson, 2009; English, Sweetser, & Ancu, 2011; Towner & Dulio, 2011b). The influence on young people's engagement with, knowledge of, and feelings about politics (Hanson et al., 2010; Towner & Dulio, 2010, 2011a) has also been a notable line of study. Researchers have reported mixed findings, reflecting patterns in political communications research more broadly. Some studies challenged common-sense assumptions about YouTube's ability to stimulate political engagement.

For example, Baumgartner and Morris (2010a) found that users of social media sites were no more likely to be politically active than users of other media. Likewise, McKinney and Rill (2009) observed that the CNN/YouTube debates were no more effective at stimulating youth engagement than a traditional general-election presidential debate. However, Ricke's (2010) analysis of voter questions submitted for the debates found that they did "provide an alternative method for political participation" (p. 211), while Schill and Kirk (2011) have positioned the YouTube debates as a "digital agora" that was both deliberative and participatory.

A smaller but equally important strand of research has analyzed the content of campaign videos on YouTube. In particular, scholars have examined the rhetorical and discursive strategies used by candidates in their videos (Church, 2010; Davisson, 2009; Duman & Locher, 2008); while others have analyzed content from both official and unofficial political sources (Hess, 2010). Despite this growing attention to how candidates, voters and other political actors are engaging with YouTube, and the effects of this use, political advertising on YouTube remains under-researched.

YOUTUBE AND CAMPAIGN ADVERTISING

A small, but vibrant, body of research is emerging in U.S. political science and communication that focuses on political advertisements on YouTube. These studies have considered each campaign cycle since 2006, extending both the concerns of new literature on social and digital media in campaigns and traditional political advertising literature. A limited number have focused specifically on campaign advertisements (de Boer et al., 2012; Ridout, Fowler, & Branstetter, 2010, 2012; Salmond, 2008, 2012). Other studies have considered YouTube ads alongside other genres of campaign videos (Cortese & Proffitt, 2012; Klotz, 2010) or as part of analyses of online political advertising more broadly (Cornfield & Kaye, 2009). Ridout and colleagues (2012) position YouTube as an ideal venue through which to understand the content and reach of new advertising forms:

> [YouTube is] a dialogic environment in which voters can and do contest the messages of the campaigns by producing their own videos to communicate directly with other voters. Individuals or other non-campaign groups routinely re-mix and subvert the messages of the campaigns, therefore radically altering the advertising landscape (p. 2).

This perspective speaks to the key concern emerging in scholarly considerations of political advertisements on YouTube; that YouTube is an interactive and open space, in which the participation of voters and other non-campaign groups may influence the campaign agenda and communication environment. In this way, studies of YouTube advertising ask questions about "Web 2.0" communication at the same time as they draw on the concerns of research into political advertising, both traditional (Diamond & Bates, 1992; Kaid & Johnston, 2000; McNair, 2011) and online (Cornfield & Kaye, 2009; Kaid, 2006). Here, exploration of the content and effects of campaign advertising—and in particular, the rise and intensification of negative or "attack" advertising (Ansolabehere & Iyengar, 1995; Geer, 2006; Johnson-Cartee & Copeland, 1991)—has been prominent.

Studies of political advertisements on YouTube extend these concerns, and often seek both to examine distinctive features of political advertising in a social media environment, and also to test the style, content and effects of YouTube ads against their more traditional counterparts (Kaid & Postelnicu, 2005; Salmond, 2012). Questions of content and production are central here, as studies seek to explore notions that participatory media spaces online would democratize conditions of production, distribution and dialogue—allowing for new genres, producers and responses to political advertising.

The possibility for new styles of campaign communication to emerge in online video-sharing is a focus of research into political ads on YouTube. A key concern here is whether campaign ads uploaded to YouTube are designed specifically for that space, as "web-only" or "web-first" content, or whether they are "repurposed" ads originally intended for television. While cyber-optimists emphasized the potential development of new web-based content styles, Cortese and Proffitt (2012) noted that early research has found most election videos on YouTube are "traditional television advertisements or national television program segments" (p. 694).

More recently, in a systematic study of major-party Senate candidates' YouTube presence, Klotz (2010) found that "repurposed 30-second television ads" dominated the most popular political videos, accounting for more than half of the top 12 videos in 2006 and three-quarters in 2008 (p. 116). Despite this finding, Klotz (2010) went on to argue that the video-sharing Web site still acted "as a repository for ads produced by candidates and parties" (p. 122), making them accessible nationwide. In a fragmented media market, where careful targeting means that some television ads are designed and broadcast only in specific areas (such as battleground states), YouTube allows voters to hold candidates accountable for their advertising beyond the borders of particular local and regional media markets.

These findings highlight a related strand of inquiry concerning the producers of political advertisements on YouTube. Towner and Dulio's (2012) warning that YouTube can be "dangerous" for campaigns because it is driven by "user-generated" or "unmediated content" is representative of this view (pp. 98–99). While the campaigns use YouTube extensively to post advertisements and other videos, "anyone else with a video camera" can also be a content creator, thereby challenging party and mainstream media dominance of campaign agendas. However, there has been little empirical mapping of content creators on YouTube, which looks not just at the extent to which "official" content is posted by candidates and parties, but also considers the extent to which "unofficial" ads are posted by independent or third-party groups (such as PACs and lobby groups) or individual citizens. Where this has been examined, Ridout and colleagues (2010) found that more than 93% of YouTube ads in their sample from the 2008 campaign were candidate-sponsored, while less than 2% were sponsored by interest groups or citizens.

Similarly, there has been limited systematic analysis of the content of political advertising on YouTube; however, questions of valence are emerging as central in the latest studies (Cortese & Proffitt, 2012; de Boer et al., 2012; Klotz, 2010). For some, the task of quantifying positive and negative content is closely linked to measures of "popularity" and voter engagement. As data is emerging about how voters share and respond to online videos (Smith & Duggan, 2012), some researchers are exploring the relationship between the negativity of online ads and their success in sparking responses (Klotz, 2010).

Cortese and Proffitt (2012) measured levels of user interaction against tone in YouTube videos posted by the McCain and Obama campaigns in 2008, finding that the McCain campaign posted significantly more negative videos than Obama and received more interactions. In addition, across the campaigns: "significantly, more people viewed, rated, made text comments on and created video responses for the negative videos compared to the other three types (positive, both and neither), yet the negative videos were rated significantly lower than the other three" (Cortese & Proffitt, 2012, p. 695).

While negative YouTube videos were more likely to promote participation, the "buzz" created by them did not mean they were "well-liked." Similarly, Ridout and colleagues' (2012) analysis of political advertising on YouTube in Senate races in 2010 found that "negative ads are particularly popular" (p. 14), generating more than half of viewership despite representing one-third of online advertising content, but did not measure voters' reactions to or feelings about these negative ads.

These participatory elements are positioned as central to YouTube's position in a "new media" landscape characterized by the potential for interactivity in the form of sharing, liking and commenting on videos, or even for political "video-exchange" (Duman & Locher, 2008). However, further research on the ability of political advertising (and other genres of political video) on YouTube to spark these interactions is needed (Holbert & Geidner, 2009). While there have been attempts to track the social media trajectories of online viral videos, such as the 2008 will.i.am "Yes We Can" clip (Vernallis, 2011; Wallsten, 2010), more attention is required to understand voters' interactions with political ads on YouTube, situated within a broader emerging field that is developing new research questions and approaches to social and participatory media (Towner & Dulio, 2012).

This chapter aims to explore some of these new questions through an analysis of YouTube political advertising during the primary stage of the 2012 presidential campaign. It links the valence of YouTube ads with the particular nature of attacks (personal or issue-based) and explores party differences and popularity. Specifically, this chapter poses and examines the following research questions:

RQ1(a): Which candidate had the most negative online campaign advertising, and
(b) which party featured more negative campaign ads?

RQ2: Were negative ads online more frequently viewed, liked, disliked, commented, and favorited than positive campaign ads?

RQ3(a): Were there differences in online ads that attacked different parties, and
(b) ads that focused on issue or personal characteristics?

RQ4: How did official online advertising compare to unofficial online advertising in terms of negativity and popularity?

METHODS

A sample of political advertisements comprised of both official YouTube channels as well as unofficial videos was found through key search terms. The sample was constructed of videos available online in mid-March 2012, and included videos from May 19, 2011, through March 13, 2012. Though this time frame does not include the entire election cycle, it does provide a lengthy examination of primary election campaigning, and notably includes the run-up to several caucuses and primaries in states that are crucial to determining the eventual presidential candidates.

Official Advertising on YouTube

In this study, "official" advertisements were those collected from the official YouTube channels of the leading Republican candidates at the time of sampling during the 2012 presidential campaign. Specifically, these channels were those of Newt Gingrich, Ron Paul, Mitt Romney, and Rick Santorum. Also included was the official YouTube channel of incumbent Democratic candidate Barack Obama. Videos were prioritized by number of views to ensure that the advertisements online most likely to be seen were incorporated into analyses. In addition, these ads were selected on the basis that one or more negative statements and/or images were present in some form of attack, comparison, or criticism.

All of the videos considered as official with this sampling procedure were either sponsored or authorized by the presidential candidate that was being promoted in each respective ad. Altogether, this produced the following breakdown of 55 official ads that were considered from each candidate's official YouTube channel: Newt Gingrich ($N = 10$), Ron Paul ($N = 14$), Mitt Romney ($N = 11$), Rick Santorum ($N = 11$), and Barack Obama ($N = 9$).

Searching Advertising on YouTube

To examine online campaign advertising more comprehensively, and outside of only officially-endorsed channels, a separate sampling technique was applied using key search terms and resulted in 18 separate ads (24.7% of the total sample). For purposes of this study, YouTube was searched with the phrases "attack advertisement president 2012" and "elections attack advertisement 2012." Much like the process of sampling the official YouTube channels, these videos were sorted by view frequency to be certain that the most prominent political advertisements that also had some negative or attack component were selected.

Duplicates of videos already present in the sample of official YouTube channels were not double-counted, and it is worth noting some professional ads sponsored by candidates that had already left the race by mid-March 2012 were drawn into this sample. In other words, in these cases and some others, not all searched videos were necessarily "unofficial" videos, as that distinction was measured by who produced an ad and whether or not it was endorsed by a candidate as being representative of their views.

Variable Categories

The codebook of Geer (2006) on attack ads in televised presidential campaigns was adapted for this study, along with some components of the Kaid and Johnston (2006) codebook for televised political advertising. Non-interpretative features included the date of upload, length in seconds, number of views, comments, likes, dislikes, and number of favorites, as well as which candidate was endorsed in the ad and if it was official or unofficial. Other interpretative aspects were categorized, and these included the overall tone, the number of negative statements and images per ad, the number of positive statements and images per ad, the format, who or what was being targeted, and whether an attack was based on issues or personal characteristics.

Following the work of Geer (2006), the overall tone was determined to be "negative," "neutral," or "positive" by one primary coder. Her level of agreement for this item, when controlling for chance in a randomly selected 15 videos (20.55% of the sample), was 0.89 when calculated with Cohen's Kappa against a second coder working independently.

More specific measures of negativity and positivity were measured by counting the number of negative and positive verbal (spoken) statements per ad along with evaluative (negative or positive) visuals. Recurrent statements and visuals were counted at every instance. Thus, the determination of the level of negativity and positivity was a cumulative figure based on frequency (i.e., recurrence or repetitiveness) instead of intensity (i.e., highly aggressive or offensive statements). In these cases, Kappa $= 0.77$ for intercoder agreement on negativity levels for both statements and visuals.

A composite positive/negative index was constructed by subtracting the total number of negative images and statements per ad from the total number of positive images and statements per ad. The range of this index was from -26 (most negative) to $+24$ (most positive), with a mean of -4.14 and standard deviation of 9.52 (skewness and kurtosis were within acceptable levels for normal distributions).

The categories of which candidate was being promoted and which candidate(s) were being targeted showed perfect agreement (Kappa $= 1.0$) and nearly perfect agreement (Kappa $= 0.91$), respectively. Coding options for these variables included all candidates' names as well as several combined options, such as "multiple

Republicans," "multiple Democrats," or "Washington in general." The nature of how opponents were being attacked in ads was also measured on the basis of personal characteristics or issue stands—or a combination of both types of attacks (Kappa = 0.84).

The last subjective variable coded in this study measured which actor(s) produced each video, regardless of whether they were found on official YouTube channels or through search terms. Categories here included officially sponsored ads that were endorsed by a candidate (and that were professionally produced by the campaign) as well as an option for having been produced by an (amateur) individual or interest group. It is worth noting that the boundary between "professional" and "non-professional" media creators was often blurred by the often comparable production quality of the ads, so the distinction of "official" versus "unofficial" advertising here is based explicitly on whether or not an ad was produced or sponsored by a candidate or if it was created by a third-party individual or organization. Kappa for this item demonstrated full agreement.

FINDINGS

This study analyzed a total of 73 presidential campaign ads that were featured on YouTube across a nearly year-long period that covered a good portion of a strongly contested Republican primary. Fifty-five of these ads were ads sampled from the official YouTube channel of a candidate that was still running at the time of data collection (mid-March 2012), and another 18 ads were found using key search terms useful to finding ads relevant to the 2012 election. Both officially-endorsed campaign ads and unofficial ads created by a third-party individual or organization were filtered by frequency of views to purposefully gather the most watched negative ads.

Before analyzing ads by candidates, parties, or negativity and positivity, some general trends can be observed. There were 331,575.93 (SD = 981,285.06) views per ad on average, along with a mean of 1,174.22 comments (SD = 3,328.06) and a mean of 311.19 "favorites" per ad (SD = 657.10). The average number of "likes" (M = 2,347.11, SD = 4719.28) was considerably less than "dislikes" (M = 10,945.79, SD = 89,349.22), with one Rick Perry ad in particular being disliked more than 8.2 million times.

When looking at these distributions across candidates, there were a number of interesting similarities and differences. To begin, the overall positive/negative index was not statistically significant ($F(5, 72)$ = 1.57, p = .181) when examined with a joint analysis of variance (ANOVA) across all candidates. In an overall assessment of negativity it is also worth noting that Tukey post–hoc tests did not identify any statistically significant pairwise differences amongst candidates as well. So while it is useful to note that Ron Paul proved to be the most negative in his YouTube advertising with an average of −7.83 (SD = 10.52), this level of combined negative images and statements subtracted from all positive images and statements was not significantly greater than that of the most positive online advertising campaign of Barack Obama (M = −0.70, SD = 9.11) that was considered here.

Though this finding suggests candidates were, overall, not differentiated on the basis of their overall negative/positive measure, the popularity of videos online also needs to be considered in relation to both factors of candidates and their levels of negativity. Starting here with only candidate-sponsored videos, the number of user comments was statistically significant across candidates ($F(5, 72) = 3.54$, $p = .007$), as was the number of ad likes ($F(5, 72) = 5.73, p = .000$), and ad favorites ($F(5, 72) = 4.81, p = .001$). Other features, namely the average number of views ($F(5, 72) = 1.22, p = .312$) and dislikes ($F(5, 72) = 1.13, p = .353$) across candidates were not statistically significant when examined with ANOVA.

Post-hoc Tukey tests indicated that Ron Paul generated significantly more comments than Mitt Romney, Rick Santorum, Newt Gingrich, and a collection of "other" candidates or organizations. The same finding was generally true of the number of audience-based liking and favoring, where Ron Paul videos were statistically greater than pairwise comparisons to the YouTube advertising of Mitt Romney, Rick Santorum, Newt Gingrich, and Barack Obama. Interestingly, these findings signal that the Ron Paul campaign was notable for not only being the most negative (albeit not to a statistically significant degree) but also for being, on average, the most commented on ($M = 3,767.67, SD = 5,896.63$), the most liked ($M = 6,622.28, SD = 5,341.51$), and the most favorited ($M = 861.22, 693.52$).

When looking more broadly at campaigning across party lines, there was not clear evidence that ads by or for Democrats were significantly more negative or positive than ads posted online that promoted Republican candidates ($t(71) = -0.93$, $p = .304$) when considered as a whole with the combined negative/positive measure. When negative images and statements per ad were isolated, however, it was observed that the Republican advertising had a significantly greater level of negativity ($t(26.91) = 2.07, p = .048$, equal variances not assumed), with an average of 11.44 negative images and statements per ad ($SD = 7.69$) compared to Democratic ads online ($M = 7.79$, $SD = 5.44$). Interestingly, though primary Republican ads on YouTube were not more viewed, on average, they did show mean levels of likes ($M = 2,688.61, SD = 5,174.29$) and favorites ($M = 358.71, SD = 717.50$) that were higher than Democratic ads to a statistically significant degree. For likes, the mean of Democratic ads was 907.93 ($SD = 1,068.07$) and ($t(70.55) = 2.43, p = .017$, equal variances not assumed) for favorites, the average for Democratic ads was 110.93 ($SD = 202.76$) with ($t(68.83) = 2.29, p = .025$, equal variances not assumed).

Negative ads, when compared only to positive ones (and not the three ads that were calculated to be perfectly neutral with equivalent numbers of negative and positive images and statements) where found to be significantly more viewed on average ($t(67.69) = 2.21, p = .031$, equal variances not assumed). The mean number of views for negative ads was 261,235.94 ($SD = 335,963.38$) compared to an average of 135,026.95 views ($SD =142,430.98$) for positive ads. Interestingly, ads that targeted the candidates from the right were most negative ($M = -6.83$, $SD = 9.49$) and significantly more so ($F(2, 72) = 3.40, p = .039$) than ads that feature attacks on the left ($M = -2.52, SD = 7.61$) and the political establishment or mainstream politics in general ($M = 0.14; SD = 10.83$) when considered jointly on the composite negative/positive index. Tukey post-hoc tests also indicated that attacks on the right were significantly more negative than attacks on mainstream politics ($p = 0.049$) in pairwise comparisons, but not ads that attacked the left ($p = 0.194$). No pairwise difference was observed between ads that attacked the left and mainstream politics (0.672).

When looking at whether ads focused on issues, personal characteristics, or a combination of the two, there was a statistically significant difference between these three groups ($F(2, 60) = 3.08$, $p = .054$). On average, issue-based attacks were the least negative ($M = -1.53$, $SD = 7.55$), followed by personal trait-based attack ads online ($M = -4.88$, $SD = 10.05$), and ads that combined both issue attacks and attacks on personal characteristics were the most negative ($M = -8.04$, $SD = 8.65$) when comparing averages of the composite negative/positive measure. Post-hoc Tukey tests indicated that in pairwise comparisons, only combined attack ads were significantly more negative than issue-only attacks ($p = 0.042$). Finally, online ads produced by third parties and not officially endorsed by candidates themselves were more negative, with an average of -8.50 ($SD = 6.17$) compared to official ads posted to YouTube, that had a mean negative/positive composite score of -3.45 ($SD = 9.64$), but this difference was only significant at the .10 level ($t(70) = 1.87$, $p = .066$).

One interesting intersection of these comparisons is where the level of negativity/positivity was measured against which actors produced online ads and who was attacked. This interaction approached statistical significance ($F(2,66) = 2.54$, $p = .087$, partial $\eta^2 = .071$, observed power $= .490$), and showed a main effect by official or unofficial ads ($F(1,66) = 6.21$, $p = .015$, partial $\eta^2 = .086$, observed power $= .690$). The divergence of how officially endorsed ads treated different parties is clear—they were most negative in their attacks on the right ($M = -7.58$, $SD = 9.70$), and increasingly less so on the left ($M = -1.67$, $SD = 7.02$) and actually quite positive in portraying establishment or mainstream politics ($M = 2.91$, $SD = 9.99$). This contrasted with ads created by third parties that actually were most positive in their attacks on the right ($M = -7.33$, $SD = 5.15$), most negative in attacking the left ($M = -11.50$, $SD = 10.61$), but still relatively negative in attacking mainstream "politics as usual" advertising ($M = -10.00$, $SD = 8.19$).

Finally, while the differences do not reach statistical significance, it is worth observing the average number of views per ad as they are situated across parties and whether they are negative or positive. Here, all ads that were below zero on the negative/positive composite measure were considered "negative" and all those ads above zero were considered "positive" ads. For Republican ads posted to YouTube, negative ads were most viewed, with 285,660.38 ($SD = 355,018.79$) views on average, whereas positive ads reached only 117,268.14 ($SD = 131,821.60$) mean views. Democratic ads, conversely, showed an average of just 133,007.63 ($SD = 171,768.55$) views for negative ads, which increased to an average of 176,464.17 ($SD = 170,192.49$) for positive ads. Again, while these differences should not be misconstrued as statistically significant, the pattern is indicative of more negative advertisements being more viewed for Republican candidates and Democrats' positive online ads being more viewed, relatively speaking.

DISCUSSION

This study intended to explore online campaign advertising as it existed in the primary season of the 2012 presidential campaign. A number of noticeable and significant differences were observed, as were several key similarities over the candidates, the parties, and the producers of online advertising, and the level of negativity or positivity found in ads posted to YouTube during this election.

To begin, when looking at RQ1a, it was clear that Ron Paul had the most negative online campaign advertising, but not to a statistically significant degree. Nonetheless, it is worth noting that Paul's online ads did generate significantly more comments, likes, and favorites than most other candidates. As to RQ1(b), ads that promoted Republican candidates were significantly more negative than ads supporting Democratic candidates, but only when comparing negative images and statements alone, and not on balance with overall levels of negativity and positivity. This finding aligns with Druckman and colleagues' (2010) observations in their multi-campaign survey of negativity on Congressional campaign Web sites that challengers would be more likely to be negative.

Also, Republican ads were significantly more liked and favorited, on average, when compared with Democratic ads, but not more viewed. This may reflect the contested nature of the Republican primary. Governor Romney did not win the nomination until August 2012 and the preceding campaign battle called on voters to engage with, and make a voting decision about, the candidates in the field. A more positive advertising style would, however, accord with a Democratic primary whose outcome was predetermined, and whose direct competitor was yet unknown.

Altogether, the results of RQ1 suggest in some ways that increased negativity, particularly on the part of Paul and Republicans more generally, was related to more interactions by the audience online. Unlike the Cortese and Proffitt (2012) findings on John McCain's online advertising in 2008, Paul seemingly was rewarded with the most comments, likes, and favorites by YouTube users. Perhaps this finding is reflective of the role that Paul played in the primary. Paul presented himself, in many ways, as an "outsider" candidate who was not representative of the mainstream of the Republican Party, and his libertarian positions were seen as more appealing to younger and anti-war voters. One possible explanation, therefore, is that his appeals matched well with those going online to YouTube in search of political information (or political entertainment).

Shah and colleagues (2007, p. 677) have noted the "mixed empirical evidence" afforded by studies into the effect of negative ads on political participation, pointing in particular to Geer's (2006) "defense of campaign negativity" as focusing voters on the central issues of the campaign. In this case, it may have been that Paul's aggressively negative campaigning was not demobilizing among this online audience but rather something many positioned as valid and worth commenting on, liking, and favoriting.

The results of examining RQ2 identified that negative ads online were more frequently viewed to a statistically significant degree than positive campaign ads.

It was also evident that online ads targeting candidates from the right were significantly more negative than ads that attacked the left or the political mainstream in general, which answered RQ3(a). The findings for RQ3(b) indicated that online ads that attacked candidates on issues were least negative, and those with combined issue and personal characteristic attacks were most negative. Ads that focused only on personal characteristics were almost exactly midway between these negativity levels, and the differences were statistically significant.

These findings raise interesting questions about the heightened negativity in combined attack ads. Perhaps as a strategy to avoid voter "backlash" against purely personal attacks, these combined ads allowed for an association between a candidate's personal characteristics and their political priorities and policies, thus possibly legitimizing the "negative" strategy. While purely personal attack ads may be off-putting and reflect poorly on the sponsoring candidate, an ad that incorporated policy elements might avoid or lessen this negative voter reaction; further research is needed to explore this proposition with greater detail.

Finally, when considering RQ4, official online advertising approached statistical significance (at $p = .066$) in being more negative than unofficial online advertising. In addition, there was an interaction that also approached statistical significance between media producers, level of negativity, and who was attacked. These findings signal the different tactics that were employed by third parties in attacking different parties in the campaign, and contribute to a deeper understanding of this otherwise under-explored area of unofficial ads both online and on television (see Brooks & Murov, 2012; Cheng & Riffe, 2008).

"Official" advertising posted online seemed to have implicitly reinforced mainstream politics while simultaneously most aggressively attacking Republican candidates, indicating a certain level of in-fighting amongst primary candidates. Conversely, "unofficial" ads were most critical of Barack Obama or other Democratic positions in general, along with negatively portraying the political establishment. This fracture suggests the augmented capacity for third-party advertising to re-order an election campaign, and there was no statistically significant difference in the average number of views of official and unofficial ads online ($t(70) = 0.26$, $p = .794$).

These findings indicate that the nearly one-quarter of ads in the sample from "unofficial" sources (a similar finding to Klotz (2010)'s proportion of "non-traditional" content producers) may have been focusing on the general campaign battle to come. In critiquing the President, his party and the "establishment" in Washington, a "time for change" message can be developed which places these negative ads into a broader political narrative. However, the sample remains dominated by "official" campaign ads, supporting previous research which has found that while YouTube offers *possibilities* for exchange and interaction, this happens mostly at the level of commenting on or sharing existing videos; ultimately the "number of truly independent videos is very small" (Klotz, 2010, p. 118) and "underlying" campaign dynamics have not been dramatically altered (Gulati & Williams, 2010, p. 106). While new producers are engaging and the campaigns and candidates are not the only (or perhaps even the dominant) voices on YouTube, political ads for the most part are being produced and uploaded by "professional" third parties rather than ordinary citizens.

Also suggested by RQ4, in terms of popularity, though the results did not achieve statistical significance, negative ads that endorsed Republicans were most viewed, on average. Amongst Democratic ads, positive ads were viewed more frequently than negative ads. Here, we can begin to draw out the links between the positive or negative tone of an advertisement and its viewing frequency. Ridout and colleagues (2012) position YouTube as a "dialogic environment" where voters "can and do contest the messages of the campaigns by producing their own videos to communicate directly with other voters" (p. 12). However, as can be observed here, this activity is not the only measure of interaction and communication between campaigns, candidates and voters on YouTube. In watching, commenting on and favoriting political ads, voters are contributing to a dynamic space where dialogue and exchange does occur, despite this being predominantly around official rather than unofficial content.

Of course, the nature of a primary campaign almost certainly had an influence on the results, and some of this advertising was about candidates from within the same party distinguishing themselves from other members of their own party rather than attacking someone from the opposition. In this regard, Obama did not have an "opposition" in the immediate sense, and so Democratic ads online could politically afford to have been more positive. Republican candidates were all "challengers" in a sense in the study of YouTube campaigning considered here and were battling for the chance to go up against the incumbent, and thus positioning themselves for a different end game.

Altogether, online advertising in the primary season of the 2012 election campaign was fairly reflective of similar findings from previous studies of traditional (televised) campaign advertising. To some extent, the patterns observed here may well indicate the normalization and embeddedness that YouTube has taken on in political campaigning. While the user benefits and the interactive options such advertising affords should surely not be discounted, they are by and large no longer "new." Thus, it is only reasonable now to situate YouTube as a permanent fixture in elections, but only as just another mediated space among many that can and does contribute to the defining features and outcomes of elections.

CHAPTER 11

The Spirals of Newly Transcending Political Voices: Social Media Purify the Atmosphere of Political Dialogues in Cyberspace

Hyun Jung Yun

According to *Wall Street Journal* analysts, social media were the fuel and engine of the Tea Party movement that became a national political phenomenon and dominated other political movements and activities in the public sphere during the 2010 midterm campaign and election (Blackmon, Levitz, Berzon, & Etter, 2010). Social media have become unavoidable channels for political communication in today's campaigns and elections. Of social media users, 66% engage in political activities and 21% belong to political or social groups on social networking sites (SNSs) that are involved in issue-oriented communications across the ideological, partisan sphere. (Rainie, Smith, Schlozman, Brady, & Verba, 2012, pp. 1–3). In surveys, 36% of SNS users said that SNSs are important in keeping up with political news and 25% responded that they use SNSs to discuss political issues and find others who share their views about political issues (Rainie & Smith, 2012).

In order to explore the political power of social media, such as Facebook and Twitter, in American politics and campaigns, the current study compares four different types of political participants who utilize social media to different degrees and with different purposes: (a) political party and civic group members who use social media for political mobilization and issue-driving under their group banner and structure; (b) politically engaged independent individuals who participate in various political discussions and forums on SNSs based on their individual values and motivations without political group affiliation; (c) politically engaged members of political or civic groups who participate in the political arena solely through traditional venues such as face-to-face meetings or writing letters to politicians; and (d) politically active independent citizens without any political group affiliation who utilize only traditional participatory methods.

Specifically, during the early campaign season of the 2012 presidential election, this study explored the demographics, political attitudes and perceptions, and opinion expression patterns of these four different categories of the politically active Americans in order to examine whether the new Internet-based communication applications of social media work as "purifying systems" that clean up the atmosphere of online political discourses, leading to a more transparent participatory democracy, and whether political group identities and reference group pressures are still important mediators for political participation in cyberspace. This study found that social media help politically underrepresented social minorities express their political views in fragmented forms and provide a digital space for political discussion in which those political outsiders can be free from any political and social constraints in their political expression.

THEORETICAL UNDERPINNINGS

Political Mavericks in Social Media

Social media are channels and platforms that provide political and social minority mavericks the opportunity to raise their political voices in the public arena. These political and social minority mavericks are independent of, often isolated from, and underrepresented in mainstream politics. Young voters, females, ethnic minorities, and third-party members (such as Green Party candidates) are more likely to utilize social media as a primary channel to express their views rather than are older citizens, males, Whites, and prominent political party or group members such as Republicans and Democrats (Brenner, 2012; Davis, 1999; Rainie & Smith, 2012). For this reason, since the 2008 American presidential campaign, social media have been rigorously adopted by politicians and governments in American politics as a channel to reach out to the aforementioned social minorities (Hayes, 2009). An even greater level of social media usage was continued throughout the 2012 presidential campaign (Rainie & Smith, 2012).

As the use of social media matures, social media have become important channels in raising political voices for political outsiders who used to be politically isolated from mainstream politics or who remained silent because limited resources prevented their entry into the traditional political arena (Kushin & Kitchener, 2009). In the context of political discussions in social media, people value individual political expression and respect diversity (Gueorguieva, 2006), and the tolerant, autonomous, and anonymous communication culture of the Internet encourages various political voices from various independent individuals and groups (Kushin & Kitchener, 2009).

Political scholars have predicted that the Internet and the Internet-based communication applications of social media will contribute to a democratic civic society by providing channels for politically underrepresented social minorities to participate in politics (Wojcieszak & Mutz, 2009). According to Papacharissi (2002) and Dahlberg (2007), Internet-based political communication can nurture grassroots democracy and encourage broader political participation across geopolitical boundaries and historical societal barriers. In political discussion in cyberspace, individual voices and crosscutting viewpoints, regardless of demographic backgrounds or partisanship, can be equally heard (Kim, 2011).

Socially marginalized members, such as African Americans and females, have adopted a nontraditional medium, the Internet, and this digital adoption has empowered these groups within society (Mehra, Merkel, & Bishop, 2004; Morahan-Martin, 2000). Other empirical studies found that more than one-fourth of young Americans utilize some form of social media to express their political views online, such as by posting political messages on their SNSs or commenting on others' walls about political issues (Vitak et al., 2011). Minority political party members were more likely to use the Internet and the Internet-based interactive communication channel of social media to convey their political platforms and issue stances as campaign promises to the public (Brenner, 2012; Gulati & Williams, 2010; Holt, 2004). These political and social minorities can not only learn about politics but also express their interests and views through social media (Brenner, 2012). Those politically active social minorities who are often alienated from mainstream politics are still very optimistic about their power to change politics via online political communication (Rainie & Smith, 2012). Those politically well-informed and engaged individuals who used to be political and social minorities in traditional offline politics would be less likely to remain silent in political discussions online (Dahlgren, 2005).

Crosscutting Spirals of Expression in the Political Grounds of Social Media

Unlike the theory of Spiral of Silence, which argued that only one spiral of dominant opinion can be heard and be prevalent, we can hear a greater number of independent, often isolated voices, just like multiple spirals of opinions crosscutting each other's views when we are on SNSs. Approximately four decades ago, Elisabeth Noelle-Neumann (1974) formulated a theory of public opinion expression called the *Spiral of Silence* which posits that individuals observe the external opinion environment and adhere to majority ideas to avoid isolation from the surrounding group. The theory further argues that individuals who found their personal opinions supported by the majority will be willing to express their own opinion, while individuals who perceive the majority in disagreement with their own views will be silent. Because those holding minority viewpoints feel reluctant to publicly express their views, others holding similar minority views will also remain silent, resulting in a "spiral of silence" where minority viewpoints and expression are silenced.

However, this political expression pattern seems a bit troublesome to fit in the new online deliberation space because this communicative context lacks a physical presence, and has less opinion conformity pressure due to the autonomy, anonymity, and tolerance of online discussion cultures. Social media users who participate in political discussions on SNSs tend to be more aggressive toward dissenting opinions due to the anonymous and autonomous nature of online contexts and more tolerant to levels of disagreement due to the prevalent norms of diversity in political discussions in cyberspace, compared to traditional offline political interactions (Kushin & Kitchener, 2009). Of politically active individuals on SNSs, 38% found their friends' political postings disagreed with their own and said that "they would challenge their friends' social networking site material about politics if they disagree with it" (Rainie & Smith, 2012, pp. 4 & 6). In other words, social and political pressure in online political communication is much weaker and less influential, and political participants on the Internet feel freer from the predominant political pressure and social convictions present in offline face-to-face political discussions (Witschge, 2004).

In addition, political discussions on SNSs are usually initiated and continued by like-minded people (Ancu & Cozma, 2009). In a political discursive context like that found on SNSs, politically active individuals often believe that their voices are part of the majority opinion, even though their views might actually be in the minority in terms of national public opinion (Schulz & Roessler, 2012). Moreover, regardless of their opinions—whether people agree with each other online or not—individuals often and easily join online political discussions and exchange crosscutting views in cyberspace (Brundidge, 2006; Wojcieszak & Mutz, 2009). Therefore, it is not always obvious whose opinions are dominant in online political discussions; those participating in politics via the Internet are less sensitive about whether their opinions are supported by the public in their online political communication (Witschge, 2004). For these reasons, unlike in traditional face-to-face political meetings, we are more likely to hear multiple political viewpoints in political discussions in cyberspace, regardless of the dominant political views and social pressures (Holt, 2004; Kushin & Kitchener, 2009).

Politically involved Internet users are political hard-cores and strong-opinion holders who are not only already politically very knowledgeable and interested (Dahlgren, 2005), but who also tend to be very skeptical and analytical (Bimber, 2003). Politically active individuals on the Internet are more likely to gather their political information not only through the medium of the Internet but also through traditional media channels, such as television, radio and newspapers (Bimber & Davis, 2003). Furthermore, social media users and bloggers who are very engaged and very opinionated are more likely to raise their political voices and more likely to strongly value freedom of expression (Swigger, 2013). These individuals are not likely to remain silent when controversial topics are injected into their online discussion zones (Davis, 1999). Even Noelle-Neumann's later work mentioned "the strength of and readiness to stand up for one's opinion," "the dual climate of opinion," and "the hard-core," and she admitted there existed different patterns of political expression for strong opinion holders (Noelle-Neumann, 1993, pp. 167–173). Political discussions in cyberspace provide more easily accessible and normatively acceptable contexts for these political hard-cores to express their political views against others' views because of the technical tools available, such as feeds embedded in SNSs and the level of anonymity and rigorous debate cultures that are often absent in traditional face-to-face political discourses (Kushin & Kitchener, 2009).

However, political discussion in cyberspace can easily turn political participants off from political and civic participation (Kushin & Kitchener, 2009). Even though about one-fourth of politically active social media users tend to become more active in politics after political discussions on an SNS, a significant number (9%) of active social media users are less likely to involve themselves in politics after political discussions with others on SNSs (Rainie & Smith, 2012). It seems much easier to avoid unwanted political interaction on SNSs by simply blocking disagreeing people, which one can do using the technical tools embedded on these sites, than it is to avoid differing opinions in offline political meetings. About 18% of political social media users "have blocked, unfriended, or hidden someone on the site because the person either posted too much about politics, disagreed with political posts, or bothered friends with political posts" (Rainie & Smith, 2012, p. 6). This implies that there could be a counter-effect of social media in meaningful political participation for some of its users.

Overall, in online political communication, people feel less pressured by views that disagree with their own and more likely to express themselves than in face-to-face interactions. Therefore, political minorities can easily express their genuine political views, and the public is more likely to hear various minority voices in online political communication. As a result, although the levels of political discussion and participation via social media still depend on types of political issues, level of interactivity, and information source credibility (Velasquez, 2012), there are multiple spirals of political expression on SNSs, embracing a greater volume of isolated voices and crosscutting views.

In-Group Identities Embedded in the Spirals of Political Discourse in Cyberspace

The socio-psychological element of in-group identities influences individuals' political attitudes and choices of political expressions. Moreover, an interpersonal in-group identity can dominate an individual's political and social attitudes and can serve as both a supportive reference and a constrained pressure when a person expresses his/her views in the public sphere. Individuals adopt the attitudes of social groups, especially a valued group that often shares their self-view (Eagly & Chaiken, 1993). These "reference groups" have greater influence on individuals when they consider publicly expressing their opinions when compared to the more anonymous general public. Oshagan (1996) found that when in-group and societal majority opinions are equally influential, people receive more influence from their reference or in-group identity. Further research showed that individuals' social identity could be a motivation to "express opinions," even when their own ideas were perceived as being in the minority (Moy, Domke, & Stamm, 2001, p. 10). People belonging to a political group were found to have a higher level of political interest and be more expressive than individuals who did not have a political group affiliation (Booth & Babchuk, 1969; Fowler & Kam, 2007). Political and social group memberships have been identified as key predictors of various forms of participatory intentions and behaviors in several studies (Moy & Scheufele, 1998; Moy et al., 2001).

Political in-group identities in cyberspace are not exceptions in that regard. Individuals who have online political in-groups are also more likely to speak up about their opinions, knowing that they have a group of supportive or like-minded people present in controversial communication climates (Brenner, 2012).

As a number of scholars argue, however, if political- and social-group pressures fade away, and organized group activities become loose in online political discussions (Witschge, 2004; Laer, 2010), individuals' political identities may be different on SNSs compared to offline. According to Rainie et al. (2012), 21% of social media users "belong to a group on a social networking site that is involved in political or social issues, or that is working to advance a cause" (p. 3). The question is, then, how are these members of online political groups influenced by their political in-groups in cyberspace?

Online in-group identities typically do not play the same role as offline in-group identities in their members' political attitudes and expressions in online political discussions. In online contexts, people can overcome geographic distance in meeting and talking to new groups of people, resulting in more diverse and controversial conversations compared to political interactions in physical, real world meetings (Stromer-Galley, 2003). Based on the fact that people tend to agree more with their group members' judgments in face-to-face interactions (Deutsch & Gerard, 1955), the group reference and pressure can be weaker or play an alternative role in political discussions in cyberspace, where individual autonomy is a prevalent norm, and a level of anonymity is often guaranteed (Witschge, 2004; Kushin & Kitchener, 2009). Kushin and Kitchener (2009), for instance, found that individual group members were sharing their views beyond, or deviating from, the established political stances and views of their reference groups in political discourses with out-group individuals on SNSs.

As with offline political affiliations (Laer, 2010), groups that are more socioeconomically affluent and educated (e.g., the ethnic majority of Whites and people under the age of 50) are also more likely to be affiliated with political and social groups on SNSs (Laer, 2010; Rainie et al., 2012). Interactions among social media users are still often embedded in their offline interpersonal ties and networks (Brenner, 2012; Baym, 2006; Kavanaugh, Carroll, Rosson, Zin, & Reese, 2006) in that the dominant, preexisting, offline political and civic groups simply move to cyberspace because of the lower transaction costs, and they continue to operate and engage in their political activities through both traditional offline and new online channels (Naughton, 2001; Boncheck, 1995; Laer, 2010).

However, newly emerging groups formed via social media are often created by political minorities and isolated individuals, such as minority party members who do not have enough resources to recruit and sustain their groups. The reason for this is that it is much more efficient to operate political activities online by creating digital zones that do not require a great level of support and monetary resources (Hayes, 2009; Naughton, 2001). In other words, the Internet helps meandering individuals come together and interact in common interests and space (Plant, 2004). For instance, young immigrants, one of the most marginalized social minority groups, can create their group identity via the Internet (Elias & Lemish, 2009). Females, who often do not have well-established political organizations that represent their specific political interests, use the Internet as a medium to express themselves, overcoming a lack of established participatory systems (Morahan-Martin, 2000).

Like Tea Party members, politically engaged and motivated individuals have joined in their political views and raised their voices as groups in social cyberspace. There are innumerable political groups in varying scales and across different political arenas on SNSs. For example, Facebook is estimated to have several thousand political groups (Williams & Gulati, 2007). In online political discussions, when political in-groups establish a level of expertise, information source credibility and more proactive interactions and feedback, such as with the Tea Party, they accelerate political discussions and expressions. In other words, political communities on SNSs with those qualities were more likely to attract others' political discussion on their social media sites (Velasquez, 2012). The minority voices nurtured, raised, and formed in cyberspace become the majority voices and transfer into mainstream offline politics, just as the Tea Party's political views and activities have created a new sensational political movement in American politics (Blackmon et al., 2010).

However, such online political group affiliations have looser political constraints than do offline political affiliations (Witschge, 2004). As discussed, these members of online political groups were more likely to express their true views, free from their political group pressure, in an autonomous and anonymous cyberspace (Kushin & Kitchener, 2009). It is important to understand the new trend in political expressiveness by online political and civic groups whose voices were often marginalized in mainstream politics and otherwise not heard, but that now appear through the new channel of social media. This study seeks to answer whether the new platforms of social media and in-group identities embedded in online political discourses accelerate political expression and participation in American politics.

METHOD

Data and Sample

For a more comprehensive comparison between politically active individuals who utilize social media and their counterparts who solely use traditional participatory methods in a consistent time frame with nationwide samples, and for a more reliable categorization of those active American citizens who have political reference groups and those who do not, two separate data sets were used. The social media user data set was gathered by the researcher and was combined with the 4th ANES 2010–2012 Evaluations of Government and Society Study (EGSS) data set, one of the most reliable national data sets.

During the early 2012 campaign season, from November of 2011 to April of 2012, politically engaged individuals who were active in social media (by posting their political views, participating in online forums, or commenting on others' political posts) were randomly selected ($n = 344$). In the process of sampling, the status of each individual as a member of a political group involved in the sample political dialogues, or as an independent commentator on the sample political discussion, was identified. From that sample, politically active citizens who were affiliated with political or nonpartisan civic groups ($n = 188$) were categorized as people who have political in-group identities or reference groups, and others who participated independently based on their individual values and motivation ($n = 67$) were identified as the type of participants without political in-group identities or reference groups.

The 4th ANES 2010–2012 Evaluations of Government and Society Study (EGSS) data set was gathered between February 18 and 23, 2012. Out of the sample of the 4th EGSS data set ($n = 1314$), politically active citizens in only traditional participatory channels and methods were identified by questioning how much they use social media: (a) Twitter, (b) Facebook, (c) Google +, (d) YouTube, or (e) Blogs, to learn about the election and questioning whether they participated in politics through traditional participatory methods in the past 12 months: (a) attended a political protest or rally; (b) contacted a government official; (c) volunteered or worked for a Presidential and/or other candidate campaign; (d) gave money to a Presidential and/or other candidate; (e) worked with others in their community to solve a problem; (f) served on a community board; (g) wrote a letter to the editor; (h) commented about politics on a message board; or, (i) helped a publicly elected official. The respondents who answered "not at all" to all the social media usages and participated in the political arena through at least one of the traditional venues, were identified as politically active individuals via traditional participatory methods ($n = 321$). Among the politically active participants via traditional channels, people who actively participated in either issue-oriented political organizations or nonpartisan civic organizations were identified as individuals with political in-group identities or reference groups ($n = 47$) and otherwise as independent political participants whose political participation were not related to any group support or pressure ($n = 270$).

Variables
Political Attitudes: Political Interests, Information Efficacy, and Cynicism
Both the 4th EGSS and the social media user surveys asked "how interested would you say you are in politics?" and "how informed do you think you are about politics?" The questions were measured on a Likert scale of 5; from 1, "not at all" to 5, "very much." The questions were used as indicators of those politically active participants' political interests and information efficacy, respectively.

Political cynicism is a complicated concept and previous researchers have often created indexes to cover multiple dimensions of the negative attitudes toward different targets (Buttel, Wilkening, & Martinson, 1977), or measured different dimensions of cynical attitudes like distrust and alienation, specifically adopted for their own studies (Citrin, 1974). Those cynicism indexes can easily cancel out the effect of single items in multiple dimensions of the negative attitudes. Moreover, specifically designed cynicism indicators per study can easily lose their explanatory power by nature of being focused on a narrower perspective. For the purpose of exploring politically active individuals, this study adopted two separate dimensions of internal powerlessness and external alienation. Individual's internal powerlessness was accessed by asking, "how much can people like you affect what the government does," and people's external alienation was measured by asking "how much do government officials care what people like you think." Both questions were asked by both the Social Media User survey and the 4th EGSS survey on an inverse Likert scale of 5; from 1 "strongly agree" to 5 "strongly disagree," representing a higher value for a higher degree of cynical attitudes.

Willingness to Express

Both the 4th EGSS and the Social Media User surveys asked people's willingness to express their political views in public. The question, "how likely/unlikely are you to attend a meeting to talk about political or social concerns" in the 4th EGSS survey and the other question, "if people have different political views from me in political discussions, I would/would not be willing to express my true political views against them" in the Social Media User survey were merged into one data set as the indicator of people's willingness to express their opinions in controversial circumstances where people disagree with each other. Both questions were measured on an inverse Likert scale of 5; from 1 "very likely to express" to 5 "very unlikely to express" indicating a higher value for more silence as the theory of the Spiral of Silence predicts. The hypothetical assumption of a controversial political atmosphere in both questions accesses the condition of the Spiral of Silence theory.

Demographic Factors: Party ID, Age, Gender, Education, and Race

For the purpose of understanding the demographics of politically engaged individuals who adopt different participatory venues with or without political affiliations, and to control mediating effects of those demographic factors in the relationship between political participation methods, status of group affiliation, political attitudes and level of political expression, the demographic factors of Party ID, age, gender, education, and race were included in the study.

Main Sources of Political Information

Survey respondents in both the fourth EGSS and the Social Media User surveys were asked to select the main source of their political information among the following sources: TV, Radio, Newspaper, Magazine, Internet, Interpersonal communication and multiple sources. The most frequently used medium to learn about politics was identified as the individual's main source of political information, and respondents who chose multiple sources were coded as multiple source users. However, data obtained from the 4th EGSS survey did not have a category of "interpersonal communication." Therefore, individuals who said that they "talk about political subjects 'a lot' at work or church with friends and family" without any primary medium usage were identified as interpersonal communicators and included in the variable categories.

RESULTS

Dynamics of Demographics

Politically active participants, via either traditional participatory methods or social media, were evenly distributed across different partisan groups: Democrats (30.4% of traditional method users; 33.8% of social media users), Independents (31.3% of traditional method users; 24.2% of social media users) and Republicans (33.2% of traditional method users; 30.6% of social media users). However, individuals with political minority party affiliations, such as the Green Party, were much more likely to use social media (70.9%) rather than traditional methods (29.1%) to participate in politics ($\chi^2 = 12.043$, $p \leq .01$). In addition, these political minorities were more likely to participate in politics as parts of their political or civic groups (65.9%) rather than as independent individuals (34.1%) ($\chi^2 = 17.759$, $p \leq .01$). This implies that we are more likely to hear political minority groups' voices through social media rather than through traditional participatory venues.

In terms of gender representation, both genders equally utilized traditional participatory channels (46.4 % of males; 50.8% of females) and the new venue of social media (53.6% of males; 49.2% of females) to express their political views in public ($\chi^2 = 1.287$, $p \leq .26$). However, unlike males who participated in politics equally as independent individuals (51.4%) or as part of political groups (48.6%), females were more likely to participate as independent individuals (67.7%) rather than as parts of those political groups (32.3%) ($\chi^2 = 15.432$, $p \leq .01$).

Racial representation among politically active citizens appeared unequally in different venues of political participations. Ethnic majority (e.g., Caucasian) respondents were more likely to use traditional venues (58.2%), such as a face-to-face meeting, to participate in politics rather than social media (41.8%). However, Black, Hispanic, and multi-ethnic groups were more likely to adopt social media (64.3% of Black; 86.3% of Hispanic; 78.9% of multi-ethnic groups) to raise their political voices than traditional participatory venues (35.6% of Black; 13.7% of Hispanic; 21.1% of multi-ethnic groups) ($\chi^2 = 67.777$, $p \leq .01$). Additionally, all ethnic minorities (67.9% of Hispanic; 56.5% of other ethnic minorities) except African Americans (25%) were more likely to participate in politics as part of their political and civic organizations, rather than engaging in individual-based participation when compared to Whites (37.2% with political group affiliations; 62.8% without any group affiliation) ($\chi^2 = 67.777$, $p \leq .01$).

Older, politically active citizens were more likely to use traditional methods to participate in politics, while politically active youth were more likely to adopt social media ($t = 21.162$, $p \leq .01$). The mean ages of politically active social media users and traditional venue users were 33.79 ($SD = 14.43$) and 57.44 ($SD = 14.19$), respectively. Education was not a statistically important demographic factor in determining the choice of political participation methods, nor was the status of an individual's group affiliation, whether the individual belonged to a political group or had any reference group.

Out of the randomly selected samples for politically engaged participants through social media or traditional participatory channels, social media users' participation was likely based on their involvement with political or nonpartisan civic organizations (73.7%), rather than based on their individual, more intrinsic motivations (26.3%). This contrasted with traditional method users who were more independently participatory (14.8% with political group affiliations; 85.2% without group affiliations) ($\chi^2 = 202.54$, $p \leq .01$).

Main Sources of Political Information

Although politically active citizens overall tended to use multiple sources to gain political information, people who participated in politics through traditional methods (64.4%) were more likely to identify multiple media sources for their political information than the counterparts who participated via social media (27.7%) ($\chi^2 = 99.32, p \leq .01$). Although multiple political information media sources were the most common way to obtain political information (50.2%) among politically active citizens, people who were affiliated with any political or civic groups (4.4%) were more likely to get their political information mainly through interpersonal communication, compared to respondents who did not identify any group affiliation (1.8%) ($\chi^2 = 12.03, p \leq .03$). This pattern was consistent for political participants who adopted only traditional participatory methods, ($\chi^2 = 14.03, p \leq .02$), but the importance of group affiliation on the source of information choice was less important for political participants via social media ($\chi^2 = 6.482, p \leq .26$).

Political Interests and Information Efficacy

Both users of traditional participatory channels and social media were interested in politics and believed that they were well informed about politics. There were no statistically significant differences in the levels of political interest and information efficacy between the two groups in that the target samples of the study were politically active individuals. When asked "how interested would you say you are in politics?" and "how informed do you think you are about politics?," both those who rely on traditional venues ($M = 3.86, SD = 1.16$ in political interest; $M = 4.01, SD = 1.11$ in political information efficacy) and those who use social media ($M = 4.07, SD = 1.13$ in political interest; $M = 4.10, SD = 1.05$ in political information efficacy) scored high on the items of political interest and information efficacy (see Tables 11.1 and 11.2).

The higher level of political information efficacy among politically active participants was consistent regardless of whether their political participation was based on their political or civic group affiliation ($M = 4.11, SD = 1.03$), or whether they were independent from such affiliations ($M = 4.00, SD = 1.14$). However, among those politically active individuals, respondents whose political participation was embedded in, or part of, political groups ($M = 4.11, SD = 1.06$) had higher levels of political interest than independent political participants ($M = 3.82, SD = 1.20$), $F(1, 538) = 5.84, p \leq .02$. Moreover, active political or civic group members who utilized traditional participatory methods to raise their political views ($M = 4.13, SD = 1.16$) tended to be more interested in politics than those members of political groups who adopted social media as their channel of communication ($M = 4.09, SD = 1.09$), $F(1, 538) = 4.72, p \leq .03$).

Political Cynicism: Internal Powerlessness and External Alienation

Two different dimensions of political cynicism, internal powerlessness and external alienation, were apparent as different among the politically active citizens in the sample. External alienation seemed a more prevalent cynical attitude than

Table 11.1 ANOVA Tests on Political Interest and Information Efficacy

	POLITICAL INTERESTS		POLITICAL INFORMATION EFFICACY	
	F	p	F	p
Intercept	66.370	0.000	67.893	0.000
Participation Channel (Social Media vs. Traditional Participatory Methods)	2.266	0.133	0.423	0.516
In-Group Identity (With vs. Without Political/Civic Group Affiliation)	5.842	0.016	0.988	0.321
Participation Channel* Group Affiliation Status	4.723	0.030	2.926	0.088
Political Party Affiliation	2.622	0.050	1.357	0.255
Gender	13.327	0.000	10.317	0.001
Race	4.366	0.002	5.024	0.001
Age	24.325	0.000	27.009	0.000
Education	2.480	0.116	10.107	0.002

Source: The combined data of the author's original study on SNS users collected between November 2011 and April 2012 ($n = 344$) with the 4th ANES 2010–2012 Evaluations of Government and Society Study (EGSS) ($n = 321$). Identical variable items in the 4th EGSS data were merged into the author's original variable items.

internal powerlessness. Regardless of having political or civic organization affiliations ($M = 3.88$, $SD = .97$ for people with political group affiliation; $M = 3.85$, $SD = .93$ for independent individuals), and despite adopting different channels for their political participation ($M = 3.90$, $SD = .92$ for traditional venue users; $M = 3.84$, $SD = .97$ for social media users), the feeling of political alienation from politics was high for all respondents (see Tables 11.3 and 11.4).

However, politically active social media users were relatively more positive about their power to influence politics ($M = 2.61$, $SD = 1.17$) and traditional participatory method adopters were more negative in their powerlessness ($M = 3.61$, $SD = 1.08$), $F(1, 538) = 45.86$, $p \leq .01$. According to the confidence internals of the leverages between internal powerlessness and external alienation, politically active participants who used either traditional participatory venues ($.02 \leq 95\%\ CI \leq .06$) or social media ($.97 \leq 95\%\ CI \leq 1.47$) tended to have higher levels of external alienation than internal powerlessness ($p \leq .01$). However, politically active social media users ($M = 1.22$, $SD = 1.36$) tended to have more distinctive attitudes of external alienation related to internal powerlessness than political participants via traditional venues ($M = .29$, $SD = 1.07$), $F(1, 536) = 34.77$, $p \leq .01$.

Political Expression
Politically engaged individuals who utilized social media to express their political voices ($M = 2.15$, $SD = .12$) were less likely to be reluctant to express their genuine political opinions when facing differing political views, compared to individuals

Table 11.2 Means and Confidence Intervals of Political Interest and Information Efficacy

		POLITICAL INTEREST		INFORMATION EFFICACY	
Traditional Participatory Methods	With Political/Civic Group Affiliation	$M = 4.13$ ($SD = .80$)	$3.78 \leq$ 95% $CI \leq 4.49$	$M = 4.165$ ($SD = .88$)	$3.83 \leq$ 95% $CI \leq 4.50$
	Without Political/Civic Group Affiliation	$M = 3.58$ ($SD = 1.18$)	$3.36 \leq$ 95% $CI \leq 3.80$	$M = 3.860$ ($SD = 1.14$)	$3.65 \leq$ 95% $CI \leq 4.07$
Social Media	With Political/Civic Group Affiliation	$M = 4.09$ ($SD = 1.09$)	$3.86 \leq$ 95% $CI \leq 4.32$	$M = 4.060$ ($SD = 1.02$)	$3.85 \leq$ 95% $CI \leq 4.28$
	Without Political/Civic Group Affiliation	$M = 4.06$ ($SD = 1.25$)	$3.74 \leq$ 95% $CI \leq 4.37$	$M = 4.139$ ($SD = 1.13$)	$3.84 \leq$ 95% $CI \leq 4.44$
		Note: 5-Point Scale: 1 = Not interested at all, 5 = Very Interested		Note: 5-Point Scale: 1 = Lowest Efficacy, 5 = Highest Efficacy	

Source: The combined data of the author's original study on SNS users collected between November 2011 and April 2012 ($n = 344$) with the 4th ANES 2010–2012 Evaluations of Government and Society Study (EGSS).

Table 11.3 ANOVA Tests on Cynicism

POLITICAL CYNICISM	INTERNAL POWERLESSNESS		EXTERNAL ALIENATION		ATTITUDE LEVERAGE B/T INTERNAL AND EXTERNAL CYNICISM	
	F	p	F	p	F	p
Intercept	126.254	0.000	220.227	0.000	1.280	0.261
Participation Channel (Social Media vs. Traditional Participatory Methods)	45.861	0.000	0.229	0.632	34.768	0.000
In-Group Identity (With vs. Without Political/ Civic Group Affiliation)	0.300	0.584	0.056	0.812	0.116	0.733
Participation Channel* Group Affiliation Status	0.369	0.544	0.084	0.772	0.126	0.722
Political Party Affiliation	4.583	0.004	5.807	0.001	0.630	0.596
Gender	1.652	0.199	0.571	0.450	3.197	0.074
Race	0.932	0.445	0.766	0.547	0.733	0.570
Age	0.401	0.527	7.267	0.007	7.182	0.008
Education	0.805	0.370	1.903	0.168	0.066	0.798

Source: The combined data of the author's original study on SNS users collected between November 2011 and April 2012 ($n = 344$) with the 4th ANES 2010–2012 Evaluations of Government and Society Study (EGSS) ($n = 321$). Identical variable items in the 4th EGSS data were merged into the author's original variable items.

who used only traditional participatory venues for political participation, such as in-person forums and physical political protests ($M = 3.56, SD = 1.29$), $F(1, 538) = 82.15, p \leq .01$ (see Tables 11.5 and 11.6).

Moreover, among these politically active participants, individuals who were affiliated with any political or civic organizations ($M = 2.64, SD = 1.24$) were less reluctant to speak out about their opinions in a political climate in which there was disagreement than independent individuals who participate in politics based on their individual values and motivations ($M = 3.07, SD = 1.36$), $F(1, 538) = 10.72, p \leq .01$. Interestingly, politically active social media users who were not affiliated with any political or civic groups ($M = 2.12, SD = 1.18$) were most likely to speak up about their political views, and independent political participants who used only traditional participatory methods to distribute their political opinions ($M = 4.02, SD = 1.19$) were most sensitive and least likely to raise their voices in a controversial political climate, $F(1, 538) = 13.75, p \leq .01$.

Table 11.4 Means and Confidence Intervals of Political Cynicism

INTERNAL POWERLESSNESS

Traditional Participatory Methods	With Political/Civic Group Affiliation	$M = 3.61$ (SD = 1.02)	$3.24 \leq 95\%\ CI \leq 3.98$
	Without Political/Civic Group Affiliation	$M = 3.61$ (SD = 1.09)	$3.39 \leq 95\%\ CI \leq 3.84$
Social Media	With Political/Civic Group Affiliation	$M = 2.69$ (SD = 1.18)	$2.45 \leq 95\%\ CI \leq 2.92$
	Without Political/Civic Group Affiliation	$M = 2.54$ (SD = 1.15)	$2.22 \leq 95\%\ CI \leq 2.87$

Note: 5-Point Scale: 1 = Lowest Cynicism, 5 = Highest Cynicism

EXTERNAL ALIENATION

Traditional Participatory Methods	With Political/Civic Group Affiliation	$M = 3.89$ (SD = .86)	$3.59 \leq 95\%\ CI \leq 4.20$
	Without Political/Civic Group Affiliation	$M = 3.90$ (SD = .93)	$3.71 \leq 95\%\ CI \leq 4.09$
Social Media	With Political/Civic Group Affiliation	$M = 3.86$ (SD = .99)	$3.67 \leq 95\%\ CI \leq 4.06$
	Without Political/Civic Group Affiliation	$M = 3.81$ (SD = .93)	$3.54 \leq 95\%\ CI \leq 4.08$

Note: 5-Point Scale: 1 = Lowest Cynicism, 5 = Highest Cynicism

LEVERAGE OF INTERNAL AND EXTERNAL CYNICISM

Traditional Participatory Methods	With Political/Civic Group Affiliation	$M = .29$ (SD = 1.17)	$-.11 \leq 95\%\ CI \leq .69$
	Without Political/Civic Group Affiliation	$M = .29$ (SD = 1.05)	$.04 \leq 95\%\ CI \leq .53$
Social Media	With Political/Civic Group Affiliation	$M = 1.18$ (SD = 1.35)	$.92 \leq 95\%\ CI \leq 1.43$
	Without Political/Civic Group Affiliation	$M = 1.27$ (SD = 1.40)	$.92 \leq 95\%\ CI \leq 1.62$

Note: Range of 10: -5 = Complete Relative Internal Cynicism, 5 = Complete Relative External Cynicism

Source: The combined data of the author's original study on SNS users collected between November 2011 and April 2012 ($n = 344$) with the 4th ANES 2010–2012 Evaluations of Government and Society Study (EGSS) ($n = 321$). Identical variable items in the 4th EGSS data were merged into the author's original variable items.

Table 11.5 ANOVA Test on Political Expression

	POLITICAL EXPRESSION	
	F	p
Intercept	105.755	0.000
Participation Channel (Social Media vs. Traditional Participatory Methods)	82.148	0.000
In-Group Identity (With vs. Without Political/Civic Group Affiliation)	10.717	0.001
Participation Channel* Group Affiliation Status	13.748	0.000
Political Party Affiliation	0.096	0.962
Gender	0.750	0.387
Race	3.839	0.004
Age	1.460	0.228
Education	1.351	0.246

Source: The combined data of the author's original study on SNS users collected between November 2011 and April 2012 ($n = 344$) with the 4th ANES 2010–2012 Evaluations of Government and Society Study (EGSS).

Table 11.6 Means and Confidence Intervals of Political Expression

		POLITICAL EXPRESSION	
Traditional Participatory Methods	With Political/Civic Group Affiliation	$M = 3.10$ ($SD = 1.55$)	$2.71 \leq 95\% \, CI \leq 3.49$
	Without Political/Civic Group Affiliation	$M = 4.02$ ($SD = 1.19$)	$3.78 \leq 95\% \, CI \leq 4.25$
Social Media	With Political/Civic Group Affiliation	$M = 2.17$ ($SD = 1.10$)	$1.92 \leq 95\% \, CI \leq 2.42$
	Without Political/Civic Group Affiliation	$M = 2.12$ ($SD = 1.18$)	$1.77 \leq 95\% \, CI \leq 2.47$

Note: 5-Point Scale, 1 = Very Unlikely Reluctant to Speak Up, 5 = Very Likely Reluctant to Speak Up

Source: The combined data of the author's original study on SNS users collected between November 2011 and April 2012 ($n = 344$) with the 4th ANES 2010–2012 Evaluations of Government and Society Study (EGSS).

DISCUSSION

The new platforms of political discourse, social media, and political reference groups embedded in the circumstance of cyberspace dialogues added more variations among politically engaged American citizens who were already interested in politics in general, were confident in their political activities, and believed in their power to influence politics despite having relatively higher cynical attitudes towards politics. Socio-economic and political minorities, such as ethnic minorities, young voters, and minority political party members were more likely to adopt social media as the venue of political expression and participation. These groups also represented themselves in the online public sphere in more organized and aggregated forms. The traditional role of a political reference group that used to help the dominant political group be louder in the sphere of traditional political discourse becomes less important in social media political dialogue, where independent and isolated voices are equally represented.

Social media are more inclusive channels and spaces for political discourse than traditional participatory venues, such as face-to-face meetings. As discussed earlier, in social media, political and social minorities such as younger people, ethnic minorities, females, and minority party members have increased their political participation to the levels of participation exhibited by political and social majorities, such as white voters and older generations. We are more likely to learn political and social minorities' opinions through social media that were not previously heard through traditional participatory channels (Holt, 2004; Rainie et al., 2012). Political communication via the Internet-based platforms of social media enhances those social minorities' political learning, interests and engagement in politics (Elin, 2003; Wojcieszak & Mutz, 2009). Those politically active mavericks online who used to be politically alienated from mainstream politics are more optimistic about their power to influence politics through social media and more expressive due to the autonomous, anonymous, and tolerant nature of online cultures and political discussions (Kushin & Kitchener, 2009).

Politically active social media users not affiliated with any political group were the most likely to express themselves in controversial atmospheres against others' views. In contrast, those independent political participants who communicate only through traditional venues, such as attending a face-to-face meeting, were least likely to share their true views in controversial political discussions. This means that in-group support would encourage the members' political expressions in offline political discussions, but not in their political participation in cyberspace. This finding implies that we can learn others' genuine opinions in online political communication even more where no group pressure exists, but we are still more likely to learn the political views of dominant groups in a face-to-face meeting. In conclusion, beyond the argument that interactions and networks via the Internet supplement traditional communication (Wellman, Hasse, & Witte, 2001), political communication through social media has transformed minority voices into majority voices and equalized these voices in the political arena, abating the argument of the Spiral of Silence. Social media are indeed new innovative engines for political and social minorities to use to run their political activities and heighten their voices. The systems of social media services purify their cyberspace by removing any socio-political hurdles that discourage independent and isolated voices from being heard.

CHAPTER 12

Evaluating Textual and Technical Interactivity in Candidate E-mail Messages during the 2012 U.S. Presidential Campaign

Andrew Paul Williams and Roxana Maiorescu

The 2012 U.S. presidential campaign was another demonstration of how political campaigns have grown to use more sophisticated and strategic means of engaging and persuading voters through Internet platforms and applications. E-campaigning has become the norm and engaging content is offered in ways that truly engage users through a two-way communication model, which is quite a contrast from when one looks back to the 1996 election when the Internet was used to merely disseminate information (see, for example, Kaid, 2002; Selnow, 1998; Stromer-Galley, 2000). Yet, this overall improvement should not come as a surprise as it was predicted by past research studies in political communication (see, for example, Margolis, Resnick, & Tu, 1997). During the 2012 U.S. campaign cycle, about 54% of Americans used the Internet to get information about the elections and/or to discuss political issues with their peers (Smith, 2012) compared to 4% of Americans who accessed online information about the elections in 1996 (Smith, 2009). In addition, during the 2012 presidential elections, 5% of Americans signed up to receive text messages directly from the candidate (Smith, 2012).

As predicted by Kaid (2002), Web offerings have multiplied, social media prevailed, mobile devices were ubiquitous, and technology advanced, all of which provided candidates with opportunities to interact with their (potential) voters in ways that were not conceivable before. In 2012, the two U.S. presidential candidates, Barack Obama and Mitt Romney, did much more than just establish their own websites. The candidates regularly e-mailed campaign information to their subscribers and maintained a highly visible presence on social media platforms such as Facebook and Twitter, and they used newer applications such as Instagram to reach voters.

Smith and Duggan (2012) conducted research for Pew about the 2012 presidential campaign and found that about 55% of registered voters watched political videos online. Out of these videos, 48% were news videos, 40% previously recorded videos of candidate speeches and/or debates, and 39% informal videos. On Election Day 2012, the Pew Internet & American Life Project found social media to play a paramount role in how voters in general, and young voters in particular, were talking about their candidate selection (Rainie, 2012; Smith & Duggan, 2012). Specifically, 22% of the registered voters let their families and friends know about how they voted on social media sites such as Facebook and Twitter. Social media platforms proved an important means by which voters attempted to persuade their peers to vote. More precisely, 30% of the registered voters were encouraged to vote for Barack Obama or Mitt Romney by friends and family via posts on Facebook or Twitter and 20% were encouraged to get out the vote (Rainie, 2012; Smith & Duggan, 2012).

Clearly the Web and social media presences were expected of the candidates in the 2012 elections, and e-mail continued to play a paramount role in reaching out to, and engaging, voters. For example, Obama's staff raised a total of $690 million, which was mostly obtained as a result of the e-mail messages sent during the campaign (Green, 2012). Behind the successful e-mail fundraising campaign was the in-depth research performed by Obama's campaign staff, which determined that a casual tone was the best way to attract donations (Green, 2012). In the 2008 presidential elections, Obama had 10 million e-mail subscribers, out of which about 3.1 million donated money for his campaign (Murray & Mosk, 2008). Both Obama and Romney tried to reach out to potential voters in swing states by using e-mail messages to connect their subscribers to Facebook friends in swing states (Beckett, 2012; Tau, 2012). Hence, e-mail played a paramount role in the 2012 campaigning efforts.

This trend is not new. Researchers have pointed to the role the Internet played in past elections. For example, Gueorguieva (2008) noted the impact YouTube and MySpace had on candidate control of messages during the 2006 elections, and Williams and Serge (2011) observed that in the 2008 campaign, social media platforms such as YouTube, Facebook, and Twitter were significant sources of information and engagement that offered the candidates many ways to focus and improve their electronic campaigning activities. The mainstreaming of the Web in the 2008 campaign, and the expectation that candidates, traditional media sources, and citizens keep up with the fast-changing technology was exemplified by the 2008 CNN/YouTube debate that allowed an unprecedented level of civic engagement compared to traditional presidential debates (McKinney & Rill, 2009).

These trends seen in the 2008 election were continued in the 2012 election campaign: 27% of registered voters used their phones to keep up with political news and information, 19% sent campaign-related text messages to their families and friends, and 5% signed up to receive text messages directly from one of the candidates (Smith, 2012). During the 2012 presidential campaign, about 55% of registered voters watched political videos online (Smith & Duggan, 2012). Out of these videos, 48% were news videos, 40% were previously recorded videos of candidate speeches and/or debates, and 39% were informal videos. On Election Day 2012, the Pew Internet & American Life Project (Smith, 2012) found social media played a paramount role in how voters, in general, and young voters, in particular, were talking about their candidate selection. Specifically, 22% of the registered voters let their family and friends know that they voted and for whom they voted on social media sites such as Facebook and Twitter. Social media platforms also proved an important means by which voters attempted to persuade their peers to vote. More precisely, 30% of the registered voters were encouraged to vote for Barack Obama or Mitt Romney by friends and family via posts on Facebook or Twitter and 20% were encourage to get out the vote (Rainie, 2012; Smith & Duggan, 2012).

Despite all of the research about other Internet offerings, literature in political communication still lacks many studies that shed light on the message strategy and interactive features of the e-mail messages sent during campaigns. Past studies pointed to the impact of online platforms such as YouTube, MySpace, Facebook, Twitter, and Tumblr in terms of information seeking and civic engagement (see, for example, Gueorguieva, 2008; McKinney & Rill, 2009). Yet, more studies are needed in order to understand the extent to which candidates make use of the features of e-mail such as interactivity to call for participation, engage voters, and potentially increase political efficacy. E-mail still represents a paramount communication tool through which users obtain news and are likely to forward it to their peers and friends—and can serve to engage recipients with websites and social media platforms and applications.

Williams (2005) argued that, "forwarding of e-mails can potentially overcome selective exposure" (p. 406). Similarly, Smith (2009) found that 47% of e-mail users forwarded e-mail messages with political content during the 2008 presidential campaign. Moreover, there is a high likelihood that a political campaign e-mail received from a friend will be forwarded multiple times (Chiu, Hsieh, Kao, & Lee, 2007), which, in turn, increases the impact and the numbers of the potential voters that the e-mail reaches. Research about the impact of e-mail during past elections showed that about 59% of e-mail users discussed the campaign via this medium and 17% discussed the campaign with their friends via e-mail on a daily basis (Smith, 2009).

Hence, it is not surprising that the presidential candidates are expected to make use of e-mail in an attempt to influence voters. In 2009 for example, 91% of all U.S. citizens were using e-mail (Jones, 2009) and, as of 2012, the Pew Research Center reported that there had not been a significant change in the number of e-mail users. Among the 91% Americans who use e-mail on a regular basis, 13% get the news via e-mail daily and 14% from time to time (Smith, 2012).

CANDIDATE USE OF E-MAIL

This chapter evaluates how the Obama and Romney presidential campaigns' used e-mail messages during the hot phase of the 2012 U.S. general election cycle. While e-mail may seem less exciting or noteworthy as compared to other Internet offerings, such as social media platforms or mobile applications, e-mail remains an essential and popular tool of communication offered by the Internet, and many citizens now access e-mail through mobile devices such as smartphones and tablets.

Stromer-Galley (2003) argued that the combination of traditional Internet use and e-mail use can foster users' information seeking and dissemination, but that past political campaigns did not utilize e-mail well. While politicians attempted to incorporate e-mail into their communications, many early political e-mail users did not integrate it effectively (Sheffer, 2003). For example, Trammell and Williams (2004) found that the 2002 Florida gubernatorial candidates' e-mail messages often failed to align with the message strategies of their websites, and interactive features were negligible in their e-mail messages. It was suggested that improvements be made to e-mail interactive features and message congruity with other campaign communication during the 2004 presidential campaign (Wiese & Gronbeck, 2005). Similarly, Williams and Trammell (2005) found from their content analysis of campaign e-mail messages from the Bush and Kerry campaigns that the candidates failed to utilize many of the interactive features with e-mail messages during the 2004 presidential campaign. Williams (2006) argued the following: "Another significant problem with many campaign [e-mail] messages was the lack of multimedia offering and incongruence with the look of the candidate Web sites" (p. 94).

Research has shown that campaign e-mail messages potentially have more impact on the recipients of a forwarded e-mail message than on recipients of direct campaign e-mail messages and that the use of e-mail is an essential part of any viral marketing strategy (Cornfield, 2004). Similarly, Polat (2005) argued that forwarding e-mails with political content was one means that individuals could take to attempt to influence governmental outcomes. Despite this potential, in an analysis of Obama and Romney 2012 campaign e-mails for *Mashable*, Prakash (2012) found that "only 0.04% of the President's e-mails were being forwarded to other readers. Romney, on the other hand, had 6% of his e-mails sent along to a new person" (para. 4). Findings pertaining to how effective e-mail is used in political communication efforts remains mixed. Nickerson (2007) suggested that the use of e-mail in campaigns for voter registration and turnout was not cost-effective, which is largely because political campaigns were not making full use of this medium's potential.

Bergan (2009) found that legislators contacted by e-mails from lobbyists were more likely to vote in favor of bills than those not contacted via e-mail. In a content analysis of the 2008 U.S. presidential candidates' use of e-mail as a campaigning tool, Williams and Serge (2011) argued that the candidates' e-mail messages were largely superficial in nature, not effective in terms of campaign message integration, and were mostly donation solicitation tools: "The candidates poor use of e-mail messages as a part of their electronic campaigning also means that they are missing myriad opportunities to communicate with and better inform citizens about important issues that can help to further educate and activate voters" (p. 54).

INTERACTIVITY

The advent of the Internet in general and of Web 2.0, in particular, forever changed how political campaigns are run by bringing about the possibility of candidates truly interacting with potential voters on a more personal level (Endres & Warnick,

2004; Selnow, 1998). During the last decade, numerous scholars have argued that the interactive features of the candidates' websites such as hyperlinks, online chats, discussion boards, and e-mail forwarding mechanisms allow candidates to engage in a two-way communication flow with potential voters (see, for example, Drummond, 2006; Stromer-Galley, 2003; Stromer-Galley & Foot, 2002; Ward & Gibson, 2003; Williams & Trammell, 2005).

During the early stages of the use of Internet in the election campaigns of 1996 and 1998, the Internet served as a means of publicity and information dissemination and, hence, only promoted a one-way communication flow (Stromer-Galley, 2000). Subsequent election campaigns made use of more interactive Internet features (Puopolo, 2001). In this respect, Foot, Schneider, Dougherty, Xenos, and Larsen (2003) contended that, during the 2000 presidential campaign, the candidates' websites entailed hyperlinks to external information in an attempt to engage visitors and gain more credibility. Yet, researchers note that it was not until the 2008 presidential campaign that the candidates made extensive use of the Internet's interactive features in general—and social media in particular (see, for example, Hanson, Haridakis, Cunningham, Sharma, & Ponder, 2010; Levy, 2008; Papacharissi, 2009; Spigel, 2009).

Undoubtedly, the advantages brought about by the evolution of the Internet and Web 2.0 are as myriad as they are unquestionable. Interactivity allows users more control over the content (Peng, Tham, & Xiaoming, 1999) and, consequently, increases their political knowledge, political engagement, and efficacy, which research has especially found to be the case among young voters (see, for example, Dalrymple & Scheufele, 2007; Drummond, 2006; Tedesco, 2006). These positive outcomes of political communication efforts can be explained by the transparency and ongoing dialogue between the users and the candidates that the Internet facilitates. The use of the Internet in political campaigns enables reaching potential voters directly, averting media influence, and focusing on the local issues that are relevant for a specific group of voters (Drummond, 2006). By engaging in online campaigning, candidates have the possibility to assess and measure their feedback almost instantly. Thus, candidates can prepare to address various concerns raised online. Furthermore, the Internet continues to allow candidates to reach multiple audiences in areas they could not reach physically (Drummond, 2006).

Technical interactivity refers to hyperlinks, chat rooms, videos, and other multimedia platforms that were found to be essential elements for political mobilization (Williams, Trammell, Postelnicu, Landreville, & Martin, 2005). In turn, hyperlinks were found to lead to the three types of online interactivity, noted earlier by McMillan (2002), namely user-to-system, user-to-user, and user-to-document (Williams et al., 2005).

The second type of interactivity studied in past political communication research about electronic platforms is textual interactivity. Endres and Warnick (2004) referred to textual interactivity as "the dimensions of expression that are strategic and rhetorically motivated" and contended that textual interactivity concerned "not only written forms of expression but also images (photograph and graphics) and multimedia texts" (p. 326). Insofar as this type of interactivity is present, it concerns the quality of the text's construction (Endres & Warnick, 2004) and can lead to interactivity provided that the users find the website content engaging (Newhagen, Cordes, & Levy, 1995). In addition, Moldoff and Williams (2007) contended that self-reflexive metacommunication can also represent a type of textual interactivity, which would lead users to engage in online dialogue and debate. Other research found that textual interactivity could lead to high recall of candidate issue stances as well as the time users spend on a candidate's Web site (Warnick, Xenos, Endres, & Gastil, 2005). However, there is a need for more studies that analyze textual interactivity in order to better understand the effects of the Internet in the election process.

Trammell, Williams, Postelnicu, and Landreville (2006) asserted that it is essential to evaluate textual and technical elements of a blog in order to properly evaluate its interactivity and argued that both the technical and the textual interactivity are paramount in online political campaigns. While past research focused on analyzing the aforementioned types of interactivity in the context of the candidates' Web sites and blogs, there is still little literature in political communication that sheds light on the extent to which candidates incorporated technical and textual interactivity in their e-mail messages. Therefore, this study seeks to evaluate the extent to which the e-mail messages sent by the candidates made use of technical and textual interactivity to call for participation/engage potential voters and/or to encourage voters for donations. Since the use of the e-mail was shown to have the potential to increase political efficacy and voter turnout, the way in which candidates use e-mail could shed light on the contribution candidates make to civic dialogue in democratic political system during a presidential election campaign.

RESEARCH QUESTIONS

RQ1: Will candidates use e-mail messages to self-promote at a higher rate than to attack the opponent?

RQ2: What types of interactivity will the candidates use in their e-mail messages?

RQ3: Which message strategies will candidates use most frequently in their e-mail messages?

RQ4: To what extent, and for what purposes, will candidates use hyperlinks in their e-mail messages?

RQ5: What issues will the candidates discuss most frequently in their e-mail messages?

METHOD

This study investigated campaign e-mail messages sent during the hot phase of the general cycle of the 2012 U.S. presidential election through the use of quantitative content analysis. The e-mail messages included in this study were official campaign communication controlled media sent from Labor Day through Election Day. The recipient signed up to receive these e-mail messages from both Obama and

Romney on the candidates' official campaign Web sites just as any ordinary citizen would do.

Sample

The universe of campaign e-mail messages received from the U.S. presidential candidates analyzed in this chapter was ($N = 154$). Sixty-two e-mail messages were received from the campaign of incumbent Democratic president Barak Obama, whereas 92 e-mail messages were received from Republican challenger Mitt Romney.

Categories

First, basic demographic information about each e-mail message was recorded. This information included the campaign from which the e-mail messages were sent, the date, and the type of author who sent the e-mail message (i.e., candidate, campaign staff, politician, celebrity, family member, or other). Tone (positive, neutral, or negative) of the e-mail message was also recorded, as was the presence of direct address (e.g., referring to the receiver as you).

Candidate message strategy of the e-mail messages was assessed through a variety of variables. For instance, the personalization of the candidate was reviewed by recording topics discussed in the e-mail; themes of horserace, issue coverage, or personality or attribute coverage; and message strategies as operationally defined in Webstyle (Banwart, 2002; Bystrom, Banwart, Kaid, & Robertson, 2004). Mention of the opponent was recorded, as was the presence of attacks or rebuttals by the sponsoring candidate. The overall strategy of the e-mail messages was determined through the use of several variables determined to be "Horserace" (campaign strategy), "Issue," (straightforward issue content) or "Attribute/Image" (focusing on the candidate or his character). Also, Kaid and Davidson (1986) identified "message strategy" as variables used in political messages.

Several aspects regarding the mention of issues in campaign e-mail messages were identified. Issues were coded as a dichotomous variable as being absent or present. These issues were war, defense or national security, economy, social issues (e.g., welfare and social security), environment, education, crime, and healthcare. E-mail messages were determined to be primarily self-promotion or attack. Candidate self-promotion e-mail messages mentioned an event, pointed readers to the campaign Web site, blog, or social media, contained an endorsement (celebrity, politician, or other), or mentioned political accomplishments of the candidate. Attack e-mail messages were those that had a negative tone, contained an attack or rebuttal, and attacked the record, stands, or personal qualities of the opponent.

Technical interactivity was measured through several dichotomous variables to record the presence of encouragement for two-way communication, viral message strategies, interactivity, and hyperlink destinations. E-mail messages were evaluated for the presence or absence of technically interactive devices such as audio, banner/image links, direct links to static downloadable material, games/quizzes, interactive graphs, actual, embedded text in body of e-mail as hyperlinks, personalized downloadable material, photo gallery, or photo slide show.

Textual interactivity was measured through several dichotomous variables to record the presence of engagement through textual elements. E-mail messages were evaluated for the presence or absence of textually interactive devices such as "call to participation/action" (directly asking the reader of the e-mail to do something), direct address (speaking directly to the e-mail recipient by name or "you"), "use of inclusive language" (to e-mail reader), and "metacommunication" (sharing information about the campaign and/or campaign communication strategies).

E-mail message strategies were measured using dichotomous categories as being present or absent. Strategies included candidate use of "calling for change," "inviting participation" in the campaign and democratic process, "emphasizing hope for the future" or "yearning for the past," containing "traditional values" such as religion or mention of morality, or the positioning of a candidate as being at the "philosophical center" of the party. Some strategies were used as a means to support the candidate or position, and in these cases the messages were examined for the use of "statistics" or "expert sources or officials" to support one's position. Attack strategies were examined by looking for candidates "attacking the record of another politician"—either in the same political party or in a different one—as well as "attacking the personal qualities" of another politician. Other appeal strategies include "identifying with the experiences of others" where candidates imply that they can relate to the everyday citizen and "emphasizing political accomplishments" where a candidate discusses previous legislation introduced or public service.

Hyperlinks were measured using dichotomous categories as being either present or absent. The types of hyperlinks coded for included links that allowed recipients to "send/forward to a friend," "forward to local media, talk radio," "vote early/request an absentee ballot," "print the e-mail/printer friendly," "donate," "respond," "sign up to volunteer, host event, etc.," "get general event information," "go to a media article," "go to candidate Web site, Link to political party Web site," "go to opponent's Web site," or "go to candidate's other online presence or identity" (e.g., Facebook, Twitter, etc.). Issue content was measured using dichotomous variables as being either present or absent. The issues coded for included war, defense/national security, the economy, social issues (e.g., welfare and social security), the environment, education, crime, and healthcare.

Coding Process and Reliability

Two trained coders analyzed the visual and textual content, textual and technical interactive elements, and multimedia present in each e-mail message. Differences were reconciled in training, and reliability was established at .97 across all categories using Holsti's method, based on a random selection of 5% of the e-mail messages coded (North, Holsti, Zaninovich, & Zinnes, 1963).

RESULTS

The first research question asked if candidates would use e-mail messages to self-promote at a higher rate than to attack the opponent. Self-promotion (emphasizing the candidates' campaign activities) was the main strategy employed and was present in 94% of the e-mail messages. Only 6% of the e-mails contained an attack of the opponent. The e-mail messages sent by the Obama campaign used self-promotion 96.7% of the time. The Romney campaign e-mail messages used self-promotion 92.2% of the time. Romney used attacks in 7.8% of his campaign's e-mail messages, and Obama used attacks in 3.3% of his e-mail messages.

The second research question asked which types of interactivity would the candidates use in their e-mail messages. There were 297 occurrences of technical interactivity and were coded as present in the candidates' e-mail messages. The Obama campaign e-mail messages contained 104 instances of technical interactivity, as compared to 193 instances of technical interactivity in the Romney campaign e-mail messages. The most frequently used form of technical interactivity was the presence of banner/image hyperlinks that merged the look of the candidates' campaign materials with the functionality of a hyperlink. Banner/image hyperlinks made up 48.1% of the total technically interactive features present in the candidates' e-mail messages. Banner/image hyperlinks made up 54.8% of the technically interactive features present in the Obama campaign e-mail messages, as compared to the Romney campaign e-mail messages, which employed banner/image hyperlinks as 45.5% of their technically interactive features. The second most frequently used form of technical interactivity was embedded hyperlinks (i.e., links that were actually integrated within the body of the text of the e-mail messages). Embedded hyperlinks made up 36.7% of the technically interactive features present in the candidate e-mail messages. Embedded hyperlinks made up 37.5% of the technically interactive features present in the Obama campaign e-mail messages, as compared to the Romney campaign e-mail messages, which employed embedded hyperlinks as 47.1% of their technically interactive features. The use of other types of technical interactivity, such as audio, interactive graphs, photo galleries, video, and personalized downloadable material, was extremely low—or completely non-existent—in the case of e-mail messages analyzed.

There were 396 occurrences of textual interactivity that were coded as present in the candidates' e-mail messages. The Obama campaign e-mail messages contained 163 instances of textual interactivity, as compared to 233 instances of textual interactivity in the Romney campaign e-mail messages. The most frequently used type of textual interactivity in both candidates' e-mail messages was the call to participation/action (i.e., directly asking the reader of the e-mail to do something). Call to participation/action made up 39.1% of the total textual interactivity present in the candidates' e-mail messages. Call to participation/action made up 15.9% of the textual interactivity present in the Obama campaign e-mail messages, as compared to the Romney campaign e-mail messages, which employed call to participation/action as 23.2% of the their textual interactivity. The second most frequently used type of textual interactivity was the use of direct address. Direct address made up 38.6% of the total textual interactivity present in the candidates' e-mail messages. Direct address made up 15.4% of the textual interactivity features present in the Obama campaign e-mail messages, as compared to the Romney campaign e-mail messages, which employed direct address as 23.23% of their textually interactive features. The third most frequently used type of textual interactivity was inclusive language. Inclusive language made up 16.66% of the total textual interactivity present in the candidates' e-mail messages. Inclusive language made up 6.5% of the textual interactivity present in the Obama campaign e-mail messages, as compared to the Romney campaign e-mail messages, which employed direct address as 10.1% of their textual interactivity features. The least frequent form of textual interactivity was metacommunication (i.e., discussing insider information about the campaign and/or campaign communication strategies). Metacommunication made up 3.2% of the textual interactivity present in the Obama campaign e-mail messages, as compared to the Romney campaign e-mail messages, which employed metacommunication as 2.3% of the their textual interactivity.

The third research question asked which message strategies candidates would use most frequently in their e-mail messages. There were 392 message strategies that were coded as present in the candidates e-mail messages. The Obama campaign e-mail messages contained 121 uses of the messages strategies analyzed in this study, as compared to 271 instances of the message strategies used in the Romney campaign e-mail messages. The most frequently used message strategy in the candidates' campaign e-mail message was inviting participation or action. Inviting participation or action made up 35.7% of the total message strategies present in the candidates' e-mail messages. Inviting participation or action made up 50.4% of the message strategies present in the Obama campaign e-mail messages, as compared to the Romney campaign e-mail messages, which employed inviting participation or action as 29.2% of their message strategies. The second most frequently used message strategy was the use of a personal tone. Personal tone made up 20.2% of the total message strategies present in the candidates' e-mail messages. Personal tone made up 18.2% of the message strategies present in the Obama e-mail messages, as compared to the Romney campaign e-mail messages, which employed personal tone as 29.2% of their message strategies. The third most frequently used message strategy was the use of inclusive language. Inclusive language made up 17.9% of the total message strategies present in the candidates' e-mail messages. Inclusive language made up 24% of the message strategies present in the Obama e-mail messages, as compared to the Romney campaign e-mail messages, which employed inclusive language as 15.1% of their message strategies.

The fourth research question asked to what extent, and for what purposes, will candidates use hyperlinks in their e-mail messages. In total, 324 hyperlinks were present in the candidate's e-mail messages. The Obama campaign e-mail messages contained 121 hyperlinks, as compared to 203 hyperlinks present in the Romney campaign e-mail messages. The most frequently used hyperlinks in the candidates' e-mail messages were fundraising hyperlinks. Hyperlinks as donation request made up 41% of the total hyperlinks present in the candidates' e-mail messages. Hyperlinks as donation requests made up 42.1% of the hyperlinks present in the Obama campaign e-mail messages, as compared to the Romney campaign e-mail messages, which employed donation hyperlinks as 40.3% of their hyperlinks. The second most frequent use of hyperlinks in the candidates' e-mail messages were hyperlinks to candidates' Web sites. Hyperlinks to candidates' Web sites made up 15.45% of the total hyperlinks present in the candidates' e-mail messages.

Hyperlinks to the Obama official candidate Web site made up 17.4% of the hyperlinks present in the Obama campaign e-mail messages, as compared to the Romney campaign e-mail messages, which employed hyperlinks to the Romney official Web site in 14.9% of the hyperlinks their e-mail messages. The third most frequent use of hyperlinks was to direct the reader to the candidates' other online presence. Hyperlinks directing readers to candidates' other online presence made up a total of 3.1% of the total hyperlinks present in the candidates' e-mail messages. Hyperlinks directing readers to Obama's other online presence made up 4.1% of the hyperlinks present in the Obama campaign e-mail messages, as compared to the Romney campaign e-mail messages, which employed hyperlinks directing readers to Romney's other online presence in 1.5% of their hyperlinks.

The fifth research question asked what issues the candidates discussed most frequently in their e-mail messages. Of the candidates' e-mail messages, 98.7% were classified as being primarily horserace, which is focusing on the campaign and campaigning such as campaign activities, debate performance, and who's ahead in the polls. Only 2.3% of the candidates' e-mail messages were classified as being issue-based. In total, the main issues present in the candidate's e-mail messages were the economy (85.3%), social issues (11.8%), defense/national security (11.8%), and healthcare (8.8%). Obama's campaign e-mail message's main issue content was: the economy (37.5%), healthcare (25%), social issues (12.5%), and defense/national security (0.0%), and Romney's e-mail messages main issue content was about the economy (100%), defense/national security (15.4%), social issues (12.5%), and healthcare (3.8%).

DISCUSSION

Despite the major advances in mobile technology, the huge shift to the use of touch-screen technology on mobile devices, and the ubiquity of social media and applications, the candidates' campaign e-mail messages analyzed in this chapter did not demonstrate much improvement in communicating campaign issue information in e-mail messages from those examined during the 2008 campaign. Instead, candidate e-mail messages appear to be primarily used as fundraising tools and offer a negligible amount of issue information to the reader.

Overall, findings suggest only minor improvements in the integration of engaging textual elements and technical features in the e-mail messages, but there are also some indications that the candidates' use of e-mail was less advanced than in prior national U.S. elections. These findings are troubling and suggest that candidates are still not harnessing the full potential that e-mail can provide. Some attempts were made to integrate the e-mail messages with other digital campaigning efforts. For example, it was encouraging to see candidates use hyperlinks to direct readers to their presence on social media platforms such as Facebook and Twitter, and to integrate YouTube video on rare occasions. However, many simple ways that e-mail can consistently connect readers to other electronic political marketing efforts were not employed in a systematic way. Constantly requesting money and linking to a Web site for a donation is almost an insult to the reader, and having icons as links to social media platforms in the signature section of an e-mail message would be something one would expect in all e-mail messages in 2012—not just in a small percentage of them.

The Obama and Romney campaigns used their e-mail messages to self-promote at a higher rate than to attack each other. This finding suggests that the e-mail was used more as a tool for reinforcement in communicating with readers than for focusing on the opponent. While one might assume that recipients of e-mail messages from a campaign were already supporters, this may not always be the case. Many citizens still rely on e-mail as a primary form of Internet usage, and it is possible that undecided voters sign up for campaign e-mail messages instead of other means of electronic communication. Just because someone signs up for an e-mail list does not ensure that he or she will vote for or donate to a given candidate, which can also be true of someone liking a Facebook page or following a Twitter account. This finding of self-promotion being more prevalent than attacks can be viewed as encouraging, but the candidates missed an opportunity to position themselves—and their respective stances—against their opponents' platforms, which could serve to better educate the e-mail recipients. While the majority of these e-mail messages' overall tone was neutral, most of these candidate-controlled communication efforts were horserace in nature, which ironically focused readers' attention on the campaign itself, which is something candidates and elected officials have been criticizing the mass media of doing for decades. Candidates can do much more with e-mail than make it a major fundraising tool.

Candidates did speak directly to the reader more often than not in their e-mail messages, which seems encouraging in regard to engaging citizens with potentially important campaign communications. However, the primary use of direct address in the e-mail messages was to directly ask the recipient to make a donation. There were only vague mentions of issues, which typically transitioned abruptly to multiple fundraising appeals. Several e-mail messages did direct the readers to visit social media sites—and to forward the e-mails to friends, but these remained rare exceptions.

Candidates did construct e-mail messages as interactive tools more often than not. All of the Obama and Romney e-mail messages contained interactive elements. However, the nature of technical interactivity was not an advancement, considering that the primary form of technical interaction was the use of banner/image links that simply guided users to the front pages of the candidates' Web sites.

The number one use of textual interactivity was the call to participation, but as previously mentioned, the request was typically just to donate money to the campaigns—not typically to become engaged with substantive content or civic activities. Therefore, the finding that candidates did use the textually interactive message strategy of inviting users to participate or take some action messages strategy most frequently in their e-mail messages is far from what an optimist could interpret as an encouraging finding in terms of voter engagement and mobilization efforts. It is unfortunate that the majority of these appeals to citizens to participate in a campaign were to visit candidate Web sites to donate money. This discouraging finding is congruent with prior U.S. campaign e-mail research (e.g., Williams & Serge, 2011; Williams & Trammell, 2005) and with Stanyer's (2005) study of e-mail messages used by British political parties during the 2005 election, which typically used e-mail to only solicit donations. While it can be argued that campaign e-mails are sent as either reinforcement or fundraising messages to recipients who are already engaged with the campaign to the extent that they would sign up for the messages, the heavy emphasis on fundraising is overlooking the possibility that an undecided voter may sign up to receive e-mails and that power of reaching recipients beyond those who signed up for the messages on the candidates web sites by the forwarding of these messages. Additionally, Foster (2012) reported that e-mail addresses from voter identification cards in nine states are sold to "political parties, organizing groups, lawmakers and campaigns who can use them to send unsolicited [e-mails]" (para. 2), which suggests that candidates can use e-mail as a way of reaching voters who have not actively requested to receive their e-mail messages.

As predicted, out of the extensive use of hyperlinks, the most prevalent was to direct readers to make a donation. Only a negligible amount of hyperlinks directed recipients of e-mail messages to news articles, issue details, and/or social media content. The majority of hyperlinks in Obama and Romney's e-mail messages were merely static campaign logo–style, banner images that typically took users to their respective official campaign Web sites without directly linking users to timely issue content. However, it was encouraging to find a few examples of hyperlinks used to integrate YouTube video and interactive features such as interactive graphs in the e-mail messages, but it is important to note that these types of true technical engagement were not frequently used. Despite the numerous reasons to use compelling hyperlinks—especially given the widespread use of smartphones and tablets with touch screens, the potential to use hypertext as an integral part of e-mail messages and create a more information-rich and truly interactive political communication tool was not met in the 2012 presidential contest. Even short e-mail messages could provide numerous links to media articles, policy information, and other candidate-controlled media content that could serve to engage and educate readers.

As expected, candidates discussed the campaign itself to a much greater extent than issues. The finding that the vast majority of e-mail messages from both the Obama and Romney campaigns were classified as horserace content that focused on the game elements of the campaign instead of important issues that affected the citizens receiving such direct campaign communications is of great concern. Also troubling is that when issues were present in these candidate-controlled media, the discussion was typically superficial in nature and was typically used as a way to request the reader, yet again, to donate more money to the campaign. This finding about excessive contribution requests is similar to Williams and Serge's (2011) results about the 2008 election campaign.

Issue content was basically present in a negligible amount of the sample of the campaign e-mail messages and it was largely vacuous when present. Thus, as found in prior e-mail scholarship, the candidates missed opportunities to educate, engage, and motivate e-mail recipients with important campaign issues—and instead made the focus the campaign itself.

Overall, it seems that the candidates are becoming more proficient with the use of electronic communication and are interested in finding ways to leverage their campaign messages across multiple platforms to maximize their communication efforts. It is this type of general advancement in e-campaigning, or techno campaigning, that makes the ways e-mail messages were used during the 2012 general election cycle not only discouraging but also similar to the ineffective use of e-mail to communicate candidates' stances about important issues facing the country during the 2004 and 2008 U.S. presidential campaigns.

It is difficult to understand why there is such a lack of integration between the candidates' use of e-mail and their other uses of the Internet, which was typically much more sophisticated and provided more multimedia options and issue information, across a variety of online channels and digital platforms. E-mail is certainly not as popular as other Internet offerings such as Facebook, Twitter, YouTube, Google+, Instagram, Tumblr, and the other popular social media platforms or applications, but e-mail is a primary means of communication for many citizens in the U.S. For example, Richtel (2010) suggested that older citizens still prefer e-mail over social media due to the better writing and communication it fosters, as compared to more casual Internet platforms. It is standard practice for many companies and media organizations to imbed icons linking to all social media accounts in their e-mail messages, and to send blog and other social media updates out to subscribers. These practices were not used by the 2012 U.S. presidential candidates in their e-mail messages. Treating e-mail as primarily a fundraising tool is a limited use of a powerful tool.

E-mail is a part of most U.S. citizens' lives, and it is can be much more effectively used as a portal to direct readers to pertinent information and timely engagement opportunities. This chapter's findings indicate the candidates made few improvements in their use of e-mail to campaign, which is particularly disheartening because they suggest that the campaigns continue to neglect to use e-mail as the powerful political marketing tool it is capable of being. As previously noted, e-mail has significant viral marketing potential and can overcome selective exposure (Williams, 2005). This potential is incredibly important, as one would hope that engaging e-mail recipients to spread the candidates' campaign messages would be as important as $20 donations.

Candidates and their staffers have the opportunity to harness the power of e-mail through better integration with Web sites, social media activity, televised ads, and all media. The use of e-mail may be perceived as commonplace and not as innovative as the many new technological advances of recent years such as Facebook and Twitter, but it is inexpensive, effective, and can have huge reach due to its use not only on personal computers but also on mobile devices. As the reach of e-mail continues to expand through citizens' accessing e-mail on smartphones and iPad and Android tablets, the candidates' poor use of e-mail messages as a vital part of their electronic campaigning also means they are missing a myriad of opportunities to communicate with and better inform citizens about important issues that can help to further educate voters about politics and the democratic process afforded to them in U.S. elections. E-mail can be used to help citizens make voting decisions—not just to raise money for campaign coffers.

CHAPTER 13

Social Network Sites and Interactivity: Differential Expression Effects in Campaign 2012

David Lynn Painter, Juliana Fernandes, Jessica Mahone, and Eisa Al Nashmi

Despite predictions of steep declines in young voter turnout during the 2012 campaign, 23 million citizens between the ages of 18 and 29 cast ballots in the general election, roughly the same number as participated in 2008 (CIRCLE, 2012; Pew, 2012). While low turnout rates among young citizens have been a chronic concern over the past several decades (Delli Carpini, 2000; Gans, 2004), voters between the ages of 18 and 29 achieved successively significant increases in turnout in both 2004 and 2008 that held steady in 2012. These relatively high levels of young voter participation not only outpaced growth among all other age groups, but also significantly influenced the outcome of the 2008 and 2012 presidential elections (CIRCLE, 2012; Kirby & Kawashima-Ginsburg, 2009).

Recent research suggests one explanation for higher turnout rates among young voters in recent elections is their rapid adoption of social networking sites (SNSs) that offer extrinsic rewards for acting in accordance with civic duty norms and that may increase social pressure on members to vote (Bond et al., 2012; Kohut, 2008; Smith & Rainie, 2008). Further, research also suggests the widespread adoption of Internet technologies and computer-mediated communication channels among young citizens may satisfy intrinsic needs, inspire confidence and a sense of urgency about participating in politics, and diminish the generation gap in civic participation (Owen, 2006; Schlozman, Verba, & Brady, 2010; Utz, 2009; Valenzuela, Park, & Kee, 2009). Indeed, young citizens' levels of confidence in their ability to cast an informed vote, or political information efficacy, and sense of urgency about participating in politics, or perceived salience of the upcoming election, are closely related to their voting behavior and may be influenced by exposure to campaign information (Delli Carpini, 2000; Gans, 2004; Kaid, Fernandes, & Painter, 2011; Kaid, McKinney, & Tedesco, 2007; Wolfinger & Rosenstone, 1980).

When investigating the effects of exposure to campaign information over the Internet, both information sources and interactivity levels must be specified to analyze their distinct effects on young voters' political information efficacy and perceptions of the election's salience. One purpose of this chapter is to provide context for the influence of social network sites by comparing exposure effects from online news election coverage, official campaign Web sites, and the candidates' Facebook pages. The second purpose of this chapter is to compare the main effects of interactivity levels on young citizens' information efficacy and perceived salience of the 2012 election.

The Internet requires more active users and offers more readily available feedback channels permitting two-way communication and user-content creation than do traditional media. Thus, research on the effects of exposure to Internet information sources must account for both "what the media do to people" as well as "what people do with the media" (Katz, 1959, p. 2; Ruggiero, 2000). Functional analyses indicate online activity may be divided into two types of conceptually distinct interactions: surveillance and expression (Bucy & Tao, 2007; Katz, Rice, & Aspden, 2001; Shah, Cho, Eveland, & Kwak, 2005; Stromer-Galley, 2000, 2004; Wang, 2007). Surveillance activities, such as clicking links, reading text, and viewing images or videos, are lower in interactivity and less influential on political communication outcomes than expressive activities, such as online messaging, posting on Facebook, or making comments on videos, blogs or Web sites (Cho et al., 2009; Tedesco, 2007). The third purpose of this chapter is to test for interaction effects and identify which information source and interactive condition exerted the greatest influence on information efficacy and the perceived salience of the election. Finally, the results of this chapter may also parse the effects of online information source and interactivity, suggesting important theoretical implications for both the Uses and Gratifications analytic framework and bi-directional communication models.

THEORETICAL FRAMEWORK

The Uses and Gratifications approach to media studies holds that personal goals may shape individual patterns of media usage. Conceptualized as active, audiences use media to monitor their society, to gather information, to pass time, or to communicate with other people (McQuail, 2005). Research in this tradition reveals specific combinations of demographic, attitudinal, and behavioral characteristics are associated with specific patterns of media usage (Johnstone, 1974; Rubin & Rubin, 1982; McLeod & Becker, 1981). The links between Internet use and political attitudes within a Uses and Gratifications framework suggest Internet users have higher levels of self-efficacy than non-users, that Internet use increases when people feel more efficacious, and that high levels of self-efficacy are also related to political interest and online participation (Gangadharbatla, 2008; Johnson & Kaye, 2002). Uses and Gratification research also suggests the motivational factors driving one's patterns of media usage may impact information processing, cognitions, and attitudes (Kim & Rubin, 1997). These usage patterns do not develop in a vacuum, however, and pre-existing knowledge of media channels or informational formats may influence perceptions, cognitions, and attitudes (Axelrod, 1973).

The perception of a media channel's utility in satisfying specific needs is important because familiarity with specific media platforms may develop into expectations of the purpose of the information presented and influence exposure effects such that different information sources may exert distinct effects (Becker & Schoenbach, 1989; Graber, 1984; Kushin & Yamamoto, 2010; Perse & Courtright, 1993). In this chapter, those exposed to election coverage by professional journalists from online news sources, campaign information published by professional operatives on candidates' Web sites, and content created collaboratively by campaign professionals and social media users on candidates' Facebook pages are expected to exert differential effects on political communication outcomes due to users' perceptions of their distinct motivations for presenting information.

Political Information Efficacy

Political information efficacy refers to one's level of "confidence in his or her own political knowledge and its sufficiency to engage the political process (to vote)" (Kaid, McKinney, & Tedesco, 2007, p. 1096). While political information efficacy theory has been used to explain why some people participate in the political process while others do not, the other basic premise of this framework is that different people will process and react to political information on different media channels in different ways. Similarly, Uses and Gratifications researchers argue that media messages may be processed differently based on the needs motivating consumption of specific media content and channels (Ruggiero, 2000).

Agenda Building: Salience of the Election

In addition to lower levels of information efficacy, young citizens in 2012 also expressed less urgency about participating in politics and relatively low perceptions of the election's salience (Pew, 2012). In the early 1970s, agenda-setting emerged as a theory that explained how the media may transfer issue salience to the public (McCombs & Shaw, 1972). This seminal theory also led scholars to examine the antecedents of media agenda-setting, developing the construct of agenda-building. In the context of political campaigns, agenda-building scholars explored the effects of various public relations efforts on public opinion (Kiousis, Mitrook, Wu, & Selzer, 2006; Kiousis & Strömbäck, 2010) and found a close relationship between public relations efforts and public opinion (Schleuder, McCombs, & Wanta, 1991). Similar to previous agenda-setting and agenda-building research that explored the manner in which issue or attribute salience was transferred from one agenda to another (e.g., from the media or the campaign to the public), this chapter measures the transfer of the 2012 election's salience from distinct online information sources to young citizens.

Online Information Sources

Online News

Uses and Gratifications research has a long tradition of examining the functions fulfilled by different news sources (e.g., Becker & Dunwoody, 1982; Culbertson, Evarts, Richard, Karin, & Stempel, 1994; Holbert, 2005). Survey research specifically focused on the motivations driving young citizens' news media use suggests this group reports much less urgent surveillance and vote guidance needs than other age groups (Pew, 2010). The young are also much more likely to consult Internet sources rather than traditional media sources, both overall and relative to those in other age groups (Diddi & LaRose, 2006). While online news Web sites present stories in a more traditional format, with a narrative directing a unidirectional flow of information, most also provide for immediate feedback, such as commenting and posting to social network and bookmark sites. Thus, similarities in content notwithstanding, structural and technological differences between the television and the Internet indicate they may also satisfy distinctly different needs, especially among the young (Kaye & Johnson, 2002, 2003).

Campaign Websites

The Howard Dean campaign's successful use of blogs and hyperlinks on its Web site during the 2004 primaries revolutionized political candidates' use of the Internet (Jenkins, 2006; Stromer-Galley & Baker, 2006). Controlled, unfiltered messaging on campaign Web sites facilitates candidates' efforts to establish ideological unity and develop closer connections with followers (Hindman, 2009). Campaign Web sites also serve as an effective fundraising and recruiting tool (Pollard, Chesebro, & Studinski, 2009). Moreover, Web sites offer "an unmediated, holistic, and representative portrait of campaigns" (Druckman, Kifer, & Parkin, 2009). Unlike news coverage, Web sites give voters a unique opportunity to access a campaign directly, enhancing unfiltered communication between politicians and their electorate (Smith & Smith, 2009). Similar to advertising, campaigns retain control of their messaging on their official Web sites, generally offering only the appearance of interactivity or two-way communication (Foot & Schneider, 2006).

Social Networking Sites

Facebook was initially launched to serve college networks beginning with Harvard in 2004, but opened its membership to the general public in 2006, and as of 2012 more than 40% of total Internet users logged on to this site on a daily basis (Alexa.com, 2012). Analyses of young citizens' orientations toward online information reveal both a preference for SNSs and a perception that these sites are more interactive than other sites (Beer, 2008; Sweetser & Weaver-Lariscy, 2007; Trammell, Williams, Postelnicu, & Landreville, 2005). This preference for SNS is based on the format's unique ability to fulfill social utility needs (Raacke & Bonds-Raacke, 2008).

In addition to satisfying social needs, sites such as Facebook are also powerful vehicles for exerting social pressure on members to act in accordance with behavioral norms (Quan-Haase & Young, 2010). Research indicates offline social pressure was distinctly effective at increasing voter turnout rates in the 2006 primary contests (Gerber, Green, & Larimer, 2008) and that social influence through Facebook significantly influenced turnout in the 2010 midterm contests (Bond et al., 2012). Therefore, this chapter finds its place in the literature by predicting exposure to candidates' Facebook pages will exert greater influence on young voters' political information efficacy and perceptions of the salience of the 2012 election than will online news coverage or official campaign Web sites. While those exposed to online news, campaign Web sites, and SNS may report significant gains in political information efficacy and the election's salience from the pretest to the posttest, we predict two distinct main effects of information source:

> H1: Those exposed to the candidates' Facebook pages will report greater gains in political information efficacy than those exposed to online news or campaign Web sites.
>
> H2: Those exposed to the candidates' Facebook pages will report greater gains in perceptions of the election's salience than those exposed to online news or campaign Web sites.

INTERACTIVITY

One of the earliest findings among media scholars was that interpersonal communication had greater effects on cognitions and attitudes than did exposure to mediated sources (Lazarsfeld, Berelson, & Gaudet, 1948; Katz & Lazarsfeld, 1955; Klapper, 1963). With the recent development and adoption of digital media platforms, however, investigations comparing effects of exposure to various online platforms may not capture the effects of interactivity in the transaction. Since Internet communications facilitate two-way communication, researchers must also control the manner in which participants interact with online information or risk drawing spurious conclusions. Moreover, replicable experimental investigations comparing the relative effects of exposure to various online stimuli under conditions with differing levels of interactivity may be the best method for testing these effects (Cho et al., 2009; Kim, 2006).

Expression Effects

Pingree (2007) argues that the expectation of future expression may be manipulated as an independent variable with participants randomly assigned to either surveillance (e.g., reading text or viewing images/videos) or expression (e.g., making comments on news coverage, forwarding campaign information, or posting on Facebook) conditions. Pingree's model predicts: "the expectation of future expression can improve attention to, cognitive processing of, and memory for received messages" independent of the nature of the expected expression (p. 446). Similar to the theoretical mechanism underlying the elaboration likelihood model, the cognitive and affective effects of information are conceptualized as greater among those who expect to express themselves than among those without such an expectation.

Political communication scholars have also adapted a theoretical framework for analyzing the effects of citizens' communication processes on relationships between elite-driven campaign communications and political outcomes (Huckfeldt, Sprague, & Levine, 2000; Just et al., 1996; Page, 1996; Pan, Shen, Paek, & Sun, 2006). This line of research on the O-S-R-O-R (Orientations-Stimulus-Reasoning-Orientations-Response) model suggests expression may trigger reasoning processes that mediate the effects of information, particularly when the expression occurs online (Shah et al., 2005). By accounting for participants' *Orientation* with a pretest, exposing them to a *Stimulus*, manipulating *Reasoning* using surveillance and expression conditions, and measuring participants' post-*Orientation*, which influence their behavioral *Responses*, this study also tests the O-S-R-O-R model by parsing the effects of expression and surveillance on three online information sources.

In his investigation of the effects of web exposure and interactive features on young adults' political information efficacy, Tedesco (2007) found that interactive features on political information Web sites positively impact young adults' political information efficacy across a variety of information sources. This investigation, on the other hand, isolates and compares the main and interaction effects of information source and interactivity by focusing on specific online platforms under surveillance and expression interactive conditions. Specifically, we expect two distinct main effects of interactivity:

> H3: Those in the expression condition will report greater gains in political information efficacy than those in the surveillance condition.
> H4: Those in the expression condition will report the greater gains in the salience of the election than those in the surveillance condition.

Finally, to identify which of the six conditions reported the greatest effects, we combine the first two sets of hypotheses to predict two interaction effects:

> H5: Those exposed to the candidates' Facebook pages in the expression condition will report the greatest gains in political information efficacy.
> H6: Those exposed to the candidates' Facebook pages in the expression condition will report the greatest gains in the salience of the election.

METHOD

Participants and Procedure

A three (online information format) by two (interactivity level) experimental design with 327 undergraduates from a large southeastern research university was used to test the hypotheses. The experiment was conducted online using Qualtrics software between October 7 and 14, 2012. Participants were randomly assigned to one of six different experimental conditions and each participant explored either online news stories about the election, the candidates' official campaign Web sites, or the candidates' *Facebook* pages. The level of interactivity was manipulated by the assigned activities for the two conditions: surveillance and expression.

All participants completed an online pretest questionnaire that included measures of political information efficacy and perceptions of the salience of the election. Upon completion of the pretest, the software directed participants to one of the six conditions, presented them with video and written instructions appropriate for their assigned level of interactivity, and exposed them to the stimulus. After completing the tasks in the assigned condition, the software directed participants to the posttest questionnaire that included items reassessing political information efficacy, perceptions of the salience of the election, and reports of online activities during exposure.

Manipulation

The online information source has three conditions: online news, the official campaign Web sites, and the candidates' Facebook pages. Participants assigned to online news were exposed to the Election Center section of the CNN and Fox News Web sites. Participants in the campaign Web sites condition explored the official Web sites of both the Barack Obama and Mitt Romney campaigns. Participants in the SNS condition explored both candidates' Facebook pages.

The level of interactivity was manipulated using two conditions: surveillance and expression. In the surveillance (low interactivity) condition, participants were instructed to spend at least five minutes reading the information, viewing the videos, and activating hyperlinks to related sites and information on each online news, campaign Web site, or SNS, depending on their assignment. Qualtrics software would not allow participants to advance in the questionnaire until five minutes of exposure had passed. In the expression (high interactivity) condition, participants were instructed not only to read or view the information, but also to express themselves during the transaction by posting content on *Facebook*; "liking" a post on a *Facebook* page, campaign Web site, or online news story; forwarding information or videos to another person; or sending the candidate or another person a message. Participants in the high interactivity condition were also instructed that they would be required to express themselves after the exposure. They were required to enter an e-mail address and a minimum one-sentence comment about the information into the item on the posttest questionnaire that forwarded the information to another person.

Dependent Variables

Political Information Efficacy

Participants' level of political information efficacy was measured in both the pretest and posttest questionnaires. As in previous studies (Kaid, McKinney, & Tedesco, 2007; Tedesco, 2007), four items from the American National Election Study (ANES, 2009) survey were used to construct the political information efficacy index: (a) I consider myself well qualified to participate in politics, (b) I think I am better informed about politics and government than most people, (c) I feel that I have a pretty good understanding of the important political issues facing our country today, and (d) If a friend asked me about the 2012 presidential election, I feel I would have enough information to help my friend figure out who to vote for. Participants rated their level of agreement with each statement on a five-point Likert scale. The Cronbach's α score for the scale was 0.88 in the pretest and 0.90 in the posttest.

Salience of the Election

In both the pretest and the posttest, participants were asked to state how salient they perceived the 2012 presidential election using six items from previous research (Zaichowsky, 1985). The items included: the upcoming election has prominent value in society; the upcoming election has significant value in society; the upcoming election has important value in society; the upcoming election is well known in society; the upcoming election has fundamental value in society; and I am concerned about the upcoming election. The Cronbach's α for the scale was 0.93 in the pretest and 0.87 in the posttest.

RESULTS

Participants and Manipulation Check

Three hundred and twenty-seven young citizens between the ages of 18 and 24 from a large southeastern research institution were randomly assigned to either the surveillance (51%) or expression (49%) interactivity condition and then randomly exposed to online news (30%), SNSs (34%), or campaign Web sites (36%). The participants were 52% female, 58% Caucasian, 18% Hispanic, 15% African-American, 7% multi-racial, and 2% Asian-American. In terms of partisanship, participants were 26% Republican, 41% Independent, 27% Democratic, and 6% identified their political party affiliation as "Other."

The manipulation of interactivity was checked by verifying all participants in the high interactivity condition expressed themselves after exposure to the stimuli. Two responses were deleted from the analysis due to their failure to comply with these directions. The manipulation of interactivity was also verified by the results of an analysis of variance test comparing the number of online activities performed by participants assigned to each condition: surveillance ($M = 37.41, SD = 3.21$) and expression ($M = 40.95, SD = 3.55$), $F(1, 323) = 23.526, p < .01$. Thus, the manipulation of interactivity was successful because those in the expression condition engaged in interactive activities and then expressed themselves after the exposure.

Main Effects of Information Source

The first group of hypotheses investigated the main effect of online information source on participant's levels of political information efficacy and perceptions of the election's salience. First, to verify that exposure to the stimuli exerted significant influence on political information efficacy, participants' pretest and posttest scores were compared. The results of a paired-samples t test revealed that participants' posttest political information efficacy levels ($M = 14.03, SD = 3.58$) were higher than their pretest levels ($M = 13.10, SD = 3.52$), and this difference was significant, $t(324) = -6.35, p < .01$. This process was also executed to determine how exposure to the stimuli affected participants' perceptions of the salience of the election. The results of a paired-samples t test revealed that participants' posttest perceptions of the election's salience ($M = 38.08, SD = 4.81$) were higher than their pretest perceptions ($M = 36.36, SD = 6.42$), and this difference was significant, $t(324) = -5.30, p < 0.01$. Second, participants' pretest political information efficacy scores were subtracted from their posttest scores to create a Political Information Efficacy Gain variable. This process was also executed across participants'

Table 13.1 Political Information Efficacy and Salience Gains by Information Source

	ONLINE NEWS N = 98	SOCIAL NETWORK N = 108	CAMPAIGN WEBSITES N = 118	F-VALUE	df	p
Information Efficacy	0.37	1.93	0.50	12.18	2	0.00
Salience	−0.42	5.09	0.40	33.19	2	0.00

Source: Campaign 2012 Interactivity Project, 327 participants, October 7–14, 2012.

posttest and pretest scores of the elections' salience to create a Salience Change variable. Once these variables were calculated, the main effects of online information source on gains in political information efficacy and perceptions of the election's salience were investigated.

The first hypothesis predicted participants exposed to the candidates' Facebook pages would report greater gains in political information efficacy than would those exposed to online news or campaign Web sites. As shown in the first row of Table 13.1, the results of an analysis of variance revealed a significant main effect of information source on gains in political information efficacy, $F(2, 319) = 12.18$, $p < 0.01$. Specifically, the results of a post hoc comparison using the Tukey HSD test revealed that the gains in political information efficacy among those exposed to the candidates' Facebook pages ($M = 1.93$, $SD = 3.79$) were significantly greater than among those exposed to online news ($M = 0.37$, $SD = 1.48$) or campaign Web sites ($M = 0.50$, $SD = 1.73$), but that the differences between online news and campaign Web sites were not significant. Thus, hypothesis one was strongly supported.

The second hypothesis predicted those exposed to the candidates' Facebook pages would report greater gains in perceptions of the election's salience than would those exposed to online news or campaign Web sites. As shown in the second row of Table 13.1, the results of an analysis of variance revealed a significant main effect of information source on gains in the election's salience, $F(2, 319) = 33.19$, $p < 0.01$. Specifically, the results of a post hoc comparison using the Tukey HSD test revealed that gains in the salience of the election among those exposed to Facebook ($M = 5.09$, $SD = 8.16$) were significantly greater than among those exposed to online news ($M = -0.42$, $SD = 3.72$) or campaign Web sites ($M = 0.40$, $SD = 2.30$), but that the differences between online news and campaign Web sites were not significant. Thus, hypothesis two was strongly supported.

Main Effects of Interactivity

The second group of hypotheses investigated the main effect of interactivity on participants' levels of political information efficacy and perceptions of the election's salience. The third hypothesis predicted those in the expression condition would report greater gains in political information efficacy than those in the surveillance condition. As shown in the first row of Table 13.2, the results of an analysis of variance revealed those in the expression condition ($M = 1.50$, $SD = 3.44$)

Table 13.2 Political Information Efficacy and Salience Gains by Interactivity Level

	SURVEILLANCE $N = 165$	EXPRESSION $N = 159$	F-VALUE	df	p
Information Efficacy	0.39	1.50	14.97	1	0.01
Salience	0.65	2.82	11.64	1	0.01

Source: Campaign 2012 Interactivity Project, 327 participants, October 7–14, 2012.

did indeed report greater gains in political information efficacy than those in the surveillance condition ($M = 0.39$, $SD = 1.33$), and this difference was significant, $F(1, 319) = 14.97$, $p < 0.01$. Thus, hypothesis three was strongly supported.

The fourth hypothesis predicted those in the expression condition would report greater gains in perceptions of the election's salience than those in the surveillance condition. As shown in the second row of Table 13.2, the results of an analysis of variance revealed a significant effect of information source on the salience of the election, $F(1,319) = 11.64$, $p < 0.01$. Specifically, perceptions of the saliency of the election were significantly higher among those in the expression condition ($M = 2.82$, $SD = 7.82$) than among those in the surveillance condition ($M = 0.65$, $SD = 2.38$). Thus, hypothesis four was strongly supported.

Interaction Between Online Information Source and Interactivity

Finally, in an attempt to specify which of the six conditions reported the greatest gains in political information efficacy and perceptions of the salience of the election, we predicted a significant interaction effect between online information source and interactivity. In Hypothesis Five, we predicted that those exposed to Facebook in the expression condition would report the greatest gains in political information efficacy. The results of a univariate analysis of variance test revealed that the interaction between online information source and interactivity was significant, $F(2, 319) = 17.16$, $p < 0.01$. As shown in Figure 13.1, an analysis of simple effects revealed that participants in the expression condition who were exposed to social network sites reported the greatest gains in political information efficacy ($M_{Expression} = 3.53$, $SD = 4.82$; $M_{Surveillance} = 0.32$, $SD = 0.31$), $F(1, 319) = 56.10$, ($p < 0.01$). No significant differences between the expression and surveillance conditions were observed for those exposed to candidate Web sites or online news. Therefore, these results provide strong support for hypothesis five.

Hypothesis six investigated the influence of online information source and level of interactivity on participants' perceptions of the salience of the election. Specifically, we predicted that those in the expression condition who were exposed to Facebook would report the greatest increases in perceptions of the salience of the election. A univariate analysis of variance revealed a significant interaction between information source and level of interactivity on perceptions of the election's salience, $F(1, 319) = 38.36$, $p < 0.01$. As shown in Figure 13.2, an analysis of simple effects revealed that those in the expression condition who were exposed to

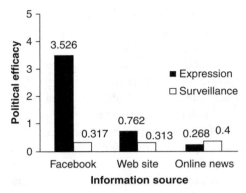

Figure 13.1 Interaction Effects on Political Information Efficacy
SOURCE: Campaign 2012 Interactivity Project, 327 participants, October 7–14, 2012.

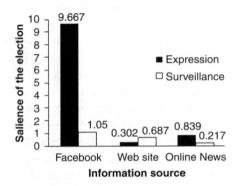

Figure 13.2 Interaction Effects on Salience of the Election
SOURCE: Campaign 2012 Interactivity Project, 327 participants, October 7–14, 2012.

SNS reported the greatest gains in saliency of the election ($M_{Expression}$ = 9.24, SD = 9.72; $M_{Surveillance}$ = 1.09, SD = 2.63), $F(1, 319)$ = 96.43, $p < 0.01$. No significant differences between expression and surveillance conditions were observed among participants exposed to campaign Web sites or online news. Therefore, these results provide strong support for hypothesis six.

DISCUSSION

These results provide compelling evidence that online information and expressive interactions enhance both political information efficacy and the election's salience. Since expressive interactions ("liking" a page, forwarding information) require one to elaborate upon and synthesize the information to a greater extent than when he or she is merely surveying the environment (clicking links, reading text, and/or viewing images/videos), expression increases cognitive recall, improving one's ability to apply information to behavioral decision-making (Nekmat, 2012). Specifically, we found the effect of expressive interaction was stronger on SNS than on online news or campaign Web sites. This result may be partially explained by the dual nature of SNS such as Facebook.

Accessing political information on online news and campaign Web sites usually occurs when one specifically seeks that information. On a social networking site (SNS), however, political information may be provided during interactions with friends, family, and acquaintances, and not as a result of a specific information search. These social interactions inherent to SNS are more likely to encourage active engagement with the information through commenting, "liking," re-posting, and sharing than when seeking and consuming information from online news and campaign Web sites. This shift from passive consumer to active participant also increases the likelihood of political participation (Shah et al., 2007). Further, the more public nature of expressive behaviors on Facebook trigger ego-involvement and a sense of commitment to a social network to a much greater extent than the relatively anonymous expressive interactions on online news or campaign Web sites.

Practically speaking, the findings in this chapter suggest it is critically important for political campaigns to use SNS such as Facebook to connect with young voters, particularly for increasing the salience of the election. While those with higher levels of political information efficacy are more likely to participate in politics than those with lower levels (Kenski & Stroud, 2006), this effect may not translate into offline participation should individuals fail to perceive the importance of their participation in the election. Stemming from a belief that politics has personal relevance, this sense of urgency about voting motivates and activates political participation (Franklin, 2001). Moreover, Druckman, Kifer, and Parkin (2010) contend candidate engagement on political issues influences the saliency of those issues in public opinion, and the Internet has a unique capacity for allowing candidates to discuss a large number of issues in greater detail without the news media filter. Taken together, this research suggests social networking sites (SNS) such as Facebook are a campaign's most powerful tool for not only increasing younger voters' confidence in their information levels, but also for persuading them of the importance of their vote in particular.

It is important to remember that the act of voting requires making two choices: first, whether or not to participate, and second, which candidates to support. Should the habit of voting and participating in politics not be developed early in life, however, disengaged young citizens are very likely to become disengaged older citizens (Putnam, 2000). Thus, analyzing the effects of online sources and interactivity on young citizens' information efficacy and perceptions of the election's salience increases our understanding of how to inspire their feelings of confidence and urgency about participating in the process. Moreover, the mediating effects of expression may be measured and compared across online information sources, testing and specifying bi-directional communication models.

As with all types of social scientific inquiry, this experimental investigation has important limitations that must be noted. First, this chapter focused on young citizens and the sample was limited to individuals in college between the ages of 18 and 24. Therefore, the conclusions may not necessarily be generalized to other age segments of the population. Second, this study did not include SNS other than

Facebook as stimulus material. Indeed, SNS such as YouTube and Twitter discussed in other chapters surely have distinct effects on political cognitions, attitudes, and behaviors also worthy of exploration. A potential third limitation was manipulating interactivity by instructing participants to either expect to express themselves or to merely survey the environment prior to exposure to the stimulus. As with all experimental investigations, this process was artificial, but it allowed for the parsing of information source, interactivity, and interaction effects in a manner that tested theoretical propositions and specified causality in each of the six conditions. Finally, this study examined the effects of interactivity and online format on two specific dependent variables: information efficacy and the election's salience. Other potential effects and behavioral outcomes were not investigated. Previous research, however, identified increased political information efficacy (Kaid, McKinney, & Tedesco, 2007) and election salience (Franklin, 2001) as strong indicators of increased probability of voting, the normative outcome at the center of this chapter's inquiry.

In light of this chapter's findings, an exploration of the links between political information efficacy and the salience of the election are warranted, especially in terms of effects resulting from exposure to campaign information. Political information efficacy, or one's confidence in his or her ability to apply political knowledge to political participation (Kaid, McKinney, & Tedesco, 2007), may increase election salience, or one's perception that his or her participation in the upcoming election is important (Franklin, 2001). Franklin's definition of salience indicates individuals must believe in the importance of their participation, and increased confidence in one's ability to participate in an informed manner may also increase the need to vote. Indeed, Rauch (2010) identified an analogous relationship among social activists who not only feel confident in their political knowledge, but also feel the need to be civically engaged because of that confidence. Determining the extent to which this recursive relationship is influenced by information, sources, and expressive behaviors among non-activists may provide compelling analysis of the relationship between these two variables.

Although previous research indicated political talk triggered reasoning processes that mediated the effects of information from a variety of online and offline sources (Kim, 2006; Shah et al., 2005; Shah et al., 2007), expression only exerted significant influence among those exposed to Facebook in this investigation. Indeed, as shown in Figures 13.1 and 13.2, the expectation and execution of expressive interactions did not exert significant influence on efficacy or saliency among those exposed to online news or campaign Web sites. Since this finding parses the conditions under which expression mediates information effects, it has important implications for the bi-directional communication models because online messaging was not a mediating factor on post-orientations or responses.

CHAPTER 14

Issue Debates in 140 Characters: Online Talk Surrounding the 2012 Debates

Dan Schill and Rita Kirk

The 2012 presidential campaigns embraced digital campaign techniques such as interactivity, immediacy, personalization, and microtargeting, and sustained engagement (for a review, see Edgerly, Bode, Kim, & Shah, 2012). The Internet and the accompanying array of social-media tools such as Facebook, Twitter, and YouTube transformed the way political campaigns are waged and the manner in which elected officials, journalists, and citizens communicate. Improvements in other information and communication technologies such as widespread cellular data networks and ubiquitous smartphone availability created improved access to these tools. The communication ecosystem during the 2012 presidential campaign was ubiquitous, immediate, dynamic, decentralized, personalized, and always on.

In the 2012 presidential election, the distinctive new communications strategy was using the social media tool Twitter. As *New York Times* reporter Ashley Parker (2012) described, "If the 2008 presidential race embraced a 24/7 news cycle, four years later politicos are finding themselves in the middle of an election most starkly defined by Twitter, complete with 24-second news cycles and pithy bursts" (para. 3). Worldwide, Twitter has grown to 500 million users sending over 350 million tweets per day (Costolo, 2012). During the 2012 election season, Twitter became the 10th most popular site on the Internet and was used heavily by people in the 18–44 age group (Alexa.com, n.d.). As election night was winding down, a photo of Barack and Michelle Obama hugging, with the caption "four more years" posted on the official Obama Twitter account, became the most retweeted image ever (with more than 800,000 RTs) and the most liked Facebook post in history (with more than 4.4 million likes and over 215,000 comments) (Scherer, 2012).

Although Twitter use now plays an important role in political campaigns, few researchers have considered how Twitter is used by campaigns and journalists, the type of communication on the service, and its impact on the political process. This chapter is a study of Twitter use during the 2012 presidential debates. Exploring the online media environment immediately before, during, and after a major

event like a presidential debate provides a unique window into our current media/
politics ecosystem.

TWITTER USE IN THE 2012 ELECTION

About 15% of all Internet users use Twitter, while 8% of online adults use the service each day (Smith & Brenner, 2012), which is nearly double the 8% of Internet
users who used Twitter in 2010. Several demographic groups have higher rates of
Twitter usage: more than a quarter (28%) of online African-Americans use Twitter,
about one quarter (26%) of Internet users ages 18–29 use Twitter, and 19% of urban
and 14% of suburban Internet users use Twitter (compared to only 8% of rural
Internet users).

   As with any new medium, users applied it to topics dominating their attention
at the time and the presidential election was the focus for many Americans in
2012. Specifically, 66% of all social media users and 39% of all American adults
used social media for political and civic activities in 2012, including "liking" or
forwarding political materials, encouraging others to vote, or posting their own
thoughts on political issues (Ranie, Smith, Schlozman, Brady, & Verba, 2012). So
it is unsurprising that there were over 31 million campaign-related tweets on Election Day, peaking at 327,452 Tweets Per Minute (TPM) during the results coverage, surpassing previous Twitter use highs (Sharp, 2012d).

   For news organizations, Twitter has become a means for engaging and directing readers and viewers to the news site for deeper knowledge. For example, CNN
invented a program permitting users to edit and share their own media clips from
the presidential debates and then post them on Facebook or Twitter. Playing
editor, users could see how their perspectives were similar to or different from that
of CNN. Users' posts on Facebook or Twitter worked as online references to CNN
so that others could use the editor tool as well or tune in to CNN for further information. This shift of focus from traditional one-way communication to a two-way
communication model is a means for engaging users.

   Politicians and political campaigns can use Twitter in various ways. Newsmakers may share policy or issue-related information by linking to their website.
Candidates can publicize campaign events and direct followers to media coverage
of their campaign. Politicians can also share personal details about their day-to-
day lives to present themselves as more likable and approachable. Research has
found that because Twitter is free and available to anyone with an Internet connection, Twitter is typically used more by minority parties and less well-known candidates in order to reach supporters (Vergeer, Hermans, & Sams, 2011).

   On Twitter, politicians can talk directly to their constituents and supporters
without going through a media outlet or other intermediary. Similar to television
advertisements and campaign websites, campaigns retain control of their messaging on Twitter and social networking sites (SNS) and generally provide only the
appearance of interactivity. While Twitter allows campaigns to build relationships
with voters and contributors, track news coverage, gather data, and respond
immediately to crises, Twitter also carries risk because it "can quickly define the

political debate, whether candidates like it or not, and a single 140-character missive can turn into a nightmare" (Parker, 2012, para. 4).

The emergent research on social networking service use and citizen engagement has shown that SNS users engage in relatively robust political talk in these spaces. For example, a study of the Coffee Party Facebook group found that SNS users participated in unprompted and significant deliberative discourse on the site (Mascaro & Goggins, 2011). While a study of college student Facebook posts during the 2008 election revealed a wide variety of divergent postings and counter postings (Fernandes, Giurcanu, Bowers, & Neely, 2010), other studies suggest SNS reach those who are less interested in politics (Utz, 2009) and that those exposed to political messages on Twitter and Facebook are likely to learn from these messages and remember them (Bode, 2012b). Online political discussion can facilitate greater offline and online political engagement (Conroy, Feezell, & Guerrero, 2012; Bode, 2012a; Valenzuela, Kim, & Gil de Zúñiga, 2012), especially when the discussion is among individuals who do not know each other well (e.g., communication outside close-knit friends and family groups) and when the discussants agree with each other (Valenzuela et al., 2012). Bode, Vraga, Borah, and Shah (forthcoming), for instance, found that adolescents who took part in political communication on SNS were more likely to engage in the classic methods of political participation (see also Vitak et al., 2011).

TWITTER, SECOND SCREENS, AND PRESIDENTIAL DEBATES

Like other social media, Twitter has become a "second screen" for those watching televised shows. In other words, viewers will have Twitter open on a laptop, tablet, or phone and tweet comments, jokes, and other responses to the television program. So pervasive is the use of Twitter that a Nielsen study found that 38% of smartphone owners and 41% of tablet owners used their device while watching television and that one in three Twitter users sent messages about the content of television shows (Bauder, 2012). These connected viewers are using their devices for a wide range of activities: 38% keep themselves busy during commercial breaks, 23% send text messages to others watching the same program, 22% use the phone to check whether what they saw on television was true, 20% visited a website that was mentioned, 11% looked up what others were saying about a program, and 11% posted their own comments online (Smith & Boyles, 2012). Much of this second screen experience resolves around major events, such as awards shows, reality television results shows, and sporting events.

This heavy use of social media while watching the debates caught the attention of political parties and news organizations anxious to engage viewers during the elections. In efforts to capitalize on the use of second screens to enhance viewership, several media organizations developed specific apps. In a Republican primary debate, Yahoo began using an app called "IntoNow." Partnering with ABC News during the broadcast, those who had the app were asked to tag the broadcast, which then permitted them to receive polling questions, stories related to candidate profiles, and access to journalists' discussions. Results of the instant polling were provided to moderators Diane Sawyer and George Stephanopoulos during the debate.

Using Twitter as a second screen during debates is also popular amongst journalists. Twitter became the go-to tool for nearly every reporter's coverage, just as campaigns and their staffs used it to draw interest in candidate messages and movements. Viewers could get the sense that they were "in the know," following the campaign as if they were on the bus (or plane) with the candidates. Tweeting and re-Tweeting messages to their followers, users could function as opinion leaders by keeping their followers informed, interested, and engaged with the election process. These journalists, campaign operatives, bloggers, activists, and engaged citizens all make up the so-called Twitterverse.

The convergence of media channels and the use of social second screens have changed traditional definitions and understandings of various media channels. As Papacharissi (2010) suggested, "In the democratic sphere of interaction, convergence simultaneously melds and blurs traditional boundaries among media, and among audiences of different media (print/TV/online/radio), audiences and publics, citizens and consumers, consumers and producers" (p. 52). The second screen phenomenon allows these converged audience members to combine several overlapping media forms (e.g., broadcast debate, news websites, campaign tweets) while concurrently creating media (e.g., tweets, e-mails) in a practice that is easily integrated with daily life (e.g., mobile, tablets, lightweight laptops).

Our analysis of the communication environment leads us to assess Twitter use among three distinct groups: journalists, political campaigns, and interested citizens.

METHOD

Based on the methodology of Parmelee and Bichard (2012), a frame analysis was conducted to determine how the campaigns and journalists used Twitter during the debates. Framing is a popular area of inquiry (Matthes, 2009) and, as stated by Dan Riffe (2004), editor of *Journalism & Mass Communication Quarterly*, "one of the most fertile areas of current research in journalism and mass communication involves the concept of 'framing'" (p. 2). Under this approach, the researchers read and systematically analyze each tweet for "keywords, stock phrases, stereotyped images, sources of information, and sentences that provide thematically reinforcing clusters of facts or judgments" (Entman, 1993, p. 52). The researchers took extensive notes while they examined the frames, keywords, and images that were present in the tweets. Both researchers agreed upon the themes that emerged.

All tweets that were posted from one hour before the debate through 90 minutes after the debate were analyzed. The Twitter accounts included for the Romney campaign were: @MittRomney, @TeamRomney (Romney campaign account), @PaulRyanVP, @RomneyResponse (Romney campaign's response account), @GGitcho (Romney's Communications Director), @AndreaMSaul (Romney's Press Secretary), and @EricFehrn (Senior Advisor to Romney). The

Obama campaign accounts analyzed were: @BarackObama, @Obama2012 (Obama campaign account), @JoeBiden, @TruthTeam2012 (Obama campaign's response account), @CBrentColburn (Obama's Communications Director), @BenLaBolt (Obama's Press Secretary), @DavidAxelrod (Senior Advisor to Obama), and @StefCutter (Obama's Deputy Campaign Manager).

To provide a sample of journalist Twitter use, Salon's list of 50 "political must-read" journalist Twitter accounts (Rayfield, 2012) was utilized. This list was selected because it provided an independent list of influential journalistic feeds and a cross-section of different types of journalists on Twitter. The sample included network news correspondents (e.g., Chuck Todd, *NBC News*), newspaper reporters (e.g., Karen Tumulty, *Washington Post*), cable television journalists (e.g., Peter Hamby, *CNN*), reporters for websites (e.g., Dave Weigel, *Slate*, @DaveWeigel), writers for politics-specific media (e.g., Maggie Haberman, *Politico*), magazine writers (e.g., Molly Ball, *The Atlantic*), wire service reporters (e.g., Kasie Hunt, *Associated Press*), writers for blogs (e.g., Ezra Klein, *Wonkblog*), reporters for opinion journalism (e.g., Adam Serwer, *Mother Jones*), and commentators (e.g., David Frum, *Daily Beast/Newsweek*).

CAMPAIGN TWITTER USE

Both candidates and their staffs used Twitter to get their message out, to attempt to influence the post-debate debate, and to provide more information to followers. Three overlapping themes emerged in these tweets: (1) the source frame, (2) the media validation frame, and (3) the framing frame.

Before exploring the themes, it should be noted that the Obama campaign was much more prolific than the Romney campaign. For example, just looking at the number of tweets from each candidate's Twitter account is revealing. Remember, these are the accounts with the largest followings and the widest reach. Obama's primary account had a total of 112 tweets during the debate period (16 in debate 1, 52 in debate 2, and 44 in debate 3), compared to only 14 for Romney's main account (4 in debate 1, 4 in debate 2, and 6 in debate 3). This is significant because continuing engagement and frequent posts are important on Twitter and the Obama campaign had 8 times as much content as the Romney campaign. For both campaigns, these messages had a substantial reach, as indicated by the number of followers and retweets of the posts. At a minimum, it was typical for the candidate's tweets to be reposted several hundreds of times, and the vast majority of posts were retweeted several thousands of times. For example, during the second debate, @BarackObama's message linking followers to a negative campaign video ("Why Mitt Romney was not an effective governor: http://t.co/BaNC4ks5") was retweeted over 3,700 times. Likewise, over 4000 people retweeted a @MittRomney attack ("As gas prices continue to rise, even @BarackObama admits he doesn't have a comprehensive energy policy").

Source Frame

The first and most pronounced frame in the candidate tweets was the source frame. Under this frame, the candidate and the campaigns framed themselves as credible transmitters of important information (Parmelee & Bichard, 2012). Throughout the debate, Twitter was used to get information out to supporters, to encourage online debate, and to influence media coverage. Just as in media effects studies of traditional advertising, the true accomplishment of Twitter campaigns is capturing the attention of otherwise inattentive voters and exposing them to information that has long been in the public domain (Stimson, 2004). This source frame was manifest in four ways: (a) tweeting evidence, (b) fact checking and rapid response, (c) the use of hashtags, and (d) tweeting debate quotes.

Both campaigns used Twitter in real time to add evidence, link to news stories, or to further elaborate on points that the candidates were making in the debate. For example, during the first debate, @TeamRomney linked to the candidates economic plan, tweeting: "@MittRomney's plan for a stronger middle class-12 million new jobs in his first term: http://t.co/QRCRZrIR." During the same debate, @Obama2012 posted, "Calculate how much you'd pay under the Romney-Ryan tax plan: http://t.co/3tDMeawR." For a viewer following the debate, these links make it easy to retrieve the detailed plans from both sides. There are many examples of the campaigns providing such elaboration. In the first debate, for instance, Stephanie Cutter tweeted: "Since the President took office, businesses created 5.1m jobs. Here's how we'll keep moving forward: http://t.co/CAjZ6Met #ForwardNotBack," while the Romney response account tweeted: "More than 23 million Americans are unemployed, underemployed, or have stopped looking for work: http://t.co/0lXx86lB #CantAfford4More."

Second, this source frame was also used to fact check the debate and respond to attacks in real time. By having both campaigns' Twitter accounts in your Twitter feed, viewers could read and click on the real time rebuttals that political consultants call "rapid response." Throughout the debates, the @TruthTeam2012 account would tweet facts and links to news stories rebutting Romney. For example, @TruthTeam2012 posted: "FACT: If Romney pays for his tax plan as he's promised, middle-class families with kids could see their taxes increase by an avg of $2,041" in the first debate. By beginning these tweets with the word "FACT," the statements are given authority and weight. During the town hall debate, Obama's primary account rebutted Romney by linking to a magazine story on Pell Grants: "Mitt says 'keep our Pell Grants growing.' But the Romney-Ryan budget 'would severely diminish Pell grants.' http://t.co/f0xSeFeM." The Romney campaign also used this technique, although with less frequency, for example, the @RomneyResponse account responded to Obama's Syria policy by tweeting, "It took months for @BarackObama to call for Mr. Assad to go, despite the Assad family's 40-year track record of hostility."

On Twitter, rapid response is measured in seconds. This is a long way from the 1992 campaign, when Bill Clinton's "War Room" was heralded for its ability to respond to attacks within the same day's news cycle. Because of social media and other changes in the media and politics ecosystem, there is no longer a news cycle at all (at least using the old definition). It appears that the campaigns had fact checking and rapid response tweets pre-written such that they could be posted on Twitter the second the issue or statement came up in the debate.

The main candidate and campaign Twitter accounts typically maintained an "above the trenches," information-providing posture, while using staff and surrogate personal accounts to launch attacks. In this way, the main accounts (which have the largest audiences) could be seen as more factual and the campaign staff accounts (which are only followed by journalists and political insiders) could engage in the spin war common among political-media elites. The prototypical combatant in this Twitter spin war was Obama's Stephanie Cutter. During the debates, Cutter tweeted with the sarcastic style common amongst those working in Washington, such as, "If ignoring MA congressional del/spkr/state prez for 4 yrs = bipartisanship then Mitt nailed it: http://t.co/DC4yEb6V #RealRomney" and "Do we think the American people want this guy in their living room for next 4 years? #testymitt." Cutter's effective use of social media like Twitter can drive conversations among opinion leaders on the topic of the moment rather than spew out canned messages.

Third, hashtags were used to establish the campaigns as an information source. A hashtag is a word or phrase prefixed with the # symbol that allows Twitter users to mark posts by topics and to organize tweets around themes. During the 2012 debates, hashtags had political and communication value. For instance, in the middle of the town hall debate, Obama referred to Romney's economic plan as a "sketchy deal." Soon after, the Obama campaign and other Twitter users began using the #sketchydeal hashtag to criticize various aspects of Romney's proposals. The hashtag (and Obama's implicit attack) echoed through the Twitterverse as #sketchydeal became a trending topic.

There are many other examples of hashtags being used to encourage discussion around a key debate moment that is favorable to one candidate or another. For example, ten minutes before the end of the final debate, the official Barack Obama Twitter feed posted: "President Obama won tonight's debate because his leadership has made us stronger, safer, & more secure. #ProudOfObama." This message was retweeted over 8,000 times and favorited over 2,400 times. Other surrogates picked up on this hashtag: Michelle Obama tweeted, "Barack's steady leadership has made us stronger and safer than we were four years ago. That was clear tonight. –mo #ProudOfObama" and Ohio Governor Ted Strickland tweeted, "Tonight, it was clear. There was only one commander in chief in the room: President Barack Obama. #ProudOfObama." The campaign also used this theme to make a fundraising pitch after the debate. The campaign linked supporters to a fundraising website, saying, "If you're #ProudOfObama tonight, help make sure this campaign has the resources it needs to win: http://t.co/LQFYSaRq" on the official Barack Obama feed.

The campaigns also attempted to influence the Twitter conversation by purchasing "Promoted Trend" ads and tags. On the day of the first debate, for example, the Romney campaign paid $120,000 for the tag #CantAfford4More to be displayed for every Twitter user to see. When the tag is clicked, the user saw this message: "Another term for @BarackObama will bring more taxes, regulations, and debt that have ground our recovery to a halt" (Mazmanian, 2012). Similarly, campaigns bought "Promoted Tweet" ads such that when a user searches for a popular word or hashtag, the promoted tweet is shown at the top of the search results. For example, when discussion peaked around the #horsesandbayonets hashtag during the second debate, the Obama campaign paid for their message to appear whenever someone clicked on the hashtag or searched for the hashtag. The message ad that appeared was, "President Obama on Romney: 'When it comes to our foreign policy, you seem to want to import the foreign policies of the 1980s.' #RomneyWrong." These promoted tweet ad buys demonstrate how the campaigns try to piggyback on Twitter trends so their position will be included in the social conversation.

Finally, the fourth way the source frame was used was to tweet quotes directly from the debate. When their candidate would say a good line, the campaigns would tweet these quotes. For instance, during the town hall debate, the main Barack Obama account tweeted, " 'Gov. Romney doesn't have a 5-point plan. He has a 1-point plan . . . to make sure that folks at the top play by a different set of rules.' " and "President Obama: 'I said I would end the war in Iraq, and I did.' #PromiseKept." By tweeting these quotes, the campaigns can encourage their followers to retweet the quotes to the followers' followers (who may not be watching the debate) and generate discussion. The two tweets that were just cited were retweeted over 5,500 and 6,000 times, respectively. This technique encourages interaction with the debate content.

As previously discussed, Twitter can be used as a two-way engagement mechanism where elected officials can respond and interact directly with citizens. During the debates, this ability of Twitter was not used by the campaigns. Overwhelmingly, tweets during the debate told their followers what to do; the campaigns did not respond to questions or retweet followers' comments with a response. For example, Joe Biden asked followers to retweet before the third debate, writing, "RT if you're ready to cheer on President Obama in tonight's debate. #StrongerWithObama http://t.co/YjiAKou8." Before the town hall debate, Obama's Brent Colburn asked followers to respond to a question, "Question of the Day—Will we see a 'severe conservative' trying to dress up like a moderate again tonight? Or will we see the #RealRomney." The campaigns also encouraged interaction by linking to images, quote photos, and charts that could be used as social media profile pictures or images on Pinterest, but again, these tactics were all one-way. This may be a missed opportunity because Utz (2009) observed that visitors to a politician's social networking site had more favorable attitudes toward that politician when that politician responded to voters' comments on their profile. The speed and complexity of debates on Twitter make two-way interaction difficult to achieve in real time.

Media Validation Frame

The second major frame used by the campaigns was citing media as third-party validation sources. Specifically, media sources were used either as a method to self-promote or as vehicles to launch attacks. When journalists would make a positive comment, the campaigns would often retweet the comment on the campaign accounts so their followers would see the tweet. For instance, when MSNBC host

Chris Matthews tweeted, "Obama won big on W policies and equal treatment for women and on taxes before that. He is way ahead. #debates," the Obama campaign retweeted the message. These compliments have more weight when coming from a journalist instead of from the campaign.

In addition to directly criticizing their opponent, both campaigns retweeted journalist tweets that were favorable to their side. For example, the main Obama account retweeted Ezra Klein's comment about Romney's math, "Yes, I heard what Romney said about his tax plan. And the numbers don't work. Math matters" in the second debate. Similarly, in the third debate, @RomneyResponse quoted the *Washington Post's* appraisal of Obama's Iran policy, "WaPo: 'The result is that President Obama is not even leading from behind on Iran; he is simply behind.' #Debates #CantAfford4More." The Obama campaign used this strategy extensively. Specifically, during the second debate Obama's Press Secretary Ben Labolt retweeted 27 media and commentator tweets that described how Obama was winning the debate. For example, Labolt retweeted NBC News correspondent Luke Russert's instant analysis, "#Obama much sharper and serious than first debate." Similarly, in the third debate, the official Obama campaign account retweeted 21 pro-Obama messages.

These critiques had more authority because they came from third party sources and the number and variety of journalists who were included created a bandwagon effect, suggesting that the elite media consensus was that Obama was winning the debates. Obviously, the reporters need to be making the tweets before the campaigns can link to them, and notably, the Obama campaign did not link to many media tweets during the first debate, when media consensus was that he performed poorly in the debate.

Framing Frame

The third major frame was used by the campaigns when they employed Twitter to try to influence viewers' and broadcasters' framing of the debate. For years, campaigns have "spun" the news and jousted via press releases, public statements, and ads, but Twitter use has escalated the campaign tit-for-tat. Starting in the Republican primaries and continuing through (and after) Election Day, campaign staffers and surrogates frequently Twitter-dueled with one-liners and back-and-forth shot-trading. The primary combatants for the presidential campaigns were Romney senior advisor Eric Fehrnstrom and Obama senior advisor David Axelrod. This is significant because previous research (Ku, Kaid, & Pfau, 2003; Tedesco, 2005) has found that candidates' online communication (e.g., websites) can set the issue agendas of the news media and of voters.

The debate spin room used to be in a gymnasium adjacent to the debate hall. In 2012, the spin room was on Twitter, where journalists, campaign communications staff, and influential citizen elites debated and co-created a narrative about what happened in a debate. Importantly, all of these exchanges occured instantly, continuously, and in real time during the debate. As Zac Moffatt, the digital director for the Romney campaign argued, "Twitter is the ultimate real-time engagement mechanism, so it's moved everything to a much faster speed. You have no choice but to be actively engaging it at all times" (cited in Parker, 2012, para. 7).

The candidates and campaigns littered their Twitter feeds with posts asserting that their candidate is "winning" the debate or otherwise scoring points. For example, before the first debate, Paul Ryan tweeted "In tonight's debate, we will see a clear choice between broken promises and bold leadership. @MittRomney is the right man to lead." The ultimate example of this was when Barack Obama's Twitter account declared that, "President Obama won tonight's debate because his leadership has made us stronger, safer & more secure. #ProudOfObama" ten minutes before the end of the third debate. This tweet was retweeted nearly 8,000 times and favorited over 2,400 times.

Using the president's Twitter account to engage in pundit-like spin is a new development, and while most Twitter users know the messages are coming from campaign staffers and not directly from the candidate, it does illustrate how old rules of decorum do not necessarily apply online. As Charlie Warzel (2012) of *Adweek* observed, "The social world has no real rules and is home to boundless speculation and wild prediction, which means that political campaigns can spin and even perform damage control from their computers well before reporters flood the spin room" (para. 4).

JOURNALIST TWITTER USE

In the United States, the typical presidential debate news cycle is well established: before the debate, journalists play-up the significance of the debates while handicapping who will win and previewing which issues and personality characteristics are likely to play a role. During this pre-debate coverage, the campaigns will attempt to lower expectations by pointing out the weaknesses of their candidate and the strength of the opposition. After the debate, as the campaign surrogates are dispatched to talk shows and the spin room, the news media determines who "won" the debate and the impact of the debate on the campaign horse race. What was new in 2012 was the news coverage during the debate. In 2012, journalists and pundits did not wait until their post-debate television appearance or the next morning's column to give their reaction; instead, many joined the hundreds of other journalists in posting real-time commentary on Twitter. This echoes a similar "real time analysis" trend established in Britain's first televised party leaders' debates in 2010 (Ampofo, Anstead, & O'Loughlin, 2012; Chadwick, 2011).

Just the fact that journalists now live-tweet the debates and use Twitter as a second screen during the debates deserves mention. In the media filing room at the debate site, the debate is shown on large monitors throughout the room and journalists sit at their assigned table and surround themselves with screens. On at least one computer, journalists will typically have a word processor open and a social media dashboard with a constantly scrolling feed of tweets and Facebook posts. The reporters will typically be composing their story while they tweet and read the tweets of other journalists. Journalists will also send and receive tweets on at least one mobile device, such as a smartphone. During a debate, journalists use Twitter like a giant focus group of other journalists where the constant stream of comments can coalesce into major themes or issues. They test out ideas and lines of argument. What resonates in this running conversation will likely end up in written pieces or television appearances. In their tweets, journalists relied on two frames: an interpretation frame and an evaluation frame.

Interpretation Frame

One of the primary functions of the news media in the United States is interpretation. The news media not only surveys the events of the day and brings them to public attention, "they also interpret the events' meanings, put them into context, and speculate about their consequences" (Graber, 2010, p. 9). From analyzing journalist tweets during the debates, it is clear that Twitter is narrowing the latitude of interpretation of what happened in the debate, what the important moments were, and the impact of the debate on the campaign. Dana Milbank (2012) from the *Washington Post* referred to this as "one of the most elaborate exercises ever undertaken in groupthink" (para. 2) which caused "conventional wisdom to be set, simplified and amplified, faster and more persuasively" (para. 3). This can help or hurt either candidate, depending on what happens in the debate and how the media discussion evolves. While Obama appeared to benefit from this quick conventional wisdom setting in the second and third debate, the news media declared Romney victorious long before the first debate ended (Stelter, 2012).

Some journalists tweeted about the news coverage or other journalist's tweets. This "meta-coverage" plays an important role as journalists test out their own framing of the event and, in return, receive nearly instantaneous feedback from their peers. On Twitter, journalists floated trial balloons and tested arguments before formalizing those ideas in a print column or broadcast appearance. This type of rapid-fire, instant analysis shifts the focus of news away from explanation and towards peanut-gallery commentary. For example, during the town hall debate, *NBC News'* Chuck Todd tweeted, "This debate is more contentious but less substantive so far" and "Wow—two questions in a row that the Obama campaign is ecstatic got asked."

Other journalists shied away from interpretation and focused on more basic reporting. Charlie Beckett (2010) observed that with live blogging on Twitter, "the journalist moves from a linear, one-off story to a story of instant witnessing" (p. 3). A good example of this "instant witnessing" is the Twitter feed of CBS News White House Correspondent Mark Knoller. Knoller used his account to post real time reporting of the debate, free of interpretation. For instance, during the town hall debate, Knoller tweeted: "Both candidates hold their own hand mikes. Pres Obama says his policies will make sure 'the future is bright' for college students" and "This debate Pres Obama wearing a red tie, Romney wearing blue. Both wearing American Flag lapel pins."

Evaluation Frame

A second major frame found in the journalist tweets is the evaluation frame. Like boxing judges, journalists appeared to be scoring the debate in real time and noted when a candidate scored a point or lost an argument. And the end product of this evaluation was deciding who was "winning" the debate. For instance Adam Serwer of the *American Prospect* wrote, "Obama talking loopholes and deductions,

Romney talking personal stories. O is not winning this debate" during the first debate. Similarly, the *Daily Caller's* Matt Lewis tweeted, "I feel like time of possession matters in this format. Being on offense matters. Whoever talks the most will likely *win*." Indicative of this play-by-play analysis was *The Hotline's* Reid Wilson. Throughout the first debate, Wilson gave his evaluations, such as, "Strong close for Romney. He wins round 1" and "Segment 2, also going Romney. He's closing well."

Some journalists no longer waited for the end of the debate to declare a winner. Ben Smith of *BuzzFeed*, one of the journalists analyzed for this chapter, posted his first reaction less than 45 minutes into the first debate by explaining, "how Mitt Romney won the first debate" (see Smith, 2012). Smith linked to this story on his Twitter feed and the story went on to gather over 96,000 total views.

Like Smith, many journalists used Twitter to link to stories or lengthier content. Twitter itself lacks the ability to convey substantive information given that users are limited to 140 characters. Even Twitter founder Jack Dorsey said, "The definition was 'a short burst of inconsequential information,' and 'chirps from birds'. And that's exactly what the product was" (cited in Sarno, 2009, para. 26). Yet in many ways, Twitter is a form of headline writing, a tease that captures reader attention and leads them to more substantive information. For many journalists, the primary function of Twitter is as a portal to other, more substantive information sources, including photos, video, and longer pieces. Tweets are similar to headline writing. The purpose is to draw readers to the full story below the headline.

There was not a great deal of direct back-and-forth through @replies or commenting on retweets. Journalists were instead more likely to offer their take on a common debate moment. And because many of these journalists follow each other on Twitter and therefore see each other's tweets in their streams, these tweets act as a form of public, collective conversation. Importantly, journalists did not typically retweet citizen comments. While viewers could respond to the journalist's posts, the journalists did not directly engage or promote such comments. Nonetheless, these media tweets may still engage viewers in new ways by making the debate (and the news coverage) more interactive and interesting. As Thurman and Walters (2012) argued, "The faster, more informal, hypertextual, and networked journalism . . . is doing more than engaging the public—it may also be making public-affairs content more palatable and going some way towards rebuilding faith in journalistic objectivity" (p. 98).

If nothing else, the chattering and back and forth amongst journalists and between journalists and the campaign are now public. The conversations between the "boys on the bus" are more transparent than ever, and they happen in real time during the debate. Because tweets are public and accessible to anyone with an Internet connection, journalists must also continually monitor and self-censor their tweets in order to meet the expectations of their followers (see Marwick & boyd, 2011).

The debate on Twitter spilled over into other media and an inter-media agenda setting effect was observed between Twitter and legacy media. On television, online, and in print, journalists and commentators frequently referenced specific tweets or Twitter trends in post-debate stories. For example, after the first debate, Brian Williams cited tweets from journalists Ron Fournier and James Fallows on

NBC and Greta Van Susteren quoted from comedian Bill Maher and Republican strategist Mike Murphy on *Fox News Channel* (see Stelter, 2012). Twitter discussion was widely covered in post-debate stories in media outlets as varied as *USA Today* (Eversley, 2012), the *LA Times* (Blake, 2012), *CBS This Morning* (Sakwa & Steers, 2012), the *Daily Beast* (Strochlic, 2012), and *Entertainment Weekly* (Hertzfeld, 2012). Even "the Old Gray Lady," *The New York Times*, covered the Twitter conversation and included tweets from Andrew Sullivan, Peggy Noonan, and Bill Maher (Shear, 2012). In the converged media ecosystem covering an American presidential election, because they cite and rely on each other as sources, new and legacy media exert a mutual inter-media agenda setting effect on each other (Meraz, 2011; Sayre, Bode, Shah, Wilcox, & Shah, 2010).

Conversations amongst journalists on Twitter during a debate are important because Americans' perceptions of debate outcomes (e.g., who was the winner of a debate) are significantly influenced by post-debate news coverage and interpersonal discussion about the debate (Brubaker & Hanson, 2009; Fridkin, Kenney, Gershon, & Woodall, 2008; Pingree, Scholl, & Quenette, 2012; Tsfati, 2003). Individuals who watched little of the actual debate are particularly influenced by this post-debate commentary. As commentator E. J. Dionne (2012) explained, "What people say during the debate—Twitter has really changed things—matters a lot. So does what happens after it's over and how it's interpreted and spun. These things can matter almost as much as the debate itself" (para. 6). Echoing Dionne, this research suggests that, for many viewers, the debate itself is less important than coverage of the debate, and Twitter increased the speed, scope, and pervasiveness of that coverage. It is likely that even politically disengaged Twitter users saw some tweets come across their feed from their friends and previous research (Brubaker & Hanson, 2009; Fridkin et al., 2008; Pingree et al., 2012; Tsfati, 2003) suggests that these tweets would be influential in opinion formation.

Research has found that seeking political information via social networking is a significant and positive predictor of people's social capital and online and offline political participatory behaviors (Gil de Zúñiga, Jung, & Valenzuela, 2012). This means that the politicians and journalists who use Twitter are communicating with an important audience. In blunt political terms, political SNS users are engaged voters and they are likely to be opinion leaders.

CITIZEN TWITTER USE

Both journalists and campaigns recognized early in the 2012 election cycle that social media and television viewing are often linked. A study by the Nielson organization found that "35 percent of people who used tablets while watching TV looked up information online about the program they were watching" (Bauder, 2012, para. 11). Just as audiences view themselves as co-producers in the outcomes of television shows, determining the fate of characters and eventually the outcomes of shows, voters using social media want the same control over their politics.

Additionally, people follow politicians on Twitter because it gives them quick, unfiltered political information and because it is easy for them to use the service as a soapbox to pass the information along to their networks (Parmelee & Bichard, 2012). Based on surveys and in-depth interviews of political Twitter users, Parmelee and Bichard (2012) argued, "Political leaders' tweets regularly cause followers to look up information and take actions that the leaders request. In addition, the relationship that followers have with the leaders often influences followers' political views as much as or more than their family and friends" (p. 205).

For the user, it is easy to engage. As tweets continuously spawn in the Twitter stream, the debate and the audience's collective response update second-by-second. Users can contribute through tweeting and retweeting and see their voices added to the data stream. The stream can be simultaneously riveting and boring, engaging and distracting, helpful and worthless. According to Twitter CEO Dick Costolo (2012), one of the biggest challenges the company faces is handling the massive amount of content it receives each day and assisting users in sifting through the content to find what they want—to find the signal amongst the Twitter noise.

There was a substantial amount of Twitter use during debates. There were 10.3 million debate specific tweets during the first debate, and after the first 15 minutes, the volume never dipped below 100,000 tweets per minute (TPM) (Figure 14.1). While not as prevalent as in the first debate, there were 7.2 million tweets during the town hall debate and the volume rarely was below 60,000 TPM (Figure 14.2). The final debate led to 6.5 million tweets, usually above 60,000 TPM (Figure 14.3). Figures 14.1, 14.2, and 14.3 show the volume of Twitter activity over each of the three debates and identify the debate moments that generated the highest peaks of online discussion. In general, Twitter activity followed a similar pattern of a slow build up in volume for the first 15 minutes of the debate, followed by a consistent number of posts continuing to the end of the debate.

Online discussion tended to be stable until a "tweetable moment" occurred in the debate. These moments corresponded to spikes in the volume graphs. Like journalists, Twitter users were most likely to write about quips and one-liners. For instance, moderator Jim Lehrer's "let's not" rejoinder to the candidates was repeated endlessly on Twitter and led to the largest spike in volume during the October 4th debate. During the second debate, the highest spike occurred when Romney slipped on a questioner's name (109,560 TPM) and when Obama pointedly told Romney, "You're the last person to get tough on China" (108,619 TPM). Likewise, in the final debate, the largest amount of discussion happened when over 100,000 viewers tweeted after Obama cuttingly reminded Romney that "we have fewer horses and bayonets" now than we did in 1916 (105,767 TPM).

One of the biggest topics of discussion was the Sesame Street character Big Bird. When, in the first debate, Romney said that although he loved Big Bird, he would cut government subsidies to PBS, more than a quarter of a million tweets were posted mentioning Big Bird (Sharp, 2012a). Supporters of Big Bird also created parody Twitter accounts such as @FiredBigBird and @SadBigBird. Several other debate topics led to Twitter memes as well. When Mitt Romney used the phrase "binders full of women," tweets mentioning "binders" spiked to over 60,000 TPM as Twitter users employed the term to attack Romney and discuss women's issues (Topsy, 2012).

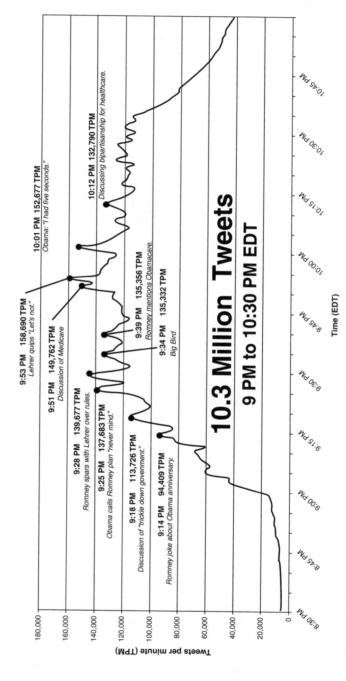

Figure 14.1 Twitter Activity Referencing the Debate, Candidates, and Related Terms during the First Presidential Debate—October 3, 2012

SOURCE: Reproduced by permission from Sharp (2012a).

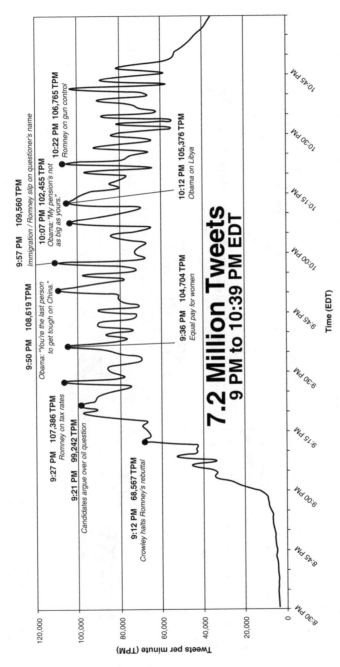

Figure 14.2 Twitter Activity Referencing the Debate, Candidates, and Related Terms during the Second Presidential Debate—October 16, 2012

SOURCE: Reproduced by permission from Sharp (2012b).

213

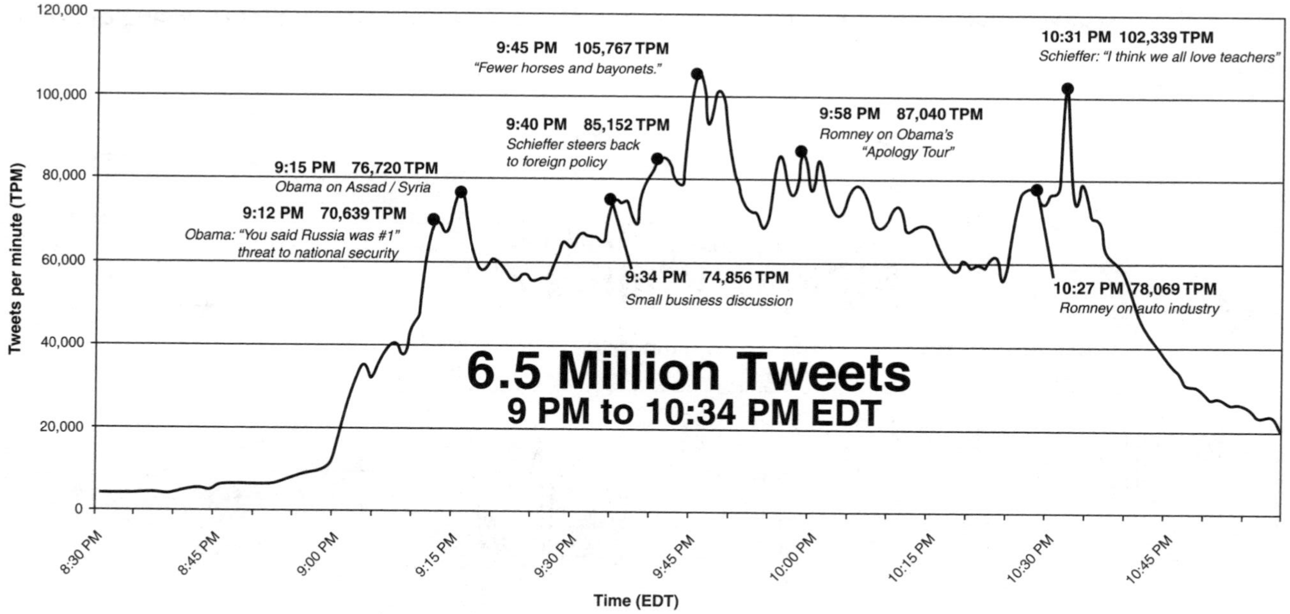
120,000
100,000
80,000
60,000
40,000
20,000
0
Tweets per minute (TPM)
9:45 PM 105,767 TPM
"Fewer horses and bayonets."
10:31 PM 102,339 TPM
Schieffer: "I think we all love teachers"
9:40 PM 85,152 TPM
Schieffer steers back
to foreign policy
9:58 PM 87,040 TPM
Romney on Obama's
"Apology Tour"
9:15 PM 76,720 TPM
Obama on Assad / Syria
9:12 PM 70,639 TPM
Obama: "You said Russia was #1"
threat to national security
9:34 PM 74,856 TPM
Small business discussion
10:27 PM 78,069 TPM
Romney on auto industry
6.5 Million Tweets
9 PM to 10:34 PM EDT
8:30 PM
8:45 PM
9:00 PM
9:15 PM
9:30 PM
9:45 PM
10:00 PM
10:15 PM
10:30 PM
10:45 PM
Time (EDT)

Figure 14.3 Twitter Activity Referencing the Debate, Candidates, and Related Terms during the Third Presidential Debate—October 22, 2012

SOURCE: Reproduced by permission from Sharp (2012c).

A wide variety of issues were discussed in viewer tweets. For instance, in the town hall debate, 28% of tweets referenced the economy, 17% focused on taxes, 16% on foreign policy, 13% on energy and the environment, and 8% on immigration (Sharp, 2012b). In the final debate, when foreign policy was the main topic, 54% of Twitter conversation related to foreign policy, 20% to the Economy, 9% to terrorism, 7% to taxes, and 4% to energy and the environment (Sharp, 2012c).

DISCUSSION

Initial analysis of the use of Twitter in the 2012 Presidential election leads to three changes in the patterns of campaign communication: (1) second screen multitasking, (2) media convergence, and (3) changes in agenda setting patterns.

Second Screen

Second screen use is changing how political debates are experienced for many citizens and how campaigns and the new media cover debates. Second screen use includes Twitter but also includes live blogs, apps, and other social media sources such as Facebook. Taken as a whole, the use of second screens during the election demonstrates a desire on the part of viewers to be a part of the political conversation, to find validation for their points of view, and to confirm for themselves in real time the veracity of candidates' claims.

To put it simply, live tweeting a debate is fun. Twitter allows you to hear the roar of the crowd, even when you might be sitting alone at home. Markus Prior (2005) warned that the proliferation of entertainment media channels has widened the engagement gap between politically active and inactive media consumers. But new technology such as live-tweeting debates and Microsoft's interactive Xbox debate feature may be lessening this gap by making politics a more interesting and attractive option for media viewers primarily interested in entertainment.

Media Convergence

This chapter finds that on Twitter during debates, the distinction between old and new media has blurred. The news media is now made up of "assemblages in which the personnel, practices, genres and temporalities of supposedly 'new' online media are increasingly integrated with those of supposedly 'old' broadcast and press media" (Chadwick, 2011, p. 24).

Convergence has also occurred between televised debates and the new media discussion surrounding the debate and influencing the post-debate coverage. Schroeder (2000) suggested that, "presidential debates are best apprehended as television shows, governed not by the rules of rhetoric or politics but by the demands of their host medium. The values of debate are the values of television: celebrity, visuals, conflict, and hype" (p. 9). While Schroeder's analysis remains true, debates are also now governed by the rules of the host medium of new and social media. Debates occur on both television and new media screens, and the values of new media are applied to this debate context: stickiness, pithiness, humor, and snark. The candidates and their staffs embrace these values in their Twitter comments. Even in the debate itself, whether it was Romney's attempts at "zingers" (see Baker & Parker, 2012) or Obama's frequently snide quips (e.g., "horses and bayonets"), the candidates appeared to be debating for social media audiences. Where candidates in past debates aimed at giving good sound bites, the candidates in 2012 seemed to be delivering "tweet bites."

Scannell (1996) asserted that "public events . . . occur simultaneously in two different places: the place of the event itself and that in which it is watched and heard" (p. 76). Because of the second screen movement and its rapid proliferation, there is now a third place (or more accurately, an unlimited number of "third places") where the mediated event is experienced simultaneously with a social feedback element. This convergent space represents a new form of media content—a political event is no longer simply a live event or a broadcasted event—now, it is a broadcast live event with accompanying live reactions and reactions to the reactions.

Traditional broadcast and print news was once one-directional and heavily filtered by media gatekeepers. This inside-out form of information sharing, where political insiders and elite journalists maintained institutional control, has been the main paradigm of journalism starting with broadsheets and continuing through radio and television news (Costolo, 2012). Twitter is different. On Twitter, a presidential debate becomes a shared experience where viewers gain multiple, unfiltered perspectives and can dialogue with other viewers in real time. Major political events can become digital agoras (Kirk & Schill, 2011) where citizens can hear what others are discussing and join the conversation. This outside-in form of news allows the observers—who Dan Gillmor (2004) called the "former audience" (p. 136)—to provide details and interpret the event instead of the participants.

Significantly, political insiders and journalists are also engaged on Twitter and putting their opinions into this virtual town square. If a user follows these Twitter accounts, major events like debates are a hybrid of inside-out and outside-in. The audience and the participants are both playing a role. The "official" news narrative is constructed in the communicative space alongside audience comments and, as discussed earlier, users can watch the news narrative evolve during the event. This interaction and co-creation produces a new type of media space. As Ampofo et al. (2012) asserted, "we now need to start thinking and attempting to theorize a form of mediatization that is driven not by elite production (and thus an elite monopoly on the production of meaning) but by ways in which elite media practices interact with socially diffuse media practices" (p. 867).

Agenda Setting

Two areas of agenda setting are worth noting. First, one clear pattern that emerged is that social media users helped determine the way media outlets targeted them and their interests. This reversal of the one-way model of communication to the two-way asymmetric model (see, e.g., Grunig, 2001) is an important shift. In part, it is important because it changes the traditional balance of power from the all-knowing media to a participant-observation model that, while taking into account media opinions, sees the news media as no more or less valid than their own individual accounts of what constitutes newsworthiness.

Second, a fruitful area for future research is the impact of groupthink among journalists. This concept in relation to Twitter has many potential tendrils but one that is particularly interesting to scholars of communication is how reporters influence each other through Twitter. Dana Milbank wrote an intriguing observation in an article for the *Washington Post*. In it, he claims that, "wire services, broadcast networks and newspapers covered major political events differently. Each outlet had its own take and tidbits. But now everybody is operating off the same script and, except for a few ideological outliers, the product is homogenous" (Milbank, 2012, p. 11). Similarly, Kevin Drum (2012) of *Mother Jones* argued that journalists should stay off Twitter until the debate is over: "Reporters should actively want to develop their own opinions about the candidates' performances. They should actively want to avoid letting the rest of the herd influence them" (para. 3).

In conclusion, many new communication mediums, including Twitter, are still in the early adoption stage and many aspects of Twitter will likely change as the service gains broader adoption (that is, if Twitter is not bought out or replaced by a competing service). So while we believe there are many long-term implications of Twitter use in political contexts, we also acknowledge that this chapter is primarily a study of Twitter as it was used during the 2012 campaign. Furthermore, we do not claim that the medium is instrumental in the victory of one candidate or another, nor do we claim that it was more important than other communication techniques. After all, "social media are only tools. They are no replacement for message, motivation, or strategy" (Metzgar & Maruggi, 2009, p. 141).

Whether it is real or merely perceived, Twitter has flattened the distance between politicians and voters and has scaled up the traditional notions of retail politics by enabling close, one-on-one interactions between newsmakers and their constituents. During the 2012 debates, Twitter was most important in establishing a communicative space amongst media, campaign, and citizen elites. Twitter is a networked distribution space, where these competing and collaborating political actors contest the media frame. Describing the impact of Twitter on political events and news, Dick Costolo, the CEO of Twitter, contended that Twitter is the modern version of the Greek Agora. Costolo (2012) said, "Twitter reinvents the Agora. We once again start to see multiple perspectives on a particular news story or event that's happening. We once again start to have a shared experience across the globe" (para. 12). During the 2012 debates, Twitter was where the shared experience happened.

CHAPTER 15

Here Comes Everybody, or Not:
An Analysis of the Social Media
Consumer of Campaign Content

Monica Ancu

Since 2008, social networking sites (SNSs) have become a campaign medium that candidates must use if they are serious about winning the election. Many voters seem to seek SNSs content from candidates, and consume it at a rate rivaling the audience of television, which is the number one source of political information in the U.S. About a week before Election Day, Obama's official YouTube channel showed a little over 253 million views, his Facebook page had over 31 million followers, and his Twitter account had over 21 million followers. Mitt Romney's YouTube channel had about 27 million views, and he recorded 10.5 million followers on Facebook and 1.5 million on Twitter. Candidates in congressional races also set up SNS profiles that reached views and followers in the hundreds of thousands and even millions, sometimes beyond the number of eligible voters in their voting district.

Such numbers, as well as numerous opinion polls, document that a majority of Americans are now active on social media sites. For example, a nationally representative survey conducted by the Pew Internet & American Life Project in August 2012 showed that about 60% of American adults were SNS users, and about 39% were engaged in some type of civic or political action through SNSs, such as consuming, creating, and disseminating political content, expressing political opinions, and encouraging others to vote (Rainie, Smith, Lehman-Schlozman, Brady, & Verba, 2012). The same survey showed that roughly one-in-five SNS users follow political candidates or elected officials, as compared to simply visiting the person's SNS page without following him or her. This number is higher among those with strong political affiliations: 32% of conservative Republicans and 27% of liberal Democrats following candidates and elected officials.

In the field of political communication, there is disagreement among researchers about the effects on voters of this widespread adoption of SNSs. Some scholars argue that these interactive tools and the direct communication between voters and candidates, or at least the illusion of direct communication, lead to increased engagement in the political process, higher campaign interest, and higher turnout on Election Day (Fernandes, Giurcanu, Bowers, & Neely, 2010; Hampton, Sessions Goulet, Rainie, & Purcell, 2011; Kes-Erkul & Erkul, 2009). Others claim that a voter's SNS activity is not connected to the person's political offline actions (Baumgartner & Morris, 2009; Fenton & Barassi, 2011; Kushin & Yamamoto, 2010; Zhou & Pinkleton, 2012).

In this chapter, eligible SNS users and U.S. voters were polled about their use of social media in relation to their demographics and offline political attitudes and behavior. One goal was to create an accurate portrait of who the politically active SNS users are, to assess these people's levels of offline political participation, and to determine the connection between exposure to SNS political content and offline political attitudes and behavior. A third goal was to see whether SNS participation can be used as a predictor for voters' offline political activities.

WHAT WE KNOW SO FAR ABOUT SNS USERS

Election 2012 was only the second U.S. general election cycle in which SNSs were part of campaign communication. In 2008, despite the enormous media buzz about SNS campaigning, social media tools were a mere novelty, used mainly by Obama as a way to support his image of as a young, atypical, and technology-savvy candidate. His SNS presence was, in reality, a timid first attempt at social media use compared to today's practices. For instance, his 2008 Twitter account had only about 112,000 supporters, and his Facebook only about two million fans, which was still higher by about 300 times that of McCain's numbers (Owyang, 2008).

At the time, SNS use by voters was also a novelty. In 2008, only 14% of all U.S. adults visited an SNS candidate page, and 85% of those visitors were under the age of 29 (Smith, 2009). So, despite the abundant research on SNS political campaigning, the picture we have today is incomplete because of the fact that, since the 2008 election cycle through 2012, the audience grew from a small group of early technology adaptors to the majority of the electorate. Early adopters tend to differ from the rest of the population in terms of age (usually younger), education (usually college or higher), income (more affluent than the average), gender (more men), social attitudes and behavior (innovators, social leaders, and risk takers) (Rogers, 1962). Therefore, this chapter investigates how voters' use of SNSs evolved from the 2008 early adopter to the 2012 average voter adopter.

WHO ARE THE POLITICALLY ACTIVE SNS USERS?

The majority of research about who uses SNSs for political purposes comes from the Pew Internet & American Life Project, which has methodically monitored the adoption and use of SNSs in political campaigns. In 2008, Smith (2009) documented that the 14% of U.S. voters who used SNSs for political purposes displayed the typical characteristics of early technology adaptors; they were predominantly Caucasian, had higher than average educations and incomes, and were more often men than women. These demographics were, however, atypical of the average 2008 SNS user, who, because of their younger age, tended to have lower income and education levels than the average American (Lenhart, 2009). Also, at the time, Blacks and Hispanics outnumbered Caucasians on social media, with men and women in equal proportions. In 2008, the top activities performed by the politically savvy SNS users were getting candidate and campaign information, joining a political group or cause, revealing vote preference, and monitoring friends' voting preference (Smith, 2009).

In 2012, political SNS users continued to show some early adopter demographics, but not all: the majority was Caucasian, younger, college educated, and affluent (Rainie et al., 2012). Almost everyone (92%) in the 18 to 29 age group used a social network to perform some political action, and 73% of the 30 to 49 age group used SNSs for political purposes. However, women outnumbered men, 75% compared to 63%, respectively. Black users matched Caucasians (both 68%), while Hispanic users outnumbered both groups (72% of all U.S. Hispanics over the age of 18 used SNSs for political purposes). Perhaps more interesting, findings point to the fact that self-identified liberals were more likely than self-identified conservatives to use SNSs for political action, although there was no significant difference between the frequency of use of Republicans and Democrats.

The most popular political activity in 2012 was to "like" campaign-related content posted by other people, which was performed by 38% of all SNS users. About 35% of SNS users encouraged people to vote, and an equal number posted their own thoughts about the campaign or a candidate. Other activities included re-posting others' posts and linking to online news about the election.

DO SNSs HAVE INFLUENCE ON OFFLINE BEHAVIOR AND ATTITUDES?

The question many commentators and political consultants have been asking is whether SNS use translates into increased political interest and offline action. The paradox is that the majority of SNS users are young people, notoriously associated with political apathy, low levels of political engagement, and low voter turnout.

Some evidence exists to suggest that SNS use does not translate in elevated political engagement. For instance, a survey of 18 to 24 year olds during the 2008 primaries showed that consumption of political news on SNSs did little to increase campaign knowledge compared to other forms of media, and that SNS use was unrelated to offline political engagement (Baumgartner & Morris, 2010). The politically active SNS users were unlikely to extend the interest and participation to offline activities such as contacting a politician, signing a petition, or contacting a media organization to express political views. Even the likelihood to vote was not positively associated with the use of SNS for political purposes (Baumgartner & Morris, 2010). Another study of SNS use in 2008 reached similar conclusions, namely, that social media participation was not significantly related to political attitudes, such as political self-efficacy or involvement (Kushin & Yamamoto, 2010).

It might be possible that SNSs, far from being an empowering and mobilizing factor, could lead to frustration and greater apathy and could be a threat, rather than an opportunity, for political participation. Through ethnographic research,

Fenton and Barassi (2011) discovered that some people used SNS political behavior (such as joining a Facebook discussion group) as a substitute for offline political action, "as they believed that political participation on SNSs distorted people's understanding of collective action by reinforcing the idea that simply joining a Facebook group was enough" (p. 187). Kushin and Yamamoto (2010) also think that exposure to political content on SNSs creates the illusion of political engagement at the expense of real action.

On the positive side, network and group membership is associated with higher political involvement (Putnam, 2000), more opportunities to be exposed to political content, and more opportunities to learn knowledge and skills that facilitate participation (Brady, Verba, & Schlozman, 1995; Leighley, 1996). Relatedly, Hanson, Haridakis, Wagstaff Cunningham, Sharma, and Ponder (2010) reported that users of social media in 2008, especially YouTube, displayed lower levels of political cynicism (a deterrent to political action) than nonusers. The authors cautioned, however, that this finding should not be taken as causal evidence, but merely as a correlation between SNS use and more positive political attitudes.

Analyzing Facebook posts by students at seven large U.S. universities, Fernandes et al. (2011) found that the students frequently mentioned offline political activities or actions that they had performed, such as registering to vote, wearing a pin or posting a sign, attending a campaign event, or purchasing a political poster. The authors argue that SNS participation translates into real activity outside the SNS community. The betterment of offline engagement by SNSs might indeed be as subtle as increasing users' self-expression and willingness to express a political opinion. Zhou and Pinkleton (2012) argue though that the positive correlation between SNSs and online political expression should not be interpreted as a sign of increased political efficacy or participation.

Yet another Pew study (Hampton et al., 2011) found that LinkedIn, Facebook, and Twitter users are more politically engaged than most people, being about three times more likely than a nonuser to attend a political rally, to try to persuade someone to vote, or to publicly express a voting preference. However, this fact does not mean these three SNSs increase political engagement. Also, higher than average levels of political engagement were not found among users of other SNSs, such as MySpace. Similar to the findings of other studies, the demographics of politically engaged SNS users were people in their 30s with above average educations.

The best news for proponents of SNSs comes from an experiment conducted during the 2010 midterm elections, when 6.3 million U.S. Facebook users were exposed to various forms of voting reminders, some static, such as a simple "I voted" button, and some social reminders which listed friends who had already voted (Aral, 2012). The experiment estimated that the social stimulus generated 559,000 additional votes compared to the group who did not see a social message. However, this study counted self-reported user votes rather than actual offline, verified ballots.

In summary, the mixed evidence on the consequence of SNS use for political purposes requires further research on the topic.

WHAT MOTIVATES SNS USERS
TO ENGAGE POLITICALLY?

One of the very first studies of political SNS use found that voters during the 2008 primaries were driven to SNSs by three motivations, namely, the desire to connect with like-minded voters, to seek information, and to pass time or for entertainment (Ancu & Cozma, 2009). A Web survey of college students similarly revealed that this group's primary Facebook motivations were socializing, entertainment, self-status seeking, and information seeking, and that the need for information gathering is positively and significantly predicted by users' need to gather information and self-status seeking (Park, Kee, & Valenzuela, 2009). In other words, those who use Facebook to look for information about political events are also likely to participate in those events or to take some other political action, such as organizing a meeting or a support party. Similar motivations were found by Hanson et al. (2010), who identified that consumption of political SNS content was driven by the following factors: the need for political evaluation of a candidate, convenient information gathering, entertaining needs, the need to find companionship, self-expression, and the need to pass time.

Beyond looking at what motivates people to seek political content on SNS, studies have also looked at what type of political activities people engage in. During the 2012 campaign, the five most popular activities were to post political content such as news about the campaign or campaign communication from candidates, to encourage friends and followers to vote, to post their own thoughts about the campaign, to ask followers to take some political action such as contacting a representative or attending a rally, and to report content created by someone else (Rainie, Smith, Lehman-Schlozman, Brady, & Verba, 2012). About 30% to 40% of American SNS users performed the activities mentioned above, but with significant racial, age, educational, and ideological gaps. Caucasian SNS users were twice more likely to use SNS for political activities than other ethnicities, a trend shared by SNS users under the age of 50 with a college education (Rainie et al., 2012). On the ideology front, liberal Democrats were more likely than conservative Republicans to use SNS tools for political activities.

With these facts in mind, the rest of this chapter will provide answers to the following questions:

RQ1: What are the demographics and political attitudes and behaviors of SNS users?

RQ2: How does use of SNS for political purposes relate to offline political attitudes and behavior?

RQ3: What are some primary motivations for using SNS for political action?

METHOD

This chapter presents data collected from 1,692 participants to an online survey conducted between October 1, 2012, to Election Day, November 6, 2012. The survey was hosted on SurveyMonkey.com and publicized on Facebook and YouTube in the comments section of the official pages of the 2012 presidential candidates and several Congressional candidates; and in the comment section of Facebook and YouTube pages with content relevant to the 2012 election; and on Twitter on the researcher's account and also as replies and direct messages to Twitter users who were, at the time, following political candidates. Responses from I.P. addresses outside the U.S. were deleted from the final data set, as well as incomplete responses or responses from those respondents who claimed to be less than 18 of age.

Sample

Through the collection process described above, 1,692 usable responses were obtained. This sample was composed of 48% men and 52% women, with a median age of 38 ($SD = 19$). In terms of ethnicity, 75% of respondents were Caucasian, 9.1% Black, 13.8% Hispanic and the remaining 2.1% other ethnicities. About 45% of respondents had completed a high school education, 42.9% had some college or had completed college, and 12.1% had post-graduate education or were in graduate school at the time of this survey.

On party affiliation, the sample was split among 28.5% Republicans, 35.6% Democrats, and 35.9% independents or other parties. Ideology trends were self-reported as 6.5% very conservative, 27.3% very conservative, 32.7% moderate, 15.4% liberal, 6% very liberal, with 12.1% of respondents skipping this question.

Measures

Political attitudes measured included political efficacy, campaign involvement, and campaign interest. To measure *political efficacy*, this study used a well-known, well-tested index with four items developed by Niemi, Craig, and Mattei (1991) and used by hundreds of other political communication studies. The index asked respondents how well qualified they were to participate in politics; if they believe they were better informed about politics and government than most people; if they had good understanding of the important political issues facing the country; and if they felt they could tell a friend enough about the presidential candidates. Responses were measured with a 1 (strongly disagree) to 5 (strongly agree) scale with Cronbach's alpha of .91.

Campaign involvement was measured with an adapted index from prior research (Horrigan, 2006; Rainie & Smith, 2008; Rainie et al., 2012) about whether or not respondents recently visited a candidate's Web site, subscribed to campaign communication such as e-mail or an RSS feed, created a piece of online content about a candidate or the campaign, talked to a friend about a candidate, donated money, volunteered, attended a rally/campaign event, displayed political paraphernalia such as a t-shirt or a sticker, watched a television debate, and registered to vote in the upcoming election. Each item was measured with a nominal measure of 0 (no) or 1 (yes), which resulted in a range of summative scores from 0 (lowest involvement) to 10 (highest involvement).

Campaign interest used a simple, self-report measure that asked respondents to rank their own campaign interest on a scale of 1 (not at all interested) to 5 (very interested).

Another set of measures asked about *participants' SNS membership*, such as how frequently they access SNS, and which ones (Facebook, Twitter, YouTube, other video-sharing SNS, Flickr and other photo-sharing SNS, Pinterest, and other). The survey also asked a *list of political activities* SNS users could engage in, such as post political content, encourage followers to vote or to take some other action, connect with political candidates, etc.

The final set of measures asked about *users' motivations* for political SNS use. This measure consisted of a 36-item scale ranging from 1 (strongly disagree) to 5 (strongly agree). The items were collected from various prior studies of online media uses and gratifications (Ancu & Cozma, 2009; Haridakis & Hanson, 2010; Hanson et al., 2010; Kaye & Johnson, 2006). The items measured use of SNS for information seeking, socializing, entertaining, convenience, decision-making, candidate evaluation, campaign education, and self-expression.

RESULTS

Demographics of Political SNS Users

The first objective of this data analysis was to describe the demographics and off-line political attitudes of 2012 SNS users, in order to understand whether political SNS users are still early technology adopter types or more majority adopters. Data analysis revealed that the younger cohorts are still the generation that embraced political SNS in the highest numbers compared to older generations (see Table 15.1).

Other demographics showed that Caucasians and Hispanics tended to be more significantly politically active than Blacks, and that the education gap still persisted with college-educated users more active than those with high school degrees or less. While the party affiliation did not produce significant differences with Republicans, Democrats and Independents equally likely to use SNS for political purposes, the ideology of voters is a predictive factor. Liberals and moderates are significantly more likely than conservatives to use SNS for political purposes.

Connection Between SNS Behavior and Offline Behavior

Research question two asked whether SNS use relates to offline political attitudes and behavior such as political efficacy, campaign involvement, and campaign interest. While Table 15.1 reports expected levels of these measures for each demographic criteria, t tests showed some interesting findings. Study participants were divided into frequent (1) and occasional/less frequent (2) SNS users to compare the means of their political efficacy, campaign involvement, and campaign interest. The frequent SNS users scored significantly higher on campaign involvement ($t(1690) = 41.05, p < .01$) and campaign interest ($t(1690) = 82.1, p < .01$) but not on political efficacy than the less frequent users ($t(1690) = 1.54$, n.s.). Those who were active on more than one SNS had the highest campaign interest ($t(1690) = 15.22, p < .01$) and campaign involvement ($t(1690) = 31.61, p < .01$). In fact, the frequent users also tended to be multiple SNS users, with 91% of them using at

Table 15.1 Sample Demographics in Connection with SNS Use for Political Purposes

N = 1,692	USES SNSs %	POLITICAL EFFICACY M (1–5)	CAMPAIGN INVOLVEMENT M (0–10)	CAMPAIGN INTEREST M (1–5)
Age				
18–29	87*	3.5*	5.1*	3.2*
30–49	71*	3.6*	7.1*	4.1*
50–64	51*	4.1*	6.3	4.0*
65+	39*	4.0*	5.9	3.7*
Gender				
Male	68	4.2*	6.2	3.6
Female	70	3.7*	6.0	3.8
Ethnicity				
Caucasian	72*	3.9	6.5	3.6
Black	54*	3.7	6.0	4.2*
Hispanic	68	3.8	6.8	3.9*
Other	52	3.7	6.3	3.6
Party				
Democrat	70	3.4	7.1*	3.7*
Republican	65	4.0*	5.7	3.4
Independent	69	3.6	6.1	3.5
Ideology				
Conservative	57*	4.0	6.4	3.1*
Liberal	78*	3.7	6.4	4.0*
Moderate	72*	3.8	6.1	3.6*
Education				
High school or less	45*	3.3	6.6	3.6
Some college up to B.A.	69*	3.8	6.7	3.6
Graduate school	73*	4.0*	6.9	3.8

Note: *Indicates statistically significant difference at $p < .05$ level or higher.
Source: Data collected by the researcher through an online survey, as explained in the Method section.

least two SNS daily. Most popular SNS are Facebook, YouTube, Twitter and some sort of photo-sharing Flickr or Instagram. The less frequent users tended to be almost exclusively (89%) users of only one network, namely Facebook.

The demographic comparison of SNS users on these three political variables did not produce any surprising results though. On all three variables, older users, men, and the better educated scored higher than the comparing categories. Caucasians and Hispanics had comparable scores, which were significantly higher than those of Black respondents. Liberals and moderates scored higher than conservatives, and Republicans scored higher than Democrats and Independents.

This finding based on party affiliation is somewhat unexpected, in the sense that prior research has not identified consistent differences in these three political attitudes along party ID.

Because prior research (Baumgartner & Morris, 2010) expressed concern that SNS users might substitute online participation for more meaningful offline action, a simple frequency analysis was further conducted on the campaign involvement measure. Looking at the top five most frequent involvement actions, it was determined that the most popular activity was indeed online (visits to candidates' campaign Web sites by 89% of respondents). Other top actions were voter registration (76%), watching political debates (61%), posting online content (59%), and talking to friends about the election (54%).

What Brings People to Political SNSs

Research question three studied the driving reasons for using SNSs for political purposes. Principal components factor analysis with varimax rotation loaded all of the 22 items into five factors (see Table 15.2).

Factor 1, *Political Decision Making*, included items such as looking for information about candidate stance on issues, information that would help voters evaluate the candidate, the campaign, and how the outcome will affect him or her personally. Factor 2 reflected social media use for *Socializing* purposes, such as connecting with like-minded supporters and the candidates directly. Factor 3 was another informational cluster that reflected use of SNS driven by *Convenience*, such as convenient and unique information being available through user-driven searches. Factor 4 bordered on socializing needs but was focused on user *Self-Expression*. The items in this cluster indicate SNS use motivated by the desire to express one's own political opinions publicly. Finally, Factor 5 was *Entertainment*, which reflects SNS use driven by the desire to pass time and have fun. These five factors combined accounted for 56.53% of the variance in people's motivations to use SNS for political purposes.

Next, the factors were entered into a series of regression analyses with the purpose of identifying demographic and attitudinal predictors for each of these motivation sets. The results show that age and education could be used as weak predictors for *Political Decision Making, Socializing,* and *Entertainment,* with significant regression beta coefficients indicating a positive relationship between these variables. Younger people and those without a college education tended to use SNS to socialize, as entertainment, and for information and guidance purposes more frequently than older and more educated groups. No other significant relationships were found between any of the other demographic variables and the five use factors.

Political efficacy, campaign involvement and campaign interest were not significantly associated with any of the factors either, except for campaign involvement and *Self-Expression*. Campaign involvement might be used to predict exposure to political content on SNS, as those respondents who reported high involvement levels also tended to use SNS for self expression more frequently than the low-involvement group.

Table 15.2 Motivations for Using SNSs for Political Purposes

I VISITED A POLITICAL CANDIDATE'S SNS PROFILE BECAUSE:	FACTOR 1 DECISION MAKING	FACTOR 2 SOCIALIZING	FACTOR 3 CONVENIENCE	FACTOR 4 SELF-EXPRESSION	FACTOR 5 ENTERTAINMENT
To see how a candidate stands on issues	.912	-.059	.104	-.021	.160
To help me decide how to vote	.897	-.043	.149	-.098	-.041
To evaluate a candidate	.895	.149	.139	.011	.085
To keep up with the campaign	.876	.183	.213	.076	-.016
To find out how the election affects me	.875	.035	.174	.139	-.112
To feel less lonely	-.020	.749	-.179	.033	.407
To meet other supporters of the candidate	.095	.678	-.239	.134	.336
To engage in direct communication with the candidate	.363	.556	.129	.247	.102
Because it's convenient to get information	.300	.145	.824	.152	.063
Because I can search for the information I want	.309	.096	.749	.082	.038
Because it's available non-stop	.171	.172	.606	.065	-.005
Because it's different information than other sources	.147	.149	.533	.033	.128
To talk to other voters	.148	.493	.068	.730	.263
To share my views	.112	.380	-.054	.669	.244
To talk about the election	.061	.366	-.080	.626	.192
To enjoy dialogue	-.008	.212	-.250	.580	.356
To inform others about a candidate or campaign	-.018	.073	-.275	.516	.089
Because it's entertaining	.072	.250	.002	.099	.885
Because it's a way to pass time	.156	.366	-.070	.190	.785
Because it keeps me from getting bored	.181	.307	-.004	.247	.741
Eigenvalue	17.747	2.125	1.665	1.214	1.096
% variance explained	56.53	6.64	5.20	3.79	3.43

N = 1,692

Source: Data collected by the researcher through an online survey, as explained in the Method section.

DISCUSSION

With a record number of American voters online, SNSs have become favorite sources of campaign information for millions of people. This has been a rapid change compared to only one prior general election, when social networks were a novelty embraced only by early adopters.

While more and more Americans used SNS to find, consume and create campaign and candidate-related content in the 2012 election cycle, it seems that the overall demographics of the political SNS users still match the 2008 early adopter profile. The most frequent political SNS user in this study's sample was a young Caucasian with a college education and liberal leaning or moderate views. The young group, 18-to-29 year olds, seems to have embraced SNS as political tools almost entirely (87% of all respondents, compared to 71% in the 30-to-49 year old group). Older users still lag significantly behind Millennials and Generation X, with only about half of 50-to-64 olds using SNS in this election cycle, a finding that matches other audience research studies into who the current SNS users are. These numbers should also be taken as counterargument to the media buzz claiming that Facebook and Twitter are universally embraced by "all" voters, when older voters clearly lag in adoption. Not only do they use SNS in smaller numbers than younger people, but they also do so less frequently. Another noteworthy difference is that older users tend to visit only one SNS while younger people have accounts on multiple sites.

The other meaning in these data is that candidates should target SNS political campaigning to younger voters, and produce content that is appropriate and relevant to this age group. It is possible that part of Obama's success on social media might have been the fact that he understood his audience. For starters, the president was more popular than his Republican rival among the 18-to-29 year old Americans who happen to be intensive SNS users, and about 60% of this age group voted for him (CIRCLE, 2012). Second, his Facebook page frequently featured informal, lighthearted content such as Vice President Biden bringing donuts to campaign volunteers; photos of Michelle Obama encouraging her husband through hugs, hand touching and even kisses; photos of the family's pet, Bo, wearing campaign attire; as well as lots of profiles of young people who declared their loyalty to Obama's campaign. The president's victory tweet, a photo of Michelle and him hugging just like a regular couple, became the most re-tweeted post ever on Twitter. In contrast, both Romney's Facebook and Twitter entries were a lot more formal, talking about policy issues and making opponent attacks. Photos of Romney and his family showed them almost exclusively in formal situations. This type of messages were very similar to media-style content and might have been appropriate for the average Romney voter, aged 45 and older (CIRCLE, 2012), but did not resonate well with the young audience which constitutes the majority of SNS users.

While young voters still rule the SNS world, it is important to recognize that older voters have increased in SNS adoption tremendously compared to the last election cycle. In 2008, only about 8% of voters over the age of 50 had SNS accounts compared to today, when 48% of those aged 50-to-64, and 34% of 65 and older use SNS (Zickhur & Madden, 2012). This adoption rate will likely continue to increase in upcoming campaigns.

However, apart from the adoption numbers, frequency of use is also an important element, and an equally dividing one between generations. This study's respondents under the age of 29 were overwhelmingly daily SNS users (72%). Frequency of use dropped dramatically with every age group older than 29. For instance, the 30-to-49 year old respondents in this study reported SNS access of only 1–2 days a week, while among the over 50 age group SNS access happens just a few times a month. In the SNS world, how frequently one reaches supporters is an essential variable. In a two-week period, the Obama campaign posted 27 Facebook entries, 404 tweets, 21 YouTube videos and 106 blog entries, while Romney had 34 Facebook posts, 16 tweets, 10 YouTube videos and 55 posts (Quimet, 2012). Someone who only logs into SNS once or twice a week, or just a few times a month, would miss the majority of the Facebook and Twitter content, as older content on these networks is very difficult to retrieve. Based on this line of reasoning, this author would argue that the truly active SNS user is the young voter, and that campaigns should focus SNS communication efforts to resonate with this public.

A final insight of demographic trivia from this study reveals another gap in SNS adoption between young and senior voters. Young voters tend to be multi-SNS users with accounts on almost all major SNS such as Facebook, Twitter, and YouTube. Older voters tend to stick to only one SNS, namely Facebook, and sometimes access YouTube but without owning a YouTube account. Not owning a YouTube login does not keep one from viewing videos, however that person would not be able to post comments, rate videos and otherwise participate in the more interactive functions of the community.

The second focus of this study was on the connection between political SNS use and offline political action. As previously discussed, prior research documents both benefits and detriments of SNS on offline political action. This chapter's findings also offer mixed evidence on how SNS impacts offline behaviors. On one hand, frequent SNS users displayed higher scores of campaign involvement and interest. On the other hand, the most frequent form of involvement was visiting a candidate's Web sites, which is just another online action. More complex forms of offline involvement such as attending campaign events, volunteering, money donations, and even offline discussion with family and friends were rather low. This being said, SNS users differ in campaign involvement and campaign interest based on demographics. In the 2012 election cycle, Democrats reported significantly higher involvement than Republicans and Independents. The 18-to-29 group had the lowest involvement, while the 30-to-49 had the highest. That the younger voter cohort is less engaged than the other age groups is not a novelty in political communication research, since apathy and lower turnout among young people is almost a cliché in scholarly literature.

On campaign interest, the most interest was displayed by the Democrat-leaning, 30-to-64 year olds of Black and Hispanic backgrounds. Traditionally, campaign interest can be predicted by factors such as age, race, gender, and education, but gender and education were not associated with campaign interest among these participants. That Black and Hispanic voters reported higher campaign interest than other groups is atypical of voter research in general, but understandable given that one of the two presidential candidates is a Black man and that immigration reform, specifically the illegal Hispanic population in the U.S., was a hot campaign topic.

Going back to the connection between SNS and offline engagement, this seems to be a complex relationship and possibly not linear. There is, however, a growing amount of evidence that points to the fact that some people perceive online activity as a form of political participation (Baumgartner & Morris, 2010; Himelboim, Weaver Lariscy, Tinkham, & Sweetser, 2012; Weaver Lariscy, Tinkham, & Sweetser, 2011). Moreover, at a time when online political activity is at its peak, as it was the case of the 2012 election, political participation offline continues to decline (Bennett & Iyengar, 2008; Putnam, 2000). If online participation increases at the expense of offline, campaigns will have an even harder time mobilizing supporters and effectively increasing Americans' participation in political life. For now, this author cautions against any optimistic claims that SNS can increase such participation. While SNS increases exposure to political content and access to other voters, including influencers such as opinion leaders, it remains to be seen if such exposure really translates into concrete political action.

The third and final purpose of this chapter was to identify the main reasons driving people to use SNS for political content. Such analysis is not novel to this area of study, and was documented in 2008, when SNS became part of a campaign cycle for the first time. This chapter's findings indicate the same reasons that drove people to SNS in 2008 remain in place. Voters seek SNS political content for informational and decision making needs, as well as socializing, self-expression and entertainment (Ancu & Cozma, 2009; Haridakis & Hanson, 2011). The difference between 2008 and 2012 might lie in what motivation is primary in a voter's mind when going to SNS. For instance, a 2008 election study found that the number one reason voters connected with political candidates on SNS was for socializing and finding other like-minded supporters of their favorite candidates (Ancu & Cozma, 2009). The current findings point to SNS users shifting primary motivation from socializing to information seeking for decision making. Socializing is still a significant factor driving the use of political SNS though.

In conclusion, if someone were to paint the portrait of an average SNS user consuming political content, that person would be an 18-to-29 year old, college-educated Caucasian who is a moderate Democrat. This person would have multiple SNS accounts and would visit other online political sources. He or she would compare on political efficacy with other demographic groups, but would have higher campaign interest and at least higher self-reported campaign involvement. However, the campaign involvement is mostly online action rather than offline behavior. This person is driven to SNS by a desire to obtain information about a candidate or campaign, but also by the need to socialize with other voters.

As SNS adoption rate continues to grow among U.S. voters as well as candidates and elected public officials, it is important to study the politically motivated SNS adopters in order to understand their attitudes, behavior, motivations to use SNS, and the effects of SNS exposure to these voters' political actions. While this study did not find clear evidence that SNS use leads to increased offline political engagement, the impressive success of Obama on social media, followed by solid youth voter turnout and his winning the youth vote, demonstrates that SNS are promising political tools with likely potential for persuasion and mobilization. Future research should continue to monitor adoption trends among the different age groups, and try to clarify the connection between online and offline political action.

CHAPTER 16

Maligned Youth or Political Activists? Young Citizen Political Engagement Using Social Media

Benjamin R. Warner, Joshua Hawthorne, and Sarah Turner McGowen

At the close of the 2012 election, election results and commentary raced across social media platforms at a rate unprecedented in previous elections. On Election Day, Twitter users made over 31 million posts regarding the political event (Sharp, 2012e). Over the course of the election, Twitter played a massive role. The first debate became the most tweeted-about U.S. political event in history (Sharp, 2012a), a record soon overtaken by Election Day itself. Over 27.7 million tweets were posted regarding the presidential and vice presidential debates alone (Sharp, 2012a, 2012b, 2012c, 2012d). Social media has become an important space for political discussion; 66% of all social media users and 39% of all American adults engage in some sort of political activity via social media (Ranie, Smith, Schlozman, Brady, & Verba, 2012).

While political engagement through social media is on the rise, it is unclear how much young people are participating. While 73% of American teens with Internet access use social networking sites (Lenhart, Purcell, Smith, & Zickuhr, 2010) and one-third of all adults between the ages of 18 and 29 use Twitter (Lenhart et al., 2010), young people have tended to engage in less political communication regardless of the medium (O'Toole, Lister, Marsh, Jones, & McDonagh, 2003). This lack of engagement may be changing, however, as youth participation has been much higher in the past two presidential contests. In the 2008 election, 49% of people between the ages of 18 and 24 voted (U.S. Census Bureau Public Information Office, 2009), and in 2012, early estimates predict that the percentage will be even higher (Kingkade, 2012). Though there are many explanations for this increase in turnout, it may not be a coincidence that young people are engaging in politics at a time when new media provide more channels for participation.

The possibility that young voters use social media as a vehicle for political engagement warrants further investigation: What types of young people are likely to talk about politics on Facebook and Twitter? What are their motivations? What is the nature of their conversations? And can researchers identify normative democratic outcomes from such political communication? This project seeks to answer some of these pressing questions. Specifically, this study focuses on which characteristics make young people more likely to engage in political communication using social media. Prior to presenting the results of our investigation, scholarship on political engagement in social media is examined.

SOCIAL MEDIA AS A DIGITAL PLACE
FOR POLITICAL ENGAGEMENT

Social media has been used in a variety of civic and political contexts in recent history. People took to the streets, mobile phones in hand, and tweeted during the political protests in Iran, Tunisia, and Egypt in 2010 and 2011 (Lotan et al., 2011; Rahimi, 2011; Tufekci & Wilson, 2012). Political debates have been annotated by users on Twitter in real time (Anstead & O'Loughlin, 2011; Hawthorne, Houston, & McKinney, 2013; Shamma, Kennedy, & Churchill, 2009). Twitter has been used between elected officials and citizens for the discussion of political controversies (Ampofo, Anstead, & O'Loughlin, 2011), and as a place to digitally protest during these controversies (Warner, Turner McGowen, & Hawthorne, 2012). Finally, many have posted regarding electoral politics (Sharp, 2012e; Tumasjan, Sprenger, Sandner, & Welpe, 2011). While the use of social media to communicate about politics is a fairly new phenomenon, the use of the Internet to communicate about politics has been heavily studied.

In general, Internet use does not decrease political engagement and, in cases where political news sites are included as an Internet-use variable, online activity is positively associated with political engagement (Boulianne, 2009). Above and beyond general Internet use, researchers who have isolated communication about politics online as a treatment or independent variable have found people were more likely to engage in politics offline when their online political communication increased (de Zúñiga, Veenstra, Vraga, & Shah, 2010; Shah, Cho, Eveland Jr., & Kwak, 2005; Tedesco, 2011; Wang, 2007). Existing research about social media, while limited, suggests this trend holds on platforms such as Facebook and Twitter (Houston, Hawthorne, & McKinney, 2012; Kushin & Yamamoto, 2010; McKinney, Houston, & Hawthorne, 2012; Tufekci & Wilson, 2012; Valenzuela, Arriagada, & Scherman, 2012; Vitak et al., 2011).

Furthermore, Gastil and Xenos (2010) have found that people with positive political and civic attitudes are more likely to engage politically and become more optimistic about the ability of political action to positively influence society following engagement. Since communicating about politics on social media leads to increased civic engagement, it may also be likely that those who are already more civically engaged are likely to participate in that type of communication. If this is the case, then it is likely that a similar reciprocal relationship between positive civic/political attitudes and political engagement, as described by Gastil and Xenos

(2010), can be observed when political engagement occurs through the use of social media.

The reciprocal relationship between online engagement and offline political participation demonstrates the important potential of social media. If democracies benefit from an engaged electorate, political uses of social media may represent a new and valuable avenue for building healthy democratic culture. The research presented here pursues the starting point of the reciprocal relationship between social media and broader political participation by seeking to identify which civic/political attitudes are most likely to generate political engagement through social media. In other words, if using Facebook and Twitter for political purposes can make young people more inclined to participate in the democratic process, what makes young people inclined to use social media to discuss politics? The following study seeks to address this question by identifying key political attitudes associated with high levels of social media engagement.

PROFILING THE POLITICALLY ENGAGED

A great deal of research has focused on why people engage politically. The field of political science has focused on traits associated with engagement (e.g., Brady, Verba, & Schlozman, 1995). Communication scholars, on the other hand, have emphasized communicative acts and variables that can be influenced by communication processes (e.g., McLeod, Scheufele, & Moy, 1999). In this way, political science tends to be descriptive, and political communication tends to be prescriptive regarding the problem of low engagement. This study focuses on the prescriptive side of the engagement problem and isolates three communication variables that influence political engagement: political cynicism, political information efficacy, and political polarization.

Political Cynicism

Political cynicism refers to the level of negative feelings associated with politics and politicians (Agger, Goldstein, & Pearl, 1961), an attitude related to external political efficacy—how responsive the government is to its constituents. Political cynicism emphasizes how much disdain people feel for politicians and politics, especially perceptions of how corrupt politicians are and how unresponsive they are to the needs of citizens.

Cappella and Jamieson (1996) found that high levels of political cynicism were more than just a healthy skepticism towards government, but rather a belief in the lack of legitimacy of government. Research has shown the relationship between cynicism and political engagement to be complex; while different beliefs about legitimacy are related to different types of political engagement, high levels of trust in the political system increase voting (Booth & Seligson, 2005). Political cynicism is the opposite of political trust (Agger et al., 1961), and it would hold that it is likely to have the opposite effect on political engagement. Therefore, this study hypothesizes that high levels of cynicism will be negatively related to political engagement through social media:

> H1: Higher levels of political cynicism will predict less political engagement on Facebook and Twitter.

Political Information Efficacy

Political information efficacy (PIE) is a form of political efficacy. Political efficacy has been divided into two categories: internal efficacy, which focuses on the ability of a person to participate effectively in politics, and external efficacy, which focuses on the responsiveness of government to citizen (Niemi, Craig, & Mattei, 1991). PIE was developed to address a missing aspect of young-voter engagement not measured by traditional internal political efficacy constructs—namely, the role of information and the confidence of the person to use that information (Tedesco, 2011). PIE thus measures the extent to which an individual believes he or she has the information and ability needed to effectively participate in politics.

PIE has been studied most often as a result or consequence of political communication (e.g., McKinney & Chattopadhyay, 2007; McKinney & Rill, 2009; Tedesco, 2011). However, high levels of PIE have also been shown to predict voting in young citizens (Kaid, McKinney, & Tedesco, 2007). Therefore, this study hypothesizes that political information efficacy will correlate to participation in political engagement through social media:

> H2: Higher levels of political information efficacy will predict greater political engagement on Facebook and Twitter.

Political Polarization

While the growth of the Internet has provided a variety of new ways for citizens to participate in politics (e.g., Boulianne, 2009), it has also provided many opportunities for citizens who are disinterested in politics to opt out. Prior (2007) argues that the proliferation of entertainment media has created a high-choice environment in which citizens can avoid news and politics altogether.

Conversely, those with strong political opinions are more motivated to seek out opportunities for engagement (Dilliplane, 2011) and participate with greater enthusiasm and fervor (Mutz, 2006). Social media provide many opportunities for highly motivated (e.g., partisan) individuals to engage in political communication but may provide fewer avenues for the disinterested to opt out. This is because while people can choose who to follow or friend, they have little control over what those that they follow actually post. Thus, even the most politically disinterested are bound to face more exposure to political discussion on Twitter or Facebook than they would in a higher-choice online environment. Nonetheless, it is still predicted that the most highly polarized individuals will have more motivation to participate and therefore engage at higher levels via social media. That is to say, more highly partisan people ought to be more likely to engage in political discussion in any medium, online or off. Social media engagement should therefore be associated with higher political polarization.

> H3: Higher levels of political polarization will predict greater levels of political engagement on Facebook and Twitter.

METHOD

Sample

Participants for this study were students at universities in Alabama, Georgia, Iowa, Kansas, Massachusetts, Missouri, Ohio, Oregon, Tennessee, Texas, Virginia, and Wisconsin. Participants were students in communication courses at various universities and were encouraged to participate (sometimes for course credit) as part of a national election research effort. Seven independent samples were collected at various times during the election. National data collection occurred on five occasions: immediately prior to each of the presidential and the vice presidential debates and once in the final ten days of the campaign. Participants in the debate studies attended debate-watch parties in person and completed the survey before the start of the debate. For the fifth national data collection effort, links were provided to students in participating communication courses ten days prior to the election. They were permitted to complete the survey any time prior to the day of the election. The two other independent samples were collected at a single major Midwestern university, once during the Republican primary campaign in March 2012 and once immediately after the presidential conventions in early September. In both instances participants were students in communication courses and were awarded course credit for their participation. A total of 2,409 students completed one of the questionnaires associated with this study. Demographic data on each independent sample is available in Appendices 16-1 and 16-2.

Procedure and Variables

All participants completed a large questionnaire pertaining to the presidential election. In each case the students completed the survey online, and all seven surveys contained a different blend of questions. Items measuring political cynicism, political information efficacy, polarization, and social media use were included in each version of the survey. Descriptive statistics and reliability scores from all seven independent samples are available in the appendix.

Cynicism

Cynicism was measured with an eight-item scale adapted from previous research (e.g., Kaid, 2003; Kaid, Johnston, & Hale, 1989; McKinney, Spiker, & Kaid, 1998; McKinney & Rill, 2009). Students were asked to indicate agreement with each of the following items on a five-point scale: *Politicians are more interested in power than in what people think; Politicians are corrupt; Politicians make promises that are never kept; Politicians cannot be trusted; Politicians are too greedy; Politicians always tell the public what they want to hear instead of what they actually plan to do; Politicians are dishonest; Politicians are more concerned about power than advocating for citizens.* Data collected during the Republican primary used a version of this measure that included all but the third item. Strong reliability was achieved in all seven independent samples.

Political Information Efficacy

Political information efficacy was measured with a five-point agreement scale using the following four items developed by Kaid et al. (2007) and used in subsequent research (e.g., Kaid, Fernandes, & Painter, 2011; McKinney & Chattopadhyay, 2007; Tedesco, 2011): *I consider myself well qualified to participate in politics; I think that I am better informed about politics and government than most people; I feel that I have a pretty good understanding of the important issues facing our country; If a friend asked me about the presidential election I feel I would have enough information to help my friend figure out who to vote for.* Data collected during the Republican primary included all but the second item of the measure. The scale achieved strong reliability in all instances.

Polarization

Following Stroud (2010), polarization was computed from feeling-thermometer evaluations of the presidential candidates. Respondents were asked to provide their feelings toward both candidates on a scale from zero to 100, where zero represented a completely unfavorable opinion and 100 represented maximum favorability. If they felt completely neutral or did not know the candidates, they were asked to provide a score of 50. Polarization was calculated by computing the absolute value of the difference between Obama and Romney's feeling-thermometer score such that, if Obama was scored 25 and Romney 100, the polarization score would be 75. This measure created a range from 0 to 100, where 0 represented no polarization (e.g., a rating of 50 for each candidate), and 100 represented maximum polarization (e.g., a 100 from one candidate and a 0 for the other).

Social Media Use

Social media use was measured with a scale adapted from Warner, Turner McGowen, and Hawthorne (2012). Respondents were asked to think about a specific political event or person and rate the likelihood of six scenarios on a 1–7 scale, from "very likely" to "very unlikely." For Facebook, the scenarios ran as follows: *Information about [subject] popped up on my Facebook timeline; I read a link or watched a video about [subject] that I saw on Facebook; I saw friends discussing [subject] on Facebook; I posted a comment in a discussion about [subject] on Facebook; I "liked" a status or comment about [subject] that I saw on Facebook; I posted a status update or shared a link about [subject]*

The scenarios for Twitter-users were as follows: *Information about [subject] showed up on my Twitter feed; I followed a link about [subject] that I saw on Twitter; My friends or acquaintances were tweeting about [subject]; I re-tweeted something about [subject]; I "favorited" a tweet that I saw about [subject]; I personally tweeted something about [subject].*

Respondents were also asked to indicate how much attention they would pay to information about the subject if it appeared both on their Facebook and Twitter stream, with the response options: *None, I would completely ignore it; Very little, I am not interested; Somewhat little, I would be unlikely to glance at it; I don't know whether I would pay attention to it or not; Some attention, I might glance at it; I would pay attention, I'd at least look it over; Quite a bit of attention, I'm very interested in these things.*

Respondents were asked about the following subjects: (a) the Republican primary (March data collection); (b) the Democratic and Republican party conventions (September data collection); (c) the candidates in general (e.g., had they seen posts about Obama or Romney) (pre-test for the first debate); (d) the first presidential debate (pre-test for the vice presidential debate); (e) the first presidential and vice presidential debate (pre-test for the Town Hall debate); (f) either of the presidential and/or vice presidential debates (the pre-test for the third presidential debate); and (g) the leaked video of Mitt Romney discussing the "47% of Americans who pay no income tax" (the final ten days of the election). In all instances both Facebook- and Twitter-use measures achieved strong reliability.

Analytic Procedures

Hypotheses were tested through structural equation modeling (SEM) with ML estimation using LISREL 8.80. SEM was used because latent modeling provides true parameter estimates that are corrected for measurement error and allows the simultaneous estimation of relationships between multiple dependent and independent variables (Brown, 2006; Kline, 2005). Using Kline's (2005) two-step process, a measurement model was specified using confirmatory factor analysis (CFA) and the structural model was fit to test the hypothesized relationships.

Model fit for the CFA was evaluated using the ML^2 statistic. Because this statistic can be excessively sensitive to model misfit and may be overly reactive to sample size, various model fit indices have been developed (Bentler & Bonett, 1980; Browne & Cudeck, 1993; Tucker & Lewis, 1973). While Hu and Bentler (1999) suggested that an RMSEA of .06 or lower and a CFI and TLI/NNFI of .95 or greater provide the best approximation of good model fit, Marsh, Hau, and Wen (2004) strongly argue against the rigid application of these criteria, as they can result in the rejection of many well-fitting and informative models. While it has been the norm in communication scholarship to adhere to Hu and Bentler's (1999) more rigid criteria (e.g., Holbert & Stephenson, 2002), this study adopts Marsh et al.'s (2004) standards for reasonable fit (i.e., RMSEA < .08, CFI & TLI/NNFI > .90). Regressed pathways were evaluated for significance iteratively, using the change in chi^2 value following Kline (2005).

While each of the measures used in the CFA have many items, a just-identified model should have three indicators for each latent construct (Holbert & Stephenson, 2002). To achieve proper identification and further reduce unreliability, items in each measure were parceled following the recommendations of Little, Cunningham, Shahar, and Widaman (2002). Cynicism was parceled such that the first, second, and sixth items were averaged into one parcel, the third, fourth, and

Table 16.1 Fit Statistics for All Models

MODEL	CHI2 (DF)	RMSEA	95% CI	TLI/NNFI	CFI
Republican Primary	78.952 (53)	.053	.025–.076	.98	.98
Conventions	111.62 (53)	.104	.077–.131	.92	.95
Candidates	97.052 (53)	.047	.032–.062	.98	.99
Debate 1	127.78 (53)	.066	.053–.083	.96	.97
Debate 1 & VP	150.26 (53)	.068	.055–.081	.96	.97
Debate 1, 2, & VP	175.28 (53)	.071	.059–.083	.95	.97
Forty-Seven Percent	204.63 (53)	.069	.060–.080	.96	.97

Source: Midwest Campaign Research Project, 2012.

seventh into another, and the fifth and eighth into the third. PIE was identified by parceling the second and third item. Both Facebook and Twitter engagement were identified by averaging the first and third; the second and seventh; and the fourth, fifth, and sixth items into separate parcels.

Parceling decisions were made based on items with overlapping specific error to reduce instances of correlated residuals. So long as item-level data analysis is not a desired outcome of modeling, Little et al. (2002) condone this parceling rationale. However, they warn that if these parcels contain unmodeled factors, parceling could misrepresent a multifaceted construct as one-dimensional. This may be the case with social media engagement, as there was some evidence in the item-level data to suggest that the third parcel represents a communication facet while the other two measure observation of political communication on social media. This distinction was not part of the rationale for this study (observing political conversation and participating in political conversation are both behaviors that have normative benefits), but it does merit future consideration. Because the items in the Facebook- and Twitter-use variables mirror each other, each parcel in the Facebook-use factor was specified to have a correlated residual with the identical parcel in the Twitter-use variable. Model fit for the CFA in all seven independent samples can be seen in Table 16.1. Strong model fit was achieved for all but one of the samples. The model acceptably approximated the data collected immediately after the conventions, but—likely because of the small sample—the RMSEA was undesirably high.

RESULTS

This study sought to test the hypotheses that individuals with more political cynicism are less likely to engage in political communication on social media while those who have greater levels of political information efficacy (PIE) and are more polarized will use social media to engage in politics more frequently. To test these hypotheses, a structural model was specified with cynicism, political information efficacy, and polarization as independent (predictor) variables and social media engagement on Facebook and Twitter as dependent variables. This structural

Table 16.2 Regression Coefficients for Prediction of Social Media Engagement

SUBJECT	N	CYNICISM	PIE	POLARIZATION
Republican Primary	176			
Facebook		.029	.483***	.107
Twitter		.008	.363***	−.085
Conventions	103			
Facebook		−.088	.537***	−.087
Twitter		.124*	.547***	.354*
Candidates	372			
Facebook		−.066	.445***	.259***
Twitter		−.172**	.323***	−.04
Debate 1	311			
Facebook		−.263***	.365***	.266**
Twitter		−.25***	.229***	.034
Debate 1 & VP	399			
Facebook		−.147**	.263***	.126
Twitter		−.255***	.193***	.055
Debate 1, 2 & VP	462			
Facebook		−.054	.341***	.06
Twitter		−.135**	.136***	.176***
Forty-Seven Percent	586			
Facebook		−.044	.358***	.197**
Twitter		−.114*	.247***	−.159*

Note: * $p < .05$, ** $p < .01$, *** $p < .001$; Results from the completely standardized solution.
Source: Midwest Campaign Research Project, 2012.

model was tested in all seven independent samples. Three of the samples asked about social media engagement regarding the presidential and vice presidential debates, and the others asked about the Republican primary, the party nominating conventions, Romney's much-discussed remarks about the 47% percent of Americans that he suggested do not pay taxes, and the candidates in general. Results of the latent regression analyses are presented in Table 16.2.

The first hypothesis predicted that people who are more cynical about politics would be less likely to use social media to politically engage. Results for this hypothesis were mixed. Cynicism negatively predicted social media engagement in five of the six cases where participants were asked about the debates (the exception was Facebook engagement in the final debate data). However, the pattern in the other four samples was much less clear. While cynical respondents exhibited less social media engagement regarding the candidates on Twitter, there was no relationship between cynicism and candidate social media engagement on Facebook. Similarly, social media engagement about Romney's "47%" remarks were negatively predicted by cynicism when Twitter was the medium, but again, there was no relationship on Facebook. Contrary to the hypothesis, participants with greater cynicism were more likely to exhibit social media engagement on Twitter regarding the conventions, though again, there was no relationship for Facebook. Finally, cynicism did not predict any level of social media engagement of the Republican primary, regardless of the medium. These results, while inconclusive, suggest that the effect of cynicism on social media engagement may depend on the topic and the medium. The decision to use social media to engage presidential debates may depend more on an individual's level of cynicism than would be the case in other contexts. Furthermore, there is limited evidence that cynicism may be a more important predictor of engagement on Twitter than on Facebook.

The second hypothesis predicted that individuals with greater political information efficacy (PIE) would exhibit more social media engagement. Data from the 2012 presidential election provides strong support for this hypothesis. As Table 16.2 demonstrates, PIE significantly predicted social media engagement for both Facebook and Twitter in all seven samples. In other words, high levels of political information efficacy predict greater levels of political engagement through social media across platform (Facebook/Twitter) and topic.

The third hypothesis predicted that people who are more polarized are also more likely to use social media to engage in politics. Data from the 2012 election provides very little support for this hypothesis. While polarization predicted greater engagement on Facebook regarding discussion of the candidates and the first debate and on Twitter regarding the conventions and the first three debates, this relationship was inconsistent and often weak. Furthermore, regarding Romney's "47%" comments, polarization positively predicted social media engagement on Facebook but negatively predicted it on Twitter. In all, more than half of the regression paths were non-significant, and of those that were significant, no interpretable pattern emerged. These findings do not confirm the third hypothesis, though a more dynamic relationship than was hypothesized here cannot be ruled out based on these results.

DISCUSSION

This study was conducted to determine which characteristics make young people most likely to use social media as a form of political participation. While young people lead other age groups in adoption and use of social media (Lenhart et al., 2010), they have been historically unengaged in politics (O'Toole et al., 2003). Results from this study demonstrate that young people do engage in political communication on Facebook and Twitter but at varying levels. It was expected that those most likely to engage in political communication through social media would be low in cynicism, high in political information efficacy (PIE), and generally more polarized than their less-engaged counterparts. This study found that PIE was clearly the most significant predictor of social media engagement, that cynicism suppressed engagement regarding political debates, and that the level of polarization had little to do with whether participants used social media as a space for political engagement.

The finding that PIE predicts social media engagement was the strongest (it was the best predictor in all but two of the 14 contexts tested) and the most consistent (it was highly significant in all 14 contexts). Apparently, so long as young people believe they have something worth saying, they are perfectly willing to express themselves through social media, regardless of their level of commitment to a particular party (polarization) or their trust in the responsiveness of the system (cynicism). Political information efficacy is an important communication variable. It reflects the amount of confidence a person has in their knowledge and ability to engage in political conversations (Kaid, McKinney, & Tedesco, 2007).

That this variable was the most important predictor of social media engagement is encouraging news for political communication researchers and educators. PIE is among the most responsive characteristics to campaign exposure. Researchers have found that exposure to presidential debates (McKinney & Chattopadhyay, 2007; McKinney & Rill, 2009; McKinney, Rill, & Gully, 2011), political advertisements (Kaid, Postelnicu, Landreville, Yun, & LeGrange, 2007), and interactive online content (Tedesco, 2007, 2011) all increase PIE. This suggests that as students are exposed to campaign messages, they will become more involved in political communication through their online networks. Furthermore, communication educators can occupy a pivotal role in fostering participation among younger voters. Political information efficacy is predicated on the belief that one has the skills and information necessary to participate effectively. This knowledge and skill set is often the focus of communication education. To the extent that educators are successful in giving students confidence in their ability to express political ideas, this study's findings suggest that they will do so through Facebook and Twitter.

While this study expected that PIE would increase social media engagement, it also predicted that cynicism would result in less communication through Twitter and Facebook, based on the fact that previous studies have identified those who trust the government and grant legitimacy to democratic institutions as being more likely to participate (Booth & Seligson, 2005), while people who mistrust politicians tend to abstain (Agger et al., 1961). However, this study's findings did not consistently support this prediction. Those who were high in cynicism were significantly less likely to use social media to learn about and discuss the debates, but they were not necessarily less likely to engage in other contexts. Respondents high in cynicism were somewhat less likely to discuss the candidates via Twitter, but no less likely to do so on Facebook. Furthermore, people high in cynicism were almost as likely to discuss the Republican primary, the conventions, and Romney's "47%" comments as were people low in cynicism. This may suggest something unique about debates; perhaps political cynics are less likely to watch political debates. It may be that cynics are disinterested in what candidates have to say because they distrust politicians. While it would be inappropriate to make broad conclusions based on these inconsistent findings, future research should explore the possibility that political communication about debates is uniquely influenced by cynicism.

It was also expected that, because moderates often use the high-choice environment created by digital media to opt out of politics and thereby cede the conversation to committed partisans (Prior, 2007), polarization would predict higher social media engagement. This study found very little evidence of this. While there were a few contexts where highly partisan individuals were more likely to participate (e.g., Facebook discussions of the candidates, the first debate, and Romney's "47%" comments; Twitter discussion of the first three debates and the conventions), a majority of contexts were not influenced by polarization. Furthermore, committed partisans were less likely to discuss Romney's 47% comments on Twitter. Given the presence of some significant findings, it would be a mistake to reject the possibility that polarization has some influence on the decision to engage in political communication via social media. However, it would also be a mistake to over-interpret the few and inconsistent relationships that emerged. Whatever role partisan polarization plays in social media engagement, this study did not find that partisans were more likely to engage than moderates.

In conclusion, the inconsistent prediction of polarization on social media engagement, the possibility that cynicism operates differently when applied to certain campaign events, and even the strong and consistent finding with political information efficacy all suggest an underlying limitation of this study. Because all seven samples were independent and cross-sectional, more dynamic relationships between the variables could not be discovered. Because campaign communication increases PIE, and PIE increases social media engagement, it may be the case that exposure to campaign messages has an indirect effect on social media engagement that is mediated by PIE. It is also likely that when individuals engage in political communication on Facebook and Twitter, they will become more confident in their political expression. The relationship is likely cyclical; people high in PIE will engage in more social media political communication, but this social media engagement will also increase PIE. None of these more dynamic variable relationships can be tested with our cross-sectional design. Furthermore, it is possible that context moderates the influence of cynicism on engagement. Future research should design experimental manipulations to isolate different political events and determine whether cynicism is more significant in some contexts than others. Finally, it seems insufficient simply to study polarization as a predictor of online engagement. While highly partisan people may have unique online communication behaviors, they were not observed in this study.

This study was further limited by the sample. University students are a specific subset of younger Americans, and a group that is more likely to be politically involved. For college students to have generally higher political information efficacy than their un-enrolled counterparts would be expected. This may not affect the relationship between PIE and social media engagement because, as a group, young people who do not attend college may be lower on both variables in a way that reflects the findings of this study. However, we cannot rule out the possibility that young people who do not attend college have unique patterns of social media engagement that differ from those identified in our sample.

Despite these limitations, these findings contribute important information to the conversation about the emerging role of social media in the political life of younger Americans. Facebook and Twitter provide unique spaces for political engagement. It is important to understand what dictates whether an individual will actualize the participatory potential of social media. These findings suggest that if students believe they have the knowledge necessary to participate effectively in political communication, they will do so regardless of their levels of cynicism or their passion about the candidates. Future research should confirm, as expected, that this relationship is reciprocal and dynamic (e.g., that political communication indirectly affects political engagement through PIE). Furthermore, researchers should continue to pursue cynicism and polarization as possible factors in the character of a young person's political engagement. More variables should also be included in future research. While cynicism, political information efficacy, and polarization are among the most important latent political attitudes, certainly other factors exist that have not been considered here. The place of social media in the broader field of political communication evolves with every election. This study advances our understanding of this evolution by demonstrating the fundamental importance of information efficacy. Whether this speaks to a larger trend toward greater youth participation remains to be seen. The past two elections saw young voters more engaged and participating at much higher levels than at any other time in a generation. To the extent that this continues, social media are certain to be major features of the American political experience.

APPENDIX 16.1: DEMOGRAPHIC DATA FOR THE SAMPLES

VARIABLE	PRIMARY	CONV.	CANDIDATE	DEB. 1	DEB. 2	DEB. 3	47%
N	176	103	372	311	399	462	586
Age							
M	20.41	19.23	20.22	20.78	20.94	20.79	20.2
SD	1.66	1.14	4.44	4.22	3.78	4.62	2.85
Sex							
Male	49 (28%)	32 (31%)	129 (35%)	135 (43%)	131 (33%)	167 (36%)	210 (36%)
Female	125 (71%)	70 (68%)	243 (65%)	171 (55%)	256 (64%)	286 (62%)	375 (64%)
Party							
Dem.	63 (36%)	34 (33%)	139 (37%)	97 (31%)	127 (32%)	157 (34%)	199 (34%)
Rep.	60 (34%)	43 (42%)	120 (32%)	123 (40%)	166 (42%)	186 (40%)	213 (36%)
Ind.	53 (30%)	26 (25%)	110 (30%)	88 (28%)	99 (25%)	112 (24%)	173 (30%)

APPENDIX 16.2: DESCRIPTIVE STATISTICS AND RELIABILITIES FOR ALL VARIABLES

VARIABLE	PRIMARY	CONVENTIONS	CANDIDATES	DEBATE (1)	(2)	(3)	47%
Polarization							
M	32.64	21.30	24.16	12.56	29.87	31.09	44.28
SD	7.59	11.84	6.03	8.65	7.37	7.47	4.78
Cynicism							
M	5.35	4.53	3.16	3.25	3.1	3.13	3.37
SD	.09	.11	.04	.04	.04	.03	.03
Cronbach's α	.898	.916	.863	.891	.883	.888	.904
PIE							
M	3.64	3.65	3.16	3.34	3.32	3.24	3.19
SD	.12	.18	.06	.06	.05	.05	.04
Cronbach's α	.915	.937	.902	.903	.904	.914	.882
Facebook							
M	1.27	1.81	2.92	4.76	4.35	3.72	2.07
SD	.29	.31	.417	.43	.4	.03	.36
Cronbach's α	.906	.877	.867	.869	.854	.844	.844
Twitter							
M	.99	.88	3.24	4.89	5.07	4.26	2.64
SD	.34	.36	.05	.64	.56	.53	.37
Cronbach's α	.923	.925	.935	.936	.932	.932	.889

Notes: Polarization was a single item and thus has no reliability statistic; all descriptive statistics are latent values. Social media engagement scores for the primary and the conventions are on a 1–4 metric, all others are on a 1–7 metric.

CHAPTER 17

YouTube and the 2012 Presidential Election: An Examination of How Obama's and Romney's Official YouTube Channels Were Used in Campaign Communication

LaChrystal D. Ricke

YouTube first became a blip on the United States' political radar during the 2006 midterm election when former U.S. senator George Allen, a Virginia Republican, was captured on video saying a racial slur. Subsequently, the video went viral on YouTube and quickly gained the attention of both the online community and the mainstream media (Karpf, 2010). This political gaffe provided the first indicator of how powerful online political video content and YouTube could be in political campaigning.

Online video in general and the YouTube platform in particular have become vital campaign and political communication tools. Online video allows for a level of image and message control outside the purview of the mainstream media; it is relatively cheap to produce, highly accessible, quick to disseminate, and easily shared via social networking sites (SNSs) (Gueorguieva, 2008). Online video also allows campaigns to position campaign-engagement tools in digital environments that their supporters are familiar with, and it has become the bedrock of digital campaign communication with supporters and undecided voters. Since the 2006 election, YouTube has become an accepted method of communication for politicians, with almost 600 candidates for U.S. political office, from the presidential race down to local races, hosting their own official YouTube channels (Michel & Pilkington, 2012). As online video and YouTube become more prominent in political campaigning, it is both interesting and important to understand the ways in which campaigns use YouTube to engage with potential voters, to advertise, and to solicit donations. This study examines the Obama and the Romney official campaign YouTube channels during the 2012 presidential campaign to see how each political team utilized this medium to engage with potential supporters.

POLITICS AND ONLINE VIDEO

In a very short period of time, social media and online video have dramatically changed the ways in which potential voters engage and interact with political campaigns. The public is increasingly turning to online video as a source of news and information, as a way to connect with candidates, and as a means of sharing political information with others through SNSs (Panagopoulos, 2009). The number of political social media users, or those Internet users who engage in politics through the use of social networks, is growing with each subsequent election cycle.

In 2008, 35% of online Americans reported having watched campaign-related videos online. This is a sharp increase from the 13% of online users who reported participating in similar activities during the 2004 presidential campaign (Smith & Rainie, 2008). The appeal of online video content for political social media users is that it allows them to watch unfiltered campaign materials such as candidate debates, speeches, and campaign announcements (Smith & Rainie, 2008). In terms of party affiliation, online Democrats were more likely to consume online videos than Republicans (51% vs. 42%) and Obama supporters were likely to engage in all manner of online political platforms more frequently than supporters of any other candidate (Smith & Rainie, 2008).

Similar gains in online video use have also been observed in non-presidential elections. In 2010, 31% of online Americans reported watching online campaign-related videos; this is, again, a sharp increase from the 19% of online adults who reported engaging in these activities during the 2006 midterm election (Smith, 2011). This increase represents a 63% growth in the number of adult Internet users watching online campaign-related videos and makes online video consumption the political activity with the greatest amount of growth (Smith, 2011). Both Democrats and Republicans were more likely to watch online political videos in 2010 than in 2006 and both were more likely to watch online videos than non-voters (Smith, 2011). However, the percentage of Republicans who engaged through online video surpassed that of Democrats (40% vs. 32%), with online video consumption amongst Republicans roughly doubling between the two election cycles (Smith, 2011). In addition, 8% of political social media users reported sharing online photo, video, or audio content related to the campaign (Smith, 2011).

Online video use was widespread during the Obama-Romney campaign. Specifically, in 2012, 66% of registered voters who use the Internet reported going online to watch campaign or other politically related videos (Smith & Duggan, 2012). In terms of the activities these users engaged in online, 40% watched previously re-corded videos of candidate speeches, press conferences, or debates, 36% watched political advertisements, and 28% watched live candidate speeches, press conferences, or debates (Smith & Duggan, 2012). Political social media users also reported the experience of engaging with online political video as being highly social, with 23% of Internet-using registered voters reporting having recommended an online political video to someone and 62% reporting having had an online political video recommended to them for viewing (Smith & Duggan, 2012). Interestingly, in an era of user-generated video content, only 1% of Internet-using registered voters reported having created their own political video. In terms of party affiliation, both Democratic and Republican voters were equally likely to watch and recommend online political videos and to have videos recommended to them (Smith & Duggan, 2012). Viewing of online videos was important amongst those voters who reported following the campaign closely, with 73% of these individuals reporting watching online political videos during the election compared to 45% of individuals who reported following the election less closely (Smith & Duggan, 2012).

The percentage of online Americans incorporating online video viewing into their normal web behavior is constantly increasing. As of May 2011, 71% of online adults reported having used video-sharing Web sites; this is a 5% increase from 2010 and a 38% increase from 2006 (Moore, 2011). On an average day, 28% of Internet users participate in some type of online video sharing site; this is up from 23% in 2010 (Moore, 2011). Additionally, non-white users, a demographic with the highest historical level of political disengagement and an often sought after voting bloc, are using online video sites at higher rates than their white counterparts, with 79% of non-whites reporting using online video sharing sites (Moore, 2011).

As Americans increasingly use online platforms to engage with political campaigns, they are discovering new ways to connect with candidates, to find out about news and events, and to share their opinions and campaign videos with others (Panagopoulos, 2009; Trammell, Williams, Postelnicu, & Landreville, 2006). This has necessitated a shift in how campaigns utilize online video and social media and has pushed campaigns to begin using these media to communicate with their supporters and potential voters in new ways.

Online video has become one of the most widely used campaign tools for communicating with and persuading voters. Through online video, campaigns can craft and distribute targeted messages, affordably advertise, and successfully fundraise (Panagopoulos, 2009). Online video offers campaigns one of the most effective ways to disseminate their messages, not just to a potential voter, but into online communities of potential voters where social networks share and discuss (Burgess & Green, 2009). It has modernized some of the more traditional aspects of political campaigning, such as get-out-the-vote efforts, political branding, and rebutting opponents' attacks (Peters, 2012). Campaigns no longer have to wait for the next news cycle to respond to opponents or other media attacks, as they can deliver their responses quickly, precisely, and directly to the voters.

Online videos have also changed the nature of political advertising and fundraising. By harnessing the power of SNSs, advertisements that are shared by friends or family gain a measure of credibility over an advertisement distributed through direct campaign marketing (Peters, 2012). This potentially increases the reach and resonance of an advertisement in ways impossible via traditional media. Online advertising, which was estimated to comprise about 10% of the campaigns' advertising budgets in 2012 (Peters, 2012), allows campaigns to target voters more aggressively based on demographic and site analyses and ad topic (Ricke, 2014). Online video has also provided new methods for political fundraising. Campaigns can now raise hundreds of millions of dollars online and are routinely breaking fundraising records for a small fraction of the cost of traditional fundraising (Panagopoulos, 2009). Through micro-targeting and social media analysis, campaigns can anticipate the issues that are likely to resonate with the voters who are likely to become donors (Ricke, 2014). This allows campaigns to develop appropriately situated online videos, to profit by requesting small donations, and to reach thousands more potential donors than through traditional fundraising strategies.

YouTube and Politics

Although YouTube made a significant impact on political campaigning during the 2006 election, it was not necessarily being used by campaigns as a communication tool that year. Potentially emboldened by the speed with which U.S. Senator Allen's infamous "Macaca moment"—a racial slur used by some Europeans toward Africans with dark complexions—spread throughout online and mainstream media, "gotcha" videos or political parodies, created and uploaded by individuals, media outlets, and politicians, became the most noticeable types of politically-oriented videos on YouTube. The campaigns of 2006 did not yet embrace the video sharing site as a platform for serious political messaging.

YouTube, as a viable mechanism for campaign and political communication, made its first substantial appearance during the 2008 presidential election. This election marked the first time that campaigns used online video as a tool for direct messaging and utilized the relationship between social media and online video to reach and attempt to persuade potential voters (Hendricks & Kaid, 2011). Campaigns began posting videos of speeches, rallies, and television commercials and attempted to leverage this new medium to engage with a specific demographic of potential voters—the political social media user. While both the Obama and McCain campaigns used social media and online video, the Obama campaign provided perhaps the first glimpse into how integral social media and online video would become to the political campaign process (Hendricks & Denton, 2010). During the election, the Obama camp unleashed an army of videographers who posted on YouTube roughly 2,000 videos of speeches, rallies, organizers going door-to-door, and of supporters sharing their personal stories. This invigorated the campaign's grassroots supporters and generated substantial page and video views (Michel & Pilkington, 2012). By the end of the 2008 election, official candidate videos were viewed nearly 200 million times and there were as many as 1 billion views of videos that were created by individuals or other groups not directly associated with the campaigns (Schwab, 2008). The successful integration of YouTube into overall campaign strategies and prolific use of it by potential voters led many to dub the 2008 presidential election "The YouTube Election" (Towner & Dulio, 2011).

By the 2012 presidential campaign, YouTube had matured into a necessary and vital campaign communication tool. During this campaign, both the Romney and Obama campaigns shifted from text to video. The campaigns produced videos with social media sharing in mind, increasingly attacked one another through video, and used the ability of online video to quickly rebut attacks and comments made by opponents (Michel & Pilkington, 2012).

Recognizing and embracing its importance and potential, President Obama announced his candidacy a full 19 months before the election with a two-minute YouTube video titled "It Begins with Us." The video featured individuals from around the country explaining the importance of actively campaigning or supporting Obama and served as the launch of the campaign's social media operation, generating over 1.3 million views (Condon, 2011). After its debut, the Obama YouTube video was prominently posted as a stand-alone advertisement, and as the only feature, other than a volunteer sign-up link, on the official campaign Web site. It appeared under the campaign's unofficial kick-off slogan, "Are You In?" Throughout the election, the Obama campaign worked to consistently upload new and dynamic videos, averaging four new videos per day (Dugan, 2012). Obama's YouTube channel, which was relied upon significantly to reach younger voters, amassed over 14.5 million hours of viewing, a figure worth roughly $47 million of television ad spending (Dugan, 2012). Approximately 3,000 videos were posted to the Obama channel, and the channel had nearly 9.2 times as many video views and 9.6 times as many followers as the Romney channel (Folliard, 2012). Additionally, Obama's official campaign Web site linked directly to its YouTube channel, making YouTube the central video hub for the campaign. Perhaps the most substantial statistic related to Obama's use of YouTube was reaching a landmark 200 million YouTube views of his online videos (Michel & Pilkington, 2012).

The Romney campaign also embraced online video and social media, but not to the same extent as the Obama campaign. Romney's campaign uploaded an average of two videos per day and ended the campaign with just over 300 videos uploaded to the Romney YouTube channel (Dugan, 2012). While substantially behind Obama in terms of video views, Romney's videos were still viewed more than 27.5 million times, reaching a substantial population (Folliard, 2012). Both campaigns also embraced video-on-demand strategies, where users of online media platforms were likely to see 30 second campaign advertisements before their selected video began, in order to reach targeted audiences. This strategy included developing and buying advertisement space on digital media platforms, such as YouTube and Hulu, in a targeted effort to reach voters who no longer consistently watch live television (Judd, 2012). Research on live television viewing estimates that as many as 45% of potential voters in key states no longer regularly consumed live television and that strategic buying could reach up to 165 million viewers a week on the web or mobile devices (Stirland, 2011). On-demand video, therefore, allows campaigns to effectively target specific voting demographics with precise messages in a manner that is cheaper to distribute and easier to track than broadcast advertisements (Christensen, 2012). Online advertisements allow campaigns to effectively target demographics through geolocation techniques, the targeting of potential voters based on their geographic location (such as in key swing states), and engage potential volunteers through click-to-call techniques, where users can connect with volunteer centers in their geographic location by clicking on links embedded in the advertisements (Stirland, 2011).

Both campaigns faced similar challenges in using YouTube and other online video. It was difficult to engage potential voters in actionable videos and to translate online engagement into offline action (Peters, 2012). One strategy both candidates used was to directly link their YouTube channels and options for sharing, donating, and volunteering, back to their main campaign Web sites, making it easier for potential voters or contributors to instantaneously take action.

It could be argued that perhaps no other media in the history of political campaigning has grown so significantly, and has had such an impact in such a short period of time. In just a few short years, the proliferation and adoption of YouTube has had a substantial impact on political campaigning in the United States. The simple scale of political video viewing underlines the growing importance of online video in political and campaign communication. In order to ascertain and understand how the presidential campaigns used their official YouTube channels to engage with potential supporters, an examination of Obama's *Obama for America* and Romney's *Believe in America* channels was conducted.

METHOD

After the impact of YouTube on the 2008 presidential election, there is much to investigate and learn about how the Obama and Romney presidential campaigns utilized the platform as part of their overarching campaign strategies during the 2012 election. An exploratory examination, such as this study, can provide insight into how YouTube was used during the campaign and offers some discussion as to the potential longevity of YouTube as a tool in political campaign communication.

To conduct this investigation, a qualitative content analysis methodology was employed to examine the official YouTube channels of both presidential candidates. This methodological approach permitted the researcher to use the data to inductively investigate the thematic and conceptual uses of YouTube videos by both campaigns and to ground discussions of the channels in the data (Krippendorff, 2003; Schreier, 2012). A frequency count was also used in order to provide insight into the rate with which certain types of political videos were used by the campaigns. This also helped inform the thematic and conceptual categories and provided a basis for equitable comparison between the two channels. However, the overarching qualitative frame allowed the video themes and concepts to function as primary content and typologies and the messages within the videos to serve as latent content.

For the purposes of this study, each candidate's YouTube Channel was treated as an independent population. This was necessary for sampling purposes because, if the channels were examined as a single population, the significant discrepancy in the number of videos between the two channels would have resulted in a majority of the videos analyzed being from the Obama channel. The final population of videos examined was 2,990 videos from *Obama for America* and 310 videos from *Believe in America*. A random sampling technique was used to select the videos examined in the final sample; the final sample, at a 95% confidence level (following Krejcie & Morgan, 1970), included 322 videos from the Obama channel and

169 videos from the Romney channel. This investigation was primarily concerned with addressing one overarching research question:

> RQ1: How did the Obama and Romney campaigns use YouTube during the 2012 presidential election?

To ascertain this, an examination of the types of political video present (i.e., informational, advertisements, engagement, fundraising, candidate-relationship building), the specific messages presented within those videos, and the ways in which the campaigns attempted to utilize YouTube to engage with potential voters were considered. The campaigns' apparent ability to address voters' primary justifications for watching online political videos, such as to gather information about the candidate or campaign, to feel more personally connected to the candidates, or to find ways to connect with the campaigns was examined. The presence of user-generated content was also taken into consideration. An investigation of these conceptual areas leads to an understanding of the ways in which YouTube was leveraged during the 2012 presidential campaign and provides insight into the effectiveness of each campaign's ability to engage potential voters and supporters through the YouTube platform. The following findings help to advance the understanding of how YouTube is used specifically during presidential elections and to illustrate specific ways that the campaigns used the medium to engage the public.

FINDINGS

The systematic investigation of Obama and Romney's official campaign YouTube channels found that, to some extent, both campaigns incorporated YouTube usage into their overall campaign strategies. However, by examining the pages, it is evident that the campaigns had different tactics for using YouTube, and arguably, achieved differing levels of effectiveness in terms of addressing users' primary motivations for watching online political videos.

The *Obama for America* channel posted nearly 3,000 videos, had over 380,000 channel subscribers, boasted over 290 million video views, and offered users a vast array of videos ranging from informational and policy explanations, to advertisements, to a video montage of President and Michelle Obama celebrating their 20th wedding anniversary. In contrast, the Romney *Believe in America* channel posted 300 videos, had 35,000 subscribers, and had roughly 33 million video views; a rough majority of the videos posted on this channel were advertisements. To provide a point of consideration and comparison, the Obama channel generated over eight times more video views than the Romney channel.

Obama for America
Obama's channel appealed to many of the stated reasons that potential voters and supporters engage with candidates through online video. Roughly 30% of the videos on the channel provided some type of information about Obama's policies, proposals, and the campaign's agenda. Gaining information is one of the primary reasons that potential voters watch online political videos (Smith & Duggan,

2012). The Obama channel provided information through a variety of methods, such as (a) briefings by Stephanie Cutter, Obama's Deputy Campaign Manager, (b) campaign strategy sessions by Obama's Campaign Manager, Jim Messina, and (c) strategically selected clips from stump speeches. The briefings by Cutter generated hundreds of thousands of views and provided users with information about Obama's political agenda and how the proposed policies would impact the American public. These videos also served to counter and rebut statements made by the Romney campaign, put them into perspective for potential Obama supporters, and encouraged supporters to speak out, specifically via social media, against false and misleading statements made by both the Romney campaign and by mainstream media outlets. These videos served the dual purpose of providing information and engaging potential supporters by distributing rapid response campaign information.

The campaign strategy sessions presented by Messina encouraged followers to get engaged with the campaign at the grassroots level and provided them with specific strategies for doing so. One particular video provided users with a strategic framework for the campaign, explaining to viewers the goals for the grassroots movement: the need to expand the electorate, (a) build something new, (b) grow the grassroots movement at the state level, (c) measure progress, and (d) work for every vote. Much like the briefing videos by Cutter, these strategy sessions served the dual purpose of providing information and telling supporters specifically how they could connect and engage with the campaign. The Obama campaign embraced the interactive aspects of social media. Information was also provided on a wide variety of topics, such as the Affordable Care Act, women's rights, the debt ceiling debate, LGBT rights, and the campaign's commitment to small businesses, minority populations, and students. This information was provided through a variety of video methods, including speech clips, direct-to-camera videos from Obama, videos from supporters such as former president Bill Clinton and former secretary of state Colin Powell and various celebrities, and videos of regular individuals discussing how these issues impacted them.

Viewing campaign advertisements is another reason that people report watching online political videos (Smith & Duggan, 2012). Advertisements comprised a substantial portion of the videos on the channel, accounting for over 54% of the total videos in the sample. There were two distinct types of advertisements present, informational advertisements, which focused primarily on Obama's agenda and/or policies and how those would positively impact the American people, and attack advertisements, which focused primarily on the flaws of the Republican candidates and/or their campaign. A wide variety of topics were broached through both types of advertisements, but the tone between the two types was, perhaps not surprisingly, vastly different. The informational advertisements focused on moving America forward and promoted themes such as "Trust," "Believers," "Facts," "Moving Forward," and "Choice." These advertisements focused on the success that the president, in conjunction with the American public, had achieved during his four years in office and provided ideas and details about how the entire country would continue to move forward in a positive direction following Obama's re-election. Attack ads were the most prominent type of political video on the channel, comprising roughly 32% of the video population. Conceptually, these ads focused on why the Republican Party was a bad choice to lead the country forward. These ads centered on themes such as "Wrong for the Middle Class," "The Cheaters," "Swiss Bank Account," "Son of Boss," and "Broken Promises," and focused collectively on ideas of criminality, gluttony, and greed.

All of the advertisements were easily sharable, which was strongly encouraged by the campaign, with one-click sharing options for both Facebook and Twitter easily accessible on every advertisement video. Interestingly, the advertising videos also served a dual purpose as fundraising videos. Stand-alone fundraising videos were not prominent on the channel, with only two being discovered in the sample. Instead, at the beginning of each advertisement on the channel, a dialogue box reading "to contribute $10 to Obama for America, text OBAMA to 62262," was superimposed over each advertisement. These fundraising messages are significant for two reasons. First, contributions were charged directly to viewers' cell phone bills, so there was no immediate out-of-pocket expense related to the donation, which may have prompted some individuals to be more likely to donate. Second, digital fundraising strategies, such as this, have contributed to campaigns being able to reach a vastly larger number of potential donors than through other forms of fundraising, thereby generating substantial amounts of money in small one-time donations, and reaching a population of donors that have likely never contributed before and who are willing to give small donations repeatedly (Ricke, 2014).

Online political video users' desire to connect with candidates and campaigns is often a reason for viewing online political videos (Smith & Duggan, 2012). Around 17% of the channel's videos were aimed at making potential supporters feel (a) engaged with the campaign, (b) engaged with other users, or (c) personally connected to the candidate. These types of videos were inclusive in nature. Some examples included videos depicting average Americans discussing why they were working to support the president's re-election bid, videos asking supporters to stand with the president as he continued his fight for American jobs, and get-out-the-vote videos encouraging unregistered voters to register through the Web site *GottaRegister.com*, which emphasized the importance of personal efficacy, of voting and the belief that an individual can overcome obstacles and achieve their goals. Examples of videos aimed at connecting viewers to other supporters include a video titled "Meet Alex" which followed Alex, a dad and Obama organizer, as he campaigned for the president and a video where 10-year-old Ian relates how he would like to meet and thank the president for bringing his father home from Iraq, which segues into clips of Obama stumping on the topic of ending the War in Iraq. These videos allowed all supporters, no matter how engaged, to feel involved in the Obama 2012 movement.

There were also many videos that served to connect supporters with Obama, the person, and not necessarily Obama, the candidate. These videos were also very inclusive, focused on the "We" of the campaign, which reminded supporters of their role in the success of the campaign, and established Obama as an average person. There were videos of Obama having dinner with teachers, army veterans, small business owners, and firefighters, video montages of the Obama family during special events, and a popular video called "The Story of Us," which compiled video clips tracking through the president's 2008 campaign, the successes of his first term in office, and into the 2012 campaign, that ended by asking the viewer if they were "In." Throughout the many videos geared towards connecting the public with the candidate as a person, there were funny clips of him signing at press conferences, of him dancing with television show host Ellen DeGeneres, and of him fist-bumping Michelle Obama. These visual image strategies helped to connect the public with the human side of the politician and made significant strides at making the candidate seem like an average person.

Another engagement and relationship-building strategy on the channel was the presence of user-generated videos and candid campaign trail videos. The channel had a tab titled "From the Field" that contained videos of official campaign staff and volunteers out on the campaign trail. These videos included (a) rallies, (b) volunteers (and the president) making calls from phone banks, (c) chronicles of the typical day of an Obama canvasser, and (d) many user generated videos illustrating different grassroots efforts from all around the country. These videos helped to show the inner-workings of the campaign, the important role that the volunteers played, how individuals from all over the country were becoming engaged, and put a personal face on the campaign.

Believe in America

Romney's channel utilized YouTube in a different manner and to a differing degree from the Obama campaign. The Romney YouTube channel used videos to provide information regarding the campaign or its agenda in approximately 4% of the videos. This information focused on the ways in which Romney would redirect the country and its leadership and how the Republican platform would alleviate some of the financial hardships that Americans had been placed under during the Obama presidency. Specific information was provided on a few policies, such as the mandate of the Affordable Care Act, but a majority of the issues discussed related to the financial hardships the country faced and Romney's plan to improve the economy and create jobs.

The channel also used both engagement and candidate-connection videos to a small degree, with approximately 4% of its videos related to relationship building. Videos that encouraged supporter engagement included a promotional-type video of a rally hosted by Romney and his running mate, Paul Ryan. The video showed throngs of supporters driving to the rally, causing traffic jams, and filling the rally's venue to capacity. Other types of engagement videos (a) depicted the Democrats for Romney grassroots effort, (b) aired testimonials from former Obama supporters discussing why they were voting for Romney in 2012, and (c) showed how specific populations, such as Catholics, could assist in the success of the campaign. There was one video specifically aimed at establishing a relationship between the candidate and supporters titled "Mitt Romney: Introduction." In this video, Romney and his wife, Ann, provide a ten minute commentary on their life and the events that helped Romney develop the values and skills he believes are necessary to lead the country.

Over 90% of the videos on the Romney Channel were advertisements. Similar to the Obama channel, these advertisements were a mixture of informational and attack ads, with the attack ads representing roughly 57% of the site's content. The informational advertisements centered on the main themes of developing a more financially productive America and the need for renewed political leadership. The attack advertisements centered around how the American public has suffered or been harmed by the policies of the Obama administration and capitalized on titles such as "Crushed by your Policies," "Can't Afford Another Term," and "Obama Isn't Working." The Romney channel also provided a one-click method for sharing advertisements and other campaign videos through Facebook, Twitter, and email. The Romney channel did not contain any user-generated videos and very few candid videos of the candidate or the campaign.

DISCUSSION

Overall, both campaigns were successful in leveraging the YouTube environment to share information, campaign messages, and advertisements with potential supporters and voters. Although both campaigns employed different methods, both channels reached a significant population via online video that would have cost the campaigns millions of dollars through more traditional media outlets. To some extent, both campaigns posted videos that addressed online video viewers' primary objectives for watching political videos, such as gathering information, watching advertisements, and connecting with the candidates and campaigns.

Even though both campaigns were successful in reaching a wide population of potential supporters through their campaign's YouTube channels, there were very few similarities in the use of YouTube between the two campaigns. The sheer number of videos posted to Obama's channel may be an indication of the campaign's sophisticated understanding of digital campaigning and of micro-targeting online videos to potential voters.

In addition to using the YouTube channel in the various methods mentioned above, the Obama channel also featured a 17-minute online documentary that was directed by an Oscar-Winning director. This documentary was essentially the launch of Obama's re-election bid and was meant to re-engage previous campaign supporters and capture the attention of new supporters in a manner that only the Obama campaigns have yet managed to accomplish. It was anticipated that the documentary would be shared through social media and email and would begin to turn the passive activity of watching online video into an early organizing and fundraising tool for the campaign (Peters, 2012). By using YouTube to release the documentary, and by integrating both organizational and fundraising functionalities into the platform, users could share, volunteer, and donate without having to click away from Obama's YouTube channel. This strategy indicates how intuitive the Obama team was regarding leveraging the digital video environment in terms of information, advertising, fundraising, and engagement.

Collectively, the Obama campaign seemed to leverage the YouTube environment more effectively. The *Obama for America* channel provided a wider range of videos that addressed the reasons political social media users report for watching online political video and produced a platform that was cohesive with the campaign's overarching media strategies. Whether by strategy or inadvertency, the Romney campaign did not utilize the YouTube platform to the extent that the Obama campaign did.

With the number of Americans using online video sharing sites increasing, and evidence that members of often highly sought after voting blocs are using online video sharing somewhat extensively (Moore, 2011), it is important that political campaigns begin increasing their level of knowledge and understanding of how to most effectively leverage online environments, such as YouTube.

Challenges

The use of YouTube in political campaigning has by no means been perfected, and it is evident that all of the potentialities of the platform for information sharing, advertising, and engagement have not been completely tapped. One of the biggest challenges for any political campaign is the ability to turn Internet-based activity, such as sharing videos, into real-world action, such as donating, volunteering, or voting. It is also difficult to measure the offline success of online campaigns because much of the data related to offline behavior stemming from digital engagement comes from self-reported data and surveys. While steps were made with many of the one-click functionalities employed by both campaigns during the 2012 election, steps still need to be taken to better translate potential supporters' online behavior into offline action. Another significant challenge is the constantly changing and evolving nature of online platforms. YouTube is first and foremost situated as a commercial enterprise and will manage its interface in the manner that is most financially beneficial to it as a company. This means that campaigns must be reactive to new and trending functionalities of the platform in order to most effectively engage supporters. This will require campaigns to be vigilant to changes and trends and consistently work to change passive online viewing experiences into reliable and measurable offline action.

The YouTube Effect

YouTube has become a fixture in campaigns and political communication. It is anticipated that as the medium continues to grow and expand, so too will the ways that the platform impacts politics and campaign communication, although its exponential and rapid growth make keeping up with YouTube usage statistics difficult. YouTube surpassed one trillion views in 2011, equating to roughly 140 views for every person on Earth, and boasts over 800 million unique user visitors who spend an estimated 4 billion hours viewing videos each month (YouTube, 2012). Approximately 72 hours of video are uploaded every minute (YouTube, 2012) and more video content is uploaded in a 60-day period than has been broadcast by the three major broadcast television networks in the past 60 years (Elliott, 2011). The social media reach of YouTube is also substantial, with 500 years of video being watched everyday on Facebook, over 700 videos shared on Twitter each minute, and 100 million people engaging in "social action" (likes, shares, comments) every week (YouTube, 2012). YouTube also has a substantial mobile technology presence, with over 20% of global views coming from mobile devices and 3 hours of video being uploaded to YouTube every minute from mobile devices (YouTube, 2012).

The YouTube Politics Channel, a political video hub that chronicled the 2012 election from the primaries through Election Day, was introduced in 2011. The channel was developed to capitalize on the public's growing desire to gather political information online and campaigns' increased use of the medium for political message distribution. It served as a one-stop online destination for political videos related to the 2012 campaign and featured horse-race-type political tracking, links to weekly "hot" political videos, and employed a third-party outlet to search and monitor user-generated content on social media platforms that were then distributed on the YouTube Politics Channel (Preston, 2011).

In conclusion, the 2012 presidential campaign had its own "Macaca Moment," the capturing of Mitt Romney's "47% comment" on video. The video, shot during a private fundraiser, went viral almost immediately and quickly became fodder for both the mainstream media and the Obama campaign (Cronkite, 2012). The video not only generated a substantial level of media attention, but also influenced the opponent's campaign strategy, and allowed the Obama campaign to capitalize on the perceived differences between Romney and the American public (Thompson, 2012). This video is a prime example of the power that online video and YouTube have in the evolving world of digital political campaigns.

The expanse and prominence of YouTube, in general, and as it relates specifically to political campaigning, is precisely why candidates and campaigns significantly benefit from understanding how to effectively implement YouTube-oriented communication strategies into overall campaign communication initiatives. YouTube is clearly not a fad; it is, in fact, growing in popularity, use, views, and functionality every day. There is no foretelling how YouTube will impact future elections or what functionalities will be available in the future for campaigns to share their messages, platforms, and stories with potential voters and supporters. However, it is anticipated that the number of political social media users who are reliant upon video as a form of information, persuasion, and engagement, will likely continue to grow, and with that, the popularity and necessity of YouTube as a method of political campaign communication will continue to expand as well.

References

Chapter 1

Adams, R. (2012). Did social media predict the 2012 presidential election results? *PRWeb .com*. Retrieved from http://www.prweb.com/releases/prwebpresidential-election/election-results/prweb10113142.htm

Alexa.com. (2012). *Top sites: The top 500 sites on the web*. Retrieved from http://www.alexa .com/topsites

Alter, J. (2013). *The center holds: Obama and his enemies*. New York: Simon & Schuster.

Balz, D. (2013, July 28). How the Obama campaign won the race for voter data. *Washington Post*. Retrieved from http://wapo.st/18HJF6R

Barbaro, M., & Shear, M. D. (2012, August 31). Before Eastwood's talk with a chair, clearance from the top. *The New York Times*. Retrieved from http://www.nytimes .com/2012/09/01/us/politics/romney-aides-scratch-their-heads-over-eastwoods-speech.html?_r=0

Brenner, J. (2012). Pew internet: Social networking. *Pew Internet and American Life Project*. Retrieved from http://pewinternet.org/Commentary/2012/March/Pew-Internet-Social-Networking-full-detail.aspx

Brown, A. (2012, January 4). GOP candidates on social media. *NewMediaRockStars.com*. Retrieved from http://newmediarockstars.com/2012/01/gops-on-social-media/

Cass, C., & Benac, N. (2012, November 12). Face of US changing; elections to look different. Associated Press. Retrieved from http://news.yahoo.com/face-us-changing-elections-look-different-143838055.html

Center for Information and Research on Civic Learning and Engagement (CIRCLE). (2012). *President Obama wins majority of youth in 2012, but not all youth vote Democratic*. Retrieved from http://www.civicyouth.org/

CIRCLE. *See* Center for Information and Research on Learning and Engagement.

Corn, D. (2012, December 31). The story behind the 47 percent video: It took months to get the scoop that rocked the 2012 election. *Mother Jones*. Retrieved from http://www .motherjones.com/politics/2012/12/story-behind-47-video

Draper, R. (2013, February 14). Can the Republicans be saved from obsolescence? *New York Times Magazine*. Retrieved from http://nyti.ms/UbxdYC

Fitzpatrick, A. (2012, December 6). The 10 best political memes of 2012. *Mashable.com.* Retrieved from http://mashable.com/2012/12/06/political-memes/

Freedland, J. (2012, November 6). How Mitt Romney's missteps kept Obama in the presidential race. *The Guardian.* Retrieved from http://www.guardian.co.uk/world/2012/nov/06/romney-missteps-obama-us-election

Friess, S. (2012, December 30). 2012's social media moments in politics. *Politico.* Retrieved from http://www.politico.com/story/2012/12/2012s-social-media-moments-in-politics-85556.html

Gallup. (2012, November 5). Romney 49%, Obama 48% in Gallup's final election survey. Retrieved from http://www.gallup.com/poll/158519/romney-obama-gallup-final-election-survey.aspx

Green, J. (2012, November 29). The science behind those Obama campaign e-mails. *Bloomberg BusinessWeek.* Retrieved from http://www.businessweek.com/articles/2012-11-29/the-science-behind-those-obama-campaign-e-mails

Green, J. (2013a, May 31). Obama's data team totally schooled Gallup. *Bloomberg Businessweek.* Retrieved from http://buswk.co/17b7Mwv

Green, J. (2013b, June 6). Obama campaign says it was 42 percent more accurate than Nate Silver. *Bloomberg Businessweek.* Retrieved from http://buswk.co/1234MQx

Harris, D. (2012, December 8). How Obama's data scientists built a volunteer army on Facebook. *Gigaom.* Retrieved from http://gigaom.com/2012/12/08/how-obamas-data-scientists-built-a-volunteer-army-on-facebook/

Hendricks, J. A., & Denton, R. E., Jr. (Eds.). (2010). *Communicator-in-chief: How Barack Obama used new media technology to win the White House.* Lanham, MD: Lexington Books.

Internet Usage and Population Statistics for North America. (2012, June 30). *Internet world stats: Usage and population statistics.* Retrieved from http://www.internetworldstats.com/stats14.htm

Johnson, S. (2012). *Future perfect: The case for progress in a networked age.* New York: Riverhead.

Judd, N. (2012a, November 19). How Obama for America made its Facebook friends into effective advocates. *TechPresident.* Retrieved from http://techpresident.com/news/23159/how-obama-america-made-its-facebook-friends-effective-advocates

Judd. N. (2012b, November 30). Obama's targeted GOTV on Facebook reached 5 million voters, Goff says. *TechPresident.* Retrieved from http://techpresident.com/news/23202/obamas-targeted-gotv-facebook-reached-5-million-voters-goff-says

Kasperkevic, J. (2012, November 7). The Tweetelection: Obama had more than just the ground game in his favor. *Timesunion.com.* Retrieved from http://blog.timesunion.com/politicssource/the-tweetelection-obama-had-more-than-just-the-ground-game-in-his-favor/2744/

Kroll, A. (2012, August 30). Clint Eastwood's bizarre "Empty Chair Obama" speech at the GOP convention. *Mother Jones.* Retrieved from http://www.motherjones.com/mojo/2012/08/video-clint-eastwood-chair-republican-convention

Lombardo, S. (2012, November 1). Election monitor: 5 days to go and trend model says Romney wins popular vote. *Huffington Post.* Retrieved from http://huff.to/QWV3mQ

Madrigal, A. C. (2012, November 16). When the nerds go marching in. *The Atlantic.* Retrieved from http://www.theatlantic.com/technology/archive/2012/11/when-the-nerds-go-marching-in/265325/2/

Mehta, S. (2011, April 18). The rise of the Internet electorate: Obama validated the use of social media as a powerful campaign tool. Now it's crucial for every candidate. *The Los*

Angeles Times. Retrieved from http://articles.latimes.com/2011/apr/18/nation/la-na-social-media-20110418

Mele, N. (2013). *The end of big: How the Internet makes David the new Goliath.* New York: St. Martin's Press.

Miller, Z. (2012, December 3). 8 new insights about the 2012 race for president. *BuzzFeed.* Retrieved from http://www.buzzfeed.com/zekejmiller/8-new-insights-about-the-2012-race-for-president

Morozov, E. (2013). *To save everything, click here: The folly of technological solutionism.* New York: PublicAffairs.

Patel, S. (2012, March 21). How the 2012 Republican primary candidates are using social media. *SearchEngineJournal.com.* Retrieved from http://www.searchenginejournal.com/how-the-2012-republican-primary-candidates-are-using-social-media/41640/

Pesante, K. (2011, April 27). GOP 2012 contenders + social media. Retrieved from http://kiarapesante.com/digital_pr/gop-2012-contenders-social-media/

Pew Research Center. (2012, August 15). *How the presidential candidates use the web and social media: Obama leads but neither candidate engages in much dialogue with voters.* Washington, DC: Pew Research Center's Project for Excellence in Journalism.

Rainie, L. (2012, September 11). Smartphone ownership update: September 2012. *Pew Internet & American Life Project.* Retrieved from http://pewinternet.org/Reports/2012/Smartphone-Update-Sept-2012.aspx

Real Clear Politics. (2012). *Real Clear Politics poll average: 2012 Republican presidential nomination.* Retrieved from http://bit.ly/eS7N8y

Remarks by the President at a Campaign Event in Roanoke, Virginia. (2012, July 13). *The White House, Office of the press secretary.* Retrieved from http://www.whitehouse.gov/the-press-office/2012/07/13/remarks-president-campaign-event-roanoke-virginia

Rodriguez, S. (2012, November 6). Obama turns to Reddit for last-minute voters. *Los Angeles Times.* Retrieved from http://articles.latimes.com/2012/nov/06/business/la-fi-tn-obama-reddit-election-20121106

Rogers, K. (2012, August 15). Obama bests Romney in the social media campaign, research shows. *The Guardian.* Retrieved from http://www.guardian.co.uk/media/2012/aug/15/obama-bests-romney-when-it-comes-to-social-media

Rutenberg, J. (2013, June 20). Data you can believe in: The Obama campaign's digital masterminds cash in. *New York Times Magazine.* Retrieved from http://nyti.ms/1bYPV9C

Scherer, M. (2012). Inside the secret world of the data crunchers who helped Obama win. *Time.* Retrieved from http://ti.me/Uj7o9o

Schmidt, E., & Cohen, J. (2013). *The new digital age: Reshaping the future of people, nations and business.* New York: Knopf.

Schouten, F. (2013, February 1). 2012 campaign hit record $7B, regulator projects. *USA Today.* Retrieved from http://www.usatoday.com/story/news/politics/2013/02/01/election-spending-7-billion/1882803/

Seib, G. F. (2011, July 5). Voting blocs to watch as 2012 nears. *The Wall Street Journal.* Retrieved from http://online.wsj.com/article/SB10001424052702303982504576425653594692390.html

Sides, J., & Vavreck, L. (2013). *The gamble: Choice and chance in the 2012 presidential election.* Princeton, NJ: Princeton University Press.

Sifry, M. L. (2012, January 6). Social media and the Republican primaries: Why social media couldn't predict the Iowa race. *CyberclassroomTV Online Education Network.* Retrieved from http://cyberclassroomtv.blogspot.com/2012/01/social-media-and-republican-primaries.html

Smith, A. (2012). 13% of online adults use Twitter: Half of Twitter users access the service "on the go" via mobile phone. *Pew Internet & American Life Project*. Retrieved from http://pewinternet.org/Reports/2011/Twitter-Update-2011.aspx

Smith, A., & Duggan, M. (2012). Online political videos and Campaign 2012. *Pew Internet & American Life Project*. Retrieved from http://www.pewinternet.org/Reports/2012/Election-2012-Video.aspx

Socialbakers.com. (2012). *United States Facebook statistics*. Retrieved from http://www.socialbakers.com/facebook-statistics/united-states

Stirland, S. L., & Judd, N. (2012, January 4). Santorum's campaign chokes online as site is overwhelmed by traffic. *TechPresident.com*. Retrieved from http://techpresident.com/news/21561/santorums-campaign-chokes-online-site-overwhelmed-traffic

Tau, B. (2013, January 13). Bill Clinton to Democrats: Don't trivialize gun culture. *Politico*. Retrieved from http://politi.co/UFr84i

Thomas, K. (2011, June 28). Obama 2012 campaign to go beyond email, text. *The Washington Times*. Retrieved from http://www.washingtontimes.com/news/2011/jun/28/obama-2012-campaign-to-go-beyond-email-text/print/

Wasserman, T. (2012, December 11). Twitter user ID numbers cross into the billions. *Mashable.com*. Retrieved from http://mashable.com/2012/12/11/twitter-1-billionth-user-id/

Winograd, M., & Hais, M. D. (2008). *Millennial makeover: MySpace, YouTube, and the future of American politics*. New Brunswick, NJ: Rutgers University Press.

YouTube. (2012). Statistics. YouTube.com. Retrieved from http://www.youtube.com/t/press_statistics

Chapter 2

Ancu, M., & Cozma, R. (2009). MySpace politics: Uses and gratifications of befriending candidates. *Journal of Broadcasting & Electric Media, 53*(4), 567–583.

Adkins, R. E., & Dowdle, A. J. (2001). How important are Iowa and New Hampshire to winning post–reform presidential nominations? *Political Research Quarterly, 54*, 431–444.

American Association for Public Opinion Research (AAPOR). (2008). *Standard definitions: Final dispositions of case codes and outcome rates for surveys*. Lenexa, KS: AAPOR. Retrieved from http://www.aapor.org/AM/Template.cfm?Section=Standard_Definitions&Template=/CM/ContentDisplay.cfm&ContentID=1273

Bachmann, I., Kaufhold, K., Lewis, S., & Gil de Zúñiga, H. (2010). News platform preference: Advancing the effects of age and media consumption on political participation. *International Journal of Internet Science, 5*(1), 34–47.

Bakker, T. P., & de Vreese, C. H. (2011). Good news for the future? Young people, Internet use and political participation. *Communication Research, 38*(4), 451–470.

Bimber, B. A., & Davis, R. (2003). *Campaigning online: The Internet in U.S. elections*. New York: Oxford University Press.

Boulianne, S. (2009). Does Internet use affect engagement? A meta-analysis of research. *Political Communication, 26*(2), 193–211.

Bucy, E., & Gregson, A. (2001). Media participation: A legitimizing mechanism of mass democracy. *New Media & Society, 3*(3), 357–380.

C-Span. (2012, September 3). Social media and 2012 election [Video file]. Retrieved from http://www.c-spanvideo.org/program/Media2

Dimitrova, D. V., Shehata, A., Strömbäck, J., & Nord, L. W. (2014). The effects of digital media on political knowledge and participation in election campaigns: Evidence from panel data. *Communication Research, 41*(1), 95–118.

Drew, D., & Weaver, D. H. (2006). Voter learning and interest in the 2004 presidential election: Did the media matter? *Journalism and Mass Communication Quarterly, 83*, 25–53.

Fitzgerald, B. (2012, November 7). Barack Obama victory photo becomes Twitter's most retweeted post ever. Retrieved from http://www.huffingtonpost.com/2012/11/07/barack-obama-twitter-most-retweeted_n_2088035.html

Foot, K., & Schneider, S. M. (2006). *Web campaigning*. Cambridge, MA: MIT Press.

Groshek, J., & Dimitrova, D. V. (2011). A cross-section of voter learning, campaign interest and intention to vote in the 2008 American election: Did Web 2.0 matter? *Communication Studies, 9*, 355–375.

Hendricks, J. A., & Denton, R. E., Jr. (Eds.). (2010). *Communicator-in-chief: How Barack Obama used new media technology to win the White House*. Lanham, MD: Lexington Books.

Hendricks, J. A., & Kaid, L. L. (Eds.) (2011). *Techno politics in presidential campaigning: New voices, new technologies, and new voters*. New York: Routledge.

Hirzalla, F., van Zoonen, L., & de Ridder, J. (2011). Internet use and political participation: Reflections on the mobilization/normalization controversy. *The Information Society, 27*(1), 1–15.

Kaye, B. K., & Johnson, T. (2002). Online and in the know: Uses and gratifications of the Web for political information. *Journal of Broadcasting & Electric Media, 46*(1), 54–71.

Kenski, K., & Stroud, N. J. (2006). Connections between Internet use and political efficacy, knowledge, and participation. *Journal of Broadcasting & Electronic Media, 50*, 173–192.

Kirk, R., & Schill, D. (2011). A digital agora: Citizen participation in the 2008 presidential debates. *American Behavioral Scientist, 55*, 325–347.

Mossberger, K., Tolbert, C. J., & McNeal, R. S. (2008). *Digital citizenship: The Internet, society, and participation*. Cambridge, MA: MIT Press.

Nielsen. (2012). *State of the media: U.S. digital consumer report, Q3-Q4 2011*. Retrieved from http://www.nielsen.com/us/en/insights/reports-downloads/2012/us-digital-consumer-report.html

O'Brien, C. (2012, December 4). Political experts discuss future of Iowa caucuses. *Iowa State Daily*. Retrieved from http://www.iowastatedaily.com/news/article_409da8e0-3dc7-11e2-ad06-0019bb2963f4.html

Plouffe, D. (2009). *The audacity to win: The inside story and lessons of Barack Obama's historic victory*. New York: Viking Press.

Prior, M. (2007). *Post-broadcast democracy: How media choice increases inequality in political involvement and polarizes elections*. New York: Cambridge University Press.

Prior, M. (2013/in press). Media and political polarization. *Annual Review of Political Science, 16*.

Quintelier, E., & Vissers, S. (2008). The effect of Internet use on political participation: An analysis of survey results for 16-year-olds in Belgium. *Social Science Computer Review, 26* (4), 411–427.

Rainie, L., & Smith, A. (2012, September 4). Politics on social networking sites. *Pew Internet & American Life Project*. Retrieved from http://pewInternet.org/~/media//Files/Reports/2012/PIP_PoliticalLifeonSocialNetworkingSites.pdf

Redlawsk, D. P., Tolbert, C. J., & Donovan, T. (2010). *Why Iowa? How caucuses and sequential elections improve the presidential nominating process*. Chicago, IL: University of Chicago Press.

Rutenberg, J., & Zeleny, J. (2012, March 8). Obama mines for voters with high tech tools. *The New York Times*. Retrieved from http://www.nytimes.com/2012/03/08/us/politics/obama-campaigns-vast-effort-to-re-enlist-08-supporters.html

Smith, A. (2011, January 27). 22% of online Americans used social networking or Twitter for politics in 2010 campaign. *Pew Internet & American Life Project.* Retrieved from http://www.pewInternet.org/Reports/2011/Politics-and-social-media/Overview.aspx

Vitak, J., Zube, P., Smock, A., Carr, C. T., Ellison, N., & Lampe, C. (2011). It's complicated: Facebook users' political participation in the 2008 election. *Cyberpsychology, Behavior, and Social Networking, 14*(3), 107–114. doi:10.1089/cyber.2009.0226

Weber, L. M., Loumakis, A., & Bergman, J. (2003). Who participates and why? An analysis of citizens on the Internet and the mass public. *Social Science Computer Review, 21,* 26–42.

Winebrenner, H., & Goldford, D. J. (2010). *The Iowa precinct caucuses: The making of a media event, third edition.* Iowa City: University of Iowa Press.

Zickhur, K., & Madden, M. (2012, June 6). Older adults and Internet use. *Pew Internet & American Life Project.* Retrieved from http://pewInternet.org/~/media//Files/Reports/2012/PIP_Older_adults_and_Internet_use.pdf

Chapter 3

Athanasopoulou, P. (2009). Relationship quality: A critical literature review and research agenda. *European Journal of Marketing, 43*(5), 583–610.

Aula, P. (2011). Meshworked reputation: Publicists' views on the reputational impacts of online communication. *Public Relations Review, 37,* 28–36.

Barnes, J. G. (1994). Close to the customer: But is it really a relationship? *Journal of Marketing Management, 10,* 79–88.

Bennett, J. B. (2001). Teaching with hospitality. *Teaching and Learning News, 10*(3), 88–89.

Bortree, D., & Seltzer, T. (2009). Dialogic strategies and outcomes: An analysis of environmental advocacy groups' Facebook profiles. *Public Relations Review, 35*(3), 317–319.

Briones, R. L., Kuch, B., Fisher Liu, B., & Jin, Y. (2011). Keeping up with the digital age: How the American Red Cross uses social media to build relationships. *Public Relations Review, 37,* 37–43.

Buttle, F. (2001). Retaining business customers through adaptation and bonding: A case study of HDoX. *Journal of Business & Industrial Marketing, 16*(7), 553–573.

Christopher, M., Payne, A., & Ballantyne, D. (2008). *Relationship marketing: Creating stakeholder value.* Oxford: Butterworth-Heinemann.

Clark, M. S., & Mills, J. (1979). Interpersonal attraction in exchange and communal relationships. *Journal of Personality and Social Psychology, 37*(1), 12–24.

Clark, M. S., & Mills, J. (1993). The difference between communal and exchange relationships: What it is and is not. *Personality and Social Psychology Bulletin, 19,* 684–691.

Coombs, W. T. (2010). Crisis communication: A developing the field. In R. L. Heath (Ed.), *The SAGE Handbook of Public Relations* (pp. 477–488). Thousand Oaks, CA: Sage Publications.

Dimitrova, D. V., Shehata, A., Strömbäck, J., & Nord, L. W. (2014). The effects of digital media on political knowledge and participation in election campaigns: Evidence from panel data. *Communication Research, 41*(1), 95–118.

Egan, J. (2011). *Relationship marketing: Exploring relational strategies in* marketing (4th ed.). Harlow, UK: Prentice Hall.

Falkheimer, J., & Heide, M. (2010). Crisis communicators in change: From plans to improvisations. In W. T. Coombs & S. J. Holladay (Eds.), *The handbook of crisis communication* (pp. 511–526). Oxford: Wiley-Blackwell.

Grönroos, C. (1996). Relationship marketing: Strategic and tactical implications. *Management Decision, 34*(3), 5–14.

Grönroos, C. (1999). Relationship marketing: Challenges for the organization. *Journal of Business Research, 46,* 327–335.

Grönroos, C. (2000). *Service management and marketing: A customer relationship management approach* (2nd ed.). Chichester, UK: John Wiley & Sons.

Grunig, L. A., Grunig, J. E., & Dozier, D. M. (2002). *Excellent public relations and effective organizations: A study of communication management in three countries.* London: Lawrence Erlbaum Associates.

Grunig, J. E., & Huang, Y. H. (2000). From organizational effectiveness to relationship indicators: Antecedents of relationships, public relations strategies, and relationship outcomes. In J. A. Ledingham & S. D. Bruning (Eds.), *Public relations as relationship management: A relational approach to the study and practice of public relations* (pp. 23–53). Mahwah, NJ: Lawrence Erlbaum Associates.

Gummesson, E. (2012). *Total relationship marketing: Marketing management, relationship strategy and CRM approaches for the network economy* (2nd ed.). Oxford: Butterworth-Heinemann.

Hallahan, K., Holtzhausen, D., van Ruler, B., Verčič, D., & Sriramesh, K. (2007). Defining strategic communication. *International Journal of Strategic Communication, 1*(1), 3–35.

Harfoush, R. (2009). *Yes we did: An inside look at how social media built the Obama brand.* Berkeley, CA: New Riders.

Heath, R. L. (2001). Shifting foundations: Public relations as relationship building. In R. L. Heath (Ed.), *Handbook of public relations* (pp. 1–9). Thousand Oaks, CA: Sage.

Hendricks, J. A., & Denton, R. E., Jr. (Eds.) (2010). *Communicator-in-chief: How Barack Obama used new media technology to win the White House.* Lanham, MD: Lexington Books.

Hendricks, J. A., & Kaid, L. L. (Eds.). (2011). *Techno politics in presidential campaigns: New voices, new technologies, and new voters.* New York: Routledge.

Holmlund, M. (2008). A definition, model, and empirical analysis of business-to-business relationship quality. *International Journal of Service Industry Management, 19*(1), 32–62.

Holsti, O. (1969). *Content analysis for the social sciences & humanities.* Reading, MA: Addison-Wesley.

Hon, L. C., & Grunig, J. E. (1999). *Guidelines for measuring relationships in public relations.* Gainesville, FL: Institute for Public Relations.

Hovland, D. I., Janis, I. L., & Kelley, H. H. (1953). *Communication and persuasion: Psychological studies of opinion change.* New Haven, CT: Yale University Press.

Hung, C. F. (2005). Exploring types of organization-public relationships and their implications for relationship management in public relations. *Journal of Public Relations Research, 17*(4), 393–426.

Hutton, J. G., Goodman, M. B., Alexander, J. B., & Genest, C. M. (2001). Reputation management: The new face of corporate public relations? *Public Relations Review, 27,* 247–261.

Kent, M. L. (2008). Critical analysis of blogging in public relations. *Public Relations Review, 34*(1), 32–40.

Kiousis, S., & Strömbäck, J. (2011). Political public relations research in the future. In J. Strömbäck & S. Kiousis (Eds.), *Political public relations: Principles and applications* (pp. 314–323). New York: Routledge.

Ledingham, J. A. (2003). Explicating relationship management as a general theory of public relations. *Journal of Public Relations Research, 15*(2), 181–198.

Ledingham, J. A. (2011). Political public relations and relationship management. In J. Strömbäck & S. Kiousis (Eds.), *Political public relations: Principles and applications* (pp. 235–253). New York: Routledge.

Ledingham, J. A., & Bruning, S. D. (1998). Relationship management in public relations: Dimensions of an organization–public relationship. *Public Relations Review, 24*(1), 55–65.

Ledingham, J. A., & Bruning, S. D. (2000). A longitudinal study of organization-public relationship dimensions: Defining the role of communication in the practice of relationship Management. In J. A. Ledingham & S. D. Bruning (Eds.), *Public relations as relationship management: A relational approach to the study and practice of public relations* (pp. 55–69). Mahwah, NJ: Lawrence Erlbaum.

Lees-Marshment, J. (2006). *Political marketing and British political parties: The party's just begun.* Manchester, UK: Manchester University Press.

Levenshus, A. (2010). Online relationship management in a presidential campaign: A case study of the Obama campaign's management of its Internet-integrated grassroots effort. *Journal of Public Relations Research, 22*(3), 313–335.

Marken, G. A. (2005). To blog or not to blog: That is the question? *Public Relations Quarterly, 50*(3), 31–33.

Metzger, E., & Maruggi, A. (2009). Social media and the 2008 U.S. presidential election. *Journal of New Communications Research, 4*(1), 141–165.

Metzler, M. S. (2001). The centrality of organizational legitimacy to public relations practice. In R. L. Heath & G. Vasquez (Eds.), *Handbook of public relations* (pp. 321–333). Thousand Oaks, CA: Sage Publications.

Morgan, R. M., & Hunt, S. D. (1994). The commitment-trust theory of relationship marketing. *Journal of Marketing, 58*, 20–38.

Morris, M. H., Brunyee, J., & Page, M. (1998). Relationship marketing in practice: Myths and realities. *Industrial Marketing Management, 27*, 359–371.

Nguyen, B., & Mutum, D. S. (2012). A review of customer relationship management: Success, advances, pitfalls and futures. *Business Process Management Journal, 18*(3), 400–419.

Park, H., & Reber, B. H. (2008). Relationship building and the use of web sites: How Fortune 500 corporations use their web sites to build relationships. *Public Relations Review, 34*(4), 409–411.

Payne, A., & Frow, P. (2005). A strategic framework for customer relationship management. *Journal of Marketing, 69*, 167–176.

Perlmutter, D. (2008). *Blogwars.* New York: Oxford University Press.

Petrocik, J. R., Benoit, W. L., & Hansen, G. J. (2003/04). Issue ownership and presidential campaign, 1952–2000. *Political Science Quarterly, 118*(4), 599–626.

Pew Research Center. (2011, July 11). *Use Facebook daily.* Retrieved from http://pewresearch.org/databank/dailynumber/?NumberID=1274

Prahalad, C. K., & Ramaswamy, V. (2004). *The future of competition: Co-creating unique value with customers.* Boston, MA: Harvard Business School Press.

Rauyruen, P., & Miller, K. E. (2007). Relationship quality as a predictor of B2B customer loyalty. *Journal of Business Research, 60*(1), 21–31.

Rybalko, S., & Seltzer, T. (2010). Dialogic communication in 140 characters or less: How Fortune 500 companies engage stakeholders using Twitter. *Public Relations Review, 36*, 336–341.

Schneider, S. M., & Foot, K. A. (2006). Web campaigning by U.S. presidential primary candidates in 2000 and 2004. In A. P. Williams & J. C. Tedesco (Eds.), *The Internet election: Perspectives on the web in campaigns 2004* (pp. 21–36). Lanham, MD: Rowman & Littlefield.

Schurr, P. H., & Ozanne, J. L. (1985). Influences on exchange processes: Buyers' preconceptions of a seller's trustworthiness and bargaining toughness. *Journal of Consumer Research, 11* (March), 939–953.

Scott, W. A. (1955). Reliability of content analysis: The case of nominal scale coding. *Public Opinion Quarterly, 19,* 321–325.

Strömbäck, J., Grandien, C., & Falasca, K. (2012). Do campaign strategies and tactics matter? Exploring party elite perceptions of what matters when explaining election outcomes. *Journal of Public Affairs, 13*(1), 41–52.

Strömbäck, J., & Kiousis, S. (2011). Political public relations: Defining and mapping an emergent field. In J. Strömbäck & S. Kiousis (Eds.), *Political public relations: Principles and applications* (pp. 1–32). New York: Routledge.

Sundar, S. S. (2007). Social psychology of interactivity in human-website interaction. In A. Joinson, K. McKenna, T. Postmes, & U.D. Reips (Eds.), *The Oxford handbook of Internet psychology* (pp. 89–104). Oxford: Oxford University Press.

Sweetser, K. D. (2011). Digital political public relations. In J. Strömbäck & S. Kiousis (Eds.), *Political public relations: Principles and applications* (pp. 293–313). New York: Routledge.

Chapter 4

Bartels, L. M. (1988). *Presidential primaries and the dynamics of public choice.* Princeton, NJ: Princeton University.

Baum, M. A. (2003). *Soft news goes to war: Public opinion and American foreign policy in the new media age.* Princeton, NJ: Princeton University Press.

Baumgartner, J., & Morris, J. S. (2007). Hard and soft new media effects on presidential candidate name recall: A case study. *Journal of Political Science, 35,* 1–29.

Baumgartner, J., & Morris, J. (2010). Who wants to be my friend? Youth, MySpace, and Facebook in the 2008 campaign. In J. A. Hendricks & R. E. Denton, Jr. (Eds.), *Communicator-in-chief: A look at how Barack Obama used new media technology to win the White House* (pp. 51–65). Lanham, MD: Lexington Books.

Bimber, B. (1998). The Internet and political transformation: Populism, community, and accelerated pluralism. *Polity, 31*(1), 133–160.

Bode, L. (2012). Facebooking it to the polls: A study in online social networking and political behavior. *Journal of Information Technology & Politics, 9*(4), 352–369.

Brenner, J. (2012). Social networking. *Pew Internet & American Life Project.* Retrieved from http://pewinternet.org/Commentary/2012/March/Pew-Internet-Social-Networking-full-detail.aspx

Ellison, N. B., Steinfield, C., & C. Lampe. (2007). The benefits of Facebook 'friends': Social capital and college students' use of online social network sites. *Journal of Computer-Mediated Communication, 12*(4), 1143–1168.

Farnsworth, S. J., & Lichter, S. R. (2011). *The nightly news nightmare: Media coverage of the U.S. presidential elections, 1988–2008.* Lanham, MD: Rowman & Littlefield.

Fernandes, J. M., Giurcanu, K. W. Bowers, & J. C. Neely. (2010). The writing on the wall: A content analysis of college students' Facebook groups for the 2008 presidential election. *Mass Communication and Society, 13*(5), 653–675.

Granovetter, M. S. (1983). The strength of weak ties: A network theory revisited. *Sociological Theory, 1*(1), 201–233.

Hanson, G., Haridakis, P. M., Cunningham, A. W., Sharma, R., & Ponder, J. D. (2010). The 2008 presidential campaign: Political cynicism in the age of Facebook, MySpace, and YouTube. *Mass Communication and Society, 13*(5), 584–607.

Johnson, T. J., & Kaye, B. K. (2003). A boost or bust for democracy? How the web influenced political attitudes and behaviors in the 1996 and 2000 presidential elections. *The International Journal of Press/Politics, 8*(3), 9–34.

Keeter, S., & Zukin, C. (1983). *Uninformed choice: The failure of the new presidential nominating system.* New York: Praeger.

Krueger, B. S. (2002). Assessing the potential of Internet political participation in the United States: A resource approach. *American Politics Research, 30*(5), 476–498.

Kushin, M. J., & Yamamoto, M. (2010). Did social media really matter? College students' use of online media and political decision making in the 2008 election. *Mass Communication and Society, 13*(5), 608–630.

Lawrence, E., Sides, J., & Farrell, H. (2010). Self-segregation or deliberation? Blog readership, participation, and polarization in American politics. *Perspectives on Politics, 8*(1), 141–157.

Lenart, S. (1997). Naming names in a Midwestern town: The salience of Democratic presidential hopefuls in early 1992. *Political Behavior, 19*(4), 365–382.

Long, J. S. (1997). *Regression models for limited and categorical dependent variables.* Thousand Oaks, CA: Sage.

Norrander, B. (1986). Selective participation: Presidential primary voters as a subset of general election voters. *American Politics Quarterly, 14,* 35–53.

Norrander, B. (1996). Presidential nomination politics in the post-reform era. *Political Research Quarterly, 49,* 875–915.

Pasek, J., More, E., & Romer, D. (2009). Realizing the social Internet? Online social networking meets offline civic engagement. *Journal of Information Technology & Politics, 6*(3–4), 197–215.

Peterson, R. A. (2001). On the use of college students in social science research: Insights from a second-order meta-analysis. *Journal of Consumer Research, 28*(3), 450–461.

Pew Research Center for People & the Press. (2008). *Biennial media consumption study.* Retrieved from http://www.people-press.org/question-search/?qid=1714233&pid=51&ccid=51#top

Pew Research Center for People & the Press (2012a). *February political survey.* Retrieved from http://www.people-press.org/question-search/?qid=1805670&pid=51&ccid=51#top

Pew Research Center for People & the Press. (2012b). *Early January communication study.* Retrieved from http://www.people-press.org/2012/01/08/early-january-2012-communications-survey/

Pfau, M., Diedrich, T., Larson, K. M., & Van Winkle, K. M. (1993). Relational and competence perceptions of presidential candidates during primary election campaigns. *Journal of Broadcasting and Electronic Media, 37,* 275–292.

Popkin, S. L. (1991). *The reasoning voter: Communication and persuasion in presidential campaigns.* Chicago: University of Chicago Press.

Porter, S. R., & Whitcomb, M. E. (2003). The impact of lottery incentives on student survey response rates. *Research in Higher Education, 44,* 389–407.

Porter, S. R., Whitcomb, M. E., & Weitzer, W. H. (2004). Multiple surveys of students and survey fatigue. *New Directions for Institutional Research, 121,* 63–73.

Prior, M. (2007). *Post-broadcast democracy: How media choice increases inequality in political involvement and polarizes elections.* New York: Cambridge University Press.

Putnam, R. D. (2000). *Bowling alone: The collapse and revival of American community.* New York: Simon and Schuster.

Quintelier, E., & Vissers, S. (2008). The effect of Internet use on political participation: An analysis of survey results for 16-year-olds in Belgium. *Social Science Computer Review, 26*(4), 411–427.

Smith, A. (2011). 22% of online Americans used social networking or Twitter for politics in 2010 campaign. *The Pew Research Center's Internet & American Life Project.* Retrieved from http://pewinternet.org/Reports/2011/Politics-and-social-media.aspx

Smith, A., & Brenner, J. (2012). Twitter use 2012. *The Pew Research Center's Internet & American Life Project*. Retrieved from http://pewinternet.org/~/media//Files/Reports/2012/PIP_Twitter_Use_2012.pdf

Smith, A., & Rainie, L. (2008). The Internet and the 2008 election. *The Pew Research Center's Internet & American Life Project*. Retrieved from http://www.pewinternet.org/~/media//Files/Reports/2008/PIP_2008_election.pdf

Steinfield, C., DiMicco, J. M., Ellison, N. B., & Lampe, C. (2009). Bowling online: Social networking and social capital within the organization. *Proceedings of the Fourth International Conference on Communities and Technologies* (pp. 245–254). New York: ACM. doi:10.1145/1556460.1556496

Stepanova, E. (2011). The role of information communication technologies in the 'Arab Spring': Implications beyond the region. *PONARS Eurasia Policy Memo no. 159*. Retrieved from http://www.gwu.edu/~ieresgwu/assets/docs/ponars/pepm_159.pdf

Sweetser, K. D., & Kaid, L. L. (2008). Stealth soapboxes: Political information efficacy, cynicism and uses of celebrity weblogs among readers. *New Media & Society, 10*(1), 67–91.

Theocharis, Y. (2011). Cuts, tweets, solidarity and mobilisation: How the Internet shaped the student occupations. *Parliamentary Affairs, 65*(1), 162–194.

Tolbert, C. J., & McNeal, R. S. (2003). Unraveling the effects of the Internet on political participation? *Political Research Quarterly, 56*(2), 175–185.

Trent, J. S., Friedenberg, R. V., & Denton, R. E., Jr. (2011). *Political campaign communication: Principles and practices*. Lanham, MD: Rowman & Littlefield.

Utz, S. (2009). The (potential) benefits of campaigning via social network sites. *Journal of Computer-Mediated Communication, 14*(2), 221–243.

Valenquela, S., Park, N., & Kee, K. (2009). Is there social capital in a social network site? Facebook use and college students' life satisfaction, trust, and participation. *Journal of Computer Mediated Communication, 14*, 875–901.

Woolley, J. K., Limperos, A. M., & Oliver, M. B. (2010). The 2008 presidential election, 2.0: A content analysis of user-generated political Facebook groups. *Mass Communication and Society, 13*(5), 631–652.

Yang, S-U., & Lim, S. (2009). The effects of blog-mediated public relations (BMPR) on relational trust. *Journal of Public Relations Research, 21*, 341–359.

Chapter 5

Ahem, R. K., Stomer-Galley, J., & Neuman, W. R. (2000). *When voters can interact and compare candidates online: Experimentally investigating political web effects*. Paper presented at the annual meeting of the International Communications Associations Annual Conference, Acapulco, Mexico.

Alfonso III, F. (2012, November 14). How Romney and Obama stack up on Tumblr. *Mashable.com*. Retrieved from http://mashable.com/2012/11/02/romney-obama-tumblr/

Andrews, P. (2003). Is blogging journalism? *Nieman Reports, 57*(3), 63–64.

Ancu, M. (2011). From soundbite to textbite: Election 2008 comments on Twitter. In J. A. Hendricks & L. L. Kaid (Eds.), *Techno politics in presidential campaigning: New voices, new technologies, and new voters* (pp. 11–21). New York: Routledge.

Baumgartner, J. C., & Morris, J. S. (2010). MyFaceTube politics: Social networking Web sites and political engagement of young adults. *Social Science Computer Review, 28*(1), 24–44.

Becker, L. B., & Dunwoody, S. (1982). Media use, public affairs knowledge and voting in a local election. *Journalism Quarterly, 59*, 212–218.

Bimber, B., & Davis, R. (2003). *Campaigning online: The Internet in U.S. elections*. New York: Oxford University Press.

Carlin, C. (2008). *The young vote: Engaging America's youth in the 2008 elections and beyond.* Washington, DC: The Brookings Institution.

Casey, C. (1996). *The hill on the net: Congress enters the information age.* Boston: AP Professional.

Chaffee, S. H., Zhao, X., & Leshner, G. (1994). Political knowledge and the campaign media of 1992. *Communication Research, 21*(3), 305–324.

CircleCount.com. (2012, November 14). *Barack Obama vs. Mitt Romney.* Retrieved from http://www.circlecount.com/

Cornfield, M. (2010). Game-changers: New technology and the 2008 presidential elections. In L. J. Sabato (Ed.), *The year of Obama: How Barack Obama won the White House* (pp. 205–230). New York: Longman.

Dalrymple, K., & Scheufele, D. (2007). Finally informing the electorate? How the Internet got people thinking about presidential politics in 2004. *The Harvard International Journal of Press/Politics, 12,* 96–111.

Davis, R. (1999). *The web of politics: The Internet's impact on the American political system.* New York: Oxford University Press.

Davis, R. (2005). Presidential campaigns fine-tune online strategies. *Journalism Studies, 6*(2), 241–244.

Delli Carpini, M. X., & Keeter, S. (1996). *What Americans know about politics and why it matters.* New Haven, CT: Yale University Press.

DiMaggio, P., Hargittai, E., Neuman, W. R., & Robinson, J. P. (2001). Social implications of the Internet. *Annual Review of Sociology, 27,* 307–336.

Drew, D., & Weaver, D. (2006). Voter learning in the 2004 presidential election: Did the media matter? *Journalism & Mass Communication Quarterly, 83,* 25–42.

Edmonds, R., Guskin, E., Rosenstiel, T., & Mitchell, A. (2012). The state of the news media 2012: An annual report on American Journalism. *The Pew Research Center's Project for Excellence in Journalism.* Retrieved from http://stateofthemedia.org/2012/newspapers-building-digital-revenues-proves-painfully-slow/newspapers-by-the-numbers/

Eveland, W. P., & Scheufele, D. A. (2000). Connecting news media use with gaps in knowledge. *Political Communication, 17*(3), 215–237.

Eveland, W. P., Marton, K., & Seo, M. (2004). Moving beyond "just the facts": The influence of online news on the content and structure of public affairs knowledge. *Communication Research, 31*(1), 82–108.

Eveland, W. P., Seo, M., & Marton, K. (2002). Learning from the news in campaign 2000: An experimental comparison of TV news, newspapers, and online news. *Media Psychology, 4,* 355–380.

Foot, K. A., & Schneider, S. M. (2002). Online action in campaign 2000: An exploratory analysis of the U.S. political Web sphere. *Journal of Broadcasting & Electronic Media, 46*(2), 222–244.

Fung, T. K. F., Vraga, E., & Thorson, K. (2011). When bloggers attack: Examining the effect of negative citizen-initiated campaigning in the 2008 presidential election. In J. A. Hendricks & L. L. Kaid (Eds.), *Techno politics in presidential campaigning: New voices, new technologies, and new voters* (pp. 83–101). New York: Routledge.

Graber, D. A. (1996). *Mass media and American politics.* Washington, DC: CQ Press.

Green, J. (2012). Obama's CEO: Jim Messina has a President to sell. *Bloomberg Business-Week.* Retrieved from http://www.businessweek.com/articles/2012-06-14/obamas-ceo-jim-messina-has-a-president-to-sell

Groshek, J., & Dimitrova, D. (2011). A Cross-section of voter learning, campaign interest and intention to vote in the 2008 American election: Did Web 2.0 matter? *Studies in Communications, 9*, 355–375.

Gueorguieva, V. (2008). Voters, MySpace, and YouTube: The impact of alternative communication channels on the 2006 election cycle and beyond. *Social Science Computer Review, 26*(3), 288–300.

Hansen, G. J., & Benoit, W. L. (2005). Presidential campaigning on the Web: The influence of candidate World Wide Web sites in the 2000 general election. *Southern Communication Journal, 70*(3), 219–229.

Haridakis, P., & Hanson, G. (2009). Social interaction and co-viewing with YouTube: Blending mass communication reception and social connection. *Journal of Broadcasting & Electronic Media, 53*(2), 317–335.

Hughes, K. A., & Hill, J. E. (1998). *Cyberpolitics: Citizen activism in the age of the Internet.* Lanham, MD: Rowman & Littlefield.

Jennings, M. K., & Zeitner, B. (2003). Internet use and civic engagement: A longitudinal analysis. *Public Opinion Quarterly, 67*, 311–334.

Johnson, T. J., & Kaye, B. K. (2004). Wag the blog: How reliance on traditional media and the Internet influence perceptions of credibility of weblogs among blog users. *Journalism & Mass Communication Quarterly, 81*(3), 622–42.

Johnson, T. J., Briama, M. A., & Sothirajah, J. (1999). Doing the traditional media sidestep: Comparing the effects of the Internet and other nontraditional media with traditional media in the 1996 presidential campaign. *Journalism & Mass Communication Quarterly, 76*(1), 99–123.

Kenski, K., & Stroud, N. J. (2006). Connections between Internet use and political efficacy, knowledge, and political participation. *Journal of Broadcasting & Electronic Media, 50*(2), 173–192.

Kohut, A., Doherty, C., Dimock, M., & Keeter, S. (2012). Trends in news consumption: 1991–2012. In changing News landscape, even television is vulnerable. *The Pew Research Center for the People & the Press.* Retrieved from http://www.people-press.org/files/legacy-pdf/2012%20News%20Consumption%20Report.pdf

Lawrence, E., Sides, J., & Farrell, H. (2010). Self-segregation or deliberation? Blog readership, participation, and polarization in American politics. *PS: Persepctives on Politics, 8*(1), 141–157.

Lowden, N. B., Anderson, P. A., Dozier, D. M., & Lauzen, M. M. (1994). Media use in the primary election: A secondary medium model. *Communication Research, 21*(3), 293–304.

Madden, M. (2007). Online video. *Pew Internet & American Life Project.* Retrieved from http://www.pewinternet.org/~/media//Files/Reports/2007/PIP_Online_Video_2007.pdf.pdf

Margolis, M., & Resnick, D. (2000). *Politics as usual: The cyberspace 'revolution'.* Thousand Oaks, CA: Sage.

McLeod, J., Scheufele, D. A., & Moy, P. (1999). Community, communication, and participation: The role of mass media and interpersonal discussion in local political participation. *Political Communication, 16*, 315–336.

Neuman, W. R. (1981). Differentiation and integration: Two dimensions of political thinking. *The American Journal of Sociology, 86*(6), 1236–1268.

Neuman, W. R., Just, M. R., & Crigler, A. N. (1992). *Common knowledge: News and the construction of political meaning.* Chicago: University of Chicago Press.

Norris, P. (2000). *A virtuous circle: Political communication in postindustrial societies.* Cambridge, England: Cambridge University Press.

Norris, P. (2001). *Digital divide: Civic engagement, information poverty, and the Internet worldwide.* New York: Cambridge University Press.

Owen, D. (2010). Media in the 2008 election: 21st century campaign, same old story. In L. J. Sabato (Ed.), *The year of Obama: How Barack Obama won the White House* (pp. 167–186). New York: Longman.

Pasek, J., More, E., & Romer, D. (2009). Realizing the social Internet? Online social networking meets offline social capital. *Journal of Information, Technology and Politics, 6*(3–4), 197–215.

Patterson, T. E. (1980). *The mass media election: How Americans choose their president.* New York: Praeger.

Patterson, T. E., & McClure, R. D. (1976). *The unseeing eye: The myth of television power in national elections.* New York: Putnam.

Pettey, G. R. (1988). The interaction of the individual's social environment, attention and interest, and public affairs media use on political knowledge holding. *Communication Research, 15*(3), 265–281.

Price, V., & Zaller, J. (1993). Who gets the news: Alternative measures of news reception and their implications for research. *Public Opinion Quarterly, 57,* 133–164.

Rainie, L., Smith, A., Scholzman, K. L., Brady, H., & Verba, S. (2012). Social media and political engagement. *Pew Research Center's Internet & American Life Project.* Retrieved from http://pewinternet.org/Reports/2012/Political-Engagement.aspx

Regan, T. (2003). Weblogs threaten and inform traditional journalism. *Nieman Reports, 57*(3), 68–70.

Rogers, R. (2005). Poignancy in the U.S. political blogosphere. *New Information Perspectives, 57*(4), 356–368.

Romano, L. (2012). Obama's data advantage. *Politico.* Retrieved from http://www.politico.com/news/stories/0612/77213.html

Rosenstiel, T., & Mitchell, A. (2012a). How the presidential candidates use the web and social media. *Pew Research Center's Project for Excellence in Journalism.* Retrieved from http://www.journalism.org/sites/journalism.org/files/DIRECT%20ACCESS%20FINAL.pdf

Rosenstiel, T., & Mitchell, A. (2012b). Social media doubles, but remains limited. *Pew Research Center's Project for Excellence in Journalism.* Retrieved from http://www.journalism.org/sites/journalism.org/files/Final.pdf

Scherer, M. (2012). Inside the secret world of the data crunchers who helped Obama win. *Time.* Retrieved from http://swampland.time.com/2012/11/07/inside-the-secret-world-of-quants-and-data-crunchers-who-helped-obama-win/

Scheufele, D. A., & Nisbet, M. C. (2002). Being a citizen online: New opportunities and dead ends. *The Harvard International Journal of Press/Politics, 7*(3), 55–75.

Schonfeld, E. (2008). *News sites attract record audience on election night.* Retrieved from http://www.techcrunch.com/2008/11/05/news-sites-attract-record-audience-on-election-night/

Selnow, G. W. (1998). *Electronic whistle-stops: The impact of the Internet in American politics.* Westport, CT: Praeger.

Shah, D., McLeod, D., & Yoon, S. (2001). Communication, context, and community: An exploration of print, broadcast, and Internet influences. *Communication Research, 28*(4), 464–506.

Singer, J. B. (2006). Journalists and news bloggers: Complements, contradictions, and challenges. In A. Bruns & J. Jacobs (Eds.), *Uses of blogs* (pp. 23–32). New York: Peter Lang.

Smith, A., & Duggan, M. (2012). Online political videos and campaign 2012. *Pew Research Center's Internet & American Life Project.* Retrieved from http://pewinternet.org/Reports/2012/Election-2012-Video.aspx

SocialBakers.com. (2012). *U.S. elections 2012.* Retrieved from http://www.socialbakers.com/elections

Sotirovic, M., & McLoed, J. (2004). Knowledge as understanding: The information processing approach to political learning. In L. L. Kaid (Ed.), *Handbook of political communication research* (pp. 357–394). Hillsdale, NJ: Lawrence Erlbaum Associates.

Tedesco, J. C., Miller, J. L., & Spiker, J. A. (1999). Presidential campaigning on the information superhighway: An exploration of content and form. In L. L. Kaid & D. G. Bystrom (Eds.), *The electronic election: Perspectives on the 1996 campaign communication* (pp. 51–63). Mahwah, NJ: Lawrence Erlbaum.

Tewksbury, D., & Althaus, S. L. (2000). Differences in knowledge acquisition among readers of the paper and online versions of a national newspaper. *Journalism & Mass Communication Quarterly, 77*(3), 457–479.

Tichenor, P. J., Donahue, G. A., & Olien, C. N. (1970). Mass media flow and differential growth in knowledge. *Public Opinion Quarterly, 34,* 159–170.

Towner, T. L., & Dulio, D. A. (2011). The web 2.0 election: Voter learning in the 2008 presidential campaign. In J. A. Hendricks & L. L. Kaid (Eds.), *Techno politics in presidential campaigning: New voices, new technologies, and new voters* (pp. 22–43). New York: Routledge.

Verba, S., Schlozman, K. L., & Brady, H. F. (1995). *Voice and equality: Civic voluntarism in American politics.* Cambridge, MA: Harvard University Press.

Wall, M. (2006). Blogging Gulf War II. *Journalism Studies, 7*(1), 111–126.

Weaver, D., & Drew, D. (1993). Voter learning in the 1990 off-year election: Did the media matter? *Journalism Quarterly, 70,* 356–368.

Wei, R., & Ven-hwei, L. (2008). News media use and knowledge about the 2006 U.S. midterm elections: Why exposure matters in voter learning. *International Journal of Public Opinion Research, 20*(3), 347–362.

Williams, C. B., & Gulati, G. J. (2008). The political impact of Facebook: Evidence from the 2006 midterm elections and 2008 nomination contest. *Politics & Technology Review, 1(1),* 11–21.

Xenos, M., & Foot, K. A. (2005). Politics as usual, or politics unusual? Position-taking and dialogue on campaign web sites in the 2002 U.S. election. *Journal of Communication, 55*(1), 169–185.

Xenos, M., & Moy, P. (2007). Direct and differential effects of the Internet on political and civic engagement. *Journal of Communication, 57,* 704–718.

Zaoh, X., & Chaffee, S. (1995). Campaign advertisements versus television news as sources of political issue information. *Public Opinion Quarterly, 58,* 41–95.

Chapter 6

Andersson, L. M., & Pearson, C. M. (1999). Tit for tat? The spiraling effect of incivility in the workplace. *The Academy of Management Review, 24,* 452–471.

Ansolabehere, S., & Iyengar, S. (1995). *Going negative: How attack ads shrink and polarize the electorate.* New York: Free Press.

Bakshy, E. (2012, November 16). The 2012 election day through the Facebook lens. *Facebook.com*. Retrieved from https://www.facebook.com/notes/facebook-data-science/the-2012-election-day-through-the-facebook-lens/10151181043778859

Baresch, B., Knight, L., Harp, D., & Yaschur, C. (2011). Friends who choose your news: An analysis of content links on Facebook. Paper presented at the annual meeting of the International Symposium on Online Journalism, Austin, TX. Retrieved from http://online.journalism.utexas.edu/2011/papers/Baresch2011.pdf

Baron, R. A., & Ball, R. L. (1974). The aggression-inhibiting influence of nonhostile humor. *The Journal of Experimental Social Psychology, 10*, 23–33.

Baum, M. (2006). The *Oprah* effect: How soft news helps inattentive citizens vote consistently. *Journal of Politics, 68*, 946–959.

Baumgartner, J. C., & Morris, J. S. (2010). MyFaceTube politics: Social networking web sites and political engagement among young adults. *Social Science Computer Review, 28*, 24–44.

Baym, G. (2005). The Daily Show: Discursive integration and the reinvention of political journalism. *Political Communication, 22*, 259–276. doi: 10.1080/10584600591006492

Baym, G. (2010). *From Cronkite to Colbert: The evolution of broadcast news*. London: Paradigm Publishers.

Bennett, W. L. (1998). The uncivic culture: Communication, identity and the rise of lifestyle politics. *P.S.: Political Science and Politics, 31*, 741–761.

Bode, L. (2010). Accidentally informed 2.0: Incidental learning on Facebook. Paper presented at the annual meeting of the Midwest Political Science Association, Chicago, IL.

Bode, L., Edgerly, S., Vraga, E. K., Sayre, B., & Shah, D. V. (2013). Digital democracy: How the Internet has changed politics. In E. Scharrer (Ed.), *Media effects/media psychology, Vol. 5. The international encyclopedia of media studies* (pp. 505–524). Boston, MA: Wiley-Blackwell.

Bode, L., Vraga, E. K., Borah, P., & Shah, D. V. (2013). A new space for political behavior: Political social networking and its democratic consequences. Accepted for publication in the *Journal of Computer-Mediated Communication*.

Bond, R. M., Fariss, C. J., Jones, J. J., Kramer, A. D. I., Marlow, C., Settle, J. E., & Fowler, J. H. (2012). A 61-million-person experiment in social influence and political mobilization. *Nature, 489*, 295–298. doi:10.1038/nature11421

Brooks, D. J., & Geer, J. G. (2007). Beyond negativity: The effects of incivility on the electorate. *American Journal of Political Science, 51*, 1–16.

CIRCLE. (2012, November 9). Updated estimate: Youth turnout was 50% in 2012; Youth turnout in battleground states was 58%. *The Center for Information and Research on Civic Learning and Engagement*. Retrieved from http://www.civicyouth.org/updated-estimate-50-of-youth-turnout-in-2012-youth-turnout-in-battleground-states-58/

Conroy, M., Feezel, J. T., & Guerrero, M. (2012). Facebook and political engagement: A study of online political group membership and offline political engagement. *Computers in Human Behavior, 28*, 1535–1546.

Edgerly, S., Vraga, E. K., Fung, T., Dalrymple, K., & Macafee, T. (2013). Directing the dialogue: The relationship between YouTube videos and the comments that they spur. Accepted for publication in the *Journal for Computer-Mediated Communication*.

Eliasoph, N. (1998). *Avoiding politics: How Americans produce apathy in everyday life*. Cambridge, UK: Cambridge University Press.

Eliasoph, N., & Lichterman, P. (2003). Culture in interaction. *American Journal of Sociology, 108*(4), 735–794.

Feldman, L., & Young, D. G. (2008). Late-night comedy as a gateway to traditional news: An analysis of time trends in news attention among late-night comedy viewers during the 2004 presidential primaries. *Political Communication, 25*, 401–422.

Fernandes, J., Giurcanu, M., Bowers, K. W., & Neely, J. C. (2010). The writing on the wall: A content analysis of college students' Facebook groups of 2008 presidential election. *Mass Communication and Society, 13*, 653–675.

Gamson, W. A. (1992). *Talking politics.* New York: Cambridge University Press.

Gil de Zuniga, H., Jung, N., & Valenzuela, S. (2012). Social media user for news and individuals' social capital, civic engagement, and political participation. *Journal of Computer-Mediated Communication, 17*, 319–336.

Glynn, C. J., Huge, M. E., & Hoffman, L. H. (2012). All the news that's fit to post: A profile of news use on social networking sites. *Computers in Human Behavior, 28*, 113–119.

Goffman, E. (1959). *The presentation of self in everyday life.* Oxford, England: Doubleday.

Harding, L. (2012, November 7). U.S. election 2012: Hug photo makes social media history. *The Guardian.* Retrieved from http://www.guardian.co.uk/media/2012/nov/07/us-election-2012-hug-photo

Hermida, A. (2010). Twittering the news: The emergence of ambient journalism. *Journalism Practice, 4(3)*, 297–308.

Hogan, B., & Quan-Haase, A. (2010). Persistence and change in social media. *Bulletin of Science, Technology & Society, 30(5)*, 309–315.

Huckfeldt, R., & Sprague, J. (1987). Networks in contexts: The social flow of political information. *American Political Science Review, 81*, 1197–1216.

Kim, J., & Kim, E. J. (2008). Theorizing dialogic deliberation: Everyday political talk as communicative action and dialogue. *Communication Theory, 18(1)*, 51–70.

Kim, Y. M., & Vishak, J. (2008). Just laugh! You don't need to remember: The effect of entertainment media on political information acquisition and information processing in political judgment. *Journal of Communication, 58*, 338–360. doi: 10.1111/j.1460-2466.2008.00388.x

Knoke, D. (1990). Networks of political action: Toward theory construction. *Social Forces, 68*, 1041–1063.

Kuiper, N. A., McKenzie, S. D., & Belanger, K. A. (1995). Cognitive appraisals and individual differences in sense of humor: Motivational and affective implications. *Personality and Individual Differences, 19(3)*, 359–372. doi: 10.1016/0191-8869(95)00072-E

Lazarsfeld, P. F., Berelson, B., & Gaudet, N. (1948). *The people's choice: How the voter makes up his mind in a presidential campaign.* New York: Duell, Sloan, and Pearce.

Marwick, A. E., & boyd, d. (2011). I tweet honestly, I tweet passionately: Twitter users, context collapse, and the imagined audience. *New Media & Society, 13(1)*, 114–133.

McPherson, M., Smith-Lovin, L., & Cook, J. M. (2001). Birds of a feather: Homophily in Social Networks. *Annual Review of Sociology, 27*, 415–444.

Miron, A. M., Brummett, B., Ruggles, B., & Brehm, J. W. (2008). Deterring anger and anger-motivated behaviors. *Basic and Applied Social Psychology, 30*, 326–338. doi: 10.1080/01973530802502259

Mutz, D. C. (2006). *Hearing the other side: Deliberative versus participatory democracy.* Cambridge, MA: Cambridge University Press.

Mutz, D. C. (2007). How the mass media divide us. In P. S. Nivola & D. W. Brady (Eds.), *Red and Blue Nation? Vol. 1* (pp. 223–248). Washington, DC: Brookings Institute Press.

Mutz, D. C., & Reeves, B. (2005). The new videomalaise: Effects of televised incivility on political trust. *American Political Science Review, 99*, 1–15.

Ng, E., & Detenber, B. (2005). The impact of synchronicity and civility in online political discussions on perceptions and intentions to participate. *Journal of Computer-Mediated Communication, 10* (3). Retrieved from http://jcmc.indiana.edu/vol10/issue3/ng.html

Papacharissi, Z. (2004). Democracy on-line: Civility, politeness, and the democratic potential of on-line political discussion groups. *New Media & Society, 6,* 259–284.

Pariser, E. (2011). *The filter bubble: What the Internet is hiding from you.* New York: Penguin Press.

Park, N., Kee, K. F., & Valenzuela, S. (2009). Being immersed in social networking environment: Facebook groups, uses and gratifications, and social outcomes. *Cyberpsychology and Behavior, 12,* 729–733.

Pew. (2010, February). Millennial: A Portrait of Generation Next. *Pew Research Center.* Retrieved from http://www.pewsocialtrends.org/files/2010/10/millennials-confident-connected-open-to-change.pdf

Pew. (2012, September). Politics on Social Networking Sites. *Pew Internet and American Life Project.* Retrieved from http://pewinternet.org/~/media//Files/Reports/2012/PIP_PoliticalLifeonSocialNetworkingSites.pdf

Prior, M. (2005). News vs. entertainment: How increasing media choice widens gaps in political knowledge and turnout. *American Journal of Political Science, 49,* 577–592.

Rainie, L., Smith, A., Schlozman, K. L., Brady, H., & Verba, S. (2012). Social media and political engagement. *Pew Research Center.* Retrieved from http://pewinternet.org/~/media//Files/Reports/2012/PIP_SocialMediaAndPoliticalEngagement_PDF.pdf

Rosen, R. J. (2012, November 8). Did Facebook give Democrats the upper hand? *The Atlantic.* Retrieved from http://www.theatlantic.com/technology/archive/12/11/did-facebook-give-democrats-the-upper-hand/264937/

Schramm, W., Lyle, J., & Parker, E. B. (1961). *Television in the lives of our children.* Stanford, CA: Stanford University Press.

Schudson, M. (1998). *The good citizen.* New York: The Free Press.

Shah, D. V., Cho, J., Nah, S., Gotlieb, M. R., Hwang, H., Lee, N., Scholl, R. M., & McLeod, D. M. (2007). Campaign ads, online messaging and participation: Extending the communication mediation model. *Journal of Communication, 57,* 676–703. doi:10.1111/j.1460-2466.2007.00363.x

Stelter, B. (2008, March 27). Finding political news online, the young pass it on. *The New York Times.* Retrieved from http://www.nytimes.com/2008/03/27/us/politics/27voters.html

Tewksbury, D., Weaver, A. J., & Maddex, B. D. (2001). Accidentally informed: Incidental exposure on the World Wide Web. *Journalism and Mass Communication Quarterly, 78,* 533–554.

Thorson, K. (2012). What does it mean to be a good citizen? Citizenship vocabularies as resources for action. *The ANNALS of the American Academy of Political and Social Science, 644(1),* 70–85.

Thorson, K., Vraga, E. K., & Ekdale, B. (2010). Credibility in context: How uncivil online commentary affects news credibility. *Mass Communication & Society. 13*(3), 289–313.

Vraga, E. K., Edgerly, S. E., Bode, L., Carr, D. J., Bard, M., Johnson, C. N., Kim, Y. M., & Shah, D. V. (2012). The correspondent, the comic, and the combatant: The consequences of host style in political talk shows. *Journalism & Mass Communication Quarterly, 89*(1), 5–22.

Vraga, E. K., Johnson, C. N., Carr, D. J., Bard, M., Bode, L., & McLaughlin, B. (2010). "Filmed in front of a live studio audience": Using laughter to offset aggression in political entertainment programming. Paper presented at the annual meeting of the Midwest Association for Public Opinion Research, Chicago, IL.

Walsh, K. C. (2004). *Talking about politics*. Chicago, IL: University of Chicago Press.

Warren, M. E. (1996). What should we expect from more democracy? Radically democratic responses to politics. *Political Theory, 24*(2), 241–270.

Wasserman, T. (2012, March 12). KONY 2012 tops 100 million views, becomes most viral video in history [STUDY]. *Mashable*. Retrieved from http://mashable.com/2012/03/12/kony-most-viral/

Wojcieszak, M., & Rojas, H. (2011). Correlates of party, ideology and issue based extremity in an era of egocentric publics. *The International Journal of Press/Politics, 16*(4), 488–507.

Wyatt, R.O., Kim, J., & Katz, E. (2000). How feeling free to talk affects ordinary political conversation, purposeful argumentation, and civic participation. *Journalism & Mass Communication Quarterly, 77*, 99–115.

Xenos, M. A., & Becker, A. B. (2009). Moments of Zen: Effects of *The Daily Show* on information seeking and political learning. *Political Communication, 26*, 317–332.

Young, D. G., & Tisinger, R. M. (2006). Dispelling late-night myths: News consumption among late-night comedy viewers and the predictors of exposure to various late-night shows. *The Harvard International Journal of Press/Politics, 11*, 113–134.

Chapter 7

Ancu, M., & Cozma, R. (2009). MySpace politics: Uses and gratifications of befriending candidates. *Journal of Broadcasting & Electronic Media, 53*(4), 567–83.

ANES. (2004). *The 2004 American National Election Study, pre- and post-election survey*. Retrieved from http://www.icpsr.umich.edu/icpsrweb/ICPSR/studies/04245/documentation

Baumgartner, J. C., & Morris, J. S. (2010). MyFaceTube politics: Social networking web sites and political engagement of young adults. *Social Science Computer Review, 28*(1), 24–44.

Bimber, B., & Davis, R. (2003). *Campaigning online: The Internet in the U.S. elections*. New York: Oxford University Press.

Conroy, M., Feezell, J. T., & Guerrero, M. (2012). Facebook and political engagement: A study of online political group membership and offline political engagement. *Computers in Human Behavior, 28*, 1535–1546.

Gil de Zúñiga, H., Jung, N., & Valenzuela, S. (2012). Social media use for news and individuals' social capital, civic engagement and political participation. *Journal of Computer-Mediated Communication, 17*, 319–336.

Hendricks, J. A., & Denton, Jr., R. E. (Eds.). (2010). *Communicator-in-chief: How Barack Obama used new media technology to win the White House*. Lanham, MD: Lexington Books.

Holbert, R. L., Lambe, J. L., Dudo, A. D., & Carlton, K. A. (2007). Primacy effects of The Daily Show and national TV news viewing: Young viewers, political gratifications, and internal political self-efficacy. *Journal of Broadcasting & Electronic Media, 51*(1), 20–38.

Ingram, M. (2012, November 27). Dick Costolo says Twitter is a reinvention of the town square, but with TV. *GigaOm*, Retrieved from http://gigaom.com/2012/11/27/dick-costolo-says-twitter-is-a-reinvention-of-the-town-square-but-with-tv/

Kavanaugh, A. L., Reese, D. D., Carroll, J. M., & Rosson, M. B. (2005). Weak ties in networked communities. *The Information Society, 21*, 119–131.

Kaye, B. K. (2005). It's a blog, blog, blog world: Users and uses of weblogs. *Atlantic Journal of Communication, 13*(2), 73–95.

Kaye, B. K., & Johnson, T. J. (2002). Online and in the know: Uses and gratifications of the Web for political information. *Journal of Broadcasting & Electronic Media, 46*(1), 54–71.

Kaye, B. K., & Johnson, T. J. (2006). The age of reasons: Motives for using different compo- nents of the Internet for political information. In A. P. Williams & J. C. Tedesco (Eds.), *The Internet election: Perspectives on the Web in campaign 2004* (pp. 147–168). Lanham, MD: Rowman & Littlefield.

Kenski, K., & Stroud, N. J. (2006). Connections between Internet use and political efficacy, knowledge, and participation. *Journal of Broadcasting & Electronic Media, 50*(2), 173–192.

Kwak, N., Shah, D. V., & Holbert, R. L. (2004). Connecting, trusting, and participating: The direct and interactive effects of social associations. *Political Research Quarterly, 57,* 643–652.

Lenhart, A., Purcell, K., Smith, A., & Zickuhr, K. (2010). Social media and young adults. *Pew Internet & American Life Project.* Retrieved from http://pewinternet.org/Reports/ 2010/Social-Media-and-Young-Adults.aspx

New Rising Media. (2012, January 31). *Editorial: Twitter is not a social network.* Retrieved from http://newrisingmedia.com/all/2012/1/31/editorial-twitter-is-not-a-social-network .html

Palmgreen, P. (1984). Uses and gratifications: A theoretical perspective. In R. N. Bostrom (Ed.), *Communication yearbook: Vol. 1* (pp. 20–55). Newbury Park, CA: Sage.

Papacharissi, Z., & Rubin, A. M. (2000). Predictors of Internet use. *Journal of Broadcasting & Electronic Media, 44*(2), 175–196.

Park, N., Kee, K. F., & Valenzuela, S. (2009). Being immersed in social networking environ- ment: Facebook groups, uses and gratifications, and social outcomes. *CyberPsychology & Behavior, 12,* 729–733.

Parmelee, J. H., & Bichard, S. L. (2011). *Politics and the Twitter revolution: How tweets influ- ence the relationship between political leaders and the public.* Lanham, MD: Lexington Books.

Postelnicu, M., & Cozma, R. (2007). *From MySpace friends to voters: Campaigning strategies on MySpace during the 2006 U.S. congressional election.* Paper presented at the annual meeting of the National Communication Association, Chicago, IL.

Rainie, L., Smith, A., Lehman Schlozman, K., Brady, H., & Verba, S. (2012). Social media and political engagement. *Pew Internet & American Life Project.* Retrieved from http:// www.pewinternet.org/Reports/2012/Political-engagement/Additional-Analysis/ Social-Media-and-Political-Engagement.aspx

Ruggiero, T. E. (2000). Uses and gratifications theory in the 21st century. *Mass Communica- tion & Society, 3*(1): 3–37.

Shah, D. V., Cho, J., Eveland, W. P., Jr., & Kwak, N. (2005). Information and expression in a digital age: Modeling Internet effects on civic participation. *Communication Research, 32,* 531–565.

Shah, D. V., Cho, J., Nah, S., Gotlieb, M. R., Hwang, H., Lee, N-J., Scholl, R.M., & McLeod, D. M. (2007). Campaign ads, online messaging, and participation: Extending the com- munication mediation model. *Journal of Communication, 57,* 676–703.

Smith, A. & Brenner, J. (2012). Twitter use 2012. *Pew Internet & American Life Project.* Retrieved from http://www.pewinternet.org/Reports/2012/Twitter-Use-2012/Findings .aspx

Sundar, S. S. (2004). Theorizing interactivity's effects. *The Information Society, 20*(5), 385–389.

Sweetser, K. D., & Weaver-Lariscy, R. (2007). *Candidates make good friends: An analysis of candidates' use of Facebook.* Paper presented at the annual meeting of the National Communication Association, Chicago, IL.

Tedesco, J. C. (2011). Political information efficacy and Internet effects in the 2008 U.S. presidential election. *American Behavioral Scientist, 55*(6), 696–713.

Tumasjan, A., Sprenger, T. O., Sandner, P. G., & Welpe, I. M. (2010, May). Predicting elections with Twitter: What 140 characters reveal about political sentiment. In *Proceedings of the fourth international AAAI conference on weblogs and social media* (pp. 178–185). Palo Alto, CA: Association for the Advancement of Artificial Intelligence.

Valenzuela, S., Park, N., & Kee, K. F. (2009). Is there social capital in a social network site? Facebook use and college students' life satisfaction, trust, and participation. *Journal of Computer-Mediated Communication, 14*, 875–901.

Vergeer, M., Hermans, L., & Sams, S. (2011). Is the voter only a tweet away? Micro blogging during the 2009 European Parliament election campaign in the Netherlands. *First Monday, 16*(8). Retrieved from http://firstmonday.org/htbin/cgiwrap/bin/ojs/index.php/fm/article/view/3540/3026

Chapter 8

Benjamin, L. M. (1987). Broadcast campaign precedents from the 1924 presidential election. *Journal of Broadcasting & Electronic Media, 31*, 449–460.

Campus, D., Pasquino, G., & Vaccari, C. (2008). Social networks, political discussion, and voting in Italy: A study of the 2006 election. *Political Communication, 25*, 423–444. doi: 10.1080/10584600802427039

Coe, K., Tewksbury, D., Bond, B. J., Drogos, K. L., Porter, R. W., Yahn, A., & Zhang, Y. (2008). Hostile news: Partisan use and perceptions of cable news programming. *Journal of Communication, 58*(2), 201–219. doi:10.1111/j.1460-2466.2008.00381.x

Cogburn, D. L., & Espinoza-Vasquez, F. K. (2011). From networked nominee to networked nation: Examining the impact of web 2.0 and social media on political participation and civic engagement in the 2008 Obama campaign. *Journal of Political Marketing, 10*(1/2), 189–213. doi: 10.1080/15377857.2011.540224

Coulter, A. (2012, October 22). *Ann Coulter on Twitter.* Retrieved from https://twitter.com/AnnCoulter/status/260581147493412865

Enda, J. (2011). Campaign coverage in the time of Twitter: How technology has transformed reporting on presidential politics. *American Journalism Review, 33*(2), 14–21.

Garramone, G. M., Harris, A. C., & Pizante, G. (1986). Predictors of motivation to use computer-mediated political communication systems. *Journal of Broadcasting & Electronic Media, 30*, 445–457.

Gayo-Avello, D. (2011). Don't turn social media into another 'Literary Digest' poll. *Communications of the ACM, 54*(10), 121–128. doi: 10.1145/2001269.2001297

Grinberg, E. (2012, October 24). Ann Coulter's backward use of the 'r-word'. *CNN.com.* Retrieved from http://www.cnn.com/2012/10/23/living/ann-coulter-obama-tweet/index.html

Hanson, G., & Haridakis, P. (2008). YouTube users watching and sharing the news: A uses and gratifications approach. *Journal of Electronic Publishing, 11.* doi: http://dx.doi.org/10.3998/3336451.0011.305

Haridakis, P., & Hanson, G. (2011). Campaign 2008: Comparing YouTube, social networking and other media use among younger voters and older voters. In J. A. Hendricks & L. L. Kaid (Eds.), *Techno politics and presidential campaigning: New technologies, new voices, new voters* (pp. 61–82). New York: Routledge.

Harwood, J. (1999). Age identification, social identity gratifications and television viewing. *Journal of Broadcasting & Electronic Media, 43*, 123–136.

Hendricks, J. A., & Kaid, L. L. (2011). Shaping the new presidential campaign. In J. A. Hendricks & L. L. Kaid (Eds.), *Techno politics and presidential campaigning: New technologies, new voices, new voters* (pp. 3–9). New York: Routledge.

Ho, S. S., Binder, A. R., Becker, A. B., Moy, P., Scheufele, D. A., Brossard, D., & Gunther, A. C. (2011). The role of perceptions of media bias in general and issue-specific political participation. *Mass Communication & Society, 14*, 343–374. doi: 10.1080/15205436.2010.491933

Hodge, K. (2010, September 27). 10 news stories that broke on Twitter first. *TechRadar.* Retrieved from http://www.techradar.com/news/world-of-tech/internet/10-news-stories-that-broke-on-twitter-first-719532

Hwang, H., Pan, Z., & Sun, Y. (2008). Influence of hostile media perception on willingness to engage in discursive activities: An examination of mediating role of media indignation. *Media Psychology, 11*, 76–97. doi: 10.1080/15213260701813454

Hwang, Y. (2012). Social diffusion of campaign effects: Campaign-generated interpersonal communication as a mediator of anti-tobacco campaign effects. *Communication Research, 39*, 120–141. doi: 10.1177/0093650210389029

Ifukor, P. (2010). "Elections" or "selections"? Blogging and twittering the Nigerian 2007 general elections. *Bulletin of Science, Technology & Society, 30*(6), 398–414. doi: 10.1177/0270467610380008

Java, A., Song, X., Finin, T., & Tseng, B. (2007, August 12). *Why we Twitter: Understanding microblogging usage and communities.* Paper presented at the proceedings of the Joint 9th WEBKDD and 1st SNA-KDD Workshop 2007, San Jose, CA.

Johnson, S. (2009, June 5). How Twitter will change the way we live. *Time, 173*, 28–33.

Johnson, T. J., & Kaye, B. K. (2003). Around the world wide web in 80 ways. *Social Science Computer Review, 21*, 304–325. doi: 10.1177/0894439303253976

Jones, D. A. (2004). Why Americans don't trust the media: A preliminary analysis. *Harvard International Journal of Press/Politics, 9*(2), 60–75. doi: 10.1177/1091191X04263461

Kaid, L. L. (2002). Political advertising and information seeking: Comparing the exposure via traditional and Internet media channels. *Journal of Advertising, 31*, 27–35.

Kaid, L. L., McKinney, M. S., & Tedesco, J. C. (2007). Political information efficacy and young voters. *American Behavioral Scientist, 50*, 1093–1111. doi: 10.1177/0002764207300040

Kaye, B. K., & Johnson, T. J. (2002). Online and in the know: Uses and gratifications of the web for political information. *Journal of Broadcasting & Electronic Media, 46*, 54–71.

Kaye, B. K., & Johnson, T. J. (2004). A web for all reasons: Uses and gratifications of Internet components for political information. *Telematics & Informatics, 21*, 197–223. doi:10.1016/S0736-5853(03)00037-6

Klapper, J. T. (1960). *The effects of mass communication.* Glencoe, IL: Free Press.

Ladhani, N. (2011). The organizing impact of social networking. *Social Policy, 40*(4), 57.

Lasswell, H. D. (1948). The structure and function of communication in society. In L. Bryson (Ed.), *The communication of ideas* (pp. 37–51). New York: Harper.

Lazarsfeld, P. F., Berelson, B., & Gaudet, H. (1944). *The people's choice: How the voter makes up his mind in a presidential campaign.* New York: Duell, Sloan, & Pearce.

Lee, E.-J., & Shin, S. Y. (2012). Are they talking to me? Cognitive and affective effects of interactivity in politicians' Twitter communication. *CyberPsychology, Behavior & Social Networking, 15*(10), 515–520. doi: 10.1089/cyber.2012.0228

Lippmann, W. (1922). *Public opinion.* New York: Macmillan.

Mad money: TV ads in the 2012 presidential campaign. (2012). Retrieved from http://www.washingtonpost.com/wp-srv/special/politics/track-presidential-campaign-ads-2012/

McLeod, J. M., & Becker, L. B. (1974). Testing the validity of gratification measures through political effects analysis. In J. G. Blumler & E. Katz (Eds.), *The uses of mass communication: Current perspectives on gratifications research* (pp. 137–164). Beverly Hills, CA: Sage.

Morris, T. (2009). *All a Twitter: A personal and professional guide to social networking with Twitter*. Indianapolis, IN: Que Publishing.

O'Brien, M. (2011). Lessons from a Twitter meltdown. *Campaigns and Elections, 32,* 305–312.

Oh, H. J., Park, J., & Wanta, W. (2011). Exploring factors in the hostile media perception: Partisanship, electoral engagement, and media use patterns. *Journalism & Mass Communication Quarterly, 88*(1), 40–54.

Papacharissi, Z., & Rubin, A. M. (2000). Predictors of Internet use. *Journal of Broadcasting & Electronic Media, 44,* 175–196.

Parker, A. (2012). *In nonstop whirlwind of campaigns, Twitter is a critical tool*. Retrieved from http://www.nytimes.com/2012/01/29/us/politics/twitter-is-a-critical-tool-in-republican-campaigns.html?pagewanted=all&_r=0

Pew Research Center. (2012a). *Further decline in credibility ratings for most news organizations*. Washington, DC: Pew Research Center. Retrieved from http://www.people-press.org/2012/08/16/further-decline-in-credibility-ratings-for-most-news-organizations/

Pew Research Center. (2012b). *In changing news landscape, even television is vulnerable: Trends in news consumption: 1991–2012*. Washington, DC: Pew Research Center. Retrieved from http://www.people-press.org/2012/09/27/in-changing-news-landscape-even-television-is-vulnerable/

Rainie, L., Smith, A., Lehman-Schlozman, K., Brady, H., & Verba, S. (2012). Social media and political engagement. *Pew Internet & American Life Project*. Washington, DC: Pew Research Center.

Rogers, E. M. (2003). *Diffusion of innovations* (5th ed.). New York: Free Press.

Smith, A., & Brenner, J. (2012, May 31). Twitter use 2012. *Pew Internet & American Life Project*. Retrieved from http://pewinternet.org/Reports/2012/Twitter-Use-2012.aspx

Sweetser, K. D., & Kaid, L. L. (2008). Stealth soapboxes: Political information efficacy, cynicism and uses of celebrity weblogs among readers. *New Media & Society, 10*(1), 67–91. doi: 10.1177/1461444807085322

Taneja, H., Webster, J. G., Malthouse, E. C., & Ksiazek, T. B. (2012). Media consumption across platforms: Identifying user-defined repertoires. *New Media & Society, 14*(6), 951–968. doi:10.1177/1461444811436146

Timpane, J. (2012, November 8). Facebook, Twitter transform this election, *Philadelphia Inquirer*. Retrieved from http://articles.philly.com/2012-11-08/news/34974563_1_twitter-tweets-social-media-obama-campaign

Van Rees, K., & Van Eijck, K. (2003). Media repertoires of selective audiences: The impact of status, gender, and age on media use. *Poetics, 31*(5–6), 465–490. doi:10.1016/j.poetic.2003.09.005

Wells, J. D. (2008). A voice in the nation: Women journalists in the early nineteenth century south. *American Nineteenth Century History, 9,* 165–182. doi: 10.1080/14664650802021766.

Wortham, J. (2012, October 8). Campaigns use social media to lure in younger voters. *New York Times*, p. B1. Retrieved from http://www.nytimes.com/2012/10/08/technology/campaigns-use-social-media-to-lure-younger-voters.html

Yang, J., & Stone, G. (2003). The powerful role of interpersonal communication in agenda setting. *Mass Communication & Society, 6,* 57–74.

Zhao, D., & Rosson, M. B. (2009). *How and why people Twitter: The role that micro-blogging plays in informal communication at work*. Paper presented at the Proceedings of the ACM 2009 International conference on Supporting group work, Sanibel Island, FL.

Chapter 9

Austin, E. W., & Pinkleton, B. E. (1999). The relation between media content evaluations and political disaffection. *Mass Communication and Society, 2*, 105–122.

Bartels, L. M. (2002). Beyond the running tally: Partisan bias in political perceptions. *Political Behavior, 24*(2), 117–150.

Bennett, L. (2003). Lifestyle politics and citizen-consumers: Identity, communication and political action. In J. Corner & D. Pels (Eds.), *Media and the restyling of politics: Consumerism, celebrity and cynicism* (pp. 137–150). London: Sage.

Benoit, W. L., McKinney, M. S., & Holbert, R. L. (2001). Beyond learning and persona: Extending the scope of presidential debate effects. *Communication Monographs, 68*(3), 259–273.

Bishop, B. (2008). *The big sort: Why the clustering of like-minded America is tearing us apart.* Boston, MA: Houghton Mifflin.

boyd, d. (2008). Can social network sites enable political action? *International Journal of Media and Cultural Politics, 4*(2), 241–244.

Brundidge, J. (2010). Encountering "difference" in the contemporary public sphere: The contribution of the Internet to the heterogeneity of political discussion networks. *Journal of Communication, 60*(4), 680–700.

Cappella, J. N., & Jamieson, K. H. (1997). *Spiral of cynicism: The press and the public good.* New York: Oxford University Press.

Clark, A. (2010). *Social media: Social uses and implications for representative democracy.* Library of Parliament: Parliamentary Information and Research Service.

Dahlberg, L. (2007). Rethinking the fragmentation of the cyberpublic: From consensus to contestation. *New Media & Society, 9*(5), 827–847.

Dahlgren, P. (2009). *Media and political engagement: Citizens, communication and democracy.* Cambridge, England: Cambridge University Press.

Dalton, R. J., Beck, P. A., & Huckfeldt, R. (1998). Partisan cues and the media: Information flows in the 1992 presidential election. *The American Political Science Review, 92*(1), 111–126.

DCI Group. (2001). *DCI group releases new state-by-state social media research.* Retrieved from http://www.dcigroup.com/blog-post/dci-group-releases-new-state-by-state-social-media-research

de Vreese, C. H. (2005). The spiral of cynicism reconsidered. *European Journal of Communication, 20*(3), 283–301.

Druckman, J. N. (2004). Priming the vote: Campaign effects in a U.S. Senate election. *Political Psychology, 25*(4), 577–594.

Eagly, A. H., & Chaiken, S. (1993). *The psychology of attitude: The social context of attitude formation and change.* Orlando, FL: Harcourt Brace Jovanovich College Publishers.

Eveland, W. P., & Shah, D. V. (2003). The Impact of individual and interpersonal factors on perceived news media bias. *Political Psychology, 24*(1), 101–117.

Gelman, A. (2008). *Red state, blue state, rich state, poor state: Why Americans vote the way they do.* Princeton, NJ: Princeton University Press.

Hanson, G., Haridakis, P. M., Cunningham, A. W., Sharma, R., & Ponder, J. D. (2010). The 2008 presidential campaign: Political cynicism in the age of Facebook, MySpace, and YouTube. *Mass Communication, 13*(5), 584–607.

Hart, R. P. (1998). *Seducing America: How television charms the modern voter.* Thousand Oaks, CA: Sage Publications.

Herrnson, P. S., Stokes-Brown, A. K., & Hindman, M. (2007). Campaign politics and the digital divide: constituency characteristics, strategic considerations, and candidate Internet use in state legislative elections. *Political Research Quarterly, 60*(1), 31–42.

Hibbing, J. R., & Theiss-Moore, E. (1995). The media's role in public negativity towards congress: Distinguishing emotional reactions and cognitive evaluations. *American Journal of Political Science, 42*(2), 475–498.

Hill, K. A., & Hughes, J. E. (1998). *Cyberpolitics: Citizen activism in the age of the Internet.* New York: Rowman & Littlefield.

Hill, D., & McKee, S. (2005). The electoral college, mobilization, and turnout in the 2000 presidential election. *American Politics Research, 33,* 700–725.

Himelboim, I., Lariscy, R. W., Tinkham, S. F., & Sweetser, K. D. (2012). Social media and online political communication: The role of interpersonal informational trust and openness. *Journal of Broadcasting & Electronic Media, 56*(1), 92–115.

Hindman, M. (2008). *The myth of digital democracy.* Princeton, NJ: Princeton University Press.

Iyengar, S., & Hahn, K. S. (2009). Red media, blue media: Evidence of ideological selectivity in media use. *Journal of Communication, 59*(1), 19–39.

Kaid, L. L. (2002). Political advertising and information seeking: Comparing exposure via traditional and Internet channels. *Journal of Advertising, 31*(1), 27–35.

Kaid, L. L., & Boydston, J. (1987). An experimental study of the effectiveness of negative political advertisements. *Communication Quarterly, 35*(2), 193–201.

Kaid, L. L., McKinney, M. S., & Tedesco, J. C. (2000). *Civic dialogue in the 1996 presidential campaign: Candidate, media, and public voices.* Cresskill, NJ: Hampton.

Kaid, L. L., McKinney, M. S., & Tedesco, J. C. (2007). Political information efficacy and young voters. *American Behavioral Scientist, 50*(9), 1093–1111.

Kim, Y. (2011). The contribution of social network sites to exposure to political difference: The relationships among SNSs, online political messaging, and exposure to cross-cutting perspectives. *Computers in Human Behavior, 27*(2), 971–977.

Lee, T. (2005). Media effects on political disengagement revisited: A multi-media approach. *Journalism & Mass Media Quarterly, 82*(2), 416–433.

Loader, B. D., & Mercea, D. (2011). Networking democracy? *Information, Communication & Society, 14*(6), 757–769.

Milbery, K., & Anderson, S. (2009). Open sourcing our way to an online commons. *Journal of Communication Inquiry, 33*(4), 393–412.

Moy, P., Pfau, M., & Kahlor, L. (1999). Media use and public confidence in democratic institutions. *Journal of Broadcasting & Electronic Media, 43*(2), 137–158.

Noelle-Neumann, E. (1993). *The spiral of silence: Public opinion—Our social skin* (2nd ed.). Chicago: The University of Chicago Press.

Oshagan, H. (1996). Reference group influence on opinion expression. *International Journal of Public Opinion Research, 8,* 335–354.

Paletz, D. (2001). *The media in American politics: Contents and consequences* (2nd ed.). New York: Longman.

Papacharissi, Z. (2002). The virtual sphere: The Internet as a public sphere. *New Media & Society, 4*(1), 9–27.

Papacharissi, Z. (2010). *A private sphere: Democracy in a digital age.* Cambridge, UK: Polity.

Parmelee, J. H., Davies, J., & McMahan, C. A. (2011). The rise of non-traditional site use for online political information. *Communication Quarterly, 59*(5), 625–640.

Patterson, T. E. (1994). *Out of order.* New York: Vintage Books.

Patterson, T. E. (2003). *The vanishing voter: Public involvement in an age of uncertainty.* New York: Vintage Books.

Pew Research Center. (1996). *News attracts most Internet users: One-in-ten voters online for campaign '96.* Retrieved from http://www.people-press.org/1996/12/16/news-attracts-most-internet-users/

Pew Research Center. (2008). *Internet overtakes newspapers as news outlet.* Retrieved from http://www.people-press.org/2008/12/23/internet-overtakes-newspapers-as-news-outlet/

Postelnicu, M., & Cozma, R. (2008, November). *Befriending the candidate: Uses and gratifications of candidate profiles on MySpace.* Paper presented at the annual meeting of the National Communication Association, San Diego, CA.

Price, V., Nir, L., & Cappella, J. N. (2006). Normative and informational influences in online political discussions. *Communication Theory, 16*(1), 47–74.

Prior, M. (2005). News v. entertainment: How increasing media choice widens gaps in political knowledge and turnout. *American Journal of Political Science, 49*(3), 594–609.

Prislin R., & Wood, W. (2005). Social influence: The role of social consensus in attitude and attitude change. In D. Albarracın, B. T. Johnson, & M. P. Zanna (Eds.), *The handbook of attitudes.* (pp. 671–706). Hillsdale, NJ: Erlbaum.

Putnam, R. D. (1995). The strange disappearance of social capital in America. *PS: Political Science & Politics, 28,* 664–683.

Rainie, R., & Smith, A. (2012). *Social networking sites and politics.* Retrieved from http://www.pewinternet.org/Reports/2012/Social-networking-and-politics.aspx

Sabato, L. J. (1993). *Feeding frenzy: How attack journalism has transformed American politics.* New York: Free Press.

Semetko, H. A. (2004). Media, public opinion, and public action. In J. Downing, D. McQuail, P. Schlesinger, & E. Wartella (Eds.), *The SAGE handbook of media studies* (pp. 351–374). Thousand Oaks, CA: Sage.

Smith, A. (2009). *The Internet's role in campaign 2008.* Retrieved from http://www.pewinternet.org/Reports/2009/6--The-Internets-Role-in-Campaign-2008.aspx

Stroud, N. J. (2010). Polarization and partisan selective exposure. *Journal of Communication, 60*(3), 556–576.

Sunstein, C. R. (2007). *Republic.com 2.0.* Princeton, NJ: Princeton University Press.

Tedesco, J. C. (2011). Political information efficacy and Internet effects in the 2008 U.S. presidential election. *American Behavioral Scientist, 55*(6), 696–713.

Tolbert, C. J., & McNeal, R. S. (2003). Unraveling the effects of the Internet on political participation. *Political Research Quarterly, 56*(2), 175–185.

Turner, J. C. (1991). *Social influence.* Belmont, CA: Thomson Brooks/Cole Publishing Co.

Weaver L. R., Tinkham, S. F., & Sweetser, K. D. (2011). Kids these days: Examining differences in political uses and gratifications, Internet political participation, political information efficacy, and cynicism on the basis of age. *American Behavioral Scientist, 55*(6), 749–764.

Williams, C. B., & Gulati, J. (2012). Social networks in political campaigns: Facebook and the congressional elections of 2006 and 2008. *New Media & Society,* Advance online publication. doi: 10.1177/1461444812457332

Wimmer, R. D., & Dominick, J. R. (2011). *Mass media research: An introduction* (9th ed.). Boston, MA: Wadsworth.

Wojcieszak, M. E., & Mutz, D. C. (2009). Online groups and political discourse: Do online discussion spaces facilitate exposure to political disagreement? *Journal of Communication, 59*(1), 40–56.

Wolak, J. (2006). Consequences of presidential battleground strategies for citizen engagement. *Political Research Quarterly, 59*(3), 353–361.

Wright, G. C. (1998). Level-of-analysis effects on explanations of voting: The case of the 1982 U.S. Senate elections. *British Journal of Political Science, 19*, 381–398.

Yaverbaum, E. (2012, August 1). 2012 election: A social media scorecard putting up the numbers for Romney and Obama. Retrieved from http://www.huffingtonpost.com/eric-yaverbaum/2012-election-a-social-me_b_1468600.html

Yun, H. J., Jasperson, A., & Kaid, L. L. (2010). The cumulative effects of televised presidential debates on voters' attitudes across red, blue, and purple political playgrounds. In M. S. McKinney & M. C. Banwart (Eds.), *Communication in the 2008 U.S. election: Digital natives elect a president* (pp. 107–120). New York: Peter Lang.

Zhang, W., Johnson, T. J., Seltzer, T., & Bichard, S. L. (2010). The influence of social networking sites on political attitudes and behavior. *Social Science Computer Review, 28*(1), 75–92.

Chapter 10

Ancu, M. (2011). From soundbite to textbite: Election'08 comments on Twitter. In J. A. Hendricks & L. L. Kaid (Eds.), *Techno politics in presidential campaigning: New voices, new technologies, and new voters* (pp. 11–21). New York: Routledge.

Ansolabehere, S., & Iyengar, S. (1995). *Going negative: How attack ads shrink and polarize the electorate*. New York: Free Press.

Bal, A. S., Campbell, C. L., Payne, N. J., & Pitt, L. (2010). Political ad portraits: A visual analysis of viewer reaction to online political spoof advertisements. *Journal of Public Affairs, 10*, 313–328.

Basulto, D. (2012, October 2). YouTube goes live, adding a new dimension to presidential debate meme machine. *Washington Post*. Retrieved from http://wapo.st/QnEwHV

Baumgartner, J. C., & Morris, J. (2010a). MyFaceTube politics: Social networking sites and political engagement of young adults. *Social Science Computer Review, 28*(1), 24–44.

Baumgartner, J. C., & Morris, J. (2010b). Who wants to be my friend? Obama, youth and social networks in the 2008 campaign. In J. A. Hendricks & R. E. Denton, Jr. (Eds.), *Communicator-in-chief: How Barack Obama used new media technology to win the White House* (pp. 51–65). Lanham, MD: Lexington Books.

Bode, L. (2012). Facebooking it to the polls: A study in online social networking and political behavior. *Journal of Information Technology and Politics, 9*(4), 352–369.

Brooks, D. J. & Murov, M. (2012). Assessing accountability in a post-Citizens United Era: The effects of attack ad sponsorship by unknown independent groups. *American Politics Research, 40*, 383–418.

Burgess, J., & Green, J. (2009). *YouTube: Online video and participatory culture*. Malden MA: Polity.

Carlson, T., & Strandberg, K. (2008). Riding the web 2.0 wave: Candidates on YouTube in the 2007 Finnish national elections. *Journal of Information Technology and Politics, 5*(2), 159–174.

Chen, P. J., & Walsh, L. (2010). E-Election 2007? Political competition online. *Australian Cultural History, 28*(1), 47–54.

Cheng, H. & Riffe, D. (2008). Attention, perception, and perceived effects: Negative political advertising in a battleground state of the 2004 Presidential election. *Mass Communication & Society, 11*, 177–196.

Church, S. H. (2010). YouTube politics: YouChoose and leadership rhetoric during the 2008 election. *Journal of Information Technology and Politics, 7*, 124–142.

Cornfield, M., & Kaye, K. (2009). Online political advertising. In C. Panagopolous (Ed.), *Politicking online: The transformation of election campaign communications* (pp. 163–176). Piscataway, NJ: Rutgers.

Cortese, J., & Proffitt, J. M. (2012). Looking back as we prepare to move forward: U.S. presidential candidates' adoption of YouTube. *Cyberpsychology, Behavior and Social Networking, 15*(12), 693–697.

Davisson, A. (2009). "I'm In!": Hillary Clinton's 2008 Democratic primary campaign on YouTube. *Journal of Visual Literacy, 28*(1), 70–91.

de Boer, N., Sutfeld, H., & Groshek, J. (2012). Social media and personal attacks: A comparative perspective on co-creation and political advertising in presidential campaigns on YouTube. *First Monday, 17*(12). Retrieved from http://firstmonday.org/htbin/cgiwrap/bin/ojs/index.php/fm/article/view/4211

Diamond, E., & Bates, S. (1992). *The spot: The rise of political advertising on television.* Cambridge, MA: MIT Press.

Druckman, J. N., Kifer, M. J. & Parkin, M. (2010). Timeless strategy meets new medium: Going negative on congressional campaign web sites, 2002–2006. *Political Communication, 27*, 88–103.

Duman, S., & Locher, M. A. (2008). So let's talk. Let's chat. Let's start a dialog: An analysis of the conversation metaphor employed in Clinton's and Obama's YouTube campaign clips. *Multilingua, 27*, 193–230.

Dylko, I. B., Beam, M. A., Landreville, K. D., & Geidner, N. (2011). Filtering 2008 U.S. Presidential election news on YouTube by elites and non-elites: An examination of the democratizing potential of the Internet. *New Media and Society, 14*(5), 832–849.

English, K., Sweetser, K. D., & Ancu, M. (2011). YouTube-ification of political talk: An examination of persuasion appeals in viral videos. *American Behavioural Scientist, 55*(6), 733–748.

Fitzgerald, B. (2012, September 8). Most popular sites 2012: Alexa ranks the 500 most-visited Web sites. *Huffington Post.* Retrieved from: http://www.huffingtonpost.com/2012/08/09/most-popular-sites-2012-alexa_n_1761365.html

Foot, K. A., & Schneider, S. (2008). *Web campaigning.* Cambridge, MA: MIT Press.

Fung, T., Vraga, A., & Thorson, K. (2011). When bloggers attack: Examining the effect of negative citizen-initiated campaigning in the 2008 presidential election. In J. A. Hendricks & L. L. Kaid (Eds.), *Techno politics in presidential campaigning: New voices, new technologies, and new voters* (pp. 83–101). New York: Routledge.

Geer, J. G. (2006). *In defense of negativity: Attack ads in presidential campaigns.* Chicago: University of Chicago Press.

Gueorguieva, V. (2008). Voters, MySpace, and YouTube: The impact of alternative communication channels on the 2006 election cycle and beyond. *Social Science Computer Review, 26*(3), 288–300.

Gulati, G., & Williams, C. B. (2009). Congressional candidates' use of YouTube in 2008: Its frequency and rationale. *Journal of Information Technology and Politics, 7*, 93–109.

Hanson, G., Haridakis, P. M., Cunningham, A. W., Sharma, R., & Ponder, J. D. (2010). The 2008 presidential campaign: Political cynicism in the age of Facebook, MySpace and YouTube. *Mass Communication and Society, 13*(5), 584–607.

Hendricks, J. A., & Denton, R. E., Jr. (Eds.). (2010) *Communicator-in-chief: How Barack Obama used new media technology to win the White House*. Lanham, MD: Lexington Books.

Hendricks, J. A., & Kaid, L. L. (Eds.). (2011). *Techno politics in presidential campaigning: New voices, new technologies, and new voters*. New York: Routledge.

Hess, A. (2010). Democracy through the polarized lens of the Camcorder: Argumentation and vernacular spectacle on YouTube in the 2008 election. *Argumentation and Advocacy, 47*(Fall), 106–122.

Holbert, R. L., & Geidner, N. (2009). The 2008 election: Highlighting the need to explore additional communication subfields to advance political communication. *Communication Studies, 60*(4), 344–358.

Johnson-Cartee, K. S., & Copeland, G. (1991). *Negative political advertising: Coming of age*. Hillsdale, NJ: Lawrence Erlbaum.

Kaid, L. L. (2006). Political web wars: The use of the Internet for political advertising. In A. P. Williams & J. C. Tedesco (Eds.). *The Internet election: Perspectives on the web in campaign 2004*. Lanham, MD: Rowman and Littlefield.

Kaid, L. L., & Johnston A. (2000). *Videostyle in presidential campaigns: Style and content of televised political advertising*. Westport, CT: Praeger.

Kaid, L. L., & Postelnicu, M. (2005). Political advertising in the 2004 Election: Comparison of traditional television and Internet messages. *American Behavioral Scientist, 49*(2), 256–278.

Kalnes, O. (2009). Norwegian parties and Web 2.0. *Journal of Information Technology and Politics, 6*, 251–266.

Karpf, D. (2010). Macaca moments reconsidered: Electoral panopticon or netroots mobilization? *Journal of Information Technology and Politics, 7*, 143–162.

Klotz, R. J. (2010). The sidetracked 2008 YouTube senate campaign. *Journal of Information Technology and Politics, 7*, 110–123.

Lev-On, A. (2012). YouTube usage in low visibility political campaigns. *Journal of Information Technology and Politics, 9*, 205–216.

Lilleker, D. G., & Jackson, N. A. (2011). The U.S. 2008: A giant step for interactivity. In D. G. Lilleker & N. A. Jackson (Eds.), *Political campaigning, elections and the Internet: Comparing the US, UK, France and Germany* (pp. 76–98). New York: Routledge.

May, A. L. (2010). WhoTube? How YouTube's news and politics space is going mainstream. *International Journal of Press/Politics, 15*(4), 499–511.

McKinney, M. S., & Rill, L. A. (2009). Not your parents' presidential debates: Examining the effects of the CNN/YouTube debates on young citizen's civic engagement. *Communication Studies, 60*(4), 392–406.

McNair, B. (2011). *An introduction to political communication* (5th ed.). New York: Routledge.

Meyer, R. (2012, August 22). 9 concrete, specific things we actually know about how social media shape elections. *The Atlantic*. Retrieved from http://www.theatlantic.com/technology/archive/2012/08/9-concrete-specific-things-we-actually-know-about-how-social-media-shape-elections/261425/

Musser, C. (2009). Political documentary, YouTube, and the 2008 U.S. presidential election: Focus on Robert Greenwald and David N. Bossie. *Studies in Documentary Film, 3*(3), 199–218.

Papacharissi, Z. (2009). The virtual geographies of social networks: A comparative analysis of Facebook, LinkedIn and ASmallWorld. *New Media and Society, 11*(1–2), 199–220.

Papacharissi, Z. (2010). *A private sphere: Democracy in a digital age*. Malden, MA: Polity.

Panagopolous, C. (2009). *Politicking online: The transformation of election campaign communications*. Piscataway, NJ: Rutgers.

Parker, R. (2012, November 15). Campaign stops: Social and anti-social media. *New York Times*. Retrieved from: http://campaignstops.blogs.nytimes.com/2012/11/15/social-and-anti-social-media/

Powell, L. (2010). Obama and Obama girl: YouTube, viral videos and the 2008 presidential campaign. In J. A. Hendricks & R. E. Denton, Jr. (Eds.). *Communicator-in-chief: How Barack Obama used new media technology to win the White House* (pp. 83–104). Lanham, MD: Lexington Books.

Ricke, L. (2010). A new opportunity for democratic engagement: The CNN-YouTube presidential candidate debates. *Journal of Information Technology and Politics, 7*, 202–215.

Ridout, T., Fowler, E., & Branstetter, J. (2010). *Political advertising in the 21st century: The rise of the YouTube ad*. Paper presented at the annual meeting of the American Political Science Association, Washington, DC.

Ridout, T., Fowler, E., & Branstetter, J. (2012). *Political advertising in the 21st century: The influence of the YouTube ad*. Paper presented at the annual meeting of the Western Political Science Association, Portland, OR.

Sabato, L. (2010). *The year of Obama: How Barack Obama won the White House*. London: Longman.

Salmond, R. (2008). RooTube: YouTube advertising in the 2007 Australian election campaign. Paper presented at the annual meeting of the American Political Science Association, Boston, MA.

Salmond, R. (2012, March 16). MeTube: Political advertising, election campaigns and YouTube. *Brookings Issues In Technology Innovation*. Retrieved from http://www.brookings.edu/research/papers/2012/03/tech-youtube-salmond

Schill, D., & Kirk, R. (2011). A digital agora: Citizen participation in the 2008 presidential debates. *American Behavioral Scientist, 55*(3), 325–347.

Schneider, S., & Foot, K. A. (2006). Web campaigning by U.S. presidential primary candidates in 2000 and 2004. In A. P. Williams & J. C. Tedesco (Eds.), *The Internet election: Perspectives on the web in campaign 2004* (pp. 21–36). Lanham, MD: Rowman and Littlefield.

Shah, D.V., Cho, J., Nah, S., Gotlieb, M. R., Hwang, H., Lee, N., Scholl, R., & McLeod, D. M. (2007). Campaign ads, online messaging, and participation: Extending the communication mediation model. *Journal of Communication 57*, 676–703.

Smith, A., & Duggan, M. (2012, November 2). Online political videos and campaign 2012. *Pew Internet and the American Life Project*. Retrieved from http://pewinternet.org/Reports/2012/Election-2012-Video.aspx

Snow, N. (2010). My fellow blogging Americans: Weblogs and the race for the White House. In J. A. Hendricks & R. E. Denton, Jr. (Eds). *Communicator-in-chief: How Barack Obama used new media technology to win the White House* (pp. 67–82). Lanham, MD: Lexington Books.

Solop, F. I. (2010). "RT@BarackObama We just made history": Twitter and the 2008 presidential election. In J. A. Hendricks & R. E. Denton Jr. (Eds.), *Communicator-in-chief: How Barack Obama used new media technology to win the White House* (pp. 37–50). Lanham, MD: Lexington Books.

Towner, T. L., & Dulio, D. A. (2010). The web 2.0 election: Voter learning in the 2008 presidential campaign. In J. A. Hendricks & L. L. Kaid (Eds.), *Techno politics in presidential campaigning: New voices, new technologies, and new voters* (pp. 22–43). New York: Routledge.

Towner, T. L., & Dulio, D. A. (2011a). An experiment of campaign effects during the You-Tube election. *New Media and Society, 13*(4), 626–44.

Towner, T. L., & Dulio, D. A. (2011b). The web 2.0 election: Does the online medium matter? *Journal of Political Marketing, 10*, 165–188.

Towner, T. L., & Dulio, D. A. (2012). New media and political marketing in the United States: 2012 and beyond. *Journal of Political Marketing, 11*(1–2), 95–119.

Tyron, C. (2008). Pop politics: Online parody videos, intertextuality, and political participation. *Popular Communication, 6*, 209–213.

van Dijck, J. (2009). Users like you? Theorizing agency in user-generated content. *Media Culture and Society, 31*(1), 41–58.

Vernallis, C. (2011). Audiovisual change: Viral web media and the Obama campaign. *Cinema Journal, 50*(4), 73–97.

Wallsten, K. (2010). "Yes We Can": How online viewership, blog discussion, campaign statements and mainstream media coverage produced a viral video phenomenon. *Journal of Information Technology and Politics, 7*, 161–181.

Williams, A. P., & Tedesco, J. C. (Eds.). (2006). *The Internet election: Perspectives on the web in campaign 2004*. Lanham, MD: Rowman and Littlefield.

Wilson, P. (2012, November 1). U.S. presidential election 2012: Targeted online video ads redefine tactics. *The Guardian Online*, Retrieved from http://www.guardian.co.uk/media-network/media-network-blog/2012/nov/01/us-presidential-election-2012-barack-obama-mitt-romney

Woolley, J. K., Limperos, A. M., & Oliver, M. (2010). The 2008 presidential election, 2.0: A content analysis of user-generated political Facebook groups. *Mass Communication and Society, 13*(5), 631–652.

Xenos, M., & Bennett, L. W. (2007). The disconnection in online politics: The youth political web sphere and U.S. election sites, 2002–2004. *Information, Community and Society, 10*(4), 443–464.

Chapter 11

American National Election Studies. (2012). *ANES 2010–2012 Evaluations of Government and Society Study (EGSS) 4* [Data file]. Retrieved from http://www.electionstudies.org/studypages/download/datacenter_all.htm

Ancu, M., & Cozma, R. (2009). MySpace politics: Uses and gratifications of befriending candidates. *Journal of Broadcasting and Electronic Media, 53*(4), 567–583.

Baym, N. K. (2006). Interpersonal life online. In L. A. Lievrouw & S. Livingstone (Eds.), *The handbook of new media* (pp. 35–54). Thousand Oaks, CA: Sage.

Bimber, B. (2003). *Information and American democracy: Technology in the evolution of political power*. New York: Cambridge University Press.

Bimber, B., & Davis, R. (2003). *Campaigning online: The Internet in U.S. elections*. New York: Oxford University Press.

Blackmon, D. A., Levitz, J., Berzon, A., & Etter, L. (2010, October 28). Birth of a movement: Tea party arose from conservatives steeped in crisis. *The Wall Street Journal.* Retrieved from http://online.wsj.com/article/SB10001424052702304173704575578332725182228.html?mod=djemTMB_t

Bonchek, M. S. (1995, April). *Grassroots in cyberspace: Recruiting members on the Internet, or do computer networks facilitate collective action? A transaction cost approach.* Paper presented at the annual meeting of the Midwest Political Science Association, Chicago, IL.

Booth, A., & Babchuk, N. (1969). Personal influence networks and voluntary association affiliation. *Sociological Inquiry, 39*(2), 179–188.

Brenner, J. (2012, November 13). *Pew Internet: Social networking* (full detail). Retrieved from http://pewinternet.org/Commentary/2012/March/Pew-Internet-Social-Networking-full-detail.aspx

Brundidge, J. (2006, June). *The contribution of the Internet to the heterogeneity of political discussion networks: Does the medium matter?* Paper presented at the annual meeting of the International Communication Association, Dresden, Germany.

Buttel, F. G., Wilkening, E. A., & Martinson, O. B. (1977). Ideology and social indication of the quality of life. *Social Indicators Research, 4,* 353–369.

Citrin, J. (1974). Comment: The political relevance of trust in government. *American Political Science Review, 68*(3), 973–988.

Davis, R. (1999). *The web of politics: The Internet's impact on the American political system.* Oxford: Oxford University Press.

Dahlgren, P. (2005). The Internet, public spheres, and political communication. *Political Communication, 22*(2), 147–162.

Dahlberg, L. (2007). Rethinking the fragmentation of the cyberpublic: From consensus to contestation. *New Media & Society, 9*(5), 827–847.

Deutsch, M., & Gerard, H. B. (1955). A study of normative and informational influences upon individual judgment. *Journal of Abnormal and Social Psychology, 51,* 629–636.

Eagly, A. H., & Chaiken, S. (1993). *The psychology of attitude: The social context of attitude formation and change.* Orlando, FL: Harcout Brace Jovanovich College Publishers.

Elias, N., & Lemish, D. (2009). Spinning the web of identity: The roles of the Internet in the lives of immigrant adolescents. *New Media & Society, 11*(4), 533–551.

Elin, L. (2003). The radicalization of Zeke Spier: How the Internet contributes to civic engagement and new forms of social capital. In M. McCarthy & M. D. Ayers (Eds.), *Cyberactivism: Online activism in theory and practice* (pp. 97–114). New York: Routledge.

Fowler, J. H., & Kam, C. D. (2007). Beyond the self: Social identity, altruism, and political participation. *The Journal of Politics, 69*(3), 813–827.

Gueorguieva, V. (2006). Voters, MySpace, and YouTube: The impact of alternative communication channels on the 2006 election cycle and beyond. *Social Science Computer Review, 26*(3), 288–300.

Gulati, G. J., & Williams, C. B. (2010). Congressional candidates' use of YouTube in 2008: Its frequency and rationale. *Journal of Information Technology & Politics, 7*(2/3), 93–109.

Hayes, R. A. (2009). *New media, new politics: Political learning efficacy and the examination of uses of social network sites for political engagement.* (Doctoral Dissertation). Michigan State University, East Lansing, MI.

Holt, R. (2004). *Dialogue on the Internet: Language, civic identity, and computer–mediated communication.* Westport, CT: Praeger Publishers.

Kavanaugh, A., Carroll, J. M., Rosson, M. B., Zin, T. T., & Reese, D. D. (2006). Community networks: Where offline communities meet online. *Journal of Computer-Mediated Communication, 10*(4), Retrieved from http://onlinelibrary.wiley.com/doi/10.1111/j.1083-6101.2005.tb00266.x/full

Kim, Y. (2011). The contribution of social network sites to exposure to political difference: The relationships among SNSs, online political messaging, and exposure to cross-cutting perspectives. *Computers in Human Behavior, 27*(2), 971–977.

Kushin, M. J., & Kitchener, K. (2009). Getting political on social network sites: Exploring online political discourse on Facebook. *First Monday, 14*(11). Retrieved from http://firstmonday.org/htbin/cgiwrap/bin/ojs/index.php/fm/article/viewArticle/2645/2350

Laer, J. V. (2010). Activists "online" and "offline": The Internet as an information channel for protest demonstrations. *Mobilization: An International Journal, 15*(3), 347–366.

Mehra, B., Merkel, C., & Bishop, A. P. (2004). The Internet for empowerment of minority and marginalized users. *New Media & Society, 6*(6), 781–802.

Morahan-Martin, J. (2000). Women and the Internet: Promise and perils. *CyberPsychology & Behavior, 3*(5), 683–691.

Moy, P., Domke, D., & Stamm, K. (2001). The spiral of silence and public opinion on affirmative action. *Journalism and Mass Communication Quarterly, 78*(1), 7–26.

Moy, P., & Scheufele, D. A. (1998, May). *Media effects on social capital and political participation.* Paper presented at the annual meeting of the American Association for Public Opinion Research, St. Louis, MO.

Naughton, J. (2001). Contested space: The Internet and global civil society. In H. Anheier, M. Glasius, & M. Kaldor (Eds.), *Global civil society* (pp.147–168). Oxford: Oxford University Press.

Noelle-Neumman, E. (1974). The spiral of silence: A theory of public opinion. *Journal of Communication, 24*(2), 43–51.

Noelle-Neumann, E. (1993). *The spiral of silence: Public opinion-our social skin.* Chicago, IL: The University of Chicago Press.

Oshagan, H. (1996). Reference group influence on opinion expression. *International Journal of Public Opinion Research, 8*(4), 335–354.

Papacharissi, Z. (2002). The virtual sphere: The Internet as a public sphere. *New Media and Society, 4*(1), 9–27.

Plant, R. (2004). Online communities. *Technology in Society, 26*(1), 51–65.

Rainie, L., & Smith, A. (2012). Politics on social networking sites. *Pew Research Center's Internet & American Life Project.* Retrieved from http://pewinternet.org/~/media//Files/Reports/2012/PIP_PoliticalLifeonSocialNetworkingSites.pdf

Rainie, L., Smith, A., Schlozman, K. L., Brady, H., & Verba, S. (2012). Social media and political engagement. *Pew Research Center's Internet & American Life Project.* Retrieved from http://pewinternet.org/~/media//Files/Reports/2012/PIP_SocialMediaAndPoliticalEngagement_PDF.pdf

Schulz, A., & Roessler, P. (2012). The spiral of silence and the Internet: Selection of online content and the perception of the public opinion climate in computer-mediated communication environments. *International Journal of Public Opinion Research, 24*(3), 346–367.

Stromer-Galley, J. (2003). Diversity of political conversation on the Internet: Users' perspectives. *Journal of Computer-Mediated Communication, 8*(3). Retrieved from http://jcmc.indiana.edu/vol8/issue3/stromergalley.html

Swigger, N. (2013). The online citizen: Is social media changing citizen's beliefs about democratic values? *Political Behavior, 35*(3), 589–603.

Velasquez, A. (2012). Social media and online political discussion: The effect of cues and informational cascades on participation in online political communities. *New Media & Society, 14*(8), 1286–1303.

Vitak, J., Zube, P., Smock, A., Carr, C. T., Ellison, N., & Lampe, C. (2011). It's complicated: Facebook users' political participation in the 2008 election. *Cyberpsychology, Behavior, and Social Networking, 14*(3), 107–114.

Wellman, B., Hasse A. Q., & Witte J. (2001). Does the Internet increase, decrease, or supplement social capital? *American Behavioral Scientist, 45*(3), 436–455.

Williams, C., & Gulati, G. (2007, August). *Social networks in political campaigns: Facebook and the 2006 midterm elections.* Paper presented at the annual meeting of the American Political Science Association, Chicago, IL.

Witschge, T. (2004). Online deliberation: Possibilities of the Internet for deliberative democracy. In P. M. Shane (Ed.), *Democracy online: The prospects for political renewal through the Internet* (pp. 109–122). New York: Routledge.

Wojcieszak, M. E., & Mutz, D. C. (2009). Online groups and political discourse: Do online discussion spaces facilitate exposure to political disagreement? *Journal of Communication, 59*(1), 40–56.

Chapter 12

Banwart, M. C. (2002). *Videostyle and webstyle in 2000: Comparing the gender differences of candidate presentation in political advertising on the Internet.* Unpublished doctoral dissertation, University of Oklahoma.

Beckett, L. (2012). *Everything we know (so far) about Obama's big data tactics. ProPublica: Journalism in the Public Interest.* Retrieved from http://www.propublica.org/article/everything-we-know-so-far-about-obamas-big-data-operation

Bergan, D. E. (2009). Does grassroots lobbying work? A field experiment measuring the effects of an e-mail lobbying campaign on legislative behavior. *American Politics Research, 37*(2), 327–352.

Bystrom, D. G., Banwart, M. C., Kaid, L. L. & Robertson, T. (2004). *Gender and political candidate communication: VideoStyle, webStyle, and newsStyle.* New York: Routledge.

Chiu, H., Hsieh, Y., Kao, Y., & Lee, M. (2007). The determinants of e-mail receivers' disseminating behaviors on the Internet. *Journal of Advertising Research, 47*(4), 524–534.

Cornfield, M. (2004). *Politics moves online: Campaigning and the Internet.* New York: The Century Foundation Press.

Dalrymple, K. E., & Scheufele, D. A. (2007). Finally informing the electorate? How the Internet got people thinking about presidential politics in 2004. *The Harvard International Journal of Press/Politics, 12*(3), 96–111.

Drummond, G. (2006). Political parties' use of web based marketing: Some preliminary findings related to first-time voters in the 2005 general election. *International Journal of Nonprofit and Voluntary Sector Marketing, 11*(3), 181–191.

Endres, D., & Warnick, B. (2004). Text-based interactivity in candidate campaign web sites: A case study from the 2002 elections. *Western Journal of Communication, 68*(3), 322–342.

Foot, K., Schneider, S., Dougherty, M., Xenos, M., & Larsen, E. (2003). Analyzing linking practices: Candidate sites in the 2002 US electoral Web sphere. *Journal of Computer-Mediated Communication, 8*(3). Retrieved from http://jcmc.indiana.edu/vol8/issue4/foot.html

Foster, K. (2012). Move over robo-calls, states sell email addresses for campaigns to reach voters. *Fox News.* Retrieved from http://www.foxnews.com/politics/2012/02/06/move-over-robo-calls-campaigns-turn-to-email-spam-to-inundate-voters/

Green, J. (2012). The science behind those Obama campaigns emails. *Bloomberg Businessweek.* Retrieved from http://www.businessweek.com/articles/2012-11-29/the-science-behind-those-obama-campaign-e-mails.

Gueorguieva, V. (2008). Voters, MySpace, and YouTube: The impact of alternative communication channels on the 2006 election cycle and beyond. *Social Science Computer Review, 26*(3), 288–300.

Hanson, G., Haridakis, P. M., Cunningham, A.W., Sharma, R., & Ponder, J. D. (2010). The 2008 presidential campaign: Political cynicism in the age of Facebook, MySpace, and YouTube. *Mass Communication and Society, 13*(5), 584–607.

Jones, S. (2009). Generations online in 2009. *Pew Internet and American Life Project.* Retrieved from http://www.pewinternet.org/Reports/2009/Generations-Online-in-2009.aspx

Kaid, L. L. (2002). Political advertising and information seeking: Comparing exposure via traditional and Internet channels. *Journal of Advertising, 31*(1), 27–35.

Kaid, L. L., & Davidson, D. K. (1986). Elements of videostyle: Candidate presentation through television advertising. In L. L. Kaid, D. Nimmo, & K. R. Sanders (Eds.), *New perspectives on political advertising* (pp. 184–209). Carbondale, IL: Southern Illinois University Press.

Levy, J. (2008). Beyond "Boxers or Briefs?": New media brings youth to politics like never before. *Phi Kappa Phi Forum, 88*(2), 14–16.

Margolis, M., Resnick, D., & Tu, C. (1997). Campaigning on the Internet: Parties and candidates on the World Wide Web in the 1996 primary season. *Harvard Journal of Press/ Politics, 2,* 59–78.

McKinney, M. S., & Rill, L. A. (2009). Not your parents' presidential debates: Examining the effects of the CNN/YouTube debates on young citizens' civic engagement. *Communication Studies, 60*(4), 392–406.

McMillan, S. J. (2002). Exploring models of interactivity from multiple research traditions: Users, documents, and systems. In L. Lievrouw & S. Livingston (Eds.), *Handbook of new media* (pp. 162–182). London: Sage.

Moldoff, J, & Williams, A. P. (2007). Metacommunication and interactivity: A content analysis of audience framing on an advocacy group's blog. *Journal of International Business Disciplines, 2*(1), 53–69.

Murray, S., & Mosk, M. (2008). Under Obama, Web would be the way. *The Washington Post.* Retrieved from http://www.washingtonpost.com/wp-dyn/content/article/2008/11/10/AR2008111000013.html

Newhagen, J. E., Cordes, J.W., & Levy, M. R. (1995). Nightly@nbc.com: Audience scope and the perception of interactivity in viewer mail on the Internet. *Journal of Communication, 45,* 164–179.

Nickerson, D. W. (2007). Does e-mail boost turnout? *Quarterly Journal of Political Science, 2*(4), 369–379.

North, R. C., Holsti, O., Zaninovich, M. G., & Zinnes, D. A. (1963). *Content analysis: A handbook with applications for the study of international crisis.* Evanston, IL: Northwestern University Press.

Papacharissi, Z. (2009). The virtual geographies of social networks: A comparative analysis of Facebook, LinkedIn and A Small World. *New Media & Society, 11*(1), 199–220.

Peng, F. Y., Tham, N. I., & Xiaoming, H. (1999). Trends in online newspapers: A look at the U.S. web. *Newspaper Research Journal, 20*(2), 52–64.

Polat, R. K. (2005). The Internet and political participation: Exploring the explanatory links. *European Journal of Communication, 20*(4), 435–459.

Prakash, N. (2012). Which presidential candidate is ruling the email election? *Mashable.* Retrieved from http://mashable.com/2012/10/18/election-emailing/

Puopolo, S. (2001). The Web and U.S. senatorial campaigns 2000. *American Behavioral Scientist, 44*(12), 2030–2047.

Rainie, L. (2012). Social media and voting. *Pew Internet and American Life Project.* Retrieved from http://pewinternet.org/Reports/2012/Social-Vote-2012.aspx

Richtel, M. (2010). E-mail gets an instant makeover. *New York Times*. Retrieved from http://www.nytimes.com/2010/12/21/technology/21email.html?_r=1&

Selnow, G. W. (1998). *Electronic whistle-stops: The impact of the Internet on American politics*. Westport, CT: Praeger.

Sheffer, M. L. (2003). State legislators' perceptions of the use of E-mail in constituent communication. *Journal of Computer Mediated Communication, 8*(4). Retrieved from http://jcmc.indiana.edu/vol8/issue4/sheffer.html

Spigel, L. (2009). My TV studies . . . now playing on a YouTube site near you. *Television & New Media, 10*(1), 149–153.

Smith, A. (2009). The Internet's role in campaign 2008. *Pew Internet and American Life Project*. Retrieved from http://www.pewinternet.org/Reports/2009/6--The-Internets-Role-in-Campaign-2008.aspx

Smith, A. (2012). Mobile politics and the 2012 election. *Pew Internet and American Life Project*. Retrieved from http://www.pewinternet.org/Reports/2011/The-Internet-and-Campaign-2010.aspx?list=1

Smith, A., & Duggan, M. (2012). Online political videos and campaigns 2012. *Pew Internet and American Life Project*. Retrieved from http://pewinternet.org/Reports/2012/Election-2012-Video.aspx

Stanyer, J. (2005). Political parties, the Internet and the 2005 general election: From Web presence to e-campaigning? *Journal of Marketing Management, 21*(9), 1049–1065.

Stromer-Galley, J. (2000). On-line interaction and why candidates avoid it. *Journal of Communication, 50*, 111–132.

Stromer-Galley, J. (2003). Diversity of political conversation on the Internet: Users' perspectives. *Journal of Computer-Mediated Communication, 8(3)* Retrieved from http://jcmc.indiana.edu/vol8/issue3/stromergalley.html

Stromer-Galley, J., & Foot, K. A. (2002). Citizen perceptions of online interactivity and implications for political campaign communication. *Journal of Computer Mediated Communication, 8*(1), Retrieved from http://www.ascusc.org/jcmc/vol18/issue1/stromerandfoot.html

Tau, B. (2012). Obama campaign emails now targeting specific individuals. Politico 44: A living diary of the Obama presidency. *Politico*. Retrieved from http://www.politico.com/politico44/2012/10/obama-campaign-emails-now-targeting-specific-individuals-139211.html

Tedesco, J. C. (2006). Web interactivity and young adult political efficacy. In A. P. Williams & J. C. Tedesco (Eds.), *The Internet election: Perspectives on the web in campaign 2004* (pp. 187–202). Lanham, MD: Rowman & Littlefield.

Trammell, K. D., Williams, A. P., Postelnicu, M., & Landreville, K. D. (2006). Evolution of online campaigning: Increasing interactivity in candidate web sites through text and technical features. *Mass Communication & Society, 9*(1), 21–44.

Trammell, K. D., & Williams, A. P. (2004). Beyond direct mail: Evaluating candidate e-mail messages in the 2002 Florida gubernatorial campaign. *Journal of eGovernment, 1*(1), 105–122.

Ward, S., & Gibson R. 2003. On-line and on message? Candidates websites in the 2001 General Election. *British Journal of Politics and International Relations, 5*(2), 188–205.

Warnick, B., Xenos, M., Endres, D., & Gastil, J. (2005). Effects of campaign-to-user and text-based interactivity in political candidate campaign Web sites. *Journal of Computer-Mediated Communication, 10*(3). Retrieved from http://jcmc.indiana.edu/vol10/issue3/warnick.html

Wiese, D. R., & Gronbeck, B. E. (2005). Campaign 2004 developments in cyber-politics. In R. E. Denton (Ed.), *The 2004 presidential campaign: A communication perspective* (pp. 352–388). Lanham, MD: Rowman & Littlefield.

Williams, A. P. (2005). The main frame: Assessing the role of the Internet in the 2004 U.S. presidential contest. In R. E. Denton, Jr. (Ed.), *The 2004 presidential campaign: A communication perspective* (pp. 389–412). Lanham, MD: Rowman & Littlefield.

Williams, A. P. (2006). Framing their fight: Candidate e-mail strategies in election 2004. In A. P. Williams & J. C. Tedesco (Eds.). *The Internet election: Perspectives on the Web in campaign 2004* (pp. 83–98). Lanham, MD: Rowman & Littlefield.

Williams, A. P., & Serge E. (2011). Evaluating candidate e-mail messages in the 2008 U.S. presidential campaign. In J. A. Hendricks & L. L. Kaid (Eds.) *Techno politics in presidential campaigning: New voices, new technologies, and new voters* (pp. 44–57). New York: Routledge.

Williams, A. P., & Trammell, K. D. (2005). Candidate campaign e-mail messages in the presidential election 2004. *American Behavioral Scientist, 49*(4), 560–574.

Williams, A. P., Trammell, K. D., Postelnicu, M., Landreville, K. D., & Martin, J. D. (2005). Blogging and hyperlinking: Use of the web to enhance viability during 2004 U.S. campaign. *Journalism Studies, 6*(2), 177–186.

Chapter 13

Alexa.com. (2012). Top sites on the web. Retrieved from http://www.alexa.com/

American National Election Study (ANES). (2009). *2008–2009 Panel study questionnaires.* Retrieved from http://www.electionstudies.org/studypages/2008_2009panel/anes2008_2009panel_qnaire.pdf

Axelrod, R. (1973). Schema theory: An information processing model of perception and cognition. *American Political Science Review, 67,* 1248–1266.

Becker, L. B., & Dunwoody, S. (1982). Media use, public affairs knowledge, and voting in a local election. *Journalism Quarterly, 59,* 212–218.

Becker, L. B., & Schoenbach, K. (1989). Audience responses to media diversification: Coping with plenty. In L. B. Becker & K. Schoenbach (Eds.), *When media content diversifies: Anticipating audience behaviors* (pp. 1–27). Hillsdale, NJ: Erlbaum.

Beer, D. D. (2008). Social network(ing) sites . . . revisiting the story so far: A response to danah boyd & Nicole Ellison. *Journal of Computer-Mediated Communication, 13,* 516–529.

Bond, R. M., Fariss, C. J., Jones, J. J., Kramer, A. D. I., Marlow, C., Settle, J. E., & Fowler, J. H. (2012, September 13). A 61-million-person experiment in social influence and political mobilization. *Nature, 61,* 295–298.

Bucy, E. P., & Tao, C. C. (2007). The mediated moderation model of interactivity. *Media Psychology, 9*(2), 647–672.

Center for Information and Research on Civic Learning and Engagement (CIRCLE). (2012, November 9). *Updated estimate: Youth turnout was 50% in 2012: Youth turnout in battleground states 58%.* Retrieved from http://www.civicyouth.org/updated-estimate-50-of-youth-turnout-in-2012-youth-turnout-in-battleground-states-58/

Cho, J., Shah, D. V., McLeod, J. M., McLeod, D. M., Scholl, R. M., & Gottlieb, M. R. (2009). Campaigns, reflection, and deliberation: Advancing an O-S-R-O-R model of communication effects. *Communication Theory, 19,* 66–88.

Culbertson, H. M., Evarts, D., Richard, P. B., Karin, S., & Stempel, G. H., III. (1994). Media use, attention to media and agenda richness. *Newspaper Research Journal, 15,* 14–29.

Delli Carpini, M. X. (2000). Gen.com: Youth, civic engagement, and the new information environment. *Political Communication, 17,* 341–349.

Diddi, A., & LaRose, R. (2006). Getting hooked on news: Uses and gratifications and the formation of news habits among college students in an Internet environment. *Journal of Broadcasting & Electronic Media, 50,* 193–210.

Druckman, J., Kifer, M., & Parkin, M. (2009). Campaign communications in U.S. congressional elections. *American Political Science Review, 103*(3), 343–366.

Druckman, J., Kifer, M., & Parkin, M. (2010). Timeless strategy meets new medium: Going negative on congressional campaign web sites, 2002–2006. *Political Communication, 27*(1), 88–103.

Foot, K. A., & Schneider, S. M. (2006). *Web campaigning.* Cambridge, MA: MIT Press.

Franklin, M. N. (2001). Electoral participation. In R. Niemi & H. Weisberg (Eds.), *Controversies in Voting Behavior* (pp. 240–258). Washington: CQ Press.

Gangadharbatla, H. (2008). Facebook me: Collective self-esteem, need to belong, and Internet self-efficacy as predictors of the igeneration's attitudes toward social networking sites. *Journal of Interactive Advertising, 8*(2), 5–15.

Gans, C. (2004). Low voter turnout and the decline of American civic participation. In M. S. McKinney, L. L. Kaid, D. G. Bystrom, & D. B. Carlin (Eds.), *Communicating politics: Engaging the public in democratic life* (pp. 80–85). New York: Peter Lang.

Gerber, A. S., Green, D. P., & Larimer, C. W. (2008). Social pressure and voter turnout: Evidence from a large-scale field experiment. *American Political Science Review, 102,* 33–48.

Graber, D. (1984). *Processing the news: How people tame the information tide.* New York: Longman.

Hindman, M. S. (2009). *The myth of digital democracy.* Princeton, NJ: Princeton University Press.

Holbert, R. L. (2005). Debate viewing as mediator and partisan reinforcement in the relationship between news use and vote choice. *Journal of Communication, 55,* 85–102.

Huckfeldt, R., Sprague, J., & Levine, J. (2000). The dynamic of collective deliberation in the 1996 election: Campaign effects on accessibility, certainty, and accuracy. *American Political Science Review, 94,* 641–651.

Jenkins, H. (2006). *Convergence culture.* New York: New York University Press.

Johnson, T. J., & Kaye, B. K. (2002). Webelievability: A path model examining how convenience and reliance predict online credibility. *Journalism & Mass Communication Quarterly, 79,* 619–642.

Johnstone, J. (1974). Social interaction and mass media use among adolescents: A case study. In J. Blumler, & E. Katz (Eds.), *The uses of mass communications: Current perspectives on gratifications research* (pp. 114–131). Beverly Hills, CA: Sage.

Just, M. R., Crigler, A. N., Alger, D. E., Cook, T. E., Kern, M., & West, D. M. (1996). *Crosstalk: Citizens, candidates, and the media in a presidential campaign.* Chicago: University of Chicago Press.

Kaid, L. L., Fernandes, J., & Painter, D. (2011). Effects of political advertising in the 2008 presidential campaign. *American Behavioral Scientist, 55*(4), 437–456.

Kaid, L. L., McKinney, M. S., & Tedesco, J. C. (2007). Introduction: Political information efficacy and young voters. *American Behavioral Scientist, 50,* 1093–1111.

Katz, E. (1959). Mass communication research and the study of popular culture: An editorial note on a possible future for this journal. *Studies in Public Communication, 3,* 1–6.

Katz, E., & Lazarsfeld, P. (1955). *Personal influence: The part played by people in the flow of mass communications.* Glencoe, IL: Free Press.

Katz, E. J., Rice, R. E., & Aspden, P. (2001). The Internet, 1995–2000: Access, civic involvement, and social interaction. *American Behavioral Scientist, 45*, 405–419.

Kaye, B. K., & Johnson, T. J. (2002). Online and in the know: Uses and gratifications of the Web for political information. *Journal of Broadcasting & Electronic Media, 46*(1), 54–71.

Kaye, B. K., & Johnson, T. J. (2003). From here to obscurity? Media substitution theory and traditional media in an online world. *Journal of the American Society for Information Science and Technology, 54*, 260–273.

Kenski, K., & Stroud, N. J. (2006). Connections between Internet use and political efficacy, knowledge, and participation. *Journal of Broadcasting & Electronic Media, 50*(2), 173–192.

Kim, J. Y. (2006). The impact of Internet use patterns on political engagement: A focus on online deliberation and virtual social capital. *Information Polity, 11*, 35–49.

Kim, J., & Rubin, A. M. (1997). The variable influence of audience on media effects. *Communication Research, 24*(2), 107–135.

Kiousis, S., Mitrook, M., Wu, X., & Seltzer, T. (2006). First- and second-level agenda-building and agenda-setting effects: Exploring the linkages among candidate news releases, media coverage, and public opinion during the 2002 Florida gubernatorial election. *Journal of Public Relations Research, 18*, 265–285.

Kiousis, S., & Strömbäck, J. (2010). The White House and public relations: Examining the linkages between presidential communications and public opinion. *Public Relations Review, 36*, 7–14.

Kirby, E. H., & Kawashima-Ginsburg, K. (2009, August 17). The youth vote in 2008. *The Center for Information and Research on Civic Learning and Engagement*. Retrieved from http://www.civicyouth.org/?page_id=241

Klapper, J. T. (1963). Mass communication research: An old road resurveyed. *Public Opinion Quarterly, 27*, 515–527.

Kohut, A. (2008, January 11). Social networking and online videos take off: Internet's broader role in campaign 2008. *The Pew Research Center for the People and the Press*. Retrieved from http://www.people-press.org/files/legacy-pdf/384.pdf

Kushin, M. J., & Yamamoto, M. (2010). Did social media really matter? College students' use of online media and political decision making in the 2008 election. *Mass Communication and Society, 13*, 608–630.

Lazarsfeld, F., Berelson, B., & Gaudet, H. (1948). *The people's choice*. New York: Columbia University Press.

McCombs, M. E., & Shaw, D. L. (1972). The agenda-setting function of the mass media. *Public Opinion Quarterly, 36*, 176–187.

McLeod, J. M., & Becker, L. B. (1981). The uses and gratifications approach. In D. D. Nimmo & K. R. Sanders (Eds.), *Handbook of political communication* (pp. 67–99). Beverly Hills, CA: Sage.

McQuail, D. (2005). *Mass communication theory*. (5th ed.). London: Sage.

Nekmat, E. (2012). Message expression effects in online social communication. *Journal of Broadcasting and Electronic Media, 56*(2), 203–224.

Owen, D. (2006). The Internet and youth civic engagement in the United States. In S. Oates, D. Owen, & R. K. Gibson (Eds.), *The Internet and politics* (pp. 17–34). New York: Routledge.

Page, B. I. (1996). *Who deliberates? Mass media in modern democracy*. Chicago: University of Chicago Press.

Pan, Z., Shen, L., Paek, H., & Sun, Y. (2006). Mobilizing political talk in a presidential campaign: An examination of campaign effects in a deliberative framework. *Communication Research, 33*, 315–345.

Perse, E. M., & Courtright, J. A. (1993). Normative images of communication media: Mass and interpersonal channels in the new media environment. *Human Communication Research, 19*, 485–503.

Pew Research Center. (2010, February). *Millenials: Portrait of generation next.* Retrieved from http://pewsocialtrends.org/files/2010/10/millennials-confident-connected open-to-change.pdf

Pew Research Center for the People and the Press. (2012, September 28). *Youth engagement falls; registration also declines.* Retrieved from http://www.people-press.org/2012/09/28/youth-engagement-falls-registration-also-declines/

Pingree, R. J. (2007). How messages affect their senders: A more general model of message effects and implications for deliberation. *Communication Theory, 17*, 439–461.

Pollard, T., Chesebro, J., & Studinski, D. (2009). The role of the Internet in presidential campaigns. *Communication Studies, 60*(5), 574–588.

Putnam, R. D. (2000). *Bowling alone: The collapse and revival of American community.* New York: Simon & Schuster.

Quan-Haase, A., & Young, A. L. (2010). Uses and gratifications of social media: A comparison of Facebook and instant messaging. *Bulletin of Science, Technology and Society, 30*, 350–361.

Raacke, J., & Bonds-Raacke, J. (2008). MySpace and Facebook: Applying the uses and gratifications theory to exploring friend-networking sites. *CyberPsychology & Behavior, 11*, 169–174.

Rauch, J. (2010). Superiority and susceptibility: How activist audiences imagine the influence of mainstream news messages on self and others. *Discourse & Communication, 4*(3), 263–277.

Rubin, A. M., & Rubin, R. (1982). Older persons' TV viewing patterns and motivations. *Communication Research, 9*, 287–313.

Ruggiero, T. E. (2000). Uses and gratifications in the 21st century. *Mass Communication & Society, 3*, 3–37.

Schleuder, J., McCombs, M., & Wanta, W. (1991). Inside the agenda-setting process: How political advertising and TV news prime viewers to think about issues and candidates. In F. Biocca (Ed.), *Television and political advertising 1: Psychological processes* (pp. 263–310). Hillsdale, NJ: Lawrence Erlbaum.

Schlozman, K. L., Verba, S., & Brady, H. E. (2010). Weapon of the strong? Participatory inequality and the Internet. *Perspectives on Politics, 8*, 487–509.

Shah, D. V., Cho, J., Eveland, W. P. Jr., & Kwak, N. (2005). Information and expression in a digital age: Modeling Internet effects on civic participation. *Communication Research, 32*, 531–565.

Shah, D. V., Cho, J., Nah, S., Gotlieb, M. R., Hwang, H., Lee, N. J., Scholl, R. M., & McLeod, D. M. (2007). Campaign ads, online messaging, and participation: Extending the communication mediation model. *Journal of Communication, 57*, 676–703.

Smith, A., & Rainie, L. (2008). The Internet and the 2008 election. *Pew Internet & American Life Project.* Washington, DC: Pew Trust. Retrieved from http://www.pewinternet.org/pdfs/PIP_2008_election.pdf

Smith, M., & Smith, B. (2009). Race and gender as peripheral cues on political campaign Web sites. *Communication Research Reports 26*(4), 347–360.

Stromer-Galley, J. (2000). On-line interaction and why candidates avoid it. *Journal of Communication, 50*(4), 111–132.

Stromer-Galley, J. (2004). Interactivity-as-Product and Interactivity-as-Process. *Information Society, 20*(5), 391–394.

Stromer-Galley, J., & Baker, A. B. (2006). Joy and sorrow of interactivity on the campaign trail: Blogs in the primary campaign of Howard Dean. In A. P. Williams & J. Tedesco (Eds.), *The Internet election: Perspectives on the web in campaign 2004* (pp. 111–132). Lanham, MD: Rowman & Littlefield.

Sweetser, K. D., & Weaver-Lariscy, R. (2007). *Candidates make good friends: An analysis of candidates' use of Facebook.* Paper presented at the annual meeting of the National Communication Association, Chicago, IL.

Tedesco, J. C. (2007). Examining Internet interactivity effects on young adult's political information efficacy. *American Behavioral Scientist, 50*, 1183–1194.

Trammell, K. D., Williams, A. P., Postelnicu, M., & Landreville, K. (2005). Evolution of online campaigning: Increasing interactivity in candidate Web sites through hyperlinks and blogs. *Mass Communication & Society, 9*(1), 21–44.

Utz, S. (2009). The (potential) benefits of campaigning via social network sites. *Journal of Computer Mediated Communication, 14*, 221–243.

Valenzuela, S., Park, N., & Kee, K. F. (2009). Is there social capital in a social network site? Facebook use and college students' life satisfaction, trust, and participation. *Journal of Computer-Mediated Communication, 14*, 875–901.

Wang, S. (2007). Political use of the Internet, political attitudes and political participation. *Asian Journal of Communication, 17*, 381–395.

Wolfinger, R. E., & Rosenstone, S. J. (1980). *Who votes?* New Haven, CT: Yale University Press.

Zaichowsky, J. L. (1985). Measuring the involvement construct. *Journal of Consumer Research, 12*, 341–352.

Chapter 14

Alexa.com. (n.d.). Twitter.com. Retrieved from http://www.alexa.com/siteinfo/twitter.com

Ampofo, L., Anstead, N., & O'Loughlin, B. (2012). Trust, confidence, credibility: Citizen responses on Twitter to opinion polls during the 2010 UK general election. *Information, Communication and Society, 14*, 850–871.

Bauder, D. (2012, December 3). Study shows growth in second screen users. *Associated Press.* Retrieved from http://bigstory.ap.org/article/study-shows-growth-second-screen-users

Baker, P., & Parker, A. (2012, September 12). Before debate, tough crowds at the practice. *New York Times*, A1. Retrieved from http://nyti.ms/OuHFZC

Beckett, C. (2010). The value of networked journalism. *POLIS: Journalism and Society.* Retrieved from http://www2.lse.ac.uk/media@lse/POLIS/documents/Polis%20papers/ValueofNetworkedJournalism.pdf

Blake, M. (2012, October 4). Big Bird's fans tweet after he's targeted in presidential debate. *Los Angeles Times*. Retrieved from http://www.latimes.com/la-et-st-big-bird-debate-mitt-romney-20121004,0,3604480.story

Bode, L. (2012a). Facebooking it to the polls: A study in online social networking and political behavior. *Journal of Information Technology & Politics, 9*(4), 352–369.

Bode, L. (2012b). *Political information 2.0: A study in political learning via social media.* (Doctoral dissertation). Retrieved from ProQuest. (3512593).

Bode, L., Vraga, E. K., Borah, P., & Shah, D. V. (forthcoming). A new space for political behavior: Political social networking and its democratic consequences. *Journal of Computer Mediated Communication.*

Brubaker, J., & Hanson, G. (2009). The effect of Fox News and CNN's postdebate commentator analysis on viewers' perceptions of presidential candidate performance. *Southern Communication Journal, 74*(4), 339–351.

Chadwick, A. (2011). Britain's first live televised party leaders' debate: From the news cycle to the political information cycle. *Parliamentary Affairs, 64*(1), 24–44.

Conroy, M., Feezell, J. T., & Guerrero, M. (2012). Facebook and political engagement: A study of online political group membership and offline political engagement. *Computers in Human Behavior, 28*, 1535–1546.

Costolo, D. (2012, November 16). The power of Twitter as a communication tool. Lecture at Gerald R. Ford School of Public Policy. University of Michigan. Retrieved from http://www.fordschool.umich.edu/video/newest/1975704207001/

Dionne, E. J. (2012, October 16). Gaming the town hall debate. *Washington Post*. Retrieved from http://wapo.st/V4mXN4

Drum, K. (2012, October 25). Okay, Twitter isn't ruining political journalism. But it sure is hurting debate coverage. *Mother Jones*. Retrieved from http://www.motherjones.com/kevin-drum/2012/10/ok-twitter-isnt-ruining-political-journalism-it-sure-hurting-debate-coverage

Edgerly, S., Bode, L., Kim, Y. M., & Shah, D. V. (2012). Campaigns go social: Are Facebook, YouTube, and Twitter changing elections? In T. N. Ridout (Ed.). *New Directions in American Politics* (pp. 82–95). New York: Routledge.

Entman, R. M. (1993). Framing: Toward clarification of a fractured paradigm. *Journal of Communication, 43*(4), 51–58.

Eversley, M. (2012, October 4). Romney's 'Big Bird' comment stirs social media. *USA Today*. Retrieved from http://usat.ly/PbAyVW

Fernandes, J., Giurcanu, M., Bowers, K. W., & Neely, J. C. (2010). The writing on the wall: A content analysis of college students' Facebook groups for the 2008 presidential election. *Mass Communication and Society, 13*, 653–675.

Fridkin, K. L., Kenney, P. J., Gershon, S. A., & Woodall, G. S. (2008). Spinning debates: The impact of the news media's coverage of the final 2004 presidential debate. *The International Journal of Press/Politics, 13*(1), 29–51.

Gil de Zúñiga, H., Jung, N., & Valenzuela, S. (2012). Social media use for news and individuals' social capital, civic engagement and political participation. *Journal of Computer-Mediated Communication, 17*, 319–336.

Gillmor, D. (2004). *We the media*. Sebastopol, CA: O'Reilly Media.

Graber, D. A. (2010). *Mass media and American politics* (8th ed.). Washington, DC: CQ Press.

Grunig, J. E. (2001). Two-way symmetrical public relations: Past, present, and future. In R. Heath (Ed.), *Handbook of public relations* (pp. 11–30). Thousand Oaks, CA: Sage.

Hertzfeld, L. (2012, October 3). Big bird winner of the debate—on social media, anyway. *Entertainment Weekly PopWatch*. Retrieved from http://popwatch.ew.com/2012/10/03/big-bird-mitt-romney-debate/

Kirk, R., & Schill, D. (2011). A digital agora: Citizen participation in the 2008 presidential debate. *American Behavioral Scientist, 55*(3), 325–347.

Ku, G., Kaid, L. L., & Pfau, M. (2003). The impact of web site campaigning on traditional news media and public information processing. *Journalism & Mass Communication, 80*(3), 528–547.

Marwick, A. E., & boyd, d. (2011). I tweet honestly, I tweet passionately: Twitter users, context collapse, and the imagined audience. *New Media & Society, 13*(1), 114–133.

Mascaro, C. M., & Goggins, S. P. (2011). Brewing up citizen engagement: The coffee party on Facebook. *Proceedings of the 5th International Conference on Communities and Technologies*. New York: ACM. doi:10.1145/2103354.2103357

Matthes, J. (2009). What's in a frame? A content analysis of media framing studies in the world's leading communication journals, 1990–2005. *Journalism & Mass Communication Quarterly, 86*(2), 349–367.

Mazmanian, A. (2012, October 3). Romney snags top Twitter ad for debate. *National Journal*. Retrieved from http://www.nationaljournal.com/tech/romney-snags-top-twitter-ad-for-debate-20121003

Meraz, S. (2011). Using time series analysis to measure intermedia agenda-setting influence in traditional media and political blog networks. *Journalism and Mass Communication Quarterly, 88*, 176–194.

Metzgar, E., & Maruggi, A. (2009). Social media and the 2008 U.S. Presidential election. *Journal of New Communications Research, 4*(1), 141–165.

Milbank, D. (2012, October 23). Trending on Twitter: Groupthink. *Washington Post*. Retrieved from http://www.washingtonpost.com/opinions/dana-milbank-trending-on-twitter-groupthink/2012/10/23/130f6208-1d54-11e2-9cd5-b55c38388962_story.html

Papacharissi, Z. A. (2010). *A private sphere: Democracy in a digital age*. Cambridge, MA: Polity.

Parmelee, J. H., & Bichard, S. L. (2012). *Politics and the Twitter revolution: How tweets influence the relationship between political leaders and the public*. Lanham, MD: Lexington Books.

Parker, A. (2012, January 28). In nonstop whirlwind of campaigns, Twitter is a critical tool. *New York Times*. Retrieved from http://nyti.ms/x5LpzK

Pingree, R. J., Scholl, R. M., & Quenette, A. M. (2012). Effects of postdebate coverage on spontaneous policy reasoning. *Journal of Communication, 62*, 643–658.

Prior, M. (2005). News vs. entertainment: How increasing media choice widens gaps in political knowledge and turnout. *American Journal of Political Science, 49*(3), 577–592.

Ranie, L., Smith, A., Schlozman, K. L., Brady, H., & Verba, S. (2012). *Social media and political engagement*. Pew Internet and American Life Project. Washington, DC: Pew Research Center. Retrieved from http://pewinternet.org/~/media//Files/Reports/2012/PIP_SocialMediaAndPoliticalEngagement_PDF.pdf

Rayfield, J. (2012, October 3). Political must-reads: Salon's Twitter 50. *Salon*. Retrieved from http://www.salon.com/2012/10/03/political_must_reads_salons_twitter_50

Riffe, D. (2004). An editorial comment. *Journalism & Mass Communication Quarterly, 81*, 2–3.

Sakwa, J. & Steers, J. (2012, October 4). Debate wrap-up: Big Bird and big trends in social media. *CBS This Morning*. Retrieved from http://www.cbsnews.com/8301-505263_162-57526216/debate-wrap-up-big-bird-and-big-trends-in-social-media/

Sarno, D. (2009, February 18). Twitter creator Jack Dorsey illuminates the site's founding document. *Los Angeles Times Technology Blog*. Retrieved from http://latimesblogs.latimes.com/technology/2009/02/twitter-creator.html

Sayre, B., Bode, L., Shah, D., Wilcox, D., & Shah, C. (2010). Agenda setting in a digital age: Tracking attention to California Proposition 8 in social media, online news, and conventional news. *Policy & Internet, 2*(2), 7–32.

Scannell, P. (1996). *Radio, television, and modern life: A phenomenological approach*. Oxford: Blackwell.

Scherer, M. (2012, December 19). 2012 person of the year: Barack Obama, the President. *Time, 180*, 51–79.

Schroeder, A. (2000). *Presidential debates: Fifty years of high risk TV*. New York: Columbia University Press.

Sharp, A. (2012a, October 4). Dispatches from the Denver debate. *Twitter Blog*. Retrieved from http://blog.twitter.com/2012/10/dispatch-from-denver-debate.html

Sharp, A. (2012b, October 16). Twitter at the town hall debate. *Twitter Blog*. Retrieved from http://blog.twitter.com/2012/10/twitter-at-town-hall-debate.html

Sharp, A. (2012c, October 22). The final 2012 presidential debate. *Twitter Blog*. Retrieved from http://blog.twitter.com/2012/10/the-final-2012-presidential-debate.html

Sharp, A. (2012d, November 6). Election Night 2012. *Twitter Blog*. Retrieved from http://blog.twitter.com/2012/11/election-night-2012.html

Shear, M. D. (2012, October 4). Debate praise for Romney as Obama is faulted as flat. *New York Times*. Retrieved from http://nyti.ms/QvkpHP

Smith, A., & Boyles, J. L. (2012). The rise of the "connected viewer". *Pew Internet & American Life Project*. Retrieved from http://pewinternet.org/Reports/2012/Connected-viewers.aspx

Smith, A., & Brenner, J. (2012). Twitter use 2012. *Pew Internet & American Life Project*. Retrieved from http://pewinternet.org/Reports/2012/Twitter-Use-2012.aspx

Smith, B. (2012, October 3). How Mitt Romney won the first debate. *BuzzFeed*. Retrieved from http://www.buzzfeed.com/bensmith/how-mitt-romney-won-the-first-debate

Stelter, B. (2012, October 4). Not waiting for pundits' take, web audience scores the candidates in an instant. *New York Times*, A22.

Stimson, J. A. (2004). *Tides of consent: How public opinion shapes American politics*. New York: Cambridge University Press.

Strochlic, N. (2012, October 4). Mitt Romney's debate performance: Best tweets about GOP nominee's love for big bird. *The Daily Beast*. Retrieved from http://thebea.st/SJ3BzS

Tedesco, J. (2005). Issue and strategy agenda setting in the 2004 presidential election: Exploring the candidate-journalist relationship. *Journalism Studies, 6*, 187–201.

Thurman, N., & Walters, A. (2012). Live blogging—Digital journalism's pivotal platform? *Digital Journalism, 1*(1), 82–101.

Topsy. (2012, October 19). Presidential debates: Big Bird and binders of women. *Topsy Blog*. Retrieved from http://about.topsy.com/2012/10/19/presidential-debates-big-bird-and-binders-of-women/

Tsfati, Y. (2003). Debating the debate: The impact of exposure to debate news coverage and its interaction with exposure to the actual debate. *The International Journal of Press/Politics, 8*(3), 70–86.

Utz, S. (2009). The (potential) benefits of campaigning via social networking site. *Journal of Computer-Mediated Communication, 14*(2), 221–243.

Valenzuela, S., Yonghwan, K., & Gil de Zúñiga, H. (2012). Social networks that matter: Exploring the role of political discussion for online political participation. *International Journal of Public Opinion Research, 24*(2), 163–184.

Vergeer, M., Hermans, L., & Sams, S. (2011). Is the voter only a tweet away? Micro blogging during the 2009 European Parliament election campaign in the Netherlands, *First Monday, 16*(8). Retrieved from http://firstmonday.org/htbin/cgiwrap/bin/ojs/index.php/fm/article/view/3540/3026

Vitak, J., Zube, P., Smock, A., Carr, C. T., Ellison, N., & Lampe, C. (2011). It's complicated: Facebook users' political participation in the 2008 election. *CyberPsychology, Behavior & Social Networking, 14*(3), 107–114.

Warzel, C. (2012, October 23). Digital lessons from the final presidential debate. *Adweek*. Retrieved from http://www.adweek.com/news/technology/digital-lessons-final-presidential-debate-144714

Chapter 15

Ancu, M., & Cozma, R. (2009). MySpace politics: Uses and gratifications of befriending candidates. *Journal of Broadcasting & Electronic Media, 53*(4), 567–583.

Aral, S. (2012). Poked to vote. *Nature, 489*, 212–213.

Baumgartner, J. C., & Morris, J. S. (2010). MyFaceTube politics: Social networking Web sites and political engagement of young adults. *Social Science Computer Review, 28*(1), 24–44. doi: 10.1177/0894439309334325

Bennett, W. L., & Iyengar, S. (2008). A new era of minimal effects? The changing foundations of political communication. *Journal of Communication, 58*(4), 707–731.

Brady, H. E., Verba, S., & Schlozman, K. L. (1995). Beyond SES: A resource model of political participation. *American Political Science Review, 89*, 271–294.

CIRCLE (The Center for Information and Research on Civic Learning and Engagement). (2012, November 7). *At least 80 electoral votes depended on youth.* Retrieved from http://www.civicyouth.org/at-least-80-electoral-votes-depended-on-youth/

Fenton, N., & Barassi, V. (2011). Alternative media and social networking sites: The politics of individualization and political participation. *The Communication Review, 14*(3), 179–196. doi: 10.1080/10714421.2011.597245

Fernandes , J., Giurcanu, M., Bowers, K. W., & Neely, J. C. (2010). The writing on the wall: A content analysis of college students' Facebook groups for the 2008 presidential election. *Mass Communication and Society, 13*(5), 653–675. doi: 10.1080/15205436.2010.516865

Hampton, K., Sessions Goulet, L., Rainie, L., & Purcell, K. (2011, June 16). Social networking sites and our lives. *Pew Internet & American Life Project.* Retrieved from http://www.pewinternet.org/Reports/2011/Technology-and-social-networks.aspx

Hanson, G., Haridakis, P. M., Wagstaff Cunningham, A., Sharma, R., & Ponder, J. D. (2010). The 2008 presidential campaign: Political cynicism in the age of Facebook, MySpace, and YouTube. *Mass Communication and Society, 13*(5), 584–607. doi: 10.1080/15205436.2010.513470

Haridakis, P., & Hanson, G. (2011). Campaign 2008: Comparing YouTube, social networking and other media use among younger voters and older voters. In J. A. Hendricks & L. L. Kaid (Eds.), *Techno politics and presidential campaigning: New voices, new technologies, new voters* (pp. 61–82). New York: Routledge.

Himelboim, I., Weaver Lariscy, R., Tinkham, S. F., & Sweetser, K. D. (2012). Social media and online political communication: The role of interpersonal informational trust and openness. *Journal of Broadcasting & Electronic Media, 56*(1), 92–115.

Horrigan, J. (2006, September 20). More Americans turn to the Internet for news about politics. *Pew Internet & American Life Project.* Retrieved from http://www.pewinternet.org/Reports/2006/More-Americans-turn-to-the-internet-for-news-about-politics.aspx

Kaye, B. K., & Johnson, T. J. (2006). The age of reasons: Motives for using different components of the Internet for political information. In A. P. Williams & J. C. Tedesco (Eds.), *The Internet election: Perspectives on the Web in campaign 2004.* Lanham, MD: Rowman & Littlefield.

Kes-Erkul, A., & Erkul, R. E. (2009). *Web 2.0 in the process of e-participation: The case of Organizing for America and the Obama administration. National Center for Digital Government.* Retrieved from http://scholarworks.umass.edu/cgi/viewcontent.cgi?article=1031&context=ncdg

Kushin, M. J., & Yamamoto, M. (2010). Did social media really matter? College students' use of online media and political decision making in the 2008 election. *Mass Communication and Society, 13*(5), 608–630. doi: 10.1080/15205436.2010.516863

Leighley, J. (1996). Group membership and the mobilization of political participation. *Journal of Politics, 58*, 447–464.

Lenhart, A. (2009). Adults and social network websites. *Pew Internet & American Life Project*. Retrieved from http://www.pewinternet.org/Reports/2009/Adults-and-Social-Network-Websites.aspx

Niemi, R. G., Craig, S. C., & Mattei, F. (1991). Measuring internal political efficacy in the 1998 National Election Study. *The American Political Science Review, 85*(4), 1407–1413.

Ouimet, M. (2012, September 12). Who's winning the 2012 social media election? *Inc.com*. Retrieved from http://www.inc.com/maeghan-ouimet/social-meda-campaigns-election-2012-obama-romney.html

Owyang, J. (2008, November 3). Snapshot of presidential candidates social networking stats. *Web-strategist.com*. Retrieved from http://www.web-strategist.com/blog/2008/11/03/snapshot-of-presidential-candidate-social-networking-stats-nov-2-2008/

Park, N., Kee, K. F., & Valenzuela, S. (2009). Being immersed in social networking environment: Facebook groups, uses and gratifications, and social outcomes. *CyberPsychology & Behavior, 12*(6), 729–733. doi:10.1089/cpb.2009.0003

Putnam, R. D. (2000). *Bowling alone: The collapse and revival of American community*. New York: Simon & Schuster.

Rainie, L., & Smith, A. (2008). The Internet and the 2008 election. *Pew Internet & American Life Project*. Retrieved from http://www.pewinternet.org/Reports/2008/The-Internet-and-the-2008-Election.aspx

Rainie, L., Smith, A., Lehman-Schlozman, K., Brady, H., & Verba, S. (2012). Social media and political engagement. *Pew Internet & American Life Project*. Retrieved from http://pewinternet.org/Reports/2012/Political-engagement/Summary-of-Findings.aspx?view=all

Rogers, E. M. (1962). *Diffusion of innovation*. New York: Free Press.

Smith, A. (2009, January 14). Adults and social network websites. *Pew Internet & American Life Project*. Retrieved from http://www.pewinternet.org/Reports/2009/Adults-and-Social-Network-Websites.aspx

Weaver Lariscy, R. A., Tinkham, S. F., & Sweetser, K. D. (2011). Kids these days: Examining differences in political uses and gratifications, Internet political participation, political information efficacy, and cynicism on the basis of age. *American Behavioral Scientist, 55*(6), 749–764.

Zhou, Y., & Pinkleton, B. E. (2012). Modeling the effects of political information source use and online expression on young adults' political efficacy. *Mass Communication and Society, 15*(6), 813–830. doi: 10.1080/15205436.2011.622064

Zickuhr, K., & Madden, M. (2012, June 6). Older adults and Internet use. *Pew Internet & American Life Project*. Retrieved from http://pewinternet.org/Reports/2012/Older-adults-and-internet-use/Summary-of-findings.aspx

Chapter 16

Agger, R. E., Goldstein, M. N., & Pearl, S. A. (1961). Political cynicism: Measurement and meaning. *The Journal of Politics, 23*, 477–506. doi:10.2307/2127102

Ampofo, L., Anstead, N., & O'Loughlin, B. (2011). Trust, confidence, credibility: Citizen responses on Twitter to opinion polls during the 2010 UK general election. *Information, Communication and Society, 14*, 850–871.

Anstead, N., & O'Loughlin, B. (2011). The emerging viewertariat and BBC Question Time. *The International Journal of Press/Politics, 16*, 440–462. doi:10.1177/1940161211415519

Bentler, P. M., & Bonett, D. G. (1980). Significance tests and goodness of fit in the analysis of covariance structures. *Psychological Bulletin, 88,* 588–606. doi:10.1037/0033-2909.88.3.588

Booth, J. A., & Seligson, M. A. (2005). Political legitimacy and participation in Costa Rica: Evidence of arena shopping. *Political Research Quarterly, 58,* 537–550. doi:10.1177/106591290505800402

Boulianne, S. (2009). Does Internet use affect engagement? A meta-analysis of research. *Political Communication, 26,* 193–211. doi:10.1080/10584600902854363

Brady, H. E., Verba, S., & Schlozman, K. L. (1995). Beyond SES: A resource model of political participation. *The American Political Science Review, 89,* 271–294. doi:10.2307/2082425

Brown, T. A. (2006). *Confirmatory factor analysis for applied research.* New York: The Guilford Press.

Browne, M. W., & Cudeck, R. (1993). Alternative ways of assessing model fit. In K. A. Bollen & J. S. Long (Eds.), *Testing structural equation models* (pp. 136–162). Newbury Park, CA: Sage.

Cappella, J. N., & Jamieson, K. H. (1996). News frames, political cynicism, and media cynicism. *Annals of the American Academy of Political and Social Science, 546,* 71–84.

de Zúñiga, H. G., Veenstra, A., Vraga, E., & Shah, D. (2010). Digital democracy: Reimagining pathways to political participation. *Journal of Information Technology & Politics, 7,* 36–51. doi:10.1080/19331680903316742

Dilliplane, S. (2011). All the news you want to hear: The impact of partisan news exposure on political participation. *Public Opinion Quarterly, 75,* 287–316. doi:10.1093/poq/nfr006

Gastil, J., & Xenos, M. (2010). Of attitudes and engagement: Clarifying the reciprocal relationship between civic attitudes and political participation. *Journal of Communication, 60,* 318–343. doi:10.1111/j.1460-2466.2010.01484.x

Hawthorne, J., Houston, J. B., & McKinney, M. S. (2013). Live-tweeting a presidential primary debate: Exploring new political conversations. *Social Science Computer Review, 31,* 552–562.

Holbert, R. L., & Stephenson, M. T. (2002). The importance of indirect effects in media effects research: Testing for mediation in structural equation modeling. *Journal of Broadcasting & Electronic Media, 47,* 556–572. doi:10.1207/s15506878jobem4704_5

Houston, J. B., Hawthorne, J., & McKinney, M. S. (2012). *Political arguments in 140 characters or less: Tweeting a Republican presidential primary debate.* Presented at the annual meeting of the National Communication Association, Orlando, FL.

Hu, L., & Bentler, P. M. (1999). Cutoff criteria for fit indexes in covariance structure analysis: Conventional criteria versus new alternatives. *Structural Equation Modeling, 6,* 1–55. doi:10.1080/10705519909540118

Kaid, L. L. (2003). Effects of political information in the 2000 presidential campaign: Comparing traditional television and Internet exposure. *American Behavioral Scientist, 46,* 677–691. doi:10.1177/0002764202238492

Kaid, L. L., Fernandes, J., & Painter, D. (2011). Effects of political advertising in the 2008 presidential campaign. *American Behavioral Scientist, 55,* 437–456. doi:10.1177/0002764211398071

Kaid, L. L., Johnston, A., & Hale, K. (1989). Mass media and political disapprobation. *Political Communication Review, 14,* 51–72.

Kaid, L. L., McKinney, M. S., & Tedesco, J. C. (2007). Political information efficacy and young voters. *American Behavioral Scientist, 50,* 1093–1111. doi:10.1177/0002764207300040

Kaid, L. L., Postelnicu, M., Landreville, K., Yun, H. J., & LeGrange, A. G. (2007). The effects of political advertising on young voters. *American Behavioral Scientist, 50*, 1137–1151.

Kingkade, T. (2012, November 7). Young voters help secure Obama victory, passage of progressive ballot measures. *Huffington Post*. Retrieved from http://www.huffingtonpost .com/2012/11/07/young-voters-2012-obama_n_2089789.html

Kline, R. B. (2011). *Principles and practice of structural equation modeling* (3rd ed.). New York: Guilford Press.

Kushin, M. J., & Yamamoto, M. (2010). Did social media really matter? College students' use of online media and political decision making in the 2008 election. *Mass Communication & Society, 13*, 608–630. doi:10.1080/15205436.2010.516863

Lenhart, A., Purcell, K., Smith, A., & Zickuhr, K. (2010). *Social media and mobile Internet use among teens and young adults*. Pew Internet and American Life Project. Washington, D.C.: Pew Research Center. Retrieved from http://pewinternet.org/Reports/2010/ Social-Media-and-Young-Adults.aspx

Little, T. D., Cunningham, W. A., Shahar, G., & Widaman, K. F. (2002). To parcel or not to parcel: Exploring the question, weighing the merits. *Structural Equation Modeling, 9*, 151–173. doi:10.1207/S15328007SEM0902_1

Lotan, G., Graeff, E., Ananny, M., Gaffney, D., Pearce, I., & boyd, d. (2011). The revolutions were tweeted: Information flows during the 2011 Tunisian and Egyptian revolutions. *International Journal of Communication, 5*, 1375–1405. doi:1932–8036/2011FEA1375

Marsh, H. W., Hau, K. T., & Wen, Z. (2004). In search of golden rules: Comment on hypothesis-testing approaches to setting cutoff values for fit indexes and dangers in overgeneralizing Hu and Bentler's (1999) findings. *Structural Equation Modeling, 11*, 320–341. doi:10.1207/s15328007sem1103_2

McKinney, M. S., & Chattopadhyay, S. (2007). Political engagement through debates: Young citizens' reactions to the 2004 presidential debates. *American Behavioral Scientist, 50*, 1169–1182. doi:10.1177/0002764207300050

McKinney, M. S., Houston, J. B., & Hawthorne, J. (2012). Live-tweeting the presidential debates: Using social media to process political campaign communication. Presented at the annual meeting of the Association for Education in Journalism and Mass Communications, Chicago, IL.

McKinney, M. S., & Rill, L. A. (2009). Not your parents' presidential debates: Examining the effects of the CNN/YouTube debates on young citizens' civic engagement. *Communication Studies, 60*, 392–406. doi:10.1080/10510970903110001

McKinney, M. S., Rill, L. A., & Gully, D. (2011). Civic engagement through presidential debates: Young citizens' attitudes of political engagement throughout the 2008 election. In M. S. McKinney & M. C. Banwart (Eds.), *Communication in the 2008 U.S. Election: Digital Natives Elect a President* (pp. 121–141). New York: Peter Lang.

McKinney, M. S., Spiker, J. A., & Kaid, L. L. (1998). DebateWatch '96 and citizen engagement: Building democracy through citizen communication. In T. J. Johnson & C. E. Hayes (Eds.), *Engaging the public: How government and the media can reinvigorate American democracy* (pp. 185–193). Lanham, MD: Rowman & Littlefield.

McLeod, J. M., Scheufele, D. A., & Moy, P. (1999). Community, communication, and participation: The role of mass media and interpersonal discussion in local political participation. *Political Communication, 16*, 315–336. doi:10.1080/105846099198659

Mutz, D. C. (2006). *Hearing the other side: Deliberative versus participatory democracy*. New York: Cambridge University Press.

Niemi, R. G., Craig, S. C., & Mattei, F. (1991). Measuring internal political efficacy in the 1988 National Election Study. *American Political Science Review, 85*, 1407–1413.

O'Toole, T., Lister, M., Marsh, D., Jones, S., & McDonagh, A. (2003). Tuning out or left out? Participation and non-participation among young people. *Contemporary Politics, 9*, 45–61.

Prior, M. (2007). *Post-broadcast democracy: How media choice increases inequality in political involvement and polarizes elections.* New York: Cambridge University Press.

Rahimi, B. (2011). The agonistic social media: Cyberspace in the formation of dissent and consolidation of state power in postelection Iran. *Communication Review, 14*, 158–178. doi:10.1080/10714421.2011.597240

Ranie, L., Smith, A., Schlozman, K. L., Brady, H., & Verba, S. (2012). *Social media and political engagement.* Pew Internet and American Life Project. Washington, D.C.: Pew Research Center. Retrieved from http://pewinternet.org/Reports/2012/Political-Engagement.aspx

Shah, D. V., Cho, J., Eveland Jr., W. P., & Kwak, N. (2005). Information and expression in a digital age: Modeling Internet effects on civic participation. *Communication Research, 32*, 531–565. doi:10.1177/0093650205279209

Shamma, D. A., Kennedy, L., & Churchill, E. F. (2009). Tweet the debates: Understanding community annotation of uncollected sources. *Proceedings of the first SIGMM workshop on Social media, WSM '09* (pp. 3–10). New York: ACM. doi:10.1145/1631144.1631148

Sharp, A. (2012a, October 4). Dispatches from the Denver debate. *Twitter Blog.* Retrieved from http://blog.twitter.com/2012/10/dispatch-from-denver-debate.html

Sharp, A. (2012b, October 12). Recapping the VP debate. *Twitter Blog.* Retrieved from http://blog.twitter.com/2012/10/recapping-vp-debate.html

Sharp, A. (2012c, October 16). Twitter at the town hall debate. *Twitter Blog.* Retrieved from http://blog.twitter.com/2012/10/twitter-at-town-hall-debate.html

Sharp, A. (2012d, October 22). The final 2012 presidential debate. *Twitter Blog.* Retrieved from http://blog.twitter.com/2012/10/the-final-2012-presidential-debate.html

Sharp, A. (2012e, November 6). Election Night 2012. *Twitter Blog.* Retrieved from http://blog.twitter.com/2012/11/election-night-2012.html

Stroud, N. J. (2010). Polarization and partisan selective exposure. *Journal of Communication, 60*, 556–576. doi:10.1111/j.1460-2466.2010.01497.x

Tedesco, J. C. (2007). Examining Internet interactivity effects on young adult political information efficacy. *American Behavioral Scientist, 50*, 1183–1194. doi:10.1177/0002764207300041

Tedesco, J. C. (2011). Political information efficacy and Internet effects in the 2008 U.S. Presidential election. *American Behavioral Scientist, 55*, 696–713. doi:10.1177/0002764211398089

Tucker, L. R., & Lewis, C. (1973). A reliability coefficient for maximum likelihood factor analysis. *Psychometrika, 38*, 1–10. doi:10.1007/BF02291170

Tufekci, Z., & Wilson, C. (2012). Social media and the decision to participate in political protest: Observations from Tahrir Square. *Journal of Communication, 62*, 363–379. doi:10.1111/j.1460-2466.2012.01629.x

Tumasjan, A., Sprenger, T. O., Sandner, P. G., & Welpe, I. M. (2011). Election forecasts with Twitter: How 140 characters reflect the political landscape. *Social Science Computer Review, 29*, 402–418. doi:10.1177/0894439310386557

U.S. Census Bureau Public Information Office. (2009). Voter turnout increases by 5 million in 2008 presidential election, U.S. Census Bureau reports. Retrieved from http://www.census.gov/newsroom/releases/archives/voting/cb09-110.html

Valenzuela, S., Arriagada, A., & Scherman, A. (2012). The social media basis of youth protest behavior: The case of Chile. *Journal of Communication, 62*, 299–314. doi:10.1111/j.1460-2466.2012.01635.x

Vitak, J., Zube, P., Smock, A., Carr, C. T., Ellison, N., & Lampe, C. (2011). It's complicated: Facebook users' political participation in the 2008 election. *CyberPsychology, Behavior & Social Networking, 14*, 107–114. doi:10.1089/cyber.2009.0226

Wang, S. I. (2007). Political use of the Internet, political attitudes and political participation. *Asian Journal of Communication, 17*, 381–395. doi:10.1080/01292980701636993

Warner, B. R., Turner McGowen, S., & Hawthorne, J. (2012). Limbaugh's social media nightmare: Facebook and Twitter as a space for political action. *Journal of Radio & Audio Media, 19*, 257–275. doi:10.1080/19376529.2012.722479

Chapter 17

Burgess, J. E., & Green, J. B. (2009). *YouTube: Online video and participatory culture*. Malden, MA: Polity.

Christensen, J. (2012, June 3). Obama outspends Romney on online ads. *CNN*. Retrieved from http://www.cnn.com/2012/06/03/politics/online-campaign-spending/index.html

Condon, S. (2011, April 4). Obama launches 2012 campaign with web video. *CBS News*. Retrieved from http://www.cbsnews.com/8301-503544_162-20050339-503544.html

Cronkite, W. (2012, October 4). Romney: "47 percent" remarks "completely wrong." *CBS News*. Retrieved from http://www.cbsnews.com/8301-250_162-57526535/romney-47-percent-remarks-completely-wrong/

Dugan, L. (2012, October 22). How has social media changed politics? *MediaBistro*. Retrieved from http://www.mediabistro.com/alltwitter/social-media-politics-infographic_b30254

Elliott, A. M. (2011, February 19). 10 fascinating YouTube facts that may surprise you. *Mashable*. Retrieved from http://mashable.com/2011/02/19/youtube-facts/

Folliard, J. (2012, November 20). 2012 presidential use online YouTube videos in campaign. *Fairfax Video Studio*. Retrieved from http://www.fairfaxvideostudio.com/news/2012-presidential-candidates-use-online-youtube-videos-in-campaign-20121120.cfm

Gueorguieva, V. (2008). Voters, MySpace, and YouTube: The impact of alternative communication channels on the 2006 election cycle and beyond. *Social Science Computer Review 26*(3): 288–300.

Hendricks, J. A., & Denton, R. E., Jr. (Eds.). (2010). *Communicator-in-chief: How Barack Obama used new media technology to win the White House*. Lanham, MD: Lexington Books.

Hendricks, J. A., & Kaid, L. L. (Eds.). (2011). *Techno politics in presidential campaigning: New voices, new technologies, and new voters*. New York: Routledge.

Judd, N. (2012, January 19). Inside Mitt Romney's digital mind. *TechPresident*. Retrieved from http://techpresident.com/news/21649/inside-mitt-romneys-digital-mind

Karpf, D. (2010). Macaca moments reconsidered: Electoral panopticon or netroots mobilization? *Journal of Information Technology and Politics, 7*(2–3), 143–162.

Krejcie, R. V., & Morgan, D. W. (1970). Determining sample size for research activities. *Educational and Psychological Measurement, 30*, 607–610.

Krippendorff, C. (2003). *Content analysis: An introduction to its methodology*. Thousand Oaks, CA: Sage.

Michel, A., & Pilkington, E. (2012, July 24). Obama passes YouTube milestone as online videos remake campaigning. *Guardian*. Retrieved from http://www.guardian.co.uk/world/2012/jul/24/obama-youtube-milestone-online-videos

Moore, K. (2011). 71% of online adults now use video-sharing sites. *Pew Internet & American Life Project*. Retrieved from http://pewinternet.org/Reports/2011/Video-sharing-sites.aspx

Panagopoulos, C. (2009). Technology and the modern political campaign: The digital pulse of the 2008 election. In C. Panagopoulos (Ed.), *Politicking Online* (pp. 1–17). Piscataway, NJ: Rutgers University Press.

Peters, J. W. (2012, March 14). With video, Obama looks to expand campaign's reach through social media. *New York Times*. Retrieved from http://www.nytimes.com/2012/03/15/us/politics/with-youtube-video-obama-looks-to-expand-social-media-reach.html?_r=0

Preston, J. (2011, October 6). New politics channel on YouTube. *Caucus*. Retrieved from http://thecaucus.blogs.nytimes.com/2011/10/06/youtube-launches-new-politics-channel/

Ricke, L. (2014). Campaigns, digital. In H. Kerric & G. J. Geoffrey (Eds.), *Encyclopedia of Social Media and Politics*. Thousand Oaks, CA: Sage.

Schreier, M. (2012). *Qualitative content analysis in practice*. Thousand Oaks, CA: Sage.

Schwab, N. (2008, November 7). In Obama-McCain race, YouTube became a serious battleground for presidential politics. *U.S. News & World Report*. Retrieved from http://www.usnews.com/news/campaign-2008/articles/2008/11/07/in-obama-mccain-race-youtube-became-a-serious-battleground-for-presidential-politics?page=2

Smith, A. (2011). The Internet and campaign 2010. *Pew Internet & American Life Project*. Retrieved from http://www.pewinternet.org/Reports/2011/The-Internet-and-Campaign-2010.aspx

Smith, A., & Duggan, M. (2012). Online political videos and campaign 2012. *Pew Internet & American Life Project*. Retrieved from http://pewinternet.org/Reports/2012/Election-2012-Video.aspx

Smith, A., & Rainie, L. (2008). The Internet and the 2008 election. *Pew Internet & American Life Project*. Retrieved from http://www.pewinternet.org/Reports/2008/The-Internet-and-the-2008-Election.aspx

Stirland, S. L. (2011, December 22). New digital targeting helps Romney campaign reach voters. *TechPresident*. Retrieved from http://techpresident.com/news/21546/youtube-facebook-romney-digital-ad-targeting

Thompson, K. (2012, October 16). Obama brings up 47 percent at very end. *Washington Post*. Retrieved from http://www.washingtonpost.com/blogs/post-politics/wp/2012/10/16/obama-brings-up-47-percent-at-very-end/

Towner, T. L., & Dulio, D. A. (2011). An experiment of campaign effects during the YouTube election. *New Media and Society, 13*(4), 626–644.

Trammell, K. D., Williams, A. P., Postelnicu, M., & Landreville, K. D. (2006). Evolution of online campaigning: Increasing interactivity in candidate Web sites and blogs through text and technical features. *Mass Communication and Society, 9*(1), 21–44.

YouTube. (2012). *Statistics*. Retrieved from http://www.youtube.com/t/press_statistics

Index

Note: page numbers followed by *f* and *t* refer to figures and tables respectively.